775
New
030?

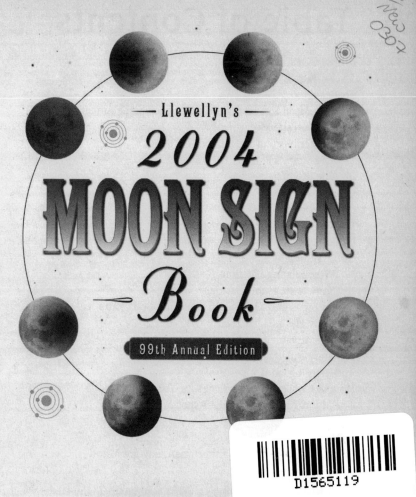

— Llewellyn's —
*2004*
MOON SIGN
*Book*
99th Annual Edition

D1565119

Copyright © 2003 Llewelly...
All rights reserved. Printed in the U.S.A.
Editor/Designer: Sharon Leah
Cover Design & Art: Kevin R. Brown
Special thanks to Aina Allen
for astrological proofreading.
ISBN 0-7387-0124-6

LLEWELLYN WORLDWIDE
P.O. Box 64383 Dept. 0124-6
St. Paul, MN 55164-0383 U.S.A.

# Table of Contents

## Home, Health, and Leisure Section

# Eclipse Dates

Dates are given in parentheses for eclipses that fall across two days due to time zone differences. Times are in Eastern Time and are rounded off to the nearest minute. The exact time of an eclipse generally differs from the exact time of a New or Full Moon. For solar eclipses, "greatest eclipse" represents the time (converted from Local Mean Time) of the Moon's maximum obscuration of the Sun as viewed from the Earth. For lunar eclipses, "middle of eclipse" represents the time at which the Moon rests at the centermost point of its journey through the shadow cast by the Earth passing between it and the Sun. Data is from *Astronomical Phenomena for the Year 2004*, prepared by the United States Naval Observatory and Her Majesty's Nautical Almanac Office (United Kingdom).

### April 19
Partial solar eclipse at 9:35 am: 29° ♈ 49'

| | | | |
|---|---|---|---|
| Eclipse begins | 7:30 am | 50° E | 70° S |
| Greatest eclipse | 9:35 am | 44° W | 62° S |
| Eclipse ends | 11:39 am | 31° W | 20° S |

### May 4
Total lunar eclipse at 4:31 pm: 14° ♏ 42'

| | | | |
|---|---|---|---|
| Moon enters penumbra | 1:51 pm | 76° W | 16° S |
| Middle of eclipse | 4:31 pm | | |
| Moon leaves penumbra | 7:10 pm | 27° W | 17° S |

### October 13
Partial solar eclipse at 11:00 pm: 21° ♎ 06'

| | | | |
|---|---|---|---|
| Eclipse begins | 8:55 pm | 94° W | 68° N |
| Greatest eclipse | 11:00 pm | 153° E | 61° N |
| Eclipse ends | 1:04 am (Oct. 14) | 171 °E | 14° N |

### October 27
Total lunar eclipse at 11:05 pm: 5° ♉ 02'

| | | | |
|---|---|---|---|
| Moon enters penumbra | 8:06 pm | 23° E | 13° N |
| Middle of eclipse | 11:05 pm | | |
| Moon leaves penumbra | 2:03 am (Oct. 28) | 76 °E | 14° N |

Note: Please check the latitude and longitude coordinates against an atlas to determine whether or not an eclipse will be visible in your area. You will also need to make the necessary time adjustments for your area. Please refer to the Time Conversions Table on page 80–81.

# 2004

## JANUARY
| S | M | T | W | T | F | S |
|---|---|---|---|---|---|---|
|   |   |   |   | 1 | 2 | 3 |
| 4 | 5 | 6 | ○ | 8 | 9 | 10 |
| 11 | 12 | 13 | ◑ | 15 | 16 | 17 |
| 18 | 19 | 20 | ● | 22 | 23 | 24 |
| 25 | 26 | 27 | 26 | ◐ | 30 | 31 |

## FEBRUARY
| S | M | T | W | T | F | S |
|---|---|---|---|---|---|---|
| 1 | 2 | 3 | 4 | 5 | ○ | 7 |
| 8 | 9 | 10 | 11 | 12 | ◑ | 14 |
| 15 | 16 | 17 | 18 | 19 | ● | 21 |
| 22 | 23 | 24 | 25 | 26 | ◐ | 28 |
| 29 |   |   |   |   |   |   |

## MARCH
| S | M | T | W | T | F | S |
|---|---|---|---|---|---|---|
|   | 1 | 2 | 3 | 4 | 5 | ○ |
| 7 | 8 | 9 | 10 | 11 | 12 | ◑ |
| 14 | 15 | 16 | 17 | 18 | 19 | ● |
| 21 | 22 | 23 | 24 | 25 | 26 | 27 |
| ◐ | 29 | 30 | 31 |   |   |   |

## APRIL
| S | M | T | W | T | F | S |
|---|---|---|---|---|---|---|
|   |   |   |   | 1 | 2 | 3 |
| 4 | ○ | 6 | 7 | 8 | 9 | 10 |
| ◐ | 12 | 13 | 14 | 15 | 16 | 17 |
| 18 | ● | 20 | 21 | 22 | 23 | 24 |
| 25 | 26 | ◐ | 28 | 29 | 30 |   |

## MAY
| S | M | T | W | T | F | S |
|---|---|---|---|---|---|---|
|   |   |   |   |   |   | 1 |
| 2 | 3 | ○ | 5 | 6 | 7 | 8 |
| 9 | 10 | ◑ | 12 | 13 | 14 | 15 |
| 16 | 17 | 18 | ● | 20 | 21 | 22 |
| 23 | 24 | 25 | 26 | ◐ | 28 | 29 |
| 30 | 31 |   |   |   |   |   |

## JUNE
| S | M | T | W | T | F | S |
|---|---|---|---|---|---|---|
|   |   | 1 | 2 | ○ | 4 | 5 |
| 6 | 7 | 8 | ◑ | 10 | 11 | 12 |
| 13 | 14 | 15 | 16 | ● | 18 | 19 |
| 20 | 21 | 22 | 23 | 24 | ◐ | 26 |
| 27 | 28 | 29 | 30 |   |   |   |

## JULY
| S | M | T | W | T | F | S |
|---|---|---|---|---|---|---|
|   |   |   |   | 1 | ○ | 3 |
| 4 | 5 | 6 | 7 | 8 | ◑ | 10 |
| 11 | 12 | 13 | 14 | 15 | 16 | ● |
| 18 | 19 | 20 | 21 | 22 | 23 | ◐ |
| 25 | 26 | 27 | 28 | 29 | 30 | ○ |

## AUGUST
| S | M | T | W | T | F | S |
|---|---|---|---|---|---|---|
| 1 | 2 | 3 | 4 | 5 | 6 | ◑ |
| 8 | 9 | 10 | 11 | 12 | 13 | 14 |
| ● | 16 | 17 | 18 | 19 | 20 | 21 |
| 22 | ◐ | 24 | 25 | 26 | 27 | 28 |
| ○ | 30 | 31 |   |   |   |   |

## SEPTEMBER
| S | M | T | W | T | F | S |
|---|---|---|---|---|---|---|
|   |   |   | 1 | 2 | 3 | 4 |
| 5 | ◑ | 7 | 8 | 9 | 10 | 11 |
| 12 | 13 | ● | 15 | 16 | 17 | 18 |
| 19 | 20 | ◐ | 22 | 23 | 24 | 25 |
| 26 | 27 | ○ | 29 | 30 |   |   |

## OCTOBER
| S | M | T | W | T | F | S |
|---|---|---|---|---|---|---|
|   |   |   |   |   | 1 | 2 |
| 3 | 4 | 5 | ◑ | 7 | 8 | 9 |
| 10 | 11 | 12 | ● | 14 | 15 | 16 |
| 17 | 18 | 19 | ◐ | 21 | 22 | 23 |
| 24 | 25 | 26 | ○ | 28 | 29 | 30 |
| 31 |   |   |   |   |   |   |

## NOVEMBER
| S | M | T | W | T | F | S |
|---|---|---|---|---|---|---|
|   | 1 | 2 | 3 | 4 | ◑ | 6 |
| 7 | 8 | 9 | 10 | 11 | ● | 13 |
| 14 | 15 | 16 | 17 | 18 | ◐ | 20 |
| 21 | 22 | 23 | 24 | 25 | ○ | 27 |
| 28 | 29 | 30 |   |   |   |   |

## DECEMBER
| S | M | T | W | T | F | S |
|---|---|---|---|---|---|---|
|   |   |   | 1 | 2 | 3 | ◑ |
| 5 | 6 | 7 | 8 | 9 | 10 | ● |
| 11 | 12 | 13 | 14 | 15 | 16 | ◐ |
| 18 | 19 | 20 | 21 | 22 | 23 | 24 |
| 25 | ○ | 27 | 28 | 29 | 30 | 31 |

# To Readers

*If you are among the rapidly increasing numbers who believe that the universe is operated upon a well-defined plan wherein each individual has a chance to advance and achieve success according to his or her degree of understanding and effort put forth toward that objective . . . this BIG little book may truly be for you a guide to victory.*

Llewellyn George

From 1906 through the 50s, electional astrology—the timing of events based on prevailing astrological influences—was the primary focus of the *Moon Sign Book*. Then, in the 1960s many of us, including astrologers, embraced psychology and personal counseling for the first time. We were also moving off the farm into cities and away from the natural cycles of nature and the Moon. We began to see the Moon as a reflection (symbol) of our "feelings" and emotions. For many, the Moon's use in the timing of events fell to the wayside.

Surely, the Moon reflects our emotional natures as it passes through its cycle as well as the twelve zodiac signs each month, but timing is still one of the Moon's primary uses. In the *Moon Sign Book*, we recognize the value of both faces of the Moon— the "time-keeper" and the "reflector" of our emotions and feelings.

Longtime readers of this almanac will notice some changes. We brought back some of material that made this almanac so unique, beginning with the calendar on page 5, which now includes Moon phase symbols to give you an "at-a-glance" perspective of the lunation cycle.

You'll still find entertaining and informative articles, like "How Not to Buy A House" on page 207 in which astrologer Marlene Utescher of Chicago writes about how one homebuyer could have saved time, money, and a lot of frustration if she had consulted with an electional astrologer before buying her house.

The economic and weather forecasts have been expanded. Electional and horary astrologer Dorothy J. Kovach of California is back with her economic forecast. She acts as a consultant to both businesses and individuals interested in finding the best times to begin projects for successful outcomes. In addition to her forecasts, Dorothy offers you Market Tips beginning on page 213.

Arizona astrologer Kris Brandt-Riske, author of *Astrometeorology: Planetary Power in Weather Forecasting* (AFA Publications), writes for eight zones instead of six this year. This change has allowed Kris to refine her weather forecasts for your zone. You'll find the weather forecasts beginning on page 307.

Along with the articles and expanded forecasts, we still have the Moon void-of-course tables, retrograde tables, the Moon Tables and Lunar Aspectarian, the Favorable and Unfavorable Days tables; and the best dates for hunting and fishing, setting eggs, planting, and doing other garden-related activities.

We are breaking with other traditions, though. Previously, the various electional activities were located in the four sections of the *Moon Sign Books*. Now, they are combined in this first section and listed alphabetically for your convenience.

In another break with tradition, the Home, Health, and Beauty Section and the Leisure and Recreation Section are now combined in the new Home, Health, and Leisure Section. We feel these changes are positive and reflect how we live and spend our time today. After all, good timing and personal success often go hand-in-hand.

Some of you will notice that the Astro Almanac is gone. While the Astro Almanac gave you an easy way to elect dates for specific activities, it was only a very general guide. Due to its general nature, the dates did not apply to all, or even a majority of readers. For example, it may have listed June 1, 4, 12, 13, and 19 as good days to sell a house, and those dates may have been perfect if you are a Sun sign Cancer, but they wouldn't have worked well at all if you are a Sun sign Capricorn. Since there is no satisfactory way to distinguish the differences for you within the scope of the tables in this almanac, we now provide you with additional information that you can use to personalize your options, beginning on page 22.

While we realize some readers may object to the changes we've made, we believe the *Moon Sign Book* is now a better tool for you; and one that will be easier to use.

# Why the *Moon Sign Book* Is Different from Some Almanacs

Readers have asked why the *Moon Sign Book* says that the Moon is in Taurus when some almanacs indicate that the Moon is Aries? It's because there are two different zodiac systems in use today: the tropical and the sidereal zodiac. The *Moon Sign Book* is based on the tropical zodiac.

The tropical zodiac takes 0 degrees of Aries to be the Spring Equinox in the Northern Hemisphere. This is the time and date when the Sun is directly overhead at noon along the equator, usually about March 20–21. The rest of the signs are positioned at 30 degree intervals from this point.

The sidereal zodiac, which is based on the location of fixed stars, uses the positions of the fixed stars to determine the starting point of 0 degrees of Aries. In this system, 0 degrees of Aries always begins at the same point. There is one problem though. The positions of the fixed stars, as seen from Earth, have changed since the constellations were named. The term "precession of the equinoxes" is used to describe the change.

Precession of the equinoxes describes an astronomical phenomenon brought about by the Earth's wobble as it rotates and orbits the Sun. The Earth's axis is inclined toward the Sun at an angle of about 23½ degrees, which creates our seasonal weather changes. Although the change is slight, because one complete circle of the Earth's axis takes 25,800 years to complete, we can actually see that the positions of the fixed stars seem to shift. The result is that each year, in the tropical system, the Spring Equinox occurs at a slightly different time.

## Does Precession Matter?

There is an accumulative difference of about 23 degrees between the Spring Equinox (0 degrees Aries in the tropical zodiac and 0 degrees Aries in the sidereal zodiac) so that 0 degrees Aries at Spring Equinox in the tropical zodiac actually occurs at about 7 degrees Pisces in the sidereal zodiac system. You can readily see that those who use the other almanacs may be planting seeds (in the garden and in their individual lives) based on the belief that it is occurring in a fruitful sign, such as Taurus, when in fact it would be occurring in Gemini, one of the most barren signs of the zodiac. So, if you wish to plant and plan activities by the Moon, it is important to follow the *Moon Sign Book*.

# A Primer on the Moon

Before we go on, there are impor-tant things to understand about the Moon, her cycles, and their corre-lation with everyday living. We'll start by looking at some basic astro-logical principles.

## How Important Is the Moon?

Everyone has seen the Moon wax (increase) and wane (decrease) over a period of approximately twenty-nine and-a-half days. This succes-sion from New Moon to New Moon is called the lunation cycle. The cycle is divided into parts, called quarters or phases. The astrological system of naming the lunar phases does not always correspond to systems used in other almanacs and calendars. It

is therefore important to follow only Llewellyn's *Moon Sign Book* or our *As-trological Calendar* for timing events defined in this book.

The Moon is the most important planet in any election. Time and ex-perience have proven that anything started when the Moon is weak by sign and aspect is unlikely to prosper.

## What Makes the Moon Weak or Strong?

When astrologers talk about the Moon's strength, they are not referring to physical strength, nor to emotional strength or weakness. The Moon's strength is an assessment of its energy in other signs—its attitude—when compared to how the Moon is ex-pressed in Cancer, the sign it rules and where it enjoys its purest form of expression. The Moon is strong in Cancer because her symbolism is closely associated with Cancer's traits of mothering, nurturing, feeling, and intuiting. The Moon's expression in Capricorn is thought to be weak because the qualities of goal setting, detachment, and achieving, which are common to Capricorn, are not in sync with the Moon's natural mode of expression.

When the Moon is not in its home sign of Cancer or the sign of its exaltation, Taurus, its strength is judged according to its position in the chart. If it is in the first, fourth, seventh, or tenth house, it will have more impact on the outcome of the election than it would have if located in the third, sixth, ninth, or twelfth house.

The Moon is considered weak when she is void-of-course (near the end of a sign and not aspecting other planets). Experience has proven that activities begun during a void-of-course Moon often have a different ending than what was expected.

In electional astrology, the worst zodiacal position of the Moon is the 30 degrees referred to as the "Via Combusta," (15 degrees Libra to 15 degrees Scorpio). This is especially unfavorable for buying, selling, travelling, and marrying.

The Moon can also be debilitated if it is in difficult aspect to Saturn, Mars, Uranus, Neptune, or Pluto.

# The Moon's Phases

The Moon's phase is important to the success of your election, too. Some elections will have better success if the Moon is in its waxing (increasing) phase, and other elections will benefit from having the Moon in its waning (decreasing) phase.

The first twelve hours after the exact moment of the New Moon are considered unfavorable for many things. The next seventy-two hours (until the time of the first quarter) are considered favorable. The twelve hours beginning with the exact time of the first quarter are unfortunate. This pattern continues throughout the Moon's cycle.

The Moon Tables (pages 56 to 78) or Llewellyn's *Astrological Calendar* can show you what sign the Moon is in, when it changes quarter phase; and the tables on pages 83–88 show when it goes void-of-course.

## First Quarter

The first quarter begins at the New Moon, when the Sun and Moon are conjoined (the Sun and Moon are in the same degree of the same zodiac sign). The New Moon phase is a time for new beginnings that favor growth. It is a time to draw things to you. During this phase, the lunar and solar forces work together, pulling things in the same direction. Toward the end of the first quarter is the best time to finalize plans. It is the time when things germinate and begin to emerge.

## Second Quarter

The second quarter begins when the Sun and Moon are ninety degrees apart (about seven days into the lunation cycle), and it ends with the Full Moon. This half Moon rises about noontime and sets near midnight, and it can be seen in the western sky during the first half of the night. It represents growth, development, and the expression of things that already exist.

If your plans are taking shape, concentrate on completing or adding to projects at this time. It should be noted that every thing has its own timeline. Events occurring now may be the result of something initiated in a different lunation cycle, year, or even a different "season" of life.

## Third Quarter

The third quarter begins at the Full Moon (about fourteen days into the lunation cycle), when the Sun is opposite the Moon, allowing its full light to shine on the Moon. Early in this phase, the Moon can be seen rising in the east at sunset, and then rising a little later each evening. The Full Moon stands for illumination, completion, unrest, and using what we worked to create. Toward the end of the third quarter is a time of maturity, fruition, and fulfillment.

## Fourth Quarter

The fourth quarter begins about day twenty-one of the lunation cycle, or halfway between the Full Moon and next New Moon. The Sun and Moon are again at ninety degrees apart, or square. A waning Moon rises at midnight and it can be seen in the east during the last half of the night, reaching the overhead position at about the time the Sun is rising. The fourth quarter is a time of disintegration, drawing back for reorganization, reflecting on what has past, and ridding yourself of what has become unnecessary in order to make room for what is new to come in.

## The Moon's Aspects

The aspects the Moon makes or will make, during the times you are considering are also important. A trine or sextile, sometimes a conjunction, are considered favorable aspects. A trine or sextile between the Sun and Moon is an excellent foundation for success. Whether or not a conjunction is favorable depends upon the planet the Moon is making a conjunction to. If it's joining the Sun, Venus, Mercury, Jupiter, or even Saturn, the aspect is favorable. If the Moon joins Pluto or Mars, however, that would not be considered favorable. There may be exceptions, but it would depend on what you are electing to do. For example, a trine to Pluto might hasten the end of a relationship you want to be free of.

It is important to avoid times when the Moon makes an aspect to or is conjoining any retrograde planet, unless, of course, you want the thing started to end in failure.

After the Moon has completed an aspect to a planet, that planetary energy has passed. For example, if the Moon squares Saturn at 10:00 am, you can disregard Saturn's influence on your activity if it will occur after that time. You should always look ahead at aspects the Moon will make on the day in question, though, because if the Moon opposes Mars at 11:30 pm on that day, you can expect events that stretch into the evening to be affected by the Moon-Mars aspect. A testy conversation might lead to an argument, or more, for example.

# A Little Lunacy

Did you know that Moon madness was taken seriously for generations? *Luna*, Latin for "Moon," forms the origin of common words like "lunacy," "loony", and "lunatic." Robert Eisle, author of *The Royal Art of Astrology*, wrote that until 1842 the Lunacy Act defined a "Lunatic" as a demented person enjoying lucid intervals during the first two phases of the Moon and afflicted with a period of fatuity in the period following after the Full Moon.

## Who's Afraid of the Big Bad Wolf?

Some people think that it's dangerous to go out at night during a Full Moon because that's when the werewolves roam.

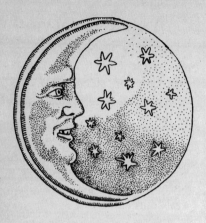

## The Moon Signs

Much agricultural work is ruled by earth signs—Virgo, Capricorn, and Taurus; and the air signs—Gemini, Aquarius, and Libra—rule flying and intellectual pursuits.

Each planet has one or two signs in which its characteristics are particularly enhanced or "dignified," and the planet is said to "rule" that sign. The Sun rules Leo and the Moon rules Cancer, for example. The ruling planet for each sign is listed below. These should not be considered complete lists. We recommend that you purchase a book of planetary rulerships for more complete information.

### Aries Moon

The energy of an Aries Moon is masculine, dry, barren, and fiery. Aries provides great start-up energy, but things started at this time may be the result of impulsive action that lacks research or necessary support. Aries lacks staying power.

Use this assertive, outgoing Moon sign for initiating changes, but have a plan in place to complete the process, or someone to pick up the reins when you're impatient to move on to the next thing. Work that requires skillful, but not necessarily patient, use of tools—hammering, cutting down trees, etc.—is appropriate in Aries. Expect things to occur rapidly but to also quickly pass. If you are prone to injury or accidents, exercise caution and good judgment in Aries related activities.

**Ruler:** Mars
**Impulse:** Action
**Rules:** Head and face
**Plants:** Aloe, buttercup, and star thistle
**Locations:** Large cities, corner houses, east, east corner rooms, east walls, and entryways
**Most compatible with:** Gemini, Leo, Sagittarius, and Aquarius

### Taurus Moon

A Taurus Moon's energy is feminine, semi-fruitful, and earthy. The Moon is exalted—very strong—in Taurus. Taurus is known as the farmer's sign because of its associations with farmland and precipitation that is typically of the day-long "soaker" type. Taurus energy is good to incorporate into your plans when patience, practicality, and perseverance are needed. Be aware, though, that you may also experience stubbornness in this sign.

Things started in Taurus tend to be long lasting and to increase in value. This can be very supportive energy in a marriage election. On the downside, the fixed energy of this sign resists change or the letting go of even the most difficult situations. A divorce following a marriage that occurred during a Taurus Moon may be difficult and costly to end. Things begun now tend to become habitual and hard to alter. If you want to make changes in something you start, it would be better to wait for Gemini.

Moon in Taurus is a good time to get a loan. However, the people in charge of money are cautious and slow to make decisions at this time.

**Ruler:** Venus
**Impulse:** Stability
**Rules:** Neck, throat, and voice
**Plants:** Columbine, daisy, cowslip, goldenrod, and violet
**Locations:** Quiet places, center rooms, middle of the block, fields, landscaped areas near a building, safes, storerooms, and southeast
**Most compatible with:** Cancer, Virgo, Capricorn, and Pisces

## Gemini Moon

A Gemini Moon's energy is masculine, dry, barren, and airy. People are more changeable than usual and may prefer to follow intellectual pursuits and play mental games rather than apply themselves to practical concerns.

This sign is not favored for agricultural matters, but it is an excellent time to prepare for activities, to run errands, write letters, and so on. Plan to use a Gemini Moon for exchanging ideas, meeting people, vacations that include a lot of walking or biking, or in situations that require versatility and quick thinking on your feet.

**Ruler:** Mercury
**Impulse:** Versatility
**Sign Rules:** Shoulders, hands, arms, lungs, and nervous system
**Plants:** Ferns, lily of the valley, vervain, yarrow, and woodbine
**Locations:** High places, grain elevators, roads of all kinds, subways, schools, and upper rooms
**Most compatible with:** Aries, Leo, Aquarius, and Libra

## Cancer Moon

In Cancer the Moon's energy is feminine, fruitful, very moist, and considered extremely strong. Use this sign when you want to grow things—flowers, fruits, vegetables, commodities, stocks, or collections—for example. This sensitive sign stimulates rapport between people. Considered the most fertile of the signs, it is often associated with mothering. You can use the Cancer Moon time to build personal friendships that support mutual growth.

Cancer is associated (through the water element) with emotions and feeings. Prominent Cancer energy promotes growth, but it can also turn people pouty and prone to withdrawing into their shells.

**Ruler:** The Moon
**Impulse:** Tenacity
**Rules:** Chest area, breasts, and stomach
**Plants:** Iris, lotus, white rose, white lily, night-blooming and water plants
**Locations:** Near water, gardens, shady places, ditches, kitchens, eating areas, grocery stores, warehouses, bathrooms, cellars, north, and north walls
**Most compatible with:** Virgo, Scorpio, Pisces, Taurus, and Leo

## Leo Moon

A Leo Moon's energy is masculine, hot, dry, fiery, and barren. Use it whenever you need to put on a show, make a presentation, or entertain colleagues or guests. This is a proud yet playful energy that exudes self-confidence and is often associated with romance.

During a Leo Moon is an excellent time to conduct fundraisers and ceremonies, or to enter into situations where you need to be straight forward, frank, and honest about something. It is advisable not to put yourself in a position of needing public approval or where you might have to cope with underhandedness, as trouble in these areas can bring out the worst Leo traits. There is

a tendency in this sign to become arrogant or self-centered.

**Ruler:** The Sun
**Impulse:** I am
**Rules:** Heart, upper back
**Plants:** Daffodil, dill, poppy, eyebright, fennel, red rose, mistletoe, marigolds, sunflower, and saffron
**Locations:** Outdoors, mountains, ballrooms, castles, dance halls, forests, stadiums, and sunrooms
**Most compatible with:** Aries, Libra, Gemini, and Sagittarius

## Virgo Moon

A Virgo Moon is feminine, dry, barren, earthy energy. It is favorable for anything that needs painstaking attention—especially those things where exactness rather than innovation is preferred.

Use this sign for activities when you must analyze information, or when you must determine the value of something. Virgo is the sign of bargain hunting. It's friendly toward agricultural matters with an emphasis on animals and harvesting vegetables. It is an excellent time to care for animals, especially training them and veterinarian work.

This sign is most beneficial when decisions have already been made and now need to be carried out. The inclination here is to see details rather than the bigger picture.

There is a tendency in this sign to overdo. Precautions should be taken to avoid becoming too dull from all work and no play. Build a little relaxation and pleasure into your routine from the beginning.

**Ruler:** Mercury
**Impulse:** Discriminating
**Rules:** Abdomen and intestines
**Plants:** Grains, azalea, lavender, skullcap, and woodbine
**Locations:** Rural areas, closets, dairies, gardens, lands that are level and productive, meadows, pantries, sick rooms, rooms that are kept locked, and southwest
**Most compatible with:** Cancer, Scorpio, Capricorn, and Taurus

## Libra Moon

The Moon's energy is masculine, semi-fruitful, and airy in Libra. This energy will benefit any attempt to bring beauty to a place of thing. Libra is considered good energy for starting things of an intellectual nature. Libra is the sign of partnership and unions, making it an excellent time to form partnerships of any kind, to make agreements, and to negotiate. Even though this sign is good for initiating things, working with a partner who will provide incentive and encouragement is crucial. A Libra Moon accentuates teamwork (particularly teams of two), and artistic work, (especially work that involves color). Make use of this sign when you are decorating your home or shopping for better quality clothing.

**Ruler:** Venus
**Impulse:** Balance
**Rules:** Lower back, kidneys, and buttocks
**Plants:** Lemon-thyme, strawberries, flowers in general
**Locations:** Beauty salons, bedrooms, boudoirs, boutiques, corner building facing west, west corner room, west wall of room, garrets, and upper airy rooms
**Most compatible with:** Aquarius, Leo, Gemini, and Sagittarius

## Scorpio Moon

The energy of a Scorpio Moon is feminine, fruitful, cold, moist energy. It is useful when intensity (that sometimes seems to border on obsession) is needed. Scorpio is considered a very psychic sign. Use this Moon sign when you must back up something you strongly believe in, such as union or employer relations. There is strong group loyalty here, but during a Scorpio Moon is a good time to end connections thoroughly. This is also a good time to conduct research.

The desire nature is so strong here that there is a tendency to manipulate situations to get what one wants, or to not see one's responsibility in an act.

**Ruler:** Pluto, Mars (traditional)
**Impulse:** Transformation
**Rules:** Reproductive organs, genitals, groin, and pelvis
**Plants:** Honeysuckle, heather, thistle, poisonous plants, and wormwood

room, vaults, and vaulted passages

**Most compatible with:** Taurus, Virgo, and Pisces

## Aquarius Moon

An Aquarius Moon's energy is masculine, barren, dry, and airy. Activities that are unique, individualistic, concerned with humanitarian issues, society as a whole, and making improvements are favored under this Moon. It is this quality of making improvements that has caused this sign to be associated with inventors and new inventions.

An Aquarius Moon promotes the gathering of social groups for friendly exchanges. People tend to react and speak from an intellectual rather than emotional viewpoint when the Moon is in this sign.

**Ruler:** Uranus, Saturn
**Impulse:** Reformer
**Rules:** Calves and ankles
**Plants:** Frankincense
**Locations:** High places where there is activity, movie theaters, airplanes, airplane hangers, and lecture halls
**Most compatible with:** Aries, Libra, Sagittarius, and Gemini

## Pisces Moon

A Pisces Moon is feminine, fruitful, cool, and moist. If you want to retreat, meditate, sleep, pray, or make that dreamed-of escape on a fantasy vacation, this is an excellent time to do it. However, things are not always what they seem to be with the Moon in Pisces. Personal boundaries tend to be fuzzy, and you may not be seeing things clearly. People tend to be idealistic under this sign, which can prevent them from seeing reality.

There is a live and let live philosophy attached to this sign, which in the idealistic world may work well enough, but chaos is frequently the result. That's why this sign is also associated with alcohol and drug abuse, drug trafficking, and counterfeiting. On the lighter side, many musicians and artists are ruled by Pisces. It's only when they move too far away from reality that the dark side of substance abuse, suicide, or crime takes away life.

**Ruler:** Jupiter and Neptune
**Impulse:** Empathetic
**Rules:** Feet
**Plants:** Water lily, water ferns, and mosses that grow in water
**Locations:** Ponds, oceans, convents, gasoline stations, hospitals, institutions, rooms with low ceilings, southeast, southeast wall, and submarines
**Most compatible with:** Taurus. Capricorn, Cancer, and Scorpio

# More About the Zodiac Signs

## Element (Triplicity)

Each of the zodiac signs is classified as belonging to the element of fire, earth, air, or water. These are the four basic elements. Aries, Sagittarius, and Leo are fire signs. Fire signs are action oriented, outgoing, energetic, and spontaneous. Taurus, Capricorn, and Virgo are earth signs. The earth signs are stable, conservative, practical, and oriented to the physical and material realm. Gemini, Aquarius, and Libra are air signs. Air signs are sociable, critical, and tend to represent intellectual responses rather than feelings. Cancer, Scorpio, and Pisces are water signs. The water signs are emotional, receptive, intuitive, and can be very sensitive.

## Quality (Quadruplicity)

Each zodiac sign is further classified as being cardinal, mutable, or fixed. There are four signs in each quadruplicity, one sign from each element.

The cardinal signs of Cancer, Aries, Libra, and Capricorn represent beginnings. They initiate new action. The cardinal signs initiate each new season in the cycle of the year.

Fixed signs want to maintain the status quo through stubbornness and persistence. Taurus, Leo, Scorpio, and Aquarius represent that between time. For example, Leo is the month when summer really is summer.

Mutable signs adapt to change and tolerate situations. Pisces, Gemini, Sagittarius, and Virgo represent the last month of each season, when things are changing in preparation for the next season.

## Nature and Fertility

In addition to a sign's element and quality, each sign is further classified as either fruitful, semi-fruitful, or barren. This classification is the most important for readers who use the gardening information in the *Moon Sign Book* because the timing of most events depends on the fertility of the sign occupied by the Moon. The water signs of Cancer, Scorpio, and Pisces are the most fruitful. The semi-fruitful signs are the earth signs Taurus and Capricorn, and the air sign Libra. The barren signs correspond to the fire signs Aries, Leo, and Sagittarius; the air signs Gemini and Aquarius; and the earth sign Virgo.

# Lunar Superstitions to Live By

Hold up a piece of money to the New Moon and you will receive money.

A girl can gain a beautiful complexion if she sleeps in the moonlight.

If there is a frost between the New Moon and Full Moon, it will not nip plants.

Plant seeds when the Moon is full and they will not do well.

Scatter manure on a field during the dark of the Moon and it will sink down into the ground.

Grass seed will not do well unless sown in the light of the Moon.

If weeds are cut in the dark of the Moon, they will not come up again.

If a wife is impregnated in the Full Moon, her husband will father a son.

Babies begotten in the light of the Moon are always girls.

A crescent Moon has its points tilting downward and since it cannot hold water, look for rain.

A crescent Moon with its points tipping downward is a wet Moon because water is pouring out of the dipper.

A kiss blown to the Moon when she is new makes dreams and wishes come true.

If a Full Moon is shining, there will not be any frost.

# Good Timing

### by Sharon Leah

*It is advantageous to make choice of days and hours at a time well constitutied by the nativity. Should the time be adverse, the choice will in no respect avail, however favourable an issue it may chance to promise.*

Ptolemy

Electional astrology is the art of "electing" times to begin any undertaking. Say, for example, you start a business. That business will experience ups and downs, as well as reach its potential, according to the promise held in the universe at the time the business was started—its birth time. The horoscope (birth chart) set for the time that a business was started would indicate its path.

So, you might ask yourself the question: if the horoscope for a business start can show success or failure, why not begin at a time that is more favorable to the venture? Well, you can.

While no time is "perfect," there are better times and better days to undertake specific activities. There are thousands of examples that prove electional astrology is not only practical, but that it can make a difference in our lives. The benefit of considering the Moon's sign and phase when planting was proven to me during two recent summers.

In two consecutive years I went out of town to attend astrology conferences at the end of May, during the time when Zone 4 gardens should be planted. Upon returning home the first year, I transplanted tomatoes into the garden and planted corn and green bean seeds, even though the *Astrological Calendar* indicated that it was the wrong Moon sign and phase to plant in.

To say the crops were bad that year would not be an understatement. The corn stalks were weak and the ears of corn that did set on were small, with deformed kernels. Rabbits ate the beans so I don't know what would have happened to them, and I don't think we got twelve good tomatoes from six plants. The best thing I can say for the effort we put into the garden that year is that weeds didn't completely take over the space.

Before leaving for the conference the second year, I glanced at the calendar and saw that I would miss the "best" planting time again, and there wouldn't be another good opportunity to plant until the third week in June. Even though it would be very late for planting, I decided to wait. What a difference it made! The tomato vines were vigorous, and the yield was phenomenal. The tomatoes were big, beautiful, and very tasty. (I didn't plant any beans for the bunnies that year.)

If you could schedule meetings so that attendees would be awake, attentive, and cooperative, wouldn't you do it? And wouldn't most of us prefer to enjoy the clothing we buy for a longer time than only the day we bought them? I hate it when I buy on a whim, only to realize days later that I'll never wear the item again.

There are rules for electing times to begin various activities. You'll find detailed instructions about how to make elections beginning on page 36.

# Personalizing Elections

The election rules provided in this almanac are based upon the planetary positions at the time for which the election is made. They do not depend on any type of birth chart. However, a birth chart based upon the time, date, and birthplace of an event does have advantages.

Why is a birth chart important if you can make elections without one? Because no election is effective for every person. For example, you may leave home at the same time as a friend to begin a trip, but each of you will have a different experience according to whether or not your birth chart favors the trip.

Not all elections require a birth chart, but the timing of very important events—business starts, marriages, etc.—would benefit from the additional accuracy a birth chart provides. To order a birth chart for yourself or a planned event, visit our website at www.llewellyn.com.

## Some Things to Consider

You've probably experienced good timing in your life. Maybe you were at the right place at the right time to meet a friend whom you hadn't seen in years. Frequently, when something like that happens, it is the result of following an intuitive impulse—that "gut instinct."

While no time is "perfect," there are definitely better times and better days to undertake specific activities. Electional astrology is a tool that can help you to align with energies, present and future, that are available due to planetary placements.

### Significators

Decide upon the important "significators" (planets, signs, and houses ruling the matter) for which the election is being made. The Moon is the most important significator in any election, so the Moon should always be "fortified" (strong by sign, and making favorable aspects to other planets). The Moon's aspects to other planets are more important than the sign the Moon is in, however.

The other important significators are the Ascendant and Midheaven with their rulers, the house ruling the election matter, and the ruler of the sign on that house cusp. Finally, any planet or sign that has a general rulership over the matter in question should be taken into consideration.

A list of significators (rulerships) begins on page 29, however, it is advisable that you purchase a book on astrological rulerships.

### Nature and Fertility

Determine the general nature of the sign that is appropriate for your election. For example, much agricultural work is ruled by the earth signs of Virgo, Capricorn, and Taurus; while the air signs—Gemini, Aquarius, and Libra—rule intellectual pursuits.

### One Final Comment

Use common sense. If you must do something, like plant your garden or take an airplane trip on a day that doesn't have the best aspects, proceed anyway, but try to minimize problems. For example, leave early for the airport to avoid being left behind due to delays in the security lanes. When you have no other choice, do the best that you can under the circumstances at the time.

# Zodiac Signs and Their Corresponding Body Parts

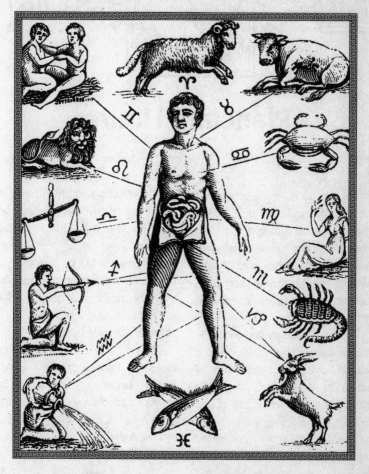

| | | | | |
|---|---|---|---|---|
| ♈ | = Aries | | ♎ | = Libra |
| ♉ | = Taurus | | ♏ | = Scorpio |
| ♊ | = Gemini | | ♐ | = Sagittarius |
| ♋ | = Cancer | | ♑ | = Capricorn |
| ♌ | = Leo | | ♒ | = Aquarius |
| ♍ | = Virgo | | ♓ | = Pisces |

# Planetary Hours

The ability to choose the "best" time for an event—meetings, marriage, trips, buying a home, and so on—to begin is one of the great benefits you can gain by using electional astrology. You've read that planets have rulership over specific days and things. Planets have rulership over specific times during each day, too.

The astrological day begins at the exact moment of local sunrise in your area, and the night begins at local sunset. The first planetary hour of the day depends on what day of the week it is. Sunday and the first planetary hour of Sunday are ruled by the Sun, the second hour is ruled by the Moon, the third hour by Mars, and so on, until the eighth hour after sunrise, which is again ruled by the Sun.

Monday and the first hour after sunrise on Monday are ruled by the Moon. The second hour is ruled by Mars, the third by Mercury, and so

on. Tuesday and the first hour after sunrise on Tuesday are ruled by Mars. Wednesday and the first hour after sunrise on Wednesday are ruled by Mercury. Thursday and the first hour after sunrise on Thursday are ruled by Jupiter. Friday and the first hour after sunrise on Friday are ruled by Venus. Saturday and the first hour after sunrise on Saturday are ruled by Saturn.

The length of a planetary hour varies, depending on the time of the year, because days are longer in summer than they are in winter (in the Northern Hemisphere). So to find the length of a planetary hour, you must first know the length of time between sunrise and sunset in hours and minutes. You divide that time by twelve, which gives you the length of a planetary hour on a specific date. It is easier to work with the time if you convert hours to sixty-minute segments. Divide the total time by twelve. Do the same to find the length of a night time planetary hour.

## The Advantage of Using Planetary Hours

It is a lot easier and less time consuming to figure out an hour table than it is to learn how to set up an election chart. There are books available, including Maria K. Simms *A Time for Magick* (Llewellyn, 2001) that have the hour tables already figured out for you. You will also find more complete information on planetary hours in the book.

Your may also find information about planetary hours on various web sites. An Internet search at the time of this writing turned up several resources. It would be best if you conducted your own search, though, because Internet addresses change frequently and without warning.

If you elect to begin an activity that involves writing, for example, you could start the letter or project on a Wednesday (Mercury rules writing and communications), or during a Mercury hour. But if you wanted to begin a courtship or some other activity that involves a woman, choosing to begin on a Friday (Venus rules courtship, women, and matters relating to women) or during a Venus hour would be to your advantage.

**Sunday is ruled by the Sun.**
**Monday is ruled by the Moon.**
**Tuesday is ruled by Mars.**
**Wednesday is ruled by Mercury.**
**Thursday is ruled by Jupiter.**
**Friday is ruled by Venus.**
**Saturday is ruled by Saturn.**

# Planetary Rulerships

Each sign and planet rules many things, including specific parts of the body. The lists that begin on the following page are not meant to be complete, but they will give you some idea about what activities are ruled over by each planet. We recommend that you refer to a book of planetary and sign rulerships if you are going to use electional astrology. There are several books on the planet rulerships available, including Rex E. Bills' *The Rulership Book* and Dr. Lee Lehman's *The Book of Rulerships*. Maria K. Simms' book *A Time for Magic* is another excellent resource if you want help with timing elections.

## The Moon

The Moon rules over things that are constantly changing: the tides, emotions and feelings, and fluctuating character. She also rules the public in general. Other things ruled by the Moon include:

Babies
Bakers and bakeries
Bars, bartenders
Baths
Breasts
Cafes
Childbirth
Cleaning
Collectors and collections
Dairys
Domestic life
Ferries
Fish
Fortunetellers
Furniture
Germination
Homes
Houseboats
Kitchens
Land
Lamps
Mariners
Midwives
Monday
Nurses
Oceans
Public opinion
Reproduction
Water pipes
Water-related occupations
Women in general

## Mercury

Driving and other forms of travel are Mercury ruled, as are most forms of communication. So, for example, hard aspects to Mercury or Mercury retrograde may result in lost letters, snarled traffic, delayed mail delivery, and faulty office equipment. Other things ruled by Mercury include:

Advertising
Agents
Amnesia
Animals, small and domestic
Animals, training
Audits
Bookcases
Books and bookstores
Communications
Commuting
Conferences
Contracts
Editors
Early education
Eyeglasses
Humor and humorists
Interviews
Invoices
Manuscripts
Neighbors
Research
Telephones
Socializing
Traffic
Vehicles
Veterinarians
Wednesday
Writing
Written agreements

## Venus

Parties and social events planned when Venus is receiving good aspects from other planets are more apt to be fun and successful. When she is receiving less favorable aspects, parties are likely to be boring or poorly attended. Other things ruled by Venus include:

Apparel, women's
Art
Art dealers and museums
Artists
Ballrooms
Banks, banking, bankers
Bank notes
Brokers
Brides, bridegrooms
Brotherhoods
Cashiers
Costumes
Customers
Dressmakers
Furnishings
Gardens, gardeners
Hotels
Jewelry
Maids, servant
Opera, opera singers
Paperhangers
Profits
Romance
Shops, shopping, shopkeepers
Social gatherings
Vacations
Wallets
Wine

## Sun

When important meetings or interviews are scheduled at a time when the Sun is making a favorable aspect to your natal Ascendant, you will make a more favorable impression on people. If the Sun is afflicted, however, business dealings should be avoided. Other things ruled by the Sun include:

Authorities
Casinos
Chief executives
Commanders
Coronations
Empires
Foremen
Games, professional
Gambling, gamblers
Grants
Government
Government service
Honors
Managers
Moneylenders
Parks, park keepers
Playgrounds
Politicians
Principals
Recreation
Resorts
Self-expression
Showboats
Speculation, speculators
Stock brokering
Stock market
Theaters

## Mars

It is best to postpone situations that could result in confrontations with someone when Mars is in hard aspect (squaring) a sensitive point in your birth chart. Fights and power struggles will likely be the outcome if Mars is feeling pressure from other planets. However, when Mars is transiting your Ascendant, it will often bring a strong sense of self-confidence to you. Other things ruled by Mars include:

Accidents
Ambition
Ammunition
Arenas
Armed forces
Atheletes
Barbers
Battles
Blacksmiths
Carpenters
Crime, criminals
Dentists, dentistry
Enemies
Firefighters, fire departments
Furnaces
Guards
Leadership
Piercing
Prizefighters
Sports, competitive
Surgery, surgeons
Tatoos
Tools, sharp
Wreckers
Wrenches
Wrestlers

## Jupiter

When you are making a very important move or life change, Jupiter is the most important planet to consider. Favorable Jupiter aspects are beneficial if you are starting an education program or publishing. Jupiter can bring about excesses such as agreeing to too much or overspending. Other things Jupiter rules include:

Accumulation
Advertising, long-range
Animals, large
Appraisals, appraisers
Assessors
Attorneys
Banquets
Benefactors
Bondsmen
Capitalism, capitalists
Celebrations
Clergy
Commerce, general
Costumes
Courts of law
Exports
Financial gain
Income
Indorsements
Inheritances
Journeys, long
Law, legal affairs
Plaintiffs
Profits
Publishing
Reimbursement
Shops and shopkeepers
Sports enthusiasts
Taxation
Vows

## Saturn

You are more apt to succeed at projects that require a long-term committment if Saturn is making good aspects to your birth chart when the work begins. If Saturn is squaring your Midheaven or Sun, failure is more likely to be the outcome. Other things Saturn rules include:

Abandoned places
Aging people
Archeology
Architects
Bankruptcy
Basements
Barriers
Builders, buildings in general
Buyers
Clothing, work
Constrictions
Contraction
Day laborers
Decomposition
Earthy occupations
Engineers
Farms, farmhands
Foreclosures
Government buildings
Hoarding
Landowners
Refrigeration
Rejection
Reservoirs
Self-control
Solitude
Subways
Tenements
Watches, watchmakers

## Uranus

This energy tends to cause unstable conditions that can have either positive or negative effects, depending on your ability to adjust to change. Uranus is impressive in its timing of events. Squares from this planet to your natal planets can bring disruption in your life. Other things Uranus rules include:

Aeronautics
Agitators
Airplanes, airports
Astrologers
Boycotts
Computers
Discrepancies
Electricians
Elevators
Explorers
Free trade
Garages, repair
Gasoline stations
Highways
Immigration
Inventions
Magic and magicians
Mechanisms
Music (electronic)
Passports
Radio
Repairpeople
Research, researchers
Revolution
Science, scientists
Telephones
Television
Transformation
Violations

## Neptune

Generally speaking, it can be said that transits by Neptune are very subtle. Changes that occur under Neptune's influence are so gradual they often go undetected until some time has passed. Neptune rules:

Actors, actresses
Addicts
Admirals
Alcohol, alcoholism
Aquariums
Artists
Baptism
Barges
Bartenders
Baths, bathing
Bayous, bays, beaches
Boats
Butterflies
Camouflage
Charity
Chemicals
Cigarettes
Confessions
Con artists
Drains
Dreams
Espionage
Fog
Liars
Magicians
Missionaries
Obsession
Prisoners
Secrets
Ships
Wasting diseases

## Pluto

The transits of Pluto are profound and have lasting consequences. You may experience big changes in life direction when this transit is interacting with your natal birth chart. Pluto rules:

Abduction
Ambulances
Autopsies
Betrayal
Coffins
Coroners
Death
Decay
Destruction
Detectives
Disasters
Espionage
Funerals
Gangs, gang leaders
Garbage
Legacies
Lewdness
Massacres
Pestilence
Petroleum
Plutonium
Poisons
Pornography
Puzzles
Rape
Satire
Septic systems
Snakes
Vandals
Viruses
Wars

# The Astrological Houses

You'll find this information about the twelve astrological houses more useful if you have a horoscope (birth chart) for yourself or the event in question. If you do not have access to a horoscope, please do not attempt to apply these additional qualifications to your elections.

Each house in the horoscope represents an area of life, and the planets found in a house will have a direct bearing on the outcome of your elections. For example, if Saturn is in the first house, you might expect something to hinder the election. Things may go slower than expected, there might be restrictions or obstacles you didn't need or expect, and so on. The planets and their aspects to other planets in other houses also influence the election. The house ruling the election is very important.

**First house** relates to you and your personal interests in an election; the business or organization in question; the home team in sports; the head.

**Second house** relates to budgets, finances, earnings, and spending power; personal possessions or resources; person(s) who handles financial matters; the ears and throat.

**Third house** relates to local travel by taxi, bus, bike, automobile, walking, and running; extended family, siblings, and neighbors; communications; shoulders, arms, lungs, and nervous system.

**Fourth house** relates to buildings, property, and real-estate investments; family, the father; endings; breast, stomach, and digestive organs.

**Fifth house** relates to children; recreation and entertaining activities; developing resources and products for speculation; gambling; creative work; the heart and upper part of the back.

**Sixth house** relates to daily routine, habits, and schedules; employees and labor unions; small animals, personal well-being and illness; the solar plexus and bowels.

**Seventh house** relates to partnerships, mergers, agreements, your opponent, and competive relationships; the public; kidneys, ovaries, and lower back.

**Eighth house** relates to loans, debts, joint finances, profits and losses from death or inheritance, sharing, borrowed money, and investments; divorce; sexuality; the muscular system, bladder, and sex organs.

**Ninth house** relates to publishing, advertising, and legal matters; foreign travel; higher education; liver and thighs.

**Tenth house** relates to career, management, status, reputation, one's public image; the government; mothers; the knees.

**Eleventh house** relates to groups of friends, organizations, and group activities; condition of employer; wishes and expectations; the ankles.

**Twelfth house** relates to secret activities, plots, and intelligence gathering; confinement, hospitals, institutions; large animals; occult matters; the feet.

# How to Choose the Best Times for Your Activities

When rules for elections refer to "favorable" and "unfavorable" aspects to your Sun sign or to other planets, please refer to the Favorable and Unfavorable Day tables and Lunar Aspectarian for more information. You'll find instructions and the tables beginning on page 50.

The material in this section came from several sources including: *The New A to Z Horoscope Maker and Delineator* by Llewellyn George (Llewellyn, 1999), *Moon Sign Book* (Llewellyn, 1945), and *Electional Astrology* (Slingshot Publishing, 2000) by Vivian Robson. Robson's book was originally published in 1937.

## Advertise (Internet)

The Moon should be conjunct, sextile, or trine Mercury or Uranus; and in the sign of Gemini, Capricorn, or Aquarius.

## Advertise (Print)

Write ads on a favorable Sun sign day while Mercury or Venus is conjunct, sextile, or trine the Moon. Hard aspects to Mars and Saturn should not occur after the time of your event. Ad campaigns produce the best results when the Moon is well aspected in Gemini (to enhance communication) or Capricorn (to build business).

## Automobiles

When buying an automobile, select a time when the Moon is conjunct, sextile, or trine to Mercury, Saturn, or Uranus; and in the sign Gemini or Capricorn.

## Animals

Take home new pets when the day is favorable to your Sun sign, or when the Moon is trine, sextile, or conjunct Mercury, Venus, or Jupiter, or in the sign of Virgo or Pisces. However, avoid days when the Moon is either square or opposing the Sun, Mars, Saturn, Uranus, Neptune, or Pluto. When selecting a pet, have the Moon well aspected by the planet that rules the animal. Cats are ruled by the Sun, dogs by Mercury, birds by Venus, horses by Jupiter, and fish by Neptune. Buy large animals when the Moon is in Sagittarius or Pisces, and making favorable aspects to Jupiter or Mercury. Buy animals smaller than sheep when the Moon is in Virgo with favorable aspects to Mercury or Venus.

## Animals (Breed)

Animals are easiest to handle when the Moon is in Taurus, Cancer, Libra, or Pisces, but try to avoid the Full Moon. To encourage healthy births, animals should be mated so births occur when the Moon is increasing in Taurus, Cancer, Pisces, or Libra. Those born during a semi-fruitful sign (Taurus and Capricorn) will

produce leaner meat. Libra yields beautiful animals for showing and racing.

## Animals (Declaw)

Declaw cats in the dark of the Moon. Avoid the week before and after the Full Moon and the sign of Pisces.

## Animals (Neuter or spay)

Have livestock and pets neutered or spayed when the Moon is in Sagittarius, Capricorn, or Pisces; after it has passed through Scorpio, the sign that rules reproductive organs. Avoid the week before and after the Full Moon.

## Animals (Sell or buy)

In either buying or selling, it is important to keep the Moon and Mercury free from conjunction or any aspect to Mars. Aspects to Mars will create discord and increase the likelihood of wrangling over price and quality. The Moon should be passing from the first quarter to full and sextile or trine Venus or Jupiter.

## Animals (Train)

Train pets when the Moon is in Virgo or when the Moon trines Mercury.

## Borrow (Money or goods)

See that the Moon is not placed between 15 degrees Libra and 15 degrees Scorpio. Let the Moon be waning and in Leo, Scorpio (16 to 30 degrees), Sagittarius, or Pisces. Venus should be in good aspect to the Moon, and the Moon should not be square, opposing, or conjunct either Saturn or Mars.

## Brewing

It is best to start brewing during the third or fourth quarter, when the Moon is in Cancer, Scorpio, or Pisces.

## Build (Start foundation)

Turning the first sod for the foundation marks the beginning of the building. For best results, excavate the site when the Moon is in the first quarter of a fixed sign and making favorable aspects to Saturn.

## Business (Start new)

When starting a business of your own, have the Moon be in Taurus, Virgo, or Capricorn, and waxing (first or second quarter). The Moon should be sextile or trine Jupiter or Saturn, but avoid oppositions or squares. The planet ruling the business should be well aspected, too.

## Buy Goods

Buy during the third quarter, when the Moon is in Taurus for quality, or in a mutable sign (Gemini, Sagittarius, Virgo, or Pisces) for savings. Good aspects from Venus or the Sun are desirable. If you are buying for yourself, it is good if the day is favorable for your Sun sign. You may also apply rules for buying specific items.

## Cakes

The Moon should be in Gemini, Libra, or Aquarius, and in good aspect to Venus or Mercury. Avoid any square, opposition, or conjunction to Saturn, which causes heaviness. If very fancy cakes are being made, the Moon is best in Libra.

## Canning

Can fruits and vegetables when the Moon is in either the third or fourth quarter, and in the water sign Cancer or Pisces. Preserves and jellies use the same quarters and the signs Cancer, Pisces, or Taurus.

## Clothing

Buy clothing on a day that is favorable for your Sun sign, and when Venus or Mercury is well aspected. Avoid aspects to Mars and Saturn. Buy your clothing when the Moon is in Taurus if you want to remain satisfied. Do not buy clothing or jewelry when the Moon is in Scorpio or Aries. See that the Moon is sextile or trine the Sun during the first or second quarters.

## Collections

Try to make collections on days when your Sun is well aspected. Avoid days when the Moon is opposing or square Mars or Saturn. If possible, the Moon should be in a cardinal sign (Aries, Cancer, Libra, or Capricorn). It is more difficult to collect when the Moon is in Taurus or Scorpio.

## Concrete

Pour concrete when the Moon is in the third quarter of the fixed signs of Taurus, Leo, or Aquarius.

## Construction (Begin new)

The Moon should be sextile or trine Jupiter. According to Hermes, no building should be begun when the Moon is in Scorpio or Pisces. The best time to begin building is when the Moon is in Aquarius.

## Consultants (Work with)

The Moon should be conjunct, sextile, or trine Mercury or Jupiter.

## Contracts (Bid on)

The Moon should be in Gemini or Capricorn, and either the Moon or Mercury should be conjunct, sextile, or trine Jupiter.

## Copyrights/Patents

The Moon should be conjunct, trine, or sextile Mercury or Jupiter.

## Cultivate

Cultivate when the Moon is in a barren sign and waning, ideally the fourth quarter in Aries, Gemini, Leo, Virgo, or Aquarius. Third quarter in the sign of Sagittarius will also work.

## Cut Timber

Timber cut during the third or fourth quarter does not become worm-eaten, it will season well, and not warp, decay, or snap during burning. Cut when the Moon is in Taurus, Gemini, Virgo, or Capricorn—especially in August. Avoid the water signs. Look for favorable aspects to Mars.

## Decorating or Home Repairs

Have the Moon in the first or second quarter, and in the sign of Libra, Gemini, or Aquarius. Avoid squares or oppositions to either Mars or Saturn. Having Venus in good aspect to Mars or Saturn is beneficial.

## Demolition

Let the Moon be in Leo, Sagittarius, or Aries, and in the third or fourth quarter.

## Dental and Dentists

Visit the dentist when the Moon is in Virgo, or pick a day marked favorable for your Sun sign Mars should be marked sextile, conjunct, or trine; and avoid squares or oppositions to Saturn, Uranus, or Jupiter.

Teeth are best removed when the Moon is in Gemini, Virgo, Sagittarius, or Pisces, and during the first or second quarter. Avoid the Full Moon! The day should be favorable for your lunar cycle, and Mars and Saturn should be marked conjunct, trine, or sextile. Fillings should be done in the third or fourth quarters in the sign of

Taurus, Leo, Scorpio, or Pisces. The same applies for dentures.

## Dressmaking

William Lilly wrote in 1676: "Make no new clothes, or first put them on when the Moon is in Scorpio or afflicted by Mars, for they will be apt to be torn and quickly worn out." Design, repair, and sew clothes in the first and second quarters of Taurus, Leo, or Libra on a day marked favorable for your Sun sign. Venus, Jupiter, and Mercury should be favorably aspected, but avoid hard aspects to Mars or Saturn.

## Egg-Setting

Eggs should be set so chicks will hatch during fruitful signs. To set eggs, subtract the number of days given for incubation or gestation from the fruitful dates. Chickens incubate in twenty-one days, turkeys and geese in twenty-eight days.

A freshly laid egg loses quality rapidly if it is not handled properly. Use plenty of clean litter in the nests to reduce the number of dirty or cracked eggs. Gather eggs daily in mild weather and at least two times daily in hot or cold weather. The eggs should be placed in a cooler immediately after gathering and stored at 50 to 55° F. Do not store eggs with foods or products that give off pungent odors since eggs may absorb the odors.

Eggs saved for hatching purposes should not be washed. Only clean and slightly soiled eggs should be saved for hatching. Dirty eggs should not be incubated. Eggs should be stored in a cool place with the large ends up. It is not advisable to store the eggs longer than one week before setting them in an incubator.

## Electronics (Buying)

Choose a day when the Moon is in an air sign (Gemini, Libra, Aquarius) and well aspected by Mercury and/or Uranus when buying electronics.

## Electronic (Repair)

The Moon should be sextile or trine Mars or Uranus in a fixed sign (Taurus, Leo, Scorpio, Aquarius).

## Electricity & Gas (Install)

The Moon should be in a fire sign, and there should be no squares, oppositions, or conjunctions with Uranus (ruler of electricity), Neptune (ruler of gas) Saturn, or Mars. Hard aspects to Mars can cause fires.

## Entertain Friends

Let the Moon be in Leo or Libra and making good aspects to Venus. Avoid squares or oppositions by either Mars or Saturn to the Moon or Venus.

## Eyes and Eyeglasses

Have your eyes tested and glasses fitted on a day marked favorable for your Sun sign, and on a day that falls during your favorable lunar cycle.

Mars should not be in aspect with the Moon. The same applies for any treatment of the eyes, which should also be started during the Moon's first or second quarter.

## Fence Posts

Set posts when the Moon is in the third or fourth quarter of the fixed sign Taurus or Leo.

## Fertilize and Compost

Fertilize when the Moon is in a fruitful sign (Cancer, Scorpio, Pisces). Organic fertilizers are best when the Moon is waning. Use chemical fertilizers when the Moon is waxing. Start compost when the Moon is in the fourth quarter in a water sign.

## Find Hidden Treasure

Let the Moon be in good aspect to Jupiter or Venus. If you erect a horoscope for this election, try to place the Moon in the fourth house.

## Find Lost Articles

Search for lost articles during the first quarter and when your Sun sign is marked favorable. Also check to see that the planet ruling the lost item is trine, sextile, or conjunct the Moon. The Moon rules household utensils; Mercury rules letters and books; and Venus rules clothing, jewelry, and money.

## Fishing

During the summer months, the best time of the day to fish is from sunrise to three hours after, and from two hours before sunset until one hour after. Fish do not bite in cooler months until the air is warm, from noon to 3 pm. Warm, cloudy days are good. The most favorable winds are from the south and southwest. Easterly winds are unfavorable. The best days of the month for fishing are when the Moon changes quarters, especially if the change occurs on a day when the Moon is in a water sign (Cancer, Scorpio, Pisces). The best period in any month is the day after the Full Moon.

## Friends

The need for friendship is greater when the Moon is in Aquarius or when Uranus aspects the Moon. Friendship prospers when Venus or Uranus is trine, sextile, or conjunct the Moon. The Moon in Gemini facilitates the chance meeting of acquaintances and friends.

## Grafting or Budding

Grafting is the process of introducing new varieties of fruit on less desirable trees. For this process you should use the increasing phase of the Moon in fruitful signs such as Cancer, Scorpio, or Pisces. Capricorn may be used, too. Cut your grafts while trees are dormant, from December to March. Keep them in a cool, dark, not too dry or too damp place. Do the grafting before the sap starts to flow and while the Moon is from new to full, and preferably while it is in Cancer, Scorpio, or Pisces. The type of plant should determine both cutting and planting times.

## Harvest Crops

Harvest root crops when the Moon is in a dry sign (Aries, Leo, Sagittarius, Gemini, Aquarius) and waning. Harvest grain for storage just after Full Moon, avoiding Cancer, Scorpio, or Pisces. Harvest in the third and fourth quarters in dry signs. Dry crops in the third quarter in fire signs.

## Habit (Breaking)

To end an undesirable habit, and this applies to ending everything from a bad relationship to smoking, start on a day when the Moon is in the fourth quarter and in the barren sign of Gemini, Leo, or Aquarius. Aries, Virgo, and Capricorn may be suitable as well, depending on the habit you want to be rid of. Make sure that your lunar cycle is favorable. Avoid lunar aspects to Mars or Jupiter. However, favorable aspects to Pluto are helpful.

## Haircuts

Haircuts are best when the Moon is in Gemini, Sagittarius, Pisces, Taurus, or Capricorn, but not in Virgo. Look for favorable aspects to Venus. For faster growth, hair should be cut when the Moon is in Cancer or Pisces

and in the first or second quarter. To make hair grow thicker, cut it when the Moon is Full or in opposition to the Sun in the signs of Taurus, Cancer, or Leo. It is best to cut hair up to the Full Moon, but not after. If you want your hair to grow more slowly, have the Moon be in Aries, Gemini, or Virgo, and in the third or fourth quarter. Have Saturn be square or opposing the Moon.

# BEAUTY SALON

Permanents, straightening, and hair coloring will take well if the Moon is in Taurus or Leo and trine or sextile Venus. Avoid hair treatments if Mars is marked as square or in opposition, especially if heat is to be used. For permanents, a trine to Jupiter is helpful. The Moon also should be in the first quarter, and check the lunar cycle for a favorable day in relation to your Sun sign.

## Health

A diagnosis is more likely to be successful when the Moon is in Aries, Cancer, Libra, or Capricorn; and less so when in Gemini, Sagittarius, Pisces, or Virgo. Begin a recuperation program when the Moon is in a cardinal or fixed sign and the day is favorable to your sign. Enter hospitals at these times, too. For surgery, see "Surgical Procedures." Buy medicines when the Moon is in Virgo or Scorpio.

## Home Furnishings (Buying)

Saturn days (Saturday) are good for buying, and Jupiter days (Thursday) are good for selling. Items bought on days when Saturn is well aspected tend to wear longer and purchases tend to be more conservative.

## Home (Buying)

If you desire a permanent home, buy when the New Moon is in a fixed sign—Taurus or Leo—for example. Each sign will affect your decision in a different way. A house bought when the Moon is in Taurus is likely to be more practical and have a country look—right down to the split-rail fence. A house purchased when the Moon is in Leo will more likely be a real showplace.

If you're buying for speculation and a quick turnover, be certain that the Moon is in a cardinal sign (Aries, Cancer, Libra, Capricorn).

Avoid buying when the Moon is in a fixed sign (Leo, Scorpio, Aquarius, Taurus).

## Home (Make repairs)

In all repairs, avoid squares, oppositions, or conjunctions to the planet ruling the place or thing to be repaired. For example, bathrooms are ruled by Scorpio and Cancer. You would not want to start a project in those rooms when the Moon or Pluto is receiving hard aspects. The front entrance, hall, dining room, and porch are ruled by the Sun. So you would want to avoid times when Saturn or Mars are square, opposing, or conjunct the Sun. Also, let the Moon be waxing.

## Home (Selling)

Make a strong effort to list your property for sale when the Sun is marked favorable in your sign and in good aspect to Jupiter. Avoid adverse aspects to as many planets as possible.

## Irrigate

Irrigate when the Moon is in Cancer, Scorpio, or Pisces.

## Job (Start new)

Jupiter and Venus should be sextile, trine, or conjunct the Moon. A day when your Sun is receiving favorable aspects is preferred.

## Legal Matters

A good aspect between the Moon and Jupiter is best for a favorable legal decision. To gain damages through a lawsuit, begin the process during the increasing Moon phases. If you are seeking to avoid payment, set a court date when the Moon is decreasing. A good aspect between the Sun and Moon strengthens your chance of success. In divorce cases, a favorable Moon-Venus aspect is best. The Moon in Cancer or Leo and well aspected by the Sun brings the best results in custody cases.

## Loan (Ask for)

A first and second quarter phase favors the lender, the third and fourth quarters favor the borrower. Good aspects of Jupiter and Venus to the Moon are favorable to both, as is having the Moon in Leo or Taurus.

## Machinery, Appliances, or Tools (Buying)

Tools, machinery, and other implements should be bought on days when your lunar cycle is favorable and when Mars and Uranus are trine, sextile, or conjunct the Moon. Any quarter of the Moon is suitable. When buying gas or electrical appliances, the Moon should be in Aquarius.

## Marriage

The best time for marriage to take place is when the Moon is increasing, but not yet full. Good signs for the Moon to be in are Taurus, Cancer, Leo, or Libra.

The Moon in Taurus produces the most steadfast marriages, but if the partners later want to separate, they may have a difficult time. Make sure that the Moon is well aspected, especially to Venus or Jupiter. Avoid aspects to Mars, Uranus, or Pluto, and the signs Aries, Gemini, Virgo, Scorpio, or Aquarius.

## Mining

Saturn rules mining. Begin work when Saturn is marked conjunct, trine, or sextile. Mine for gold when the Sun is marked conjunct, trine, or sextile. Mercury rules quicksilver, Venus rules copper, Jupiter rules tin, Saturn rules lead and coal, Uranus rules radioactive elements, Neptune rules oil, the Moon rules water. Mine for these items when the ruling planet is marked conjunct, trine, or sextile.

## Mow Lawn

Mow in the first and second quarters (waxing phase) to increase growth and lushness, and in the third and fourth quarters (waning phase) to decrease growth.

## Move to New Home

If you have a choice, and sometimes we don't, make sure that Mars is not aspecting the Moon. Move on a day favorable to your Sun sign, or when the Moon is conjunct, sextile, or trine the Sun.

## Negotiate

When you are choosing a time to negotiate, consider what the meeting is about and what you want to have happen. If it is agreement or compromise between two parties that you desire, have the Moon be in the sign of Libra. When you are making contracts, it is best to have the Moon in the same element. For example, if your concern is communication, then elect a time when the Moon is in an air sign. If, on the other hand, your concern is about possessions, an earth sign would be more appropriate. Fixed signs are unfavorable, with the exception of Leo; so are cardinal signs, except for Capricorn. If you are negotiating the end of something, use the rules that apply to ending habits.

## Occupational Training

When you begin training, see that your lunar cycle is favorable that day, and that the planet ruling your occupation is marked conjunct or trine.

## Paint

The best time to paint buildings is during the waning phase of the Moon, and in the sign Libra or Aquarius. If the weather is hot, paint when the Moon is in Taurus. If the weather is cold, paint when the Moon is in Leo. Schedule the painting to start in the fourth quarter as the wood is drier and paint will penetrate wood better. Avoid painting around the New Moon, though, as the wood is likely to be damp, making the paint subject to scalding when hot weather hits it. If the temperature is below 70° F, it is not advisable to paint while the Moon is in Cancer, Scorpio, or Pisces as the paint is apt to creep, check, or run.

## Party (Host or attend)

The best time for parties is when the Moon is in Gemini, Leo, Libra, or Sagittarius, with good aspects to Venus and Jupiter. There should be no aspects between the Moon and Mars or Saturn.

## Pick Mushrooms

Mushrooms, one of the most promising traditional medicines in the world, should be gathered at the Full Moon.

## Plant

Root crops, like carrots and potatoes, are best if planted in the sign Taurus or Capricorn. Beans, peas, tomatoes, peppers, and other fruit-bearing plants, are best if planted in a sign that supports seed growth. Leaf plants, like lettuce, broccoli, or cauliflower, are best planted when the Moon is in a water sign.

It is recommended that you transplant during a decreasing Moon, when forces are then streaming into the lower part of the plant. This helps root growth.

For complete instructions on planting by the Moon, see Gardening by the Moon on page 280, A Guide to Planting (pages 286–91), Gardening Dates (page 292–99, and Companion Planting Guide (303–06).

## Promotion (Ask for)

Choose a day when your Sun sign is favorable. Mercury should be marked conjunct, trine, or sextile. Avoid days when Mars or Saturn is aspected.

## Prune

Prune during the third and fourth quarter of a Scorpio Moon to retard growth and to promote better fruit. Prune when the Moon is in cardinal Capricorn to promote healing.

## Roof a Building

Begin roofing a building during the third or fourth quarter, when the Moon is in Aries or Aquarius. Shin-

gles laid during the New Moon have a tendency to curl at the edges.

## Romance

The same principles hold true for starting a relationship as for marriage. However, since there is less control of when a romance starts, it is sometimes necessary to study it after the fact. Romances begun under an increasing Moon are more likely to be permanent or satisfying, while those begun during the decreasing Moon will tend to transform the participants. The tone of the relationship can be guessed from the sign the Moon is in. Romances begun with the Moon in Aries may be impulsive. Those begun in Capricorn will take greater effort to bring to a desirable conclusion, but they may be very rewarding. Good aspects between the Moon and Venus will have a positive influence on the relationship. Avoid unfavorable aspects to Mars, Uranus, and Pluto. A decreasing Moon, particularly the fourth quarter, facilitates ending a relationship, and causes the least pain.

## Sauerkraut
The best-tasting sauerkraut is made just after the Full Moon in the fruitful signs of Cancer, Scorpio, or Pisces.

## Select a Child's Sex
Count from the last day of menstruation to first day of the next cycle and divide the interval between the two dates into halves. Pregnancy in the first half produces females, but copulation should take place with the Moon in a feminine sign. Pregnancy in the latter half, up to three days before the beginning of menstruation, produces males, but copulation should take place with the Moon in a masculine sign. The three-day period before the next period again produces females.

## Sell or Canvas
Begin these activities during a day favorable to your Sun sign. Otherwise, sell on days when Jupiter, Mercury, or Mars is trine, sextile, or conjunct the Moon. Avoid days when Saturn is square or opposing the Moon, for that always hinders business and causes discord. If the Moon is passing from the first quarter to full. It is best to have the Moon swift in motion and in good aspect with Venus and/or Jupiter.

## Sign Papers
Sign contracts or agreements when the Moon is increasing in a fruitful sign and on a day when the Moon is making favorable aspects to Mercury. Avoid days when Mars, Saturn, or Neptune are square or opposite the Moon.

## Spray and Weed
Spray pests and weeds during the fourth quarter when the Moon is in the barren sign Leo or Aquarius, and making favorable aspects to Pluto. Weed during a waning Moon in a barren sign. For the best days to kill weeds and pests, see pages 301–02.

## Staff (Fire)
Have the Moon in the third or fourth quarter, but not full; the Moon should not be square any planets.

## Staff (Hire)
The Moon should be in the first or second quarter, and preferably in the sign of Gemini or Virgo. The Moon should be conjunct, trine, or sextile Mercury or Jupiter.

## Stocks (Buying)
The Moon should be in Taurus or Capricorn, and there should be a sextile or trine to Jupiter or Saturn.

## Surgical Procedures
The flow of blood, like ocean tides, appears to be related to Moon phases. To reduce hemorrhage after a sur-

gery, schedule it within one week before or after a New Moon.

Schedule surgery to occur during the increase of the Moon if possible, as wounds heal better and vitality is greater than during the decrease of the Moon. Avoid surgery within one week before or after the Full Moon. Select a date when the Moon is past the sign governing the part of the body involved in the operation. For example, abdominal operations should be done when the Moon is in Sagittarius, Capricorn, or Aquarius. To find the signs and the body parts they rule, turn to the chart on page 25. The further removed the Moon sign is from the sign ruling the afflicted part of the body, the better.

For successful operations, do not operate when the Moon is applying to any aspect of Mars (this tends to promote inflammation and complications). See the lunar aspectarian (pages 57–79) to determine days with negative Mars aspects and positive Venus and Jupiter aspects. Never operate with the Moon in the same sign as a person's Sun sign or Ascendant. Let the Moon be in a fixed sign and avoid square or opposing aspects. The Moon should not be void-of-course.

Cosmetic surgery should be done in the increase of the Moon, when the Moon is not square or in opposition to Mars. Avoid days when the Moon is square or opposing Saturn or the Sun.

## Travel (Air)

Start long trips when the Moon is making favorable aspects to the Sun. For enjoyment, aspects to Jupiter are preferable; for visiting, look for favorable aspects to Mercury. To prevent accidents, avoid squares or oppositions to Mars, Saturn, Uranus, or Pluto. Choose a day when the Moon is in Sagittarius or Gemini and well aspected to Mercury, Jupiter, or Uranus. Avoid adverse aspects of Mars, Saturn, or Uranus.

## Travel (Automobile)

Start your journey on a day when the Moon is not in a fixed sign, and when it is marked favorable to your ruler, or to Mercury or Uranus. For automobile travels, choose a day when the Moon is in Gemini and making good aspects to Mercury.

## Wean Children

To wean a child successfully, do so when the Moon is in Sagittarius, Capricorn, Aquarius, or Pisces—signs that do not rule vital human organs. By observing this astrological rule, much trouble for parents and child may be avoided.

## Weight (Reducing)

If you want to lose weight, the best time to get started is when the Moon is in the third or fourth quarter, and in the barren sign of Virgo. Review the section on Using the Moon Tables beginning on page 50 to help you select a date that is favorable to begin your weight loss program.

## Wine and Drinks Other Than Beer

It is best to start brewing when the Moon is in Pisces or Taurus. Sextiles or trines to Venus are favorable, but avoid aspects to Mars or Saturn.

## Write

Write for pleasure or publication when the Moon is in Gemini. Mercury should be making favorable aspects to Uranus and Neptune to promote ingenuity, and in retrograde motion.

# The Moon Tables:
## Using the Aspectarian and Moon Tables

Timing activities is one of the most important things you can do to ensure their success. In many Eastern countries, timing by the planets is so important that practically no event takes place without first setting up a chart for it. Weddings have occurred in the middle of the night because that was when the influences were best. You may not want to take it that far, but you can still make use of the influences of the Moon whenever possible. It's easy and it works!

In the *Moon Sign Book* you will find the information you need to plan just about any activity: weddings, fishing, making purchases, cutting your hair, traveling, and more. Not all of the things you do will fall on favorable days, but we provide the guidelines you need to pick the best day out of the several from which you have to choose. The primary method in the *Moon Sign Book* for choosing your own dates is

to use the Moon Tables that begin on page 56. Following are instructions, examples, and directions on how to read the Moon Tables; and more advanced information on using the tables containing the lunar aspectarian and favorable and unfavorable days (found on odd numbered pages opposite the Moon Tables), Moon void-of-course, and retrograde information to choose the dates that are best for you personally.

To enhance your understanding of the directions given below, we highly recommend that you read the sections of this book called Why the *Moon Sign Book* is Different From Some Almanacs on page 8, Understanding Lunar Astrology on page 10, Retrogrades on page 89, and Moon Void-of-Course on page 82. It's not essential that you read these before you try the examples below, but reading them will deepen your understanding of the date-choosing process.

# The Five Basic Steps

## Step 1: Directions for Choosing Dates

Look up the directions for choosing dates for the activity that you wish to begin, then go to step 2.

## Step 2: Check the Moon Tables

You'll find two tables for each month of the year beginning on page 56. The Moon Tables on the left-hand pages include the day and date, the sign the Moon is in, the element of that sign, the nature of the sign, the Moon's phase, and the times that it changes sign or phase. If there is a time listed after a date, that time is the time when the Moon moves into that zodiac sign. Until then, the Moon is considered to be in the sign for the previous day.

The abbreviation *Full* signifies Full Moon and *New* signifies New Moon. The times listed directly after the abbreviation are the times when the Moon changes sign. The times listed after the phase indicate when the Moon changes phase.

If you know the month you would like to begin your activity, turn directly to that month. You will be using the Moon's sign and phase information most often when you begin choosing your own dates. All times are listed in Eastern Time, and are adjusted for Daylight Saving Time. Use the Time Zone Conversions chart and table on page 80–81 to convert time to your own time zone.

When you have found some dates that meet the criteria for the correct Moon phase and sign for your activity, you may have completed the process. For certain simple activities, such as getting a haircut, the phase and sign information is all that is needed. If the directions for your activity include information on certain lunar aspects, however, you should consult the Lunar Aspectarian. An example of this would be if the directions told you not to perform a certain activity when the Moon is square (Q) Jupiter.

## Step 3: Check the Lunar Aspectarian

On the pages opposite the Moon Tables you will find tables containing the Lunar Aspectarian and Favorable and Unfavorable Days. The Lunar Aspectarian gives the aspects (or angles) of the Moon to the other planets. In a nutshell, it tells where the Moon is in relation to the other planets in the sky. Some placements of the Moon in relation to other planets are favorable, while others are not. To use the Lunar Aspectarian, which is the left half of this table, find the planet that the directions list as favorable for your activity, and run down the column to the date desired. For example, you should avoid aspects to Mars if you are planning surgery. You would look for Mars across the top and then run down that column looking for days where there are no aspects to Mars (as signified by empty boxes). If you want to find a favorable aspect (sextile [X] or trine [T]) to Mercury, run your finger down the column under Mercury until you find an X or T. Adverse aspects to planets are squares [Q] or oppositions [O]. A conjunction [C] is sometimes beneficial, sometimes not, depending on the activity or planets involved.

## Step 4: Favorable and Unfavorable Days

The tables that list favorable and unfavorable days are helpful when you want to choose your personal best dates because your Sun sign is taken into consideration. The twelve Sun signs are listed on the right side of the tables. Once you have determined which days meet your criteria for phase, sign, and aspects, you can determine whether or not those days are positive for you by checking the favorable and unfavorable days for your Sun sign.

To find out if a day is positive for you, find your Sun sign and then look down the column. If it is marked *F*, it is very favorable. The Moon is in the same sign as your Sun on a favorable day. If it is marked *f*, it is slightly favorable; *U* is very unfavorable; and *u* means slightly unfavorable. A day marked very unfavorable (*U*) indicates that the Moon is in the sign opposing your Sun.

Once you have selected good dates for the activity you are about to begin, you can go straight to the examples section beginning on the next page. If you are up to the challenge, though, and would like to learn how to fine-tune your selections even further, read on.

## Step 5: Void-of-Course Moon and Retrogrades

This last step is perhaps the most advanced portion of the procedure. It is generally considered poor timing to make decisions, sign important papers, or start special activities during a Moon void-of-course period or during a Mercury retrograde. Once you have chosen the best date for your activity based on steps one through four, you can check the Void-of-Course tables, beginning on page 83, to find out if any of the dates you have chosen have void periods.

The Moon is said to be void-of-course after it has made its last aspect to a planet within a particular sign, but before it has moved into the next sign. Put simply, the Moon is "resting" during the void-of-course period, so activities initiated at this time generally don't come to fruition. You will notice that there are many void periods during the year, and it is nearly impossible to avoid all of them. Some people choose to ignore these altogether and do not take them into consideration when planning activities.

Next, you can check the Table of Retrograde Periods on page 89 to see what planets are retrograde during your chosen date(s).

A planet is said to be retrograde when it appears to move backward in the sky as viewed from the Earth. Generally, the farther a planet is away from the Sun, the longer it can stay retrograde. Some planets will retrograde for several months at a time. Avoiding retrogrades is not as important in lunar planning as avoiding the Moon void-of-course, with the exception of the planet Mercury.

Mercury rules thought and communication, so it is advisable not to sign important papers, initiate important business or legal work, or make crucial decisions during these times. As with the Moon void-of-course, it is difficult to avoid all planetary retrogrades when beginning events, and you may choose to ignore this step of the process. Following are some examples using some or all of the steps outlined above.

## Using What You've Learned

Let's say you need to make an appointment to have your hair cut. Your hair is thin and you would like it to look thicker. You find the directions for hair care and you see that for thicker hair you should cut hair while the Moon is Full and in the sign of Taurus, Cancer, or Leo. You should avoid the Moon in Aries, Gemini, or Virgo. We'll say that it is the month of January. Look up January in the Moon Tables. The Full Moon falls on January 7 at 10:40 am. The Moon moves into the sign of Leo January 8 at 10:38 pm, and remains in Leo until January 10 at 9:37 pm, so January 8 meets both the phase and sign criteria.

Let's move on to a more difficult example using the sign and phase of the Moon. You want to buy a permanent home. After checking the instructions for purchasing a house (Home, Buying), you'll read that it says you should buy a home when the Moon is in Taurus, Cancer, or Leo. You need to get a loan, so you should also look under "Loans." Here it says that the third and fourth Moon quarters favor the borrower (you). You are going to buy the house in June. Look up June in the Moon Tables. The Moon is in the third quarter June 4–9, the fourth quarter June 9–17. The Moon is in Taurus from 9:37 pm on June 12 until 9:44 am on June 15. The best days for obtaining a loan would be June 13–14, while the Moon is in Taurus.

Just match up the best sign and phase (quarter) to come up with the best date. With all activities, be sure to check the Favorable and Unfavorable Days for your Sun sign in the table adjoining the Lunar Aspectarian. If there is a choice between several dates, pick the one most favorable for you (marked F under your Sun sign). Because buying a home is an important business decision, you may also wish to see if there are Moon voids or a Mercury retrograde during these dates.

Now let's look at an example that uses signs, phases, and aspects. Our example this time is starting new home construction. We will use March as the example month. Looking under "Build, Start Foundation" you'll see that the Moon should be in the first quarter of the fixed sign of Taurus or Leo. You should select a time when the Moon is not making unfavorable aspects to Saturn. (Good aspects are sextiles and trines, marked X and T. Conjunctions are usually considered good if they are not conjunctions to Mars, Saturn, or Neptune.) Look in the July Moon Table. You will see that the Moon is in the first quarter July 17–24. The Moon is in Leo between 4:56 pm on July 17 and 3:44 am on July 20. Now, look to the lunar aspectarian for July. We see that there are no squares or oppositions to Sat-

urn on July 17–19. In addition, there are no negative aspects to Mars on these dates. If you wanted to start building your house in July, the best dates would be July 17–19.

## A Note About Time and Time Zones

All tables in the *Moon Sign Book* use Eastern time. Therefore, it is necessary for you to calculate the difference between your time zone and the Eastern Time Zone when you use tables that show specific times (the Moon Tables and Moon Void-of-Course, for example). Please refer to the Time Conversion Chart on page 81 for help with time conversions. In addition.

*Note:* The *Moon Sign Book* now observes Daylight Saving Time. This is a change from previous years when only Eastern Standard Time was used for the entire year.

### How Does the Time Matter?

Due to the three-hour time difference between the east and west coasts of the United States, those of you living on the East Coast may be, for example, under the influence of a Virgo Moon, while those of you living on the West Coast will still have a Leo Moon influence. Indicating these subtle, but very important, differences within the scope of the tables in this almanac is very cumbersome.

To minimize difficulties and the confusion that does arise, we have chosen to follow a commonly held belief among astrologers: whatever sign the Moon is in at the start of a day—12:00 am Eastern Time—is considered the dominant influence of the day. That sign is indicated in the Moon Tables. If the date you select for an activity shows the Moon changing signs (see the Moon Tables), you can decide how important the sign change may be for your specific election and adjust your election date and time accordingly.

## Use Common Sense

Some activities depend on outside factors. Obviously, you can't go out and plant when there is a foot of snow on the ground. You should adjust to the conditions at hand. If the weather was bad during the first quarter, when it was best to plant crops, do it during the second quarter while the Moon is in a fruitful sign. If the Moon is not in a fruitful sign during the first or second quarter, choose a day when it is in a semi-fruitful sign. The best advice is to choose either the sign or phase that is most favorable when the two don't coincide.

## To Summarize

In order to make the most of your activities, check with the *Moon Sign Book*. First, look up the activity under the proper heading, then look for the information given in the tables (the Moon Tables, Lunar Aspectarian, or Favorable and Unfavorable Days). Choose the best date considering the number of positive factors in effect. If most of the dates are favorable, there is no problem choosing the one that will fit your schedule. However, if there aren't any really good dates, pick the ones with the least number of negative influences.

Please keep in mind that the information found here applies in the broadest sense to the events you want to plan or are considering. To be the most effective, when you use electional astrology, you should also consider your own birth chart in relation to a chart drawn for the time or times you have under consideration.

The best advice we can offer you is: read the entire introduction to each section. We provide examples using current Moon and aspect tables so that you can follow along and get familiar with the process. At first, using the tables may seem confusing because there are several factors to take into account, but if you read the directions carefully and practice, you'll get improved results in no time.

Due to the general nature of this information, we do not guarantee any specific outcomes.

# January Moon Table

| Date | Sign | Element | Nature | Phase |
|------|------|---------|--------|-------|
| 1 Thu. 12:02 am | Taurus | Earth | Semi-fruitful | 2nd |
| 2 Fri. | Taurus | Earth | Semi-fruitful | 2nd |
| 3 Sat. 12:58 pm | Gemini | Air | Barren | 2nd |
| 4 Sun. | Gemini | Air | Barren | 2nd |
| 5 Mon. | Gemini | Air | Barren | 2nd |
| 6 Tue. 1:38 am | Cancer | Water | Fruitful | 2nd |
| 7 Wed. | Cancer | Water | Fruitful | Full 10:40 am |
| 8 Thu. 12:38 pm | Leo | Fire | Barren | 3rd |
| 9 Fri. | Leo | Fire | Barren | 3rd |
| 10 Sat. 9:37 pm | Virgo | Earth | Barren | 3rd |
| 11 Sun. | Virgo | Earth | Barren | 3rd |
| 12 Mon. | Virgo | Earth | Barren | 3rd |
| 13 Tue. 4:38 am | Libra | Air | Semi-fruitful | 3rd |
| 14 Wed. | Libra | Air | Semi-fruitful | 4th 11:46 pm |
| 15 Thu. 9:33 am | Scorpio | Water | Fruitful | 4th |
| 16 Fri. | Scorpio | Water | Fruitful | 4th |
| 17 Sat. 12:18 pm | Sagittarius | Fire | Barren | 4th |
| 18 Sun. | Sagittarius | Fire | Barren | 4th |
| 19 Mon. 1:24 pm | Capricorn | Earth | Semi-fruitful | 4th |
| 20 Tue. | Capricorn | Earth | Semi-fruitful | 4th |
| 21 Wed. 2:11 pm | Aquarius | Air | Barren | New 4:05 pm |
| 22 Thu. | Aquarius | Air | Barren | 1st |
| 23 Fri. 4:29 pm | Pisces | Water | Fruitful | 1st |
| 24 Sat. | Pisces | Water | Fruitful | 1st |
| 25 Sun. 10:06 pm | Aries | Fire | Barren | 1st |
| 26 Mon. | Aries | Fire | Barren | 1st |
| 27 Tue. | Aries | Fire | Barren | 1st |
| 28 Wed. 7:46 am | Taurus | Earth | Semi-fruitful | 1st |
| 29 Thu. | Taurus | Earth | Semi-fruitful | 2nd 1:03 am |
| 30 Fri. 8:18 pm | Gemini | Air | Barren | 2nd |
| 31 Sat. | Gemini | Air | Barren | 2nd |

# January

**Lunar Aspectarian**      **Favorable and Unfavorable Days**

| | Sun | Mercury | Venus | Mars | Jupiter | Saturn | Uranus | Neptune | Pluto | Aries | Taurus | Gemini | Cancer | Leo | Virgo | Libra | Scorpio | Sagittarius | Capricorn | Aquarius | Pisces |
|---|---|---|---|---|---|---|---|---|---|---|---|---|---|---|---|---|---|---|---|---|---|
| 1 | T | | | | | X | X | Q | | F | | f | u | f | | U | | f | u | f | |
| 2 | | | Q | | T | | | | | | F | | f | u | f | | U | | f | u | f |
| 3 | | | | | | | | Q | | | F | | f | u | f | | U | | f | u | f |
| 4 | | | | X | | | | T | | f | | F | | f | u | f | | U | | f | u |
| 5 | | O | T | | | Q | | | O | f | | F | | f | u | f | | U | | f | u |
| 6 | | | | | | C | T | | | f | | F | | f | u | f | | U | | f | u |
| 7 | O | | | Q | X | | | | | u | f | | F | | f | u | f | | U | | f |
| 8 | | | | | | | | | | u | f | | F | | f | u | f | | U | | f |
| 9 | | | | T | | | | O | | f | u | f | | F | | f | u | f | | U | |
| 10 | | T | O | | | | | O | T | f | u | f | | F | | f | u | f | | U | |
| 11 | | | | | | X | | | | | f | u | f | | F | | f | u | f | | U |
| 12 | T | | | | C | | | | Q | | f | u | f | | F | | f | u | f | | U |
| 13 | | Q | | | | Q | | | | | f | u | f | | F | | f | u | f | | U |
| 14 | Q | | | O | | | | T | X | U | | f | u | f | | F | | f | u | f | |
| 15 | | X | T | | | T | | | | U | | f | u | f | | F | | f | u | f | |
| 16 | | | | | X | T | | Q | | | U | | f | u | f | | F | | f | u | f |
| 17 | X | | Q | | | | | Q | | | U | | f | u | f | | F | | f | u | f |
| 18 | | | | T | Q | | | X | C | f | | U | | f | u | f | | F | | f | u |
| 19 | | C | | | | | X | | | f | | U | | f | u | f | | F | | f | u |
| 20 | | | X | | T | O | | | | u | f | | U | | f | u | f | | F | | f |
| 21 | C | | Q | | | | | | | u | f | | U | | f | u | f | | F | | f |
| 22 | | | | | | | | C | | f | u | f | | U | | f | u | f | | F | |
| 23 | | | | X | | | | C | X | f | u | f | | U | | f | u | f | | F | |
| 24 | | X | C | | | T | | | | | f | u | f | | U | | f | u | f | | F |
| 25 | | | | O | | | | | Q | | f | u | f | | U | | f | u | f | | F |
| 26 | X | | | | Q | | X | | | F | | f | u | f | | U | | f | u | f | |
| 27 | | Q | | C | | | | | T | F | | f | u | f | | U | | f | u | f | |
| 28 | | | | | | X | X | | | F | | f | u | f | | U | | f | u | f | |
| 29 | Q | T | X | | T | | | Q | | | F | | f | u | f | | U | | f | u | f |
| 30 | | | | | | | | Q | | | F | | f | u | f | | U | | f | u | f |
| 31 | T | | | | | | | T | | f | | F | | f | u | f | | U | | f | u |

# February Moon Table

| Date | Sign | Element | Nature | Phase |
|------|------|---------|--------|-------|
| 1 Sun. | Gemini | Air | Barren | 2nd |
| 2 Mon. 9:03 am | Cancer | Water | Fruitful | 2nd |
| 3 Tue. | Cancer | Water | Fruitful | 2nd |
| 4 Wed. 7:50 pm | Leo | Fire | Barren | 2nd |
| 5 Thu. | Leo | Fire | Barren | 2nd |
| 6 Fri. | Leo | Fire | Barren | Full 3:47 am |
| 7 Sat. 4:03 am | Virgo | Earth | Barren | 3rd |
| 8 Sun. | Virgo | Earth | Barren | 3rd |
| 9 Mon. 10:12 am | Libra | Air | Semi-fruitful | 3rd |
| 10 Tue. | Libra | Air | Semi-fruitful | 3rd |
| 11 Wed. 2:58 pm | Scorpio | Water | Fruitful | 3rd |
| 12 Thu. | Scorpio | Water | Fruitful | 3rd |
| 13 Fri. 6:35 pm | Sagittarius | Fire | Barren | 4th 8:39 am |
| 14 Sat. | Sagittarius | Fire | Barren | 4th |
| 15 Sun. 9:14 pm | Capricorn | Earth | Semi-fruitful | 4th |
| 16 Mon. | Capricorn | Earth | Semi-fruitful | 4th |
| 17 Tue. 11:27 pm | Aquarius | Air | Barren | 4th |
| 18 Wed. | Aquarius | Air | Barren | 4th |
| 19 Thu. | Aquarius | Air | Barren | 4th |
| 20 Fri. 2:27 am | Pisces | Water | Fruitful | New 4:18 am |
| 21 Sat. | Pisces | Water | Fruitful | 1st |
| 22 Sun. 7:45 am | Aries | Fire | Barren | 1st |
| 23 Mon. | Aries | Fire | Barren | 1st |
| 24 Tue. 4:30 pm | Taurus | Earth | Semi-fruitful | 1st |
| 25 Wed. | Taurus | Earth | Semi-fruitful | 1st |
| 26 Thu. | Taurus | Earth | Semi-fruitful | 1st |
| 27 Fri. 4:22 am | Gemini | Air | Barren | 2nd 10:24 pm |
| 28 Sat. | Gemini | Air | Barren | 2nd |
| 29 Sun. 5:12 pm | Cancer | Water | Fruitful | 2nd |

# February

## Lunar Aspectarian     Favorable and Unfavorable Days

| | Sun | Mercury | Venus | Mars | Jupiter | Saturn | Uranus | Neptune | Pluto | Aries | Taurus | Gemini | Cancer | Leo | Virgo | Libra | Scorpio | Sagittarius | Capricorn | Aquarius | Pisces |
|---|---|---|---|---|---|---|---|---|---|---|---|---|---|---|---|---|---|---|---|---|---|
| 1 | | | Q | | Q | | | | O | f | | F | | f | u | f | | U | | f | u |
| 2 | | | X | | | C | T | | | f | | F | | f | u | f | | U | | f | u |
| 3 | | | | X | | | | | | u | f | | F | f | u | f | | | U | | f |
| 4 | | O | T | Q | | | | | | u | f | | F | f | u | f | | | U | | f |
| 5 | | | | | | | | O | | f | u | f | | F | | f | u | f | | U | |
| 6 | O | | | | | | | | T | f | u | f | | F | | f | u | f | | U | |
| 7 | | | | T | X | | O | | | f | u | f | | F | | f | u | f | | U | |
| 8 | | | | | C | | | | Q | | f | u | f | | F | | f | u | f | | U |
| 9 | | T | O | | | Q | | | | | f | u | f | | F | | f | u | f | | U |
| 10 | | | | | | | | T | | U | | f | u | f | | F | | f | u | f | |
| 11 | T | | | | | T | | | X | U | | f | u | f | | F | | f | u | f | |
| 12 | | Q | | O | X | T | | Q | | | U | | f | u | f | | F | | f | u | f |
| 13 | Q | | | | | Q | | | | | U | | f | u | f | | F | | f | u | f |
| 14 | | X | T | | Q | | | X | | f | | U | | f | u | f | | F | | f | u |
| 15 | X | | | | | | | | C | f | | U | | f | u | f | | F | | f | u |
| 16 | | | Q | T | T | O | X | | | u | f | | U | | f | u | f | | F | | f |
| 17 | | | | | | | | | | u | f | | U | | f | u | f | | F | | f |
| 18 | | | X | Q | | | | C | | f | u | f | | U | | f | u | f | | F | |
| 19 | | C | | | | | | X | | f | u | f | | U | | f | u | f | | F | |
| 20 | C | | | X | | T | C | | | f | u | f | | U | | f | u | f | | F | |
| 21 | | | | O | | | | | Q | f | u | f | | U | | f | u | f | | | F |
| 22 | | | | | | Q | | | | f | u | f | | U | | f | u | f | | | F |
| 23 | | | C | | | | X | | | F | | f | u | f | | U | | f | u | f | |
| 24 | | X | | | | | X | | T | F | | f | u | f | | U | | f | u | f | |
| 25 | X | | | C | T | X | | Q | | | F | | f | u | f | | U | | f | u | f |
| 26 | | | | | | | | | | | F | | f | u | f | | U | | f | u | f |
| 27 | Q | Q | | | | Q | | | | | F | | f | u | f | | U | | f | u | f |
| 28 | | | | | Q | | | T | | f | | F | | f | u | f | | U | | f | u |
| 29 | | | X | | | | | T | O | f | | F | | f | u | f | | U | | f | u |

# March Moon Table

| Date | Sign | Element | Nature | Phase |
|------|------|---------|--------|-------|
| 1 Mon. | Cancer | Water | Fruitful | 2nd |
| 2 Tue. | Cancer | Water | Fruitful | 2nd |
| 3 Wed. 4:18 am | Leo | Fire | Barren | 2nd |
| 4 Thu. | Leo | Fire | Barren | 2nd |
| 5 Fri. 12:18 pm | Virgo | Earth | Barren | 2nd |
| 6 Sat. | Virgo | Earth | Barren | Full 6:14 pm |
| 7 Sun. 5:31 pm | Libra | Air | Semi-fruitful | 3rd |
| 8 Mon. | Libra | Air | Semi-fruitful | 3rd |
| 9 Tue. 9:03 pm | Scorpio | Water | Fruitful | 3rd |
| 10 Wed. | Scorpio | Water | Fruitful | 3rd |
| 11 Thu. 11:57 pm | Sagittarius | Fire | Barren | 3rd |
| 12 Fri. | Sagittarius | Fire | Barren | 3rd |
| 13 Sat. | Sagittarius | Fire | Barren | 4th 4:01 pm |
| 14 Sun. 2:51 am | Capricorn | Earth | Semi-fruitful | 4th |
| 15 Mon. | Capricorn | Earth | Semi-fruitful | 4th |
| 16 Tue. 6:10 am | Aquarius | Air | Barren | 4th |
| 17 Wed. | Aquarius | Air | Barren | 4th |
| 18 Thu. 10:26 am | Pisces | Water | Fruitful | 4th |
| 19 Fri. | Pisces | Water | Fruitful | 4th |
| 20 Sat. 4:29 pm | Aries | Fire | Barren | New 5:41 pm |
| 21 Sun. | Aries | Fire | Barren | 1st |
| 22 Mon. | Aries | Fire | Barren | 1st |
| 23 Tue. 1:10 am | Taurus | Earth | Semi-fruitful | 1st |
| 24 Wed. | Taurus | Earth | Semi-fruitful | 1st |
| 25 Thu. 12:35 pm | Gemini | Air | Barren | 1st |
| 26 Fri. | Gemini | Air | Barren | 1st |
| 27 Sat. | Gemini | Air | Barren | 1st |
| 28 Sun. 1:23 am | Cancer | Water | Fruitful | 2nd 6:48 pm |
| 29 Mon. | Cancer | Water | Fruitful | 2nd |
| 30 Tue. 1:07 pm | Leo | Fire | Barren | 2nd |
| 31 Wed. | Leo | Fire | Barren | 2nd |

# March

**Lunar Aspectarian**                **Favorable and Unfavorable Days**

| | Sun | Mercury | Venus | Mars | Jupiter | Saturn | Uranus | Neptune | Pluto | Aries | Taurus | Gemini | Cancer | Leo | Virgo | Libra | Scorpio | Sagittarius | Capricorn | Aquarius | Pisces |
|---|---|---|---|---|---|---|---|---|---|---|---|---|---|---|---|---|---|---|---|---|---|
| 1 | T | T | | | X | C | | | | u | f | | F | | f | u | f | | U | | f |
| 2 | | | Q | X | | | | | | u | f | | F | | f | u | f | | U | | f |
| 3 | | | | | | | | | | u | f | | F | | f | u | f | | U | | f |
| 4 | | | | Q | | | | 0 | T | f | u | f | | F | | f | u | f | | U | |
| 5 | | | T | | | X | 0 | | | f | u | f | | F | | f | u | f | | U | |
| 6 | 0 | 0 | | | C | | | | | | f | u | f | | F | | f | u | f | | U |
| 7 | | | | T | | | | | Q | | f | u | f | | F | | f | u | f | | U |
| 8 | | | | | Q | | T | | | U | | f | u | f | | F | | f | u | f | |
| 9 | | | | | | | | X | | U | | f | u | f | | F | | f | u | f | |
| 10 | | 0 | | | X | T | T | Q | | | U | | f | u | f | | F | | f | u | f |
| 11 | T | T | | | 0 | | | | | | U | | f | u | f | | F | | f | u | f |
| 12 | | | | | Q | | Q | | | f | | U | | f | u | f | | F | | f | u |
| 13 | Q | | | | | | X | C | | f | | U | | f | u | f | | F | | f | u |
| 14 | | Q | T | | | 0 | X | | | f | | U | | f | u | f | | F | | f | u |
| 15 | X | | | | T | | | | | u | f | | U | | f | u | f | | F | | f |
| 16 | | X | | T | | | | | | u | f | | U | | f | u | f | | F | | f |
| 17 | | | Q | | | | | C | X | f | u | f | | U | | f | u | f | | F | |
| 18 | | | Q | | | T | C | | | f | u | f | | U | | f | u | f | | F | |
| 19 | | | X | | 0 | | | | | | f | u | f | | U | | f | u | f | | F |
| 20 | C | | | X | | | | | Q | | f | u | f | | U | | f | u | f | | F |
| 21 | | | | | | Q | | X | | F | | f | u | f | | U | | f | u | f | |
| 22 | | C | | | | | | | T | F | | f | u | f | | U | | f | u | f | |
| 23 | | | | | T | X | X | | | F | | f | u | f | | U | | f | u | f | |
| 24 | | | C | | | | | Q | | | F | | f | u | f | | U | | f | u | f |
| 25 | | | | C | | | Q | | | | F | | f | u | f | | U | | f | u | f |
| 26 | X | | | | Q | | | T | | f | | F | | f | u | f | | U | | f | u |
| 27 | | X | | | | | | | 0 | f | | F | | f | u | f | | U | | f | u |
| 28 | Q | | | | X | C | T | | | f | | F | | f | u | f | | U | | f | u |
| 29 | | | | | | | | | | u | f | | F | | f | u | f | | U | | f |
| 30 | | Q | X | | | | | | | u | f | | F | | f | u | f | | U | | f |
| 31 | T | | | | X | | | 0 | | f | u | f | | F | | f | u | f | | U | |

# April Moon Table

| Date | Sign | Element | Nature | Phase |
|------|------|---------|--------|-------|
| 1 Thu. 9:45 pm | Virgo | Earth | Barren | 2nd |
| 2 Fri. | Virgo | Earth | Barren | 2nd |
| 3 Sat. | Virgo | Earth | Barren | 2nd |
| 4 Sun. 3:52 am | Libra | Air | Semi-fruitful | 2nd |
| 5 Mon. | Libra | Air | Semi-fruitful | Full 7:03 am |
| 6 Tue. 6:24 am | Scorpio | Water | Fruitful | 3rd |
| 7 Wed. | Scorpio | Water | Fruitful | 3rd |
| 8 Thu. 7:50 am | Sagittarius | Fire | Barren | 3rd |
| 9 Fri. | Sagittarius | Fire | Barren | 3rd |
| 10 Sat. 9:33 am | Capricorn | Earth | Semi-fruitful | 3rd |
| 11 Sun. | Capricorn | Earth | Semi-fruitful | 4th 11:46 pm |
| 12 Mon. 12:33 pm | Aquarius | Air | Barren | 4th |
| 13 Tue. | Aquarius | Air | Barren | 4th |
| 14 Wed. 5:24 pm | Pisces | Water | Fruitful | 4th |
| 15 Thu. | Pisces | Water | Fruitful | 4th |
| 16 Fri. | Pisces | Water | Fruitful | 4th |
| 17 Sat. 12:24 am | Aries | Fire | Barren | 4th |
| 18 Sun. | Aries | Fire | Barren | 4th |
| 19 Mon. 9:43 am | Taurus | Earth | Semi-fruitful | New 9:21 am |
| 20 Tue. | Taurus | Earth | Semi-fruitful | 1st |
| 21 Wed. 9:10 pm | Gemini | Air | Barren | 1st |
| 22 Thu. | Gemini | Air | Barren | 1st |
| 23 Fri. | Gemini | Air | Barren | 1st |
| 24 Sat. 9:56 am | Cancer | Water | Fruitful | 1st |
| 25 Sun. | Cancer | Water | Fruitful | 1st |
| 26 Mon. 10:14 pm | Leo | Fire | Barren | 1st |
| 27 Tue. | Leo | Fire | Barren | 2nd 1:32 pm |
| 28 Wed. | Leo | Fire | Barren | 2nd |
| 29 Thu. 8:00 am | Virgo | Earth | Barren | 2nd |
| 30 Fri. | Virgo | Earth | Barren | 2nd |

# April

## Lunar Aspectarian     Favorable and Unfavorable Days

| | Sun | Mercury | Venus | Mars | Jupiter | Saturn | Uranus | Neptune | Pluto | Aries | Taurus | Gemini | Cancer | Leo | Virgo | Libra | Scorpio | Sagittarius | Capricorn | Aquarius | Pisces |
|---|---|---|---|---|---|---|---|---|---|---|---|---|---|---|---|---|---|---|---|---|---|
| 1 | | T | Q | | | | | | T | f | u | f | | F | | f | u | f | | U | |
| 2 | | | | Q | C | X | 0 | | | | f | u | f | | F | | f | u | f | | U |
| 3 | | | | | | | | | Q | | f | u | f | | F | | f | u | f | | U |
| 4 | | | T | T | | Q | | | | | f | u | f | | F | | f | u | f | | U |
| 5 | 0 | | | | | | | T | X | U | | f | u | f | | F | | f | u | f | |
| 6 | | 0 | | | X | T | T | | | U | | f | u | f | | F | | f | u | f | |
| 7 | | | | | | | | Q | | | U | | f | u | f | | F | | f | u | f |
| 8 | | | 0 | | | | Q | | | | U | | f | u | f | | F | | f | u | f |
| 9 | T | | | 0 | Q | | | X | C | f | | U | | f | u | f | | F | | f | u |
| 10 | | T | | | | 0 | X | | | f | | U | | f | u | f | | F | | f | u |
| 11 | Q | | | | T | | | | | u | f | | U | | f | u | f | | F | | f |
| 12 | | Q | | | | | | | | u | f | | U | | f | u | f | | F | | f |
| 13 | | | T | T | | | | | C | f | u | f | | U | | f | u | f | | F | |
| 14 | X | X | | | | | | | X | f | u | f | | U | | f | u | f | | F | |
| 15 | | | Q | Q | 0 | T | C | | | | f | u | f | | U | | f | u | f | | F |
| 16 | | | | | | | | Q | | | f | u | f | | U | | f | u | f | | F |
| 17 | | | | | Q | | | | | F | | f | u | f | | U | | f | u | f | |
| 18 | | | X | X | | | | X | T | F | | f | u | f | | U | | f | u | f | |
| 19 | C | C | | | | | X | | | F | | f | u | f | | U | | f | u | f | |
| 20 | | | | | T | X | | Q | | | F | | f | u | f | | U | | f | u | f |
| 21 | | | | | | | | | | | F | | f | u | f | | U | | f | u | f |
| 22 | | | | | Q | | Q | | | f | | F | | f | u | f | | U | | f | u |
| 23 | | X | C | C | | | | T | 0 | f | | F | | f | u | f | | U | | f | u |
| 24 | X | | | | | | T | | | f | | F | | f | u | f | | U | | f | u |
| 25 | | | | | X | C | | | | u | f | | F | | f | u | f | | U | | f |
| 26 | | Q | | | | | | | | u | f | | F | | f | u | f | | U | | f |
| 27 | Q | | | | | | | | | f | u | f | | F | | f | u | f | | U | |
| 28 | | T | X | X | | | | 0 | T | f | u | f | | F | | f | u | f | | U | |
| 29 | | | | | 0 | | | | | f | u | f | | F | | f | u | f | | U | |
| 30 | T | | Q | | C | X | | | Q | | f | u | f | | F | | f | u | f | | U |

# May Moon Table

| Date | Sign | Element | Nature | Phase |
|------|------|---------|--------|-------|
| 1 Sat. 2:03 pm | Libra | Air | Semi-fruitful | 2nd |
| 2 Sun. | Libra | Air | Semi-fruitful | 2nd |
| 3 Mon. 4:38 pm | Scorpio | Water | Fruitful | 2nd |
| 4 Tue. | Scorpio | Water | Fruitful | Full 4:33 pm |
| 5 Wed. 5:08 pm | Sagittarius | Fire | Barren | 3rd |
| 6 Thu. | Sagittarius | Fire | Barren | 3rd |
| 7 Fri. 5:17 pm | Capricorn | Earth | Semi-fruitful | 3rd |
| 8 Sat. | Capricorn | Earth | Semi-fruitful | 3rd |
| 9 Sun. 6:46 pm | Aquarius | Air | Barren | 3rd |
| 10 Mon. | Aquarius | Air | Barren | 3rd |
| 11 Tue. 10:52 pm | Pisces | Water | Fruitful | 4th 7:04 am |
| 12 Wed. | Pisces | Water | Fruitful | 4th |
| 13 Thu. | Pisces | Water | Fruitful | 4th |
| 14 Fri. 6:02 am | Aries | Fire | Barren | 4th |
| 15 Sat. | Aries | Fire | Barren | 4th |
| 16 Sun. 3:57 pm | Taurus | Earth | Semi-fruitful | 4th |
| 17 Mon. | Taurus | Earth | Semi-fruitful | 4th |
| 18 Tue. | Taurus | Earth | Semi-fruitful | 4th |
| 19 Wed. 3:47 am | Gemini | Air | Barren | New 12:52 am |
| 20 Thu. | Gemini | Air | Barren | 1st |
| 21 Fri. 4:35 pm | Cancer | Water | Fruitful | 1st |
| 22 Sat. | Cancer | Water | Fruitful | 1st |
| 23 Sun. | Cancer | Water | Fruitful | 1st |
| 24 Mon. 5:07 am | Leo | Fire | Barren | 1st |
| 25 Tue. | Leo | Fire | Barren | 1st |
| 26 Wed. 3:52 pm | Virgo | Earth | Barren | 1st |
| 27 Thu. | Virgo | Earth | Barren | 2nd 3:57 am |
| 28 Fri. 11:22 pm | Libra | Air | Semi-fruitful | 2nd |
| 29 Sat. | Libra | Air | Semi-fruitful | 2nd |
| 30 Sun. | Libra | Air | Semi-fruitful | 2nd |
| 31 Mon. 3:08 am | Scorpio | Water | Fruitful | 2nd |

# May

**Lunar Aspectarian**     **Favorable and Unfavorable Days**

| | Sun | Mercury | Venus | Mars | Jupiter | Saturn | Uranus | Neptune | Pluto | Aries | Taurus | Gemini | Cancer | Leo | Virgo | Libra | Scorpio | Sagittarius | Capricorn | Aquarius | Pisces |
|---|---|---|---|---|---|---|---|---|---|---|---|---|---|---|---|---|---|---|---|---|---|
| 1 | | | | Q | | | | | | | f | u | f | | F | | f | u | f | | U |
| 2 | | | | | | Q | | T | | U | | f | u | f | | F | | f | u | f | |
| 3 | | 0 | T | T | | | | | X | U | | f | u | f | | F | | f | u | f | |
| 4 | 0 | | | | X | T | T | Q | | | U | | f | u | f | | F | | f | u | f |
| 5 | | | | | | | | | | | U | | f | u | f | | F | | f | u | f |
| 6 | | | | | Q | | Q | X | | f | | U | | f | u | f | | F | | f | u |
| 7 | | T | 0 | 0 | | | | | C | f | | U | | f | u | f | | F | | f | u |
| 8 | | | | | T | | 0 | X | | u | f | | U | | f | u | f | | F | | f |
| 9 | T | Q | | | | | | | | u | f | | U | | f | u | f | | F | | f |
| 10 | | | | | | | | C | | f | u | f | | U | | f | u | f | | F | |
| 11 | Q | X | T | | | | | | X | f | u | f | | U | | f | u | f | | F | |
| 12 | | | | T | 0 | | T | C | | | f | u | f | | U | | f | u | f | | F |
| 13 | X | | Q | | | | | | Q | | f | u | f | | U | | f | u | f | | F |
| 14 | | | Q | | | | | | | | f | u | f | | U | | f | u | f | | F |
| 15 | | | | | Q | | | X | T | F | | f | u | f | | U | | f | u | f | |
| 16 | | C | X | | | | | | | F | | f | u | f | | U | | f | u | f | |
| 17 | | | | X | T | | X | X | Q | | F | | f | u | f | | U | | f | u | f |
| 18 | | | | | | | | | | | F | | f | u | f | | U | | f | u | f |
| 19 | C | | | | Q | | Q | | | f | | F | | f | u | f | | U | | f | u |
| 20 | | | | | | | | T | 0 | f | | F | | f | u | f | | U | | f | u |
| 21 | | | C | | | | | | | f | f | F | | f | u | f | | U | | f | u |
| 22 | | X | | C | X | C | T | | | u | f | | F | | f | u | f | | U | | f |
| 23 | | | | | | | | | | u | f | | F | | f | u | f | | U | | f |
| 24 | X | | | | | | | | | u | f | | F | | f | u | f | | U | | f |
| 25 | | Q | | | | | 0 | T | | f | u | f | | F | | f | u | f | | U | |
| 26 | | | X | | | | | | | f | u | f | | F | | f | u | f | | U | |
| 27 | Q | T | | X | C | X | 0 | | | | f | u | f | | F | | f | u | f | | U |
| 28 | | | Q | | | | | Q | | | f | u | f | | F | | f | u | f | | U |
| 29 | T | | | | | Q | | | | U | | f | u | f | | F | | f | u | f | |
| 30 | | | T | Q | | | | T | X | U | | f | u | f | | F | | f | u | f | |
| 31 | | | | | X | T | T | | | U | | f | u | f | | F | | f | u | f | |

# June Moon Table

| Date | Sign | Element | Nature | Phase |
|------|------|---------|--------|-------|
| 1 Tue. | Scorpio | Water | Fruitful | 2nd |
| 2 Wed. 3:52 am | Sagittarius | Fire | Barren | 2nd |
| 3 Thu. | Sagittarius | Fire | Barren | Full 12:20 am |
| 4 Fri. 3:12 am | Capricorn | Earth | Semi-fruitful | 3rd |
| 5 Sat. | Capricorn | Earth | Semi-fruitful | 3rd |
| 6 Sun. 3:10 am | Aquarius | Air | Barren | 3rd |
| 7 Mon. | Aquarius | Air | Barren | 3rd |
| 8 Tue. 5:38 am | Pisces | Water | Fruitful | 3rd |
| 9 Wed. | Pisces | Water | Fruitful | 4th 4:02 pm |
| 10 Thu. 11:49 am | Aries | Fire | Barren | 4th |
| 11 Fri. | Aries | Fire | Barren | 4th |
| 12 Sat. 9:37 pm | Taurus | Earth | Semi-fruitful | 4th |
| 13 Sun. | Taurus | Earth | Semi-fruitful | 4th |
| 14 Mon. | Taurus | Earth | Semi-fruitful | 4th |
| 15 Tue. 9:44 am | Gemini | Air | Barren | 4th |
| 16 Wed. | Gemini | Air | Barren | 4th |
| 17 Thu. 10:37 pm | Cancer | Water | Fruitful | New 4:27 pm |
| 18 Fri. | Cancer | Water | Fruitful | 1st |
| 19 Sat. | Cancer | Water | Fruitful | 1st |
| 20 Sun. 11:05 am | Leo | Fire | Barren | 1st |
| 21 Mon. | Leo | Fire | Barren | 1st |
| 22 Tue. 10:10 pm | Virgo | Earth | Barren | 1st |
| 23 Wed. | Virgo | Earth | Barren | 1st |
| 24 Thu. | Virgo | Earth | Barren | 1st |
| 25 Fri. 6:50 am | Libra | Air | Semi-fruitful | 2nd 3:08 pm |
| 26 Sat. | Libra | Air | Semi-fruitful | 2nd |
| 27 Sun. 12:13 pm | Scorpio | Water | Fruitful | 2nd |
| 28 Mon. | Scorpio | Water | Fruitful | 2nd |
| 29 Tue. 2:15 pm | Sagittarius | Fire | Barren | 2nd |
| 30 Wed. | Sagittarius | Fire | Barren | 2nd |

# June

## Lunar Aspectarian

## Favorable and Unfavorable Days

| | Sun | Mercury | Venus | Mars | Jupiter | Saturn | Uranus | Neptune | Pluto | Aries | Taurus | Gemini | Cancer | Leo | Virgo | Libra | Scorpio | Sagittarius | Capricorn | Aquarius | Pisces |
|---|---|---|---|---|---|---|---|---|---|---|---|---|---|---|---|---|---|---|---|---|---|
| 1 | | 0 | | T | | | | Q | | | U | | f | u | f | | F | | f | u | f |
| 2 | | | | Q | | Q | | | | | U | | f | u | f | | F | | f | u | f |
| 3 | 0 | | 0 | | | | | X | C | f | | U | | f | u | f | | F | | f | u |
| 4 | | | | T | 0 | X | | | | f | | U | | f | u | f | | F | | f | u |
| 5 | | | | 0 | | | | | | u | f | | U | | f | u | f | | F | | f |
| 6 | | T | | | | | | | | u | f | | U | | f | u | f | | F | | f |
| 7 | T | | T | | | | | C | X | f | u | f | | U | | f | u | f | | F | |
| 8 | | Q | | | | | C | | | f | u | f | | U | | f | u | f | | F | |
| 9 | Q | | Q | T | 0 | T | | | Q | | f | u | f | | U | | f | u | f | | F |
| 10 | | | | | | | | | | | f | u | f | | U | | f | u | f | | F |
| 11 | | X | X | | | Q | X | | | F | | f | u | f | | U | | f | u | f | |
| 12 | X | | | Q | | | | | T | F | | f | u | f | | U | | f | u | f | |
| 13 | | | | T | | X | | | | | F | | f | u | f | | U | | f | u | f |
| 14 | | | | X | | X | | Q | | | F | | f | u | f | | U | | f | u | f |
| 15 | | | | | | Q | | | | | F | | f | u | f | | U | | f | u | f |
| 16 | | | C | Q | | | | T | | f | | F | | f | u | f | | U | | f | u |
| 17 | C | C | | | | | | | 0 | f | | F | | f | u | f | | U | | f | u |
| 18 | | | | X | | T | | | | u | f | | F | | f | u | f | | U | | f |
| 19 | | | | | | C | | | | u | f | | F | | f | u | f | | U | | f |
| 20 | | | C | | | | | | | u | f | | F | | f | u | f | | U | | f |
| 21 | | | X | | | | | 0 | | f | u | f | | F | | f | u | f | | U | |
| 22 | | | | | | | | | T | f | u | f | | F | | f | u | f | | U | |
| 23 | X | X | Q | | C | | 0 | | | | f | u | f | | F | | f | u | f | | U |
| 24 | | | | | | X | | Q | | | f | u | f | | F | | f | u | f | | U |
| 25 | Q | | | X | | | | | | | f | u | f | | F | | f | u | f | | U |
| 26 | | Q | T | | Q | | | T | X | U | | f | u | f | | F | | f | u | f | |
| 27 | T | | | Q | | | T | | | U | | f | u | f | | F | | f | u | f | |
| 28 | | T | | | X | T | | Q | | | U | | f | u | f | | F | | f | u | f |
| 29 | | | T | | | | | | | | U | | f | u | f | | F | | f | u | f |
| 30 | | | 0 | Q | | | Q | X | C | f | | U | | f | u | f | | F | | f | u |

# July Moon Table

| Date | Sign | Element | Nature | Phase |
|------|------|---------|--------|-------|
| 1 Thu. 2:01 pm | Capricorn | Earth | Semi-fruitful | 2nd |
| 2 Fri. | Capricorn | Earth | Semi-fruitful | Full 7:09 am |
| 3 Sat. 1:22 pm | Aquarius | Air | Barren | 3rd |
| 4 Sun. | Aquarius | Air | Barren | 3rd |
| 5 Mon. 2:26 pm | Pisces | Water | Fruitful | 3rd |
| 6 Tue. | Pisces | Water | Fruitful | 3rd |
| 7 Wed. 7:03 pm | Aries | Fire | Barren | 3rd |
| 8 Thu. | Aries | Fire | Barren | 3rd |
| 9 Fri. | Aries | Fire | Barren | 4th 3:34 am |
| 10 Sat. 3:51 am | Taurus | Earth | Semi-fruitful | 4th |
| 11 Sun. | Taurus | Earth | Semi-fruitful | 4th |
| 12 Mon. 3:45 pm | Gemini | Air | Barren | 4th |
| 13 Tue. | Gemini | Air | Barren | 4th |
| 14 Wed. | Gemini | Air | Barren | 4th |
| 15 Thu. 4:40 am | Cancer | Water | Fruitful | 4th |
| 16 Fri. | Cancer | Water | Fruitful | 4th |
| 17 Sat. 4:56 pm | Leo | Fire | Barren | New 7:24 am |
| 18 Sun. | Leo | Fire | Barren | 1st |
| 19 Mon. | Leo | Fire | Barren | 1st |
| 20 Tue. 3:44 am | Virgo | Earth | Barren | 1st |
| 21 Wed. | Virgo | Earth | Barren | 1st |
| 22 Thu. 12:39 pm | Libra | Air | Semi-fruitful | 1st |
| 23 Fri. | Libra | Air | Semi-fruitful | 1st |
| 24 Sat. 7:08 pm | Scorpio | Water | Fruitful | 2nd 11:37 pm |
| 25 Sun. | Scorpio | Water | Fruitful | 2nd |
| 26 Mon. 10:48 pm | Sagittarius | Fire | Barren | 2nd |
| 27 Tue. | Sagittarius | Fire | Barren | 2nd |
| 28 Wed. 11:57 pm | Capricorn | Earth | Semi-fruitful | 2nd |
| 29 Thu. | Capricorn | Earth | Semi-fruitful | 2nd |
| 30 Fri. 11:54 pm | Aquarius | Air | Barren | 2nd |
| 31 Sat. | Aquarius | Air | Barren | Full 2:05 pm |

# July

**Lunar Aspectarian**      **Favorable and Unfavorable Days**

| Day | Sun | Mercury | Venus | Mars | Jupiter | Saturn | Uranus | Neptune | Pluto | Aries | Taurus | Gemini | Cancer | Leo | Virgo | Libra | Scorpio | Sagittarius | Capricorn | Aquarius | Pisces |
|---|---|---|---|---|---|---|---|---|---|---|---|---|---|---|---|---|---|---|---|---|---|
| 1 | | | | | | | | | | f | | U | | f | u | f | | F | | f | u |
| 2 | 0 | | | | T | 0 | X | | | u | f | | U | | f | u | f | | F | | f |
| 3 | | | 0 | 0 | | | | | | u | f | | U | | f | u | f | | F | | f |
| 4 | | | T | | | | | C | X | f | u | f | | U | | f | u | f | | F | |
| 5 | | | | | | | | | | f | u | f | | U | | f | u | f | | F | |
| 6 | T | | Q | | 0 | T | C | | | | f | u | f | | U | | f | u | f | | F |
| 7 | | | | | | | | | Q | | f | u | f | | U | | f | u | f | | F |
| 8 | | T | X | T | | | | X | | F | | f | u | f | | U | | f | u | f | |
| 9 | Q | | | | | Q | | | T | F | | f | u | f | | U | | f | u | f | |
| 10 | | | | | | | | X | | F | | f | u | f | | U | | f | u | f | |
| 11 | X | Q | | Q | T | X | | Q | | | F | | f | u | f | | U | | f | u | f |
| 12 | | | | | | | | | | | F | | f | u | f | | U | | f | u | f |
| 13 | | X | C | X | Q | | | Q | T | f | | F | | f | u | f | | U | | f | u |
| 14 | | | | | | | | | 0 | f | | F | | f | u | f | | U | | f | u |
| 15 | | | | | | | | T | | f | | F | | f | u | f | | U | | f | u |
| 16 | | | | | | X | C | | | u | f | | F | | f | u | f | | U | | f |
| 17 | C | | | | | | | | | u | f | | F | | f | u | f | | U | | f |
| 18 | | | X | | | | | 0 | | f | u | f | | F | | f | u | f | | U | |
| 19 | | C | | C | | | | | T | f | u | f | | F | | f | u | f | | U | |
| 20 | | | | | | | | 0 | | f | u | f | | F | | f | u | f | | U | |
| 21 | | | Q | | C | X | | | Q | f | u | f | | F | | f | u | f | | | U |
| 22 | X | | | | | | | | | f | u | f | | F | | f | u | f | | | U |
| 23 | | | T | X | | Q | | T | | U | | f | u | f | | F | | f | u | f | |
| 24 | Q | X | | | | | | | X | U | | f | u | f | | F | | f | u | f | |
| 25 | | | | | | T | Q | | | | U | | f | u | f | | F | | f | u | f |
| 26 | | | Q | | X | T | | | | | U | | f | u | f | | F | | f | u | f |
| 27 | T | Q | | | | | Q | X | | f | | U | | f | u | f | | F | | f | u |
| 28 | | | 0 | T | Q | | | | C | f | | U | | f | u | f | | F | | f | u |
| 29 | | T | | | | | X | | | u | f | | U | | f | u | f | | F | | f |
| 30 | | | | | T | 0 | | | | u | f | | U | | f | u | f | | F | | f |
| 31 | 0 | | | | | | | C | | f | u | f | | U | | f | u | f | | F | |

# August Moon Table

| Date | Sign | Element | Nature | Phase |
|------|------|---------|--------|-------|
| 1 Sun. | Aquarius | Air | Barren | 3rd |
| 2 Mon. 12:34 am | Pisces | Water | Fruitful | 3rd |
| 3 Tue. | Pisces | Water | Fruitful | 3rd |
| 4 Wed. 3:59 am | Aries | Fire | Barren | 3rd |
| 5 Thu. | Aries | Fire | Barren | 3rd |
| 6 Fri. 11:26 am | Taurus | Earth | Semi-fruitful | 3rd |
| 7 Sat. | Taurus | Earth | Semi-fruitful | 4th  6:01 pm |
| 8 Sun. 10:33 pm | Gemini | Air | Barren | 4th |
| 9 Mon. | Gemini | Air | Barren | 4th |
| 10 Tue. | Gemini | Air | Barren | 4th |
| 11 Wed. 11:20 am | Cancer | Water | Fruitful | 4th |
| 12 Thu. | Cancer | Water | Fruitful | 4th |
| 13 Fri. 11:30 pm | Leo | Fire | Barren | 4th |
| 14 Sat. | Leo | Fire | Barren | 4th |
| 15 Sun. | Leo | Fire | Barren | New 9:24 pm |
| 16 Mon. 9:49 am | Virgo | Earth | Barren | 1st |
| 17 Tue. | Virgo | Earth | Barren | 1st |
| 18 Wed. 6:09 pm | Libra | Air | Semi-fruitful | 1st |
| 19 Thu. | Libra | Air | Semi-fruitful | 1st |
| 20 Fri. | Libra | Air | Semi-fruitful | 1st |
| 21 Sat. 12:37 am | Scorpio | Water | Fruitful | 1st |
| 22 Sun. | Scorpio | Water | Fruitful | 1st |
| 23 Mon. 5:08 am | Sagittarius | Fire | Barren | 2nd 6:12 am |
| 24 Tue. | Sagittarius | Fire | Barren | 2nd |
| 25 Wed. 7:46 am | Capricorn | Earth | Semi-fruitful | 2nd |
| 26 Thu. | Capricorn | Earth | Semi-fruitful | 2nd |
| 27 Fri. 9:08 am | Aquarius | Air | Barren | 2nd |
| 28 Sat. | Aquarius | Air | Barren | 2nd |
| 29 Sun. 10:33 am | Pisces | Water | Fruitful | Full 10:22 pm |
| 30 Mon. | Pisces | Water | Fruitful | 3rd |
| 31 Tue. 1:46 pm | Aries | Fire | Barren | 3rd |

# August

## Lunar Aspectarian    Favorable and Unfavorable Days

| | Sun | Mercury | Venus | Mars | Jupiter | Saturn | Uranus | Neptune | Pluto | Aries | Taurus | Gemini | Cancer | Leo | Virgo | Libra | Scorpio | Sagittarius | Capricorn | Aquarius | Pisces |
|---|---|---|---|---|---|---|---|---|---|---|---|---|---|---|---|---|---|---|---|---|---|
| 1 | | | T | 0 | | | | | X | f | u | f | | U | | f | u | f | | F | |
| 2 | | 0 | | | | | C | | | f | u | f | | U | | f | u | f | | F | |
| 3 | | | Q | | 0 | T | | | Q | | f | u | f | | U | | f | u | f | | F |
| 4 | | | | | | | | | | | f | u | f | | U | | f | u | f | | F |
| 5 | T | | | | | Q | | X | T | F | | f | u | f | | U | | f | u | f | |
| 6 | | | X | T | | | | X | | F | | f | u | f | | U | | f | u | f | |
| 7 | Q | T | | | | | | | Q | | F | | f | u | f | | U | | f | u | f |
| 8 | | | Q | T | X | | | | | | F | | f | u | f | | U | | f | u | f |
| 9 | | Q | | | | | | Q | | f | | F | | f | u | f | | U | | f | u |
| 10 | X | | | | | Q | | T | 0 | f | | F | | f | u | f | | U | | f | u |
| 11 | | | C | X | | | T | | | f | | F | | f | u | f | | U | | f | u |
| 12 | | X | | | | | | | | u | f | | F | | f | u | f | | U | | f |
| 13 | | | | | | X | C | | | u | f | | F | | f | u | f | | U | | f |
| 14 | | | | | | | | | | f | u | f | | F | | f | u | f | | U | |
| 15 | C | | | | | | | 0 | T | f | u | f | | F | | f | u | f | | U | |
| 16 | | C | | C | | | | 0 | | f | u | f | | F | | f | u | f | | U | |
| 17 | | | X | | | | | | Q | | f | u | f | | F | | f | u | f | | U |
| 18 | | | | | | C | X | | | | f | u | f | | F | | f | u | f | | U |
| 19 | | | Q | | | | | T | | U | | f | u | f | | F | | f | u | f | |
| 20 | X | | | | | Q | | | X | U | | f | u | f | | F | | f | u | f | |
| 21 | | X | | X | | | T | | | U | | f | u | f | | F | | f | u | f | |
| 22 | | | T | | X | T | | Q | | | U | | f | u | f | | F | | f | u | f |
| 23 | Q | Q | | Q | | Q | | | | | U | | f | u | f | | F | | f | u | f |
| 24 | | | | | Q | | | X | C | f | | U | | f | u | f | | F | | f | u |
| 25 | T | T | | | | | X | | | f | | U | | f | u | f | | F | | f | u |
| 26 | | | 0 | T | T | | 0 | | | u | f | | U | | f | u | f | | F | | f |
| 27 | | | | | | | | | | u | f | | U | | f | u | f | | F | | f |
| 28 | | | | | | | C | X | | f | u | f | | U | | f | u | f | | F | |
| 29 | 0 | 0 | | | | | C | | | f | u | f | | U | | f | u | f | | F | |
| 30 | | | | 0 | | | | | Q | | f | u | f | | U | | f | u | f | | F |
| 31 | | | T | | 0 | T | | | | | f | u | f | | U | | f | u | f | | F |

# September Moon Table

| Date | Sign | Element | Nature | Phase |
|------|------|---------|--------|-------|
| 1 Wed. | Aries | Fire | Barren | 3rd |
| 2 Thu. 8:16 pm | Taurus | Earth | Semi-fruitful | 3rd |
| 3 Fri. | Taurus | Earth | Semi-fruitful | 3rd |
| 4 Sat. | Taurus | Earth | Semi-fruitful | 3rd |
| 5 Sun. 6:24 am | Gemini | Air | Barren | 3rd |
| 6 Mon. | Gemini | Air | Barren | 4th 11:10 am |
| 7 Tue. 6:50 pm | Cancer | Water | Fruitful | 4th |
| 8 Wed. | Cancer | Water | Fruitful | 4th |
| 9 Thu. | Cancer | Water | Fruitful | 4th |
| 10 Fri. 7:06 am | Leo | Fire | Barren | 4th |
| 11 Sat. | Leo | Fire | Barren | 4th |
| 12 Sun. 5:16 pm | Virgo | Earth | Barren | 4th |
| 13 Mon. | Virgo | Earth | Barren | 4th |
| 14 Tue. | Virgo | Earth | Barren | New 10:29am |
| 15 Wed. 12:54 am | Libra | Air | Semi-fruitful | 1st |
| 16 Thu. | Libra | Air | Semi-fruitful | 1st |
| 17 Fri. 6:25 am | Scorpio | Water | Fruitful | 1st |
| 18 Sat. | Scorpio | Water | Fruitful | 1st |
| 19 Sun. 10:30 am | Sagittarius | Fire | Barren | 1st |
| 20 Mon. | Sagittarius | Fire | Barren | 1st |
| 21 Tue. 1:35 pm | Capricorn | Earth | Semi-fruitful | 2nd 11:54 am |
| 22 Wed. | Capricorn | Earth | Semi-fruitful | 2nd |
| 23 Thu. 4:10 pm | Aquarius | Air | Barren | 2nd |
| 24 Fri. | Aquarius | Air | Barren | 2nd |
| 25 Sat. 6:55 pm | Pisces | Water | Fruitful | 2nd |
| 26 Sun. | Pisces | Water | Fruitful | 2nd |
| 27 Mon. 10:57 pm | Aries | Fire | Barren | 2nd |
| 28 Tue. | Aries | Fire | Barren | Full 9:09 am |
| 29 Wed. | Aries | Fire | Barren | 3rd |
| 30 Thu. 5:24 am | Taurus | Earth | Semi-fruitful | 3rd |

# September

## Lunar Aspectarian — Favorable and Unfavorable Days

| | Sun | Mercury | Venus | Mars | Jupiter | Saturn | Uranus | Neptune | Pluto | Aries | Taurus | Gemini | Cancer | Leo | Virgo | Libra | Scorpio | Sagittarius | Capricorn | Aquarius | Pisces |
|---|---|---|---|---|---|---|---|---|---|---|---|---|---|---|---|---|---|---|---|---|---|
| 1 | | | | | | | | X | | F | | f | u | f | | U | | f | u | f | |
| 2 | | T | Q | | | Q | | | T | F | | f | u | f | | U | | f | u | f | |
| 3 | T | | | | | | X | Q | | | F | | f | u | f | | U | | f | u | f |
| 4 | | Q | | | T | T | X | | | | F | | f | u | f | | U | | f | u | f |
| 5 | | | X | | | | | Q | | | F | | f | u | f | | U | | f | u | f |
| 6 | Q | | | Q | | | | T | 0 | f | | F | | f | u | f | | U | | f | u |
| 7 | | X | | Q | | | | | | f | | F | | f | u | f | | U | | f | u |
| 8 | | | | | | | T | | | u | f | | F | | f | u | f | | U | | f |
| 9 | X | | | X | | C | | | | u | f | | F | | f | u | f | | U | | f |
| 10 | | | C | X | | | | | | u | f | | F | | f | u | f | | U | | f |
| 11 | | | | | | | | 0 | T | f | u | f | | F | | f | u | f | | U | |
| 12 | | C | | | | | | | | f | u | f | | F | | f | u | f | | U | |
| 13 | | | | | | 0 | | | | | f | u | f | | F | | f | u | f | | U |
| 14 | C | | | | C | C | X | | Q | | f | u | f | | F | | f | u | f | | U |
| 15 | | | X | | | | | | | U | | f | u | f | | F | | f | u | f | |
| 16 | | | | | | Q | | T | X | U | | f | u | f | | F | | f | u | f | |
| 17 | | | | | | | | T | | U | | f | u | f | | F | | f | u | f | |
| 18 | | X | Q | | | | | Q | | | U | | f | u | f | | F | | f | u | f |
| 19 | X | | | X | X | T | Q | | | | U | | f | u | f | | F | | f | u | f |
| 20 | | Q | T | | | | | X | C | f | | U | | f | u | f | | F | | f | u |
| 21 | Q | | | Q | Q | | X | | | f | | U | | f | u | f | | F | | f | u |
| 22 | | T | | | | | | | | u | f | | U | | f | u | f | | F | | f |
| 23 | T | | | T | T | 0 | | | | u | f | | U | | f | u | f | | F | | f |
| 24 | | | | | | | | C | | f | u | f | | U | | f | u | f | | F | |
| 25 | | | 0 | | | | | | X | f | u | f | | U | | f | u | f | | F | |
| 26 | | | | | | | C | | | | f | u | f | | U | | f | u | f | | F |
| 27 | | 0 | | | | T | | | Q | | f | u | f | | U | | f | u | f | | F |
| 28 | 0 | | | 0 | 0 | | | X | | F | | f | u | f | | U | | f | u | f | |
| 29 | | | T | | | Q | | | T | F | | f | u | f | | U | | f | u | f | |
| 30 | | | | | | | X | | | F | | f | u | f | | U | | f | u | f | |

# October Moon Table

| Date | Sign | Element | Nature | Phase |
|------|------|---------|--------|-------|
| 1 Fri. | Taurus | Earth | Semi-fruitful | 3rd |
| 2 Sat. 2:55 pm | Gemini | Air | Barren | 3rd |
| 3 Sun. | Gemini | Air | Barren | 3rd |
| 4 Mon. | Gemini | Air | Barren | 3rd |
| 5 Tue. 2:54 am | Cancer | Water | Fruitful | 3rd |
| 6 Wed. | Cancer | Water | Fruitful | 4th 6:12 am |
| 7 Thu. 3:23 pm | Leo | Fire | Barren | 4th |
| 8 Fri. | Leo | Fire | Barren | 4th |
| 9 Sat. | Leo | Fire | Barren | 4th |
| 10 Sun. 2:00 am | Virgo | Earth | Barren | 4th |
| 11 Mon. | Virgo | Earth | Barren | 4th |
| 12 Tue. 9:32 am | Libra | Air | Semi-fruitful | 4th |
| 13 Wed. | Libra | Air | Semi-fruitful | New 10:48 pm |
| 14 Thu. 2:10 pm | Scorpio | Water | Fruitful | 1st |
| 15 Fri. | Scorpio | Water | Fruitful | 1st |
| 16 Sat. 4:58 pm | Sagittarius | Fire | Barren | 1st |
| 17 Sun. | Sagittarius | Fire | Barren | 1st |
| 18 Mon. 7:07 pm | Capricorn | Earth | Semi-fruitful | 1st |
| 19 Tue. | Capricorn | Earth | Semi-fruitful | 1st |
| 20 Wed. 9:38 pm | Aquarius | Air | Barren | 2nd 5:59 pm |
| 21 Thu. | Aquarius | Air | Barren | 2nd |
| 22 Fri. | Aquarius | Air | Barren | 2nd |
| 23 Sat. 1:13 am | Pisces | Water | Fruitful | 2nd |
| 24 Sun. | Pisces | Water | Fruitful | 2nd |
| 25 Mon. 6:24 am | Aries | Fire | Barren | 2nd |
| 26 Tue. | Aries | Fire | Barren | 2nd |
| 27 Wed. 1:37 pm | Taurus | Earth | Semi-fruitful | Full 11:07 pm |
| 28 Thu. | Taurus | Earth | Semi-fruitful | 3rd |
| 29 Fri. 11:11 pm | Gemini | Air | Barren | 3rd |
| 30 Sat. | Gemini | Air | Barren | 3rd |
| 31 Sun. | Gemini | Air | Barren | 3rd |

# October

## Lunar Aspectarian        Favorable and Unfavorable Days

| | Sun | Mercury | Venus | Mars | Jupiter | Saturn | Uranus | Neptune | Pluto | Aries | Taurus | Gemini | Cancer | Leo | Virgo | Libra | Scorpio | Sagittarius | Capricorn | Aquarius | Pisces |
|---|---|---|---|---|---|---|---|---|---|---|---|---|---|---|---|---|---|---|---|---|---|
| 1 | | | | | | | | Q | | | F | | f | u | f | | U | | f | u | f |
| 2 | | | Q | T | T | X | Q | | | | F | | f | u | f | | U | | f | u | f |
| 3 | T | T | | | | | | T | | f | | F | | f | u | f | | U | | f | u |
| 4 | | | | | | | | O | | f | | F | | f | u | f | | U | | f | u |
| 5 | | | X | Q | Q | | T | | | f | | F | | f | u | f | | U | | f | u |
| 6 | Q | Q | | | | | | | | u | f | | F | | f | u | f | | U | | f |
| 7 | | | | | | X | C | | | u | f | | F | | f | u | f | | U | | f |
| 8 | X | | | X | | | | O | | f | u | f | | F | | f | u | f | | U | |
| 9 | | X | | | | | | T | | f | u | f | | F | | f | u | f | | U | |
| 10 | | | C | | | | | O | | f | u | f | | F | | f | u | f | | U | |
| 11 | | | | | | | | Q | | | f | u | f | | F | | f | u | f | | U |
| 12 | | | | | C | X | | | | | f | u | f | | F | | f | u | f | | U |
| 13 | C | | | C | | | | T | X | U | | f | u | f | | F | | f | u | f | |
| 14 | | C | | | | Q | T | | | U | | f | u | f | | F | | f | u | f | |
| 15 | | | X | | | | | Q | | | U | | f | u | f | | F | | f | u | f |
| 16 | | | | | | T | Q | | | | U | | f | u | f | | F | | f | u | f |
| 17 | | | Q | X | X | | X | | | f | | U | | f | u | f | | F | | f | u |
| 18 | X | | | | | | | C | | f | | U | | f | u | f | | F | | f | u |
| 19 | | X | | Q | Q | | X | | | u | f | | U | | f | u | f | | F | | f |
| 20 | Q | | T | | | O | | | | u | f | | U | | f | u | f | | F | | f |
| 21 | | Q | | | T | | C | | | f | u | f | | U | | f | u | f | | F | |
| 22 | | | T | | | | | X | | f | u | f | | U | | f | u | f | | F | |
| 23 | T | T | | | | | C | | | f | u | f | | U | | f | u | f | | F | |
| 24 | | | O | | | | | Q | | | f | u | f | | U | | f | u | f | | F |
| 25 | | | | | O | T | | | | | f | u | f | | U | | f | u | f | | F |
| 26 | | | O | | | | X | T | | F | | f | u | f | | U | | f | u | f | |
| 27 | O | | | | Q | X | | | | F | | f | u | f | | U | | f | u | f | |
| 28 | | | | | | | | Q | | | F | | f | u | f | | U | | f | u | f |
| 29 | | O | | | | | X | | | | F | | f | u | f | | U | | f | u | f |
| 30 | | | T | | T | | Q | | | f | | F | | f | u | f | | U | | f | u |
| 31 | | | | T | | | | T | O | f | | F | | f | u | f | | U | | f | u |

# November Moon Table

| Date | Sign | Element | Nature | Phase |
|------|------|---------|--------|-------|
| 1 Mon. 9:53 am | Cancer | Water | Fruitful | 3rd |
| 2 Tue. | Cancer | Water | Fruitful | 3rd |
| 3 Wed. 10:32 pm | Leo | Fire | Barren | 3rd |
| 4 Thu. | Leo | Fire | Barren | 3rd |
| 5 Fri. | Leo | Fire | Barren | 4th 12:53 am |
| 6 Sat. 10:00 am | Virgo | Earth | Barren | 4th |
| 7 Sun. | Virgo | Earth | Barren | 4th |
| 8 Mon. 6:23 pm | Libra | Air | Semi-fruitful | 4th |
| 9 Tue. | Libra | Air | Semi-fruitful | 4th |
| 10 Wed. 11:05 pm | Scorpio | Water | Fruitful | 4th |
| 11 Thu. | Scorpio | Water | Fruitful | 4th |
| 12 Fri. | Scorpio | Water | Fruitful | New 9:27 am |
| 13 Sat. 12:56 am | Sagittarius | Fire | Barren | 1st |
| 14 Sun. | Sagittarius | Fire | Barren | 1st |
| 15 Mon. 1:33 am | Capricorn | Earth | Semi-fruitful | 1st |
| 16 Tue. | Capricorn | Earth | Semi-fruitful | 1st |
| 17 Wed. 2:39 am | Aquarius | Air | Barren | 1st |
| 18 Thu. | Aquarius | Air | Barren | 1st |
| 19 Fri. 5:38 am | Pisces | Water | Fruitful | 2nd 12:50 am |
| 20 Sat. | Pisces | Water | Fruitful | 2nd |
| 21 Sun. 11:11 am | Aries | Fire | Barren | 2nd |
| 22 Mon. | Aries | Fire | Barren | 2nd |
| 23 Tue. 7:16 pm | Taurus | Earth | Semi-fruitful | 2nd |
| 24 Wed. | Taurus | Earth | Semi-fruitful | 2nd |
| 25 Thu. | Taurus | Earth | Semi-fruitful | 2nd |
| 26 Fri. 5:25 am | Gemini | Air | Barren | Full 3:07 pm |
| 27 Sat. | Gemini | Air | Barren | 3rd |
| 28 Sun. 5:10 pm | Cancer | Water | Fruitful | 3rd |
| 29 Mon. | Cancer | Water | Fruitful | 3rd |
| 30 Tue. | Cancer | Water | Fruitful | 3rd |

# November

| | Sun | Mercury | Venus | Mars | Jupiter | Saturn | Uranus | Neptune | Pluto | Aries | Taurus | Gemini | Cancer | Leo | Virgo | Libra | Scorpio | Sagittarius | Capricorn | Aquarius | Pisces |
|---|---|---|---|---|---|---|---|---|---|---|---|---|---|---|---|---|---|---|---|---|---|
| 1 | | | Q | | | | | T | | f | | F | | f | u | f | | U | | f | u |
| 2 | T | | | | Q | | | | | u | f | | F | | f | u | f | | U | | f |
| 3 | | T | | Q | | C | | | | u | f | | F | | f | u | f | | U | | f |
| 4 | | | X | | X | | | O | | f | u | f | | F | | f | u | f | | U | |
| 5 | Q | | | | | | | | T | f | u | f | | F | | f | u | f | | U | |
| 6 | | Q | | X | | O | | | | f | u | f | | F | | f | u | f | | U | |
| 7 | X | | | | | | | | | | f | u | f | | F | | f | u | f | | U |
| 8 | | | | | | | X | | Q | | f | u | f | | F | | f | u | f | | U |
| 9 | | X | C | | C | | | T | | U | | f | u | f | | F | | f | u | f | |
| 10 | | | | C | | Q | | | X | U | | f | u | f | | F | | f | u | f | |
| 11 | | | | | | T | Q | | | | U | | f | u | f | | F | | f | u | f |
| 12 | C | | | | | T | | | | | U | | f | u | f | | F | | f | u | f |
| 13 | | C | | | X | | | Q | X | | U | | f | u | f | | F | | f | u | f |
| 14 | | | X | | | | | | C | f | | U | | f | u | f | | F | | f | u |
| 15 | | | | X | Q | | X | | | f | | U | | f | u | f | | F | | f | u |
| 16 | X | | Q | | | | O | | | u | f | | U | | f | u | f | | F | | f |
| 17 | | | Q | T | | | | | | u | f | | U | | f | u | f | | F | | f |
| 18 | | X | T | | | | | C | X | f | u | f | | U | | f | u | f | | F | |
| 19 | Q | | | T | | C | | | | f | u | f | | U | | f | u | f | | F | |
| 20 | | Q | | | | | | | Q | | f | u | f | | U | | f | u | f | | F |
| 21 | T | | | | T | | | | | | f | u | f | | U | | f | u | f | | F |
| 22 | | | | | O | | X | | | F | | f | u | f | | U | | f | u | f | |
| 23 | | T | O | | | Q | | | T | F | | f | u | f | | U | | f | u | f | |
| 24 | | | O | | | | X | Q | | | F | | f | u | f | | U | | f | u | f |
| 25 | | | | | X | | | | | | F | | f | u | f | | U | | f | u | f |
| 26 | O | | | | | | Q | | | | F | | f | u | f | | U | | f | u | f |
| 27 | | | | | T | | | T | | f | | F | | f | u | f | | U | | f | u |
| 28 | | O | | | | T | | | O | f | | F | | f | u | f | | U | | f | u |
| 29 | | | T | T | Q | | | | | u | f | | F | | f | u | f | | U | | f |
| 30 | | | | | | C | | | | u | f | | F | | f | u | f | | U | | f |

# December Moon Table

| Date | Sign | Element | Nature | Phase |
|------|------|---------|--------|-------|
| 1 Wed. 5:50 am | Leo | Fire | Barren | 3rd |
| 2 Thu. | Leo | Fire | Barren | 3rd |
| 3 Fri. 6:00 pm | Virgo | Earth | Barren | 3rd |
| 4 Sat. | Virgo | Earth | Barren | 4th 7:53 pm |
| 5 Sun. | Virgo | Earth | Barren | 4th |
| 6 Mon. 3:46 am | Libra | Air | Semi-fruitful | 4th |
| 7 Tue. | Libra | Air | Semi-fruitful | 4th |
| 8 Wed. 9:43 am | Scorpio | Water | Fruitful | 4th |
| 9 Thu. | Scorpio | Water | Fruitful | 4th |
| 10 Fri. 11:54 am | Sagittarius | Fire | Barren | 4th |
| 11 Sat. | Sagittarius | Fire | Barren | New 8:29 pm |
| 12 Sun. 11:42 am | Capricorn | Earth | Semi-fruitful | 1st |
| 13 Mon. | Capricorn | Earth | Semi-fruitful | 1st |
| 14 Tue. 11:10 am | Aquarius | Air | Barren | 1st |
| 15 Wed. | Aquarius | Air | Barren | 1st |
| 16 Thu. 12:24 pm | Pisces | Water | Fruitful | 1st |
| 17 Fri. | Pisces | Water | Fruitful | 1st |
| 18 Sat. 4:52 pm | Aries | Fire | Barren | 2nd 11:40 am |
| 19 Sun. | Aries | Fire | Barren | 2nd |
| 20 Mon. | Aries | Fire | Barren | 2nd |
| 21 Tue. 12:52 am | Taurus | Earth | Semi-fruitful | 2nd |
| 22 Wed. | Taurus | Earth | Semi-fruitful | 2nd |
| 23 Thu. 11:32 am | Gemini | Air | Barren | 2nd |
| 24 Fri. | Gemini | Air | Barren | 2nd |
| 25 Sat. 11:38 pm | Cancer | Water | Fruitful | 2nd |
| 26 Sun. | Cancer | Water | Fruitful | Full 10:06 am |
| 27 Mon. | Cancer | Water | Fruitful | 3rd |
| 28 Tue. 12:14 pm | Leo | Fire | Barren | 3rd |
| 29 Wed. | Leo | Fire | Barren | 3rd |
| 30 Thu. | Leo | Fire | Barren | 3rd |
| 31 Fri. 12:33 am | Virgo | Earth | Barren | 3rd |

# December

**Lunar Aspectarian**    **Favorable and Unfavorable Days**

| | Sun | Mercury | Venus | Mars | Jupiter | Saturn | Uranus | Neptune | Pluto | Aries | Taurus | Gemini | Cancer | Leo | Virgo | Libra | Scorpio | Sagittarius | Capricorn | Aquarius | Pisces |
|---|---|---|---|---|---|---|---|---|---|---|---|---|---|---|---|---|---|---|---|---|---|
| 1 | | | | | | | | | | u | f | | F | | f | u | f | | U | | f |
| 2 | T | | Q | Q | X | | | O | | f | u | f | | F | | f | u | f | | U | |
| 3 | | T | | | | | | | T | f | u | f | | F | | f | u | f | | U | |
| 4 | Q | | | | | O | | | | | f | u | f | | F | | f | u | f | | U |
| 5 | | Q | X | X | | X | | | Q | | f | u | f | | F | | f | u | f | | U |
| 6 | | | | | | | | | | | f | u | f | | F | | f | u | f | | U |
| 7 | X | X | | | C | | | T | X | U | | f | u | f | | F | | f | u | f | |
| 8 | | | | | | Q | T | | | U | | f | u | f | | F | | f | u | f | |
| 9 | | | C | C | | | | Q | | | U | | f | u | f | | F | | f | u | f |
| 10 | | | | | | T | Q | | | | U | | f | u | f | | F | | f | u | f |
| 11 | C | C | | | X | | | X | C | f | | U | | f | u | f | | F | | f | u |
| 12 | | | | | | | X | | | f | | U | | f | u | f | | F | | f | u |
| 13 | | | | X | Q | | | | | u | f | | U | | f | u | f | | F | | f |
| 14 | | | X | | O | | | | | u | f | | U | | f | u | f | | F | | f |
| 15 | | X | | | T | | | C | X | f | u | f | | U | | f | u | f | | F | |
| 16 | X | | Q | Q | | | C | | | f | u | f | | U | | f | u | f | | F | |
| 17 | | Q | | | | | | | | | f | u | f | | U | | f | u | f | | F |
| 18 | Q | | T | T | T | | | Q | | | f | u | f | | U | | f | u | f | | F |
| 19 | | T | | | O | | | X | | F | | f | u | f | | U | | f | u | f | |
| 20 | | | | | | Q | | | T | F | | f | u | f | | U | | f | u | f | |
| 21 | T | | | | | | X | | | F | | f | u | f | | U | | f | u | f | |
| 22 | | | | | | | | Q | | | F | | f | u | f | | U | | f | u | f |
| 23 | | | | O | | X | Q | | | | F | | f | u | f | | U | | f | u | f |
| 24 | | O | O | | T | | | T | | f | | F | | f | u | f | | U | | f | u |
| 25 | | | – | | | | | | O | f | | F | | f | u | f | | U | | f | u |
| 26 | O | | | | | | T | | | u | f | | F | | f | u | f | | U | | f |
| 27 | | | | Q | | | | | | u | f | | F | | f | u | f | | U | | f |
| 28 | | | T | | | C | | | | u | f | | F | | f | u | f | | U | | f |
| 29 | | T | T | | X | | | | O | f | u | f | | F | | f | u | f | | U | |
| 30 | | | | | | | | T | | f | u | f | | F | | f | u | f | | U | |
| 31 | T | | | Q | | | O | | | f | u | f | | F | | f | u | f | | U | |

# Time Zone Map

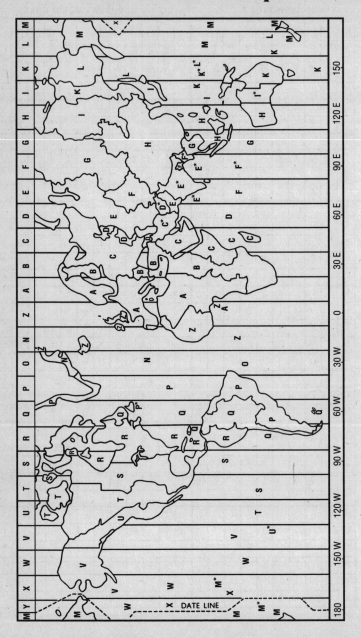

# Time Zone Conversions

## World Time Zones
### (Compared to Eastern Time)

| | | | |
|---|---|---|---|
| (R) | EST—Used | (C*) | Add 8½ hours |
| (S) | CST—Subtract 1 hour | (D) | Add 9 hours |
| (T) | MST—Subtract 2 hours | (D*) | Add 9½ hours |
| (U) | PST—Subtract 3 hours | (E) | Add 10 hours |
| (V) | Subtract 4 hours | (E*) | Add 10½ hours |
| (V*) | Subtract 4½ hours | (F) | Add 11 hours |
| (W) | Subtract 5 hours | (F*) | Add 11½ hours |
| (X) | Subtract 6 hours | (G) | Add 12 hours |
| (Y) | Subtract 7 hours | (H) | Add 13 hours |
| (Q) | Add 1 hour | (I) | Add 14 hours |
| (P) | Add 2 hours | (I*) | Add 14½ hours |
| (P*) | Add 2½ hours | (K) | Add 15 hours |
| (O) | Add 3 hours | (K*) | Add 15½ hours |
| (N) | Add 4 hours | (L) | Add 16 hours |
| (Z) | Add 5 hours | (L*) | Add 16½ hours |
| (A) | Add 6 hours | (M) | Add 17 hours |
| (B) | Add 7 hours | (M*) | Add 17½ hours |
| (C) | Add 8 hours | | |

## Important!

All times given in the *Moon Sign Book* are set in Eastern Time. The conversions shown here are for standard times only. Use the time zone conversions chart and table to calculate the difference in your time zone. You must make the adjustment for your time zone and adjust for Daylight Saving Time where applicable.

# Moon Void-of-Course

*by Kim Rogers-Gallagher*

The Moon makes a loop around the Earth in about twenty-eight days, moving through each of the signs in two and a half days (or so). As she passes through the thirty degrees of each sign, she "visits" with the planets in numerical order by forming angles or aspects with them. Because she moves one degree in just two to two-and-a-half hours, her influence on each planet lasts only a few hours, then she moves along. As she approaches the late degrees of the sign she's passing through, she eventually reaches the planet that's in the highest degree of any sign, and forms what will be her final aspect before leaving the sign. From this point until she actually enters the new sign, she is referred to as void-of-course, or void.

Think of it this way: the Moon is the emotional "tone" of the day, carrying feelings with her particular to the sign she's "wearing" at the moment. After she has contacted each of the planets, she symbolically "rests" before changing her costume, so her instinct is temporarily on hold. It's during this time that many people feel "fuzzy" or "vague"—scattered, even. Plans or decisions we make now will usually not pan out. Without the instinctual "knowing" the Moon provides as she touches each planet, we tend to be unrealistic or exercise poor judgment. The traditional definition of the void Moon is that "nothing will come of this," and it seems to be true. Actions initiated under a void Moon are often wasted, irrelevant, or incorrect—usually because information is hidden, missing, or has been overlooked.

Although it's not a good time to initiate plans, routine tasks seem to go along just fine. However, this period is really ideal for what the Moon does best: reflection. It's at this time that we can assimilate what the world has tossed at us over the past few days.

On the lighter side, remember that there are other good uses for the void Moon. This is the time period when the universe seems to be most open to loopholes. It's a great time to make plans you don't want to fulfill or schedule things you don't want to do. See the table on pages 83–88 for a schedule of the 2004 Moon void-of-course times.

# Moon Void-of-Course Tables

| Last Aspect | | Moon enters New Sign | | |
|:---:|:---:|:---:|:---:|:---:|
| **Date** | **Time** | **Date** | **Sign** | **Time** |
| | | *January* | | |
| 2 | 2:21 pm | 3 | Gemini | 12:58 pm |
| 5 | 6:14 pm | 6 | Cancer | 1:38 am |
| 7 | 3:00 pm | 8 | Leo | 12:38 pm |
| 10 | 5:00 pm | 10 | Virgo | 9:37 pm |
| 13 | 3:01 am | 13 | Libra | 4:38 am |
| 14 | 11:46 pm | 15 | Scorpio | 9:33 am |
| 17 | 6:48 am | 17 | Sagittarius | 12:18 pm |
| 18 | 10:58 pm | 19 | Capricorn | 1:24 pm |
| 21 | 12:34 am | 21 | Aquarius | 2:11 pm |
| 23 | 4:33 am | 23 | Pisces | 4:29 pm |
| 25 | 6:09 am | 25 | Aries | 10:06 pm |
| 27 | 11:59 pm | 28 | Taurus | 7:46 am |
| 29 | 9:04 pm | 30 | Gemini | 8:18 pm |
| | | *February* | | |
| 2 | 7:56 am | 2 | Cancer | 9:03 am |
| 4 | 12:52 pm | 4 | Leo | 7:50 pm |
| 6 | 12:38 pm | 7 | Virgo | 4:03 am |
| 8 | 7:23 pm | 9 | Libra | 10:12 am |
| 11 | 12:42 am | 11 | Scorpio | 2:58 pm |
| 13 | 8:39 am | 13 | Sagittarius | 6:35 pm |
| 15 | 3:20 pm | 15 | Capricorn | 9:14 pm |
| 16 | 12:00 pm | 17 | Aquarius | 11:27 pm |
| 19 | 12:34 pm | 20 | Pisces | 2:27 am |
| 21 | 5:10 pm | 22 | Aries | 7:45 am |
| 24 | 1:55 pm | 24 | Taurus | 4:30 pm |
| 25 | 9:55 pm | 27 | Gemini | 4:22 am |
| 29 | 5:08 am | 29 | Cancer | 5:12 pm |

## Last Aspect          Moon enters New Sign

| | | March | | |
|---|---|---|---|---|
| 2 | 10:42 pm | 3 | Leo | 4:18 am |
| 5 | 12:13 pm | 5 | Virgo | 12:18 pm |
| 7 | 3:49 am | 7 | Libra | 5:31 pm |
| 9 | 7:43 am | 9 | Scorpio | 9:03 pm |
| 11 | 11:11 pm | 11 | Sagittarius | 11:57 pm |
| 13 | 4:01 pm | 14 | Capricorn | 2:51 am |
| 16 | 12:34 am | 16 | Aquarius | 6:10 am |
| 18 | 7:15 am | 18 | Pisces | 10:26 am |
| 20 | 3:57 pm | 20 | Aries | 4:29 pm |
| 22 | 10:14 am | 23 | Taurus | 1:10 am |
| 24 | 5:29 pm | 25 | Gemini | 12:35 pm |
| 27 | 5:44 pm | 28 | Cancer | 1:23 am |
| 30 | 11:00 am | 30 | Leo | 1:07 pm |
| | | April | | |
| 1 | 6:56 pm | 1 | Virgo | 9:45 pm |
| 3 | 1:23 pm | 4 | Libra | 3:52 am |
| 5 | 5:26 pm | 6 | Scorpio | 6:24 am |
| 7 | 7:06 am | 8 | Sagittarius | 7:50 am |
| 9 | 8:30 pm | 10 | Capricorn | 9:33 am |
| 11 | 11:46 pm | 12 | Aquarius | 12:33 pm |
| 14 | 3:27 pm | 14 | Pisces | 5:24 pm |
| 16 | 9:43 am | 17 | Aries | 12:24 am |
| 19 | 9:21 am | 19 | Taurus | 9:43 am |
| 20 | 3:36 pm | 21 | Gemini | 9:10 pm |
| 23 | 7:22 pm | 24 | Cancer | 9:56 am |
| 26 | 5:56 am | 26 | Leo | 10:14 pm |
| 28 | 10:08 pm | 29 | Virgo | 8:00 am |

| Last Aspect | | Moon enters New Sign | | |
|---|---|---|---|---|
| | | **May** | | |
| 1 | 7:31 am | 1 | Libra | 2:03 pm |
| 3 | 12:49 pm | 3 | Scorpio | 4:38 pm |
| 4 | 5:36 pm | 5 | Sagittarius | 5:08 pm |
| 7 | 7:50 am | 7 | Capricorn | 5:17 pm |
| 9 | 9:03 am | 9 | Aquarius | 6:46 pm |
| 11 | 3:31 pm | 11 | Pisces | 10:52 pm |
| 13 | 10:14 pm | 14 | Aries | 6:02 am |
| 16 | 8:17 am | 16 | Taurus | 3:57 pm |
| 19 | 12:52 am | 19 | Gemini | 3:47 am |
| 20 | 12:52 am | 20 | Gemini | 3:47 am |
| 21 | 8:13 am | 21 | Cancer | 4:35 pm |
| 22 | 2:58 pm | 24 | Leo | 5:07 am |
| 26 | 5:42 am | 26 | Virgo | 3:52 pm |
| 28 | 12:17 pm | 28 | Libra | 11:22 pm |
| 30 | 3:09 pm | 31 | Scorpio | 3:08 am |
| | | **June** | | |
| 1 | 5:15 pm | 2 | Sagittarius | 3:52 am |
| 3 | 1:12 pm | 4 | Capricorn | 3:12 am |
| 5 | 8:28 am | 6 | Aquarius | 3:10 am |
| 7 | 2:09 pm | 8 | Pisces | 5:38 am |
| 9 | 7:37 pm | 10 | Aries | 11:49 am |
| 12 | 7:31 am | 12 | Taurus | 9:37 pm |
| 14 | 10:34 pm | 15 | Gemini | 9:44 am |
| 17 | 4:27 pm | 17 | Cancer | 10:37 pm |
| 20 | 6:46 am | 20 | Leo | 11:05 am |
| 22 | 3:54 am | 22 | Virgo | 10:10 pm |
| 24 | 1:19 pm | 25 | Libra | 6:50 am |
| 26 | 7:41 pm | 27 | Scorpio | 12:13 pm |
| 28 | 8:57 pm | 29 | Sagittarius | 2:15 pm |

| | | | | |
|---|---|---|---|---|
| 30 | 10:53 pm | 1 | Capricorn | 2:01 pm |
| | | **July** | | |
| 3 | 10:25 am | 3 | Aquarius | 1:22 pm |
| 4 | 10:15 pm | 5 | Pisces | 2:26 pm |
| 7 | 1:30 am | 7 | Aries | 7:03 pm |
| 9 | 8:52 am | 10 | Taurus | 3:51 am |
| 11 | 7:29 pm | 12 | Gemini | 3:45 pm |
| 14 | 8:33 am | 15 | Cancer | 4:40 am |
| 17 | 7:24 am | 17 | Leo | 4:56 pm |
| 19 | 2:50 pm | 20 | Virgo | 3:44 am |
| 21 | 5:48 pm | 22 | Libra | 12:39 pm |
| 24 | 5:54 pm | 24 | Scorpio | 7:08 pm |
| 26 | 6:48 am | 26 | Sagittarius | 10:48 pm |
| 28 | 11:06 am | 28 | Capricorn | 11:57 pm |
| 30 | 7:21 am | 30 | Aquarius | 11:54 pm |
| | | **August** | | |
| 1 | 4:51 pm | 2 | Pisces | 12:34 am |
| 3 | 10:58 pm | 4 | Aries | 3:59 am |
| 6 | 9:59 am | 6 | Taurus | 11:26 am |
| 8 | 8:46 pm | 8 | Gemini | 10:33 pm |
| 10 | 3:59 pm | 11 | Cancer | 11:20 am |
| 13 | 6:17 am | 13 | Leo | 11:30 pm |
| 15 | 9:24 pm | 16 | Virgo | 9:49 am |
| 18 | 3:15 am | 18 | Libra | 6:09 pm |
| 20 | 9:39 pm | 21 | Scorpio | 12:37 am |
| 22 | 4:53 pm | 23 | Sagittarius | 5:08 am |
| 25 | 7:13 am | 25 | Capricorn | 7:46 am |
| 26 | 10:58 pm | 27 | Aquarius | 9:08 am |
| 29 | 5:23 am | 29 | Pisces | 10:33 am |

| --- | --- | --- | --- | --- |
| 31 | 4:28 am | 31 | Aries | 1:46 pm |
| | | **September** | | |
| 2 | 12:17 pm | 2 | Taurus | 8:16 pm |
| 5 | 2:56 am | 5 | Gemini | 6:24 am |
| 7 | 2:08 pm | 7 | Cancer | 6:50 pm |
| 10 | 12:41 am | 10 | Leo | 7:06 am |
| 11 | 9:22 pm | 12 | Virgo | 5:16 pm |
| 14 | 8:55 pm | 15 | Libra | 12:54 am |
| 16 | 9:31 pm | 17 | Scorpio | 6:25 am |
| 19 | 8:24 am | 19 | Sagittarius | 10:30 am |
| 21 | 12:19 pm | 21 | Capricorn | 1:35 pm |
| 23 | 3:41 pm | 23 | Aquarius | 4:10 pm |
| 25 | 2:25 am | 25 | Pisces | 6:55 pm |
| 27 | 9:12 pm | 27 | Aries | 10:57 pm |
| 29 | 9:53 pm | 30 | Taurus | 5:24 am |
| | | **October** | | |
| 2 | 12:34 pm | 2 | Gemini | 2:55 pm |
| 4 | 6:28 am | 5 | Cancer | 2:54 am |
| 7 | 8:13 am | 7 | Leo | 3:23 pm |
| 9 | 6:42 am | 10 | Virgo | 2:00 am |
| 12 | 3:32 am | 12 | Libra | 9:32 am |
| 14 | 10:22 am | 14 | Scorpio | 2:10 pm |
| 16 | 11:43 am | 16 | Sagittarius | 4:58 pm |
| 18 | 11:46 am | 18 | Capricorn | 7:07 pm |
| 20 | 5:59 pm | 20 | Aquarius | 9:38 pm |
| 22 | 8:20 am | 23 | Pisces | 1:13 am |
| 25 | 1:17 am | 25 | Aries | 6:24 am |
| 27 | 8:24 am | 27 | Taurus | 1:37 pm |
| 29 | 5:50 pm | 29 | Gemini | 11:11 pm |

## Last Aspect                    Moon enters New Sign

| | | | | |
|---|---|---|---|---|
| 31 | 8:21 pm | 1 | Cancer | 9:53 am |
| | | **November** | | |
| 3 | 9:00 pm | 3 | Leo | 10:32 pm |
| 6 | 3:45 am | 6 | Virgo | 10:00 am |
| 8 | 1:32 pm | 8 | Libra | 6:23 pm |
| 10 | 11:02 pm | 10 | Scorpio | 11:05 pm |
| 12 | 8:34 pm | 13 | Sagittarius | 12:56 am |
| 14 | 10:58 am | 15 | Capricorn | 1:33 am |
| 16 | 10:07 pm | 17 | Aquarius | 2:39 am |
| 19 | 12:50 am | 19 | Pisces | 5:38 am |
| 21 | 10:35 am | 21 | Aries | 11:11 am |
| 23 | 1:47 pm | 23 | Taurus | 7:16 pm |
| 25 | 11:37 pm | 26 | Gemini | 5:25 am |
| 28 | 10:04 am | 28 | Cancer | 5:10 pm |
| 30 | 11:28 pm | 1 | Leo | 5:50 am |
| | | **December** | | |
| 3 | 9:52 am | 3 | Virgo | 6:00 pm |
| 5 | 9:28 pm | 6 | Libra | 3:46 am |
| 8 | 3:41 am | 8 | Scorpio | 9:43 am |
| 10 | 6:03 am | 10 | Sagittarius | 11:54 am |
| 11 | 11:03 pm | 12 | Capricorn | 11:42 am |
| 14 | 6:43 am | 14 | Aquarius | 11:10 am |
| 16 | 3:33 am | 16 | Pisces | 12:24 pm |
| 18 | 11:40 am | 18 | Aries | 4:52 pm |
| 21 | 12:16 am | 21 | Taurus | 12:52 am |
| 23 | 8:41 am | 23 | Gemini | 11:32 am |
| 25 | 8:30 am | 25 | Cancer | 11:38 pm |
| 28 | 2:34 am | 28 | Leo | 12:14 pm |
| 30 | 9:54 am | 31 | Virgo | 12:33 am |

# Retrograde Periods

**Eastern Time (ET)** in regular type, **Pacific Time (PT)** in bold type

| Planet | Begin | ET | PT | End | ET | PT |
|---|---|---|---|---|---|---|
| Saturn | 10/25/03 | 7:42 pm | **4:42 pm** | 03/07/04 | 11:51 am | **8:51 am** |
| Mercury | 12/17/03 | 11:02 am | **8:02 am** | 01/06/04 | 8:44 am | **5:44 am** |
| Jupiter | 01/03/04 | 6:57 pm | **3:57 pm** | 05/04/04 | 11:06 pm | **8:06 pm** |
| Pluto | 03/24/04 | 10:09 am | **7:09 am** | 08/30/04 | 3:38 pm | **12:38 pm** |
| Chiron | 04/01/04 04/02/04 | 1:12 am | **10:12 pm** | 09/26/04 | 1:20 pm | **10:20 am** |
| Mercury | 04/06/04 | 4:28 pm | **1:28 pm** | 04/30/04 | 9:05 am | **6:05 am** |
| Neptune | 05/17/04 | 8:13 am | **5:13 am** | 10/24/03 | 7:56 am | **4:56 am** |
| Venus | 05/17/04 | 6:29 pm | **3:29 pm** | 06/29/04 | 7:16 pm | **4:16 pm** |
| Uranus | 06/10/04 | 11:47 am | **8:47 am** | 11/11/04 | 2:12 pm | **11:12 am** |
| Mercury | 08/09/04 | 8:32 pm | **5:32 pm** | 09/02/04 | 9:09 am | **6:09 am** |
| Saturn | 11/07/04 11/08/04 | 1:54 am | **10:54 pm** | 03/21/05 | 9:54 pm | **6:54 pm** |
| Mercury | 11/30/04 | 7:17 am | **4:17 am** | 12/19/04 12/20/04 | 1:28 am | **10:28 pm** |

| | 03 Dec | 04 Jan | Feb | Mar | Apr | May | Jun | Jul | Aug | Sep | Oct | Nov | 04 Dec | 05 Jan |
|---|---|---|---|---|---|---|---|---|---|---|---|---|---|---|
| ☿ | | | | | | | | | | | | | | |
| ♀ | | | | | | | | | | | | | | |
| ♂ | | | | | | | | | | | | | | |
| ♃ | | | | | | | | | | | | | | |
| ♄ | | | | | | | | | | | | | | |
| ⚷ | | | | | | | | | | | | | | |
| ♅ | | | | | | | | | | | | | | |
| ♆ | | | | | | | | | | | | | | |
| ♇ | | | | | | | | | | | | | | |

# Find Your Moon Sign

Every year we give tables for the position of the Moon during that year, but it is more complicated to provide tables for the Moon's position in any given year because of its continuous movement. However, the problem was solved by Grant Lewi in *Astrology for the Millions*, which is available from Llewellyn Worldwide.

## Grant Lewi's System

### Step 1:
Find your birth year in the natal Moon tables. (pages 93–103).

### Step 2:
Run down the left-hand column and see if your birth date is there.

### Step 3:
If your birth date is in the left-hand column, run over this line until you come to the column under your birth year. Here you will find a number. This is your base number. Write it down, and go directly to the direc-

tion under the heading "What to Do with Your Base Number" on page 91.

### Step 4:
If your birth date is not in the left-hand column, get a pencil and paper. Your birth date falls between two numbers in the left-hand column. Look at the date closest after your birth date; run across this line to your birth year. Write down the number you find there, and label it "top number." Directly beneath it on your piece of paper write the number printed just above it in the table. Label this "bottom number." Subtract the bottom number from the top number. If the top number is smaller, add 360 and subtract. The result is your difference.

### Step 5:
Go back to the left-hand column and find the date before your birth date. Determine the number of days between this date and your birth date. Write this down and label it "intervening days."

## Step 6:

Note which group your difference (found at step 4) falls in.

| Difference | Daily Motion |
|------------|--------------|
| 80–87 | 12 degrees |
| 88–94 | 13 degrees |
| 95–101 | 14 degrees |
| 102–106 | 15 degrees |

*Note:* If you were born in a leap year and use the difference between February 26 and March 5, then the daily motion is slightly different. If you fall into this category and your difference use the figures below.

| Difference | Daily Motion |
|------------|--------------|
| 94–99 | 12 degrees |
| 100–108 | 13 degrees |
| 109–115 | 14 degrees |
| 115–122 | 15 degrees |

## Step 7:

Write down the "daily motion" corresponding to your place in the proper table of difference above. Multiply daily motion by the number labeled "intervening days" (found at step 5).

## Step 8:

Add the result of step 7 to your bottom number (under step 4). This is your base number. If it is more than 360, subtract 360 from it and call the result your base number.

## What to Do with Your Base Number

Turn to the Table of Base Numbers on page 92 and locate your base number in it. At the top of the column you will find the sign your Moon was in. In the far left-hand column you will find the degree the Moon occupied at 7:00 am of your birth date if you were born under Eastern Standard Time (EST). Refer to the Time Zone Conversions chart and table on page 81 to adjust information for your time zone.

If you don't know the hour of your birth, accept this as your Moon's sign and degree. If you do know the hour of your birth, get the exact degree as follows:

If you were born after 7:00 am EST, determine the number of hours after the time that you were born. Divide this by two, rounding up if necessary. Add this to your base number, and the result in the table will be the exact degree and sign of the Moon on the year, month, date, and hour of your birth.

If you were born before 7:00 am EST, determine the number of hours before the time that you were born. Divide this by two. Subtract this from your base number, and the result in the table will be the exact degree and sign of the Moon on the year, month, date, and hour of your birth.

# Table of Base Numbers

| | ♈ (13) | ♉ (14) | ♊ (15) | ♋ (16) | ♌ (17) | ♍ (18) | ♎ (19) | ♏ (20) | ♐ (21) | ♑ (22) | ♒ (23) | ♓ (24) |
|---|---|---|---|---|---|---|---|---|---|---|---|---|
| 0° | 0 | 30 | 60 | 90 | 120 | 150 | 180 | 210 | 240 | 270 | 300 | 330 |
| 1° | 1 | 31 | 61 | 91 | 121 | 151 | 181 | 211 | 241 | 271 | 301 | 331 |
| 2° | 2 | 32 | 62 | 92 | 122 | 152 | 182 | 212 | 242 | 272 | 302 | 332 |
| 3° | 3 | 33 | 63 | 93 | 123 | 153 | 183 | 213 | 243 | 273 | 303 | 333 |
| 4° | 4 | 34 | 64 | 94 | 124 | 154 | 184 | 214 | 244 | 274 | 304 | 334 |
| 5° | 5 | 35 | 65 | 95 | 125 | 155 | 185 | 215 | 245 | 275 | 305 | 335 |
| 6° | 6 | 36 | 66 | 96 | 126 | 156 | 186 | 216 | 246 | 276 | 306 | 336 |
| 7° | 7 | 37 | 67 | 97 | 127 | 157 | 187 | 217 | 247 | 277 | 307 | 337 |
| 8° | 8 | 38 | 68 | 98 | 128 | 158 | 188 | 218 | 248 | 278 | 308 | 338 |
| 9° | 9 | 39 | 69 | 99 | 129 | 159 | 189 | 219 | 249 | 279 | 309 | 339 |
| 10° | 10 | 40 | 70 | 100 | 130 | 160 | 190 | 220 | 250 | 280 | 310 | 340 |
| 11° | 11 | 41 | 71 | 101 | 131 | 161 | 191 | 221 | 251 | 281 | 311 | 341 |
| 12° | 12 | 42 | 72 | 102 | 132 | 162 | 192 | 222 | 252 | 282 | 312 | 342 |
| 13° | 13 | 43 | 73 | 103 | 133 | 163 | 193 | 223 | 253 | 283 | 313 | 343 |
| 14° | 14 | 44 | 74 | 104 | 134 | 164 | 194 | 224 | 254 | 284 | 314 | 344 |
| 15° | 15 | 45 | 75 | 105 | 135 | 165 | 195 | 225 | 255 | 285 | 315 | 345 |
| 16° | 16 | 46 | 76 | 106 | 136 | 166 | 196 | 226 | 256 | 286 | 316 | 346 |
| 17° | 17 | 47 | 77 | 107 | 137 | 167 | 197 | 227 | 257 | 287 | 317 | 347 |
| 18° | 18 | 48 | 78 | 108 | 138 | 168 | 198 | 228 | 258 | 288 | 318 | 248 |
| 19° | 19 | 49 | 79 | 109 | 139 | 169 | 199 | 229 | 259 | 289 | 319 | 349 |
| 20° | 20 | 50 | 80 | 110 | 140 | 170 | 200 | 230 | 260 | 290 | 320 | 350 |
| 21° | 21 | 51 | 81 | 111 | 141 | 171 | 201 | 231 | 261 | 291 | 321 | 351 |
| 22° | 22 | 52 | 82 | 112 | 142 | 172 | 202 | 232 | 262 | 292 | 322 | 352 |
| 23° | 23 | 53 | 83 | 113 | 143 | 173 | 203 | 233 | 263 | 293 | 323 | 353 |
| 24° | 24 | 54 | 84 | 114 | 144 | 174 | 204 | 234 | 264 | 294 | 324 | 354 |
| 25° | 25 | 55 | 85 | 115 | 145 | 175 | 205 | 235 | 265 | 295 | 325 | 355 |
| 26° | 26 | 56 | 86 | 116 | 146 | 176 | 206 | 236 | 266 | 296 | 326 | 356 |
| 27° | 27 | 57 | 87 | 117 | 147 | 177 | 207 | 237 | 267 | 297 | 327 | 357 |
| 28° | 28 | 58 | 88 | 118 | 148 | 178 | 208 | 238 | 268 | 298 | 328 | 358 |
| 29° | 29 | 59 | 89 | 119 | 149 | 179 | 209 | 239 | 269 | 299 | 329 | 359 |

| Month | Date | 1901 | 1902 | 1903 | 1904 | 1905 | 1906 | 1907 | 1908 | 1909 | 1910 |
|---|---|---|---|---|---|---|---|---|---|---|---|
| Jan. | 1 | 55 | 188 | 308 | 76 | 227 | 358 | 119 | 246 | 39 | 168 |
| Jan. | 8 | 149 | 272 | 37 | 179 | 319 | 82 | 208 | 350 | 129 | 252 |
| Jan. | 15 | 234 | 2 | 141 | 270 | 43 | 174 | 311 | 81 | 213 | 346 |
| Jan. | 22 | 327 | 101 | 234 | 353 | 138 | 273 | 44 | 164 | 309 | 84 |
| Jan. | 29 | 66 | 196 | 317 | 84 | 238 | 6 | 128 | 255 | 50 | 175 |
| Feb. | 5 | 158 | 280 | 46 | 188 | 328 | 90 | 219 | 359 | 138 | 259 |
| Feb. | 12 | 241 | 12 | 149 | 279 | 51 | 184 | 319 | 90 | 221 | 356 |
| Feb. | 19 | 335 | 111 | 242 | 2 | 146 | 283 | 52 | 173 | 317 | 94 |
| Feb. | 26 | 76 | 204 | 326 | 92 | 248 | 13 | 136 | 264 | 60 | 184 |
| Mar. | 5 | 166 | 288 | 57 | 211 | 336 | 98 | 229 | 21 | 147 | 267 |
| Mar. | 12 | 249 | 22 | 157 | 300 | 60 | 194 | 328 | 110 | 230 | 5 |
| Mar. | 19 | 344 | 121 | 250 | 24 | 154 | 293 | 60 | 195 | 325 | 105 |
| Mar. | 26 | 86 | 212 | 334 | 116 | 258 | 22 | 144 | 288 | 69 | 192 |
| Apr. | 2 | 175 | 296 | 68 | 219 | 345 | 106 | 240 | 29 | 155 | 276 |
| Apr. | 9 | 258 | 31 | 167 | 309 | 69 | 202 | 338 | 118 | 240 | 13 |
| Apr. | 16 | 352 | 132 | 258 | 33 | 163 | 304 | 68 | 204 | 334 | 115 |
| Apr. | 23 | 96 | 220 | 342 | 127 | 267 | 31 | 152 | 299 | 77 | 201 |
| Apr. | 30 | 184 | 304 | 78 | 227 | 354 | 114 | 250 | 38 | 164 | 285 |
| May | 7 | 267 | 40 | 177 | 317 | 78 | 210 | 348 | 126 | 249 | 21 |
| May | 14 | 1 | 142 | 266 | 42 | 172 | 313 | 76 | 212 | 344 | 124 |
| May | 21 | 104 | 229 | 350 | 138 | 275 | 40 | 160 | 310 | 85 | 210 |
| May | 28 | 193 | 313 | 87 | 236 | 2 | 123 | 259 | 47 | 172 | 294 |
| Jun. | 4 | 277 | 48 | 187 | 324 | 88 | 219 | 358 | 134 | 258 | 30 |
| Jun. | 11 | 11 | 151 | 275 | 50 | 182 | 322 | 85 | 220 | 355 | 132 |
| Jun. | 18 | 112 | 238 | 359 | 149 | 283 | 48 | 169 | 320 | 93 | 218 |
| Jun. | 25 | 201 | 322 | 96 | 245 | 11 | 133 | 267 | 57 | 180 | 304 |
| Jul. | 2 | 286 | 57 | 197 | 333 | 97 | 228 | 8 | 142 | 267 | 40 |
| Jul. | 9 | 21 | 160 | 283 | 58 | 193 | 330 | 94 | 228 | 6 | 140 |
| Jul. | 16 | 121 | 247 | 7 | 159 | 291 | 57 | 178 | 330 | 102 | 226 |
| Jul. | 23 | 209 | 332 | 105 | 255 | 18 | 143 | 276 | 66 | 188 | 314 |
| Jul. | 30 | 295 | 66 | 206 | 341 | 105 | 239 | 17 | 151 | 275 | 51 |
| Aug. | 6 | 32 | 168 | 292 | 66 | 204 | 338 | 103 | 237 | 17 | 148 |
| Aug. | 13 | 130 | 255 | 17 | 168 | 301 | 65 | 188 | 339 | 111 | 234 |
| Aug. | 20 | 217 | 341 | 113 | 265 | 27 | 152 | 285 | 76 | 197 | 323 |
| Aug. | 27 | 303 | 77 | 215 | 350 | 113 | 250 | 25 | 160 | 283 | 62 |
| Sep. | 3 | 43 | 176 | 301 | 75 | 215 | 346 | 111 | 246 | 27 | 157 |
| Sep. | 10 | 139 | 263 | 27 | 176 | 310 | 73 | 198 | 347 | 121 | 242 |
| Sep. | 17 | 225 | 350 | 123 | 274 | 35 | 161 | 294 | 85 | 205 | 331 |
| Sep. | 24 | 311 | 88 | 223 | 358 | 122 | 261 | 33 | 169 | 292 | 73 |
| Oct. | 1 | 53 | 185 | 309 | 85 | 224 | 355 | 119 | 256 | 35 | 166 |
| Oct. | 8 | 149 | 271 | 36 | 185 | 320 | 81 | 207 | 356 | 130 | 250 |
| Oct. | 15 | 233 | 359 | 133 | 283 | 44 | 169 | 305 | 93 | 214 | 339 |
| Oct. | 22 | 319 | 99 | 231 | 7 | 130 | 271 | 42 | 177 | 301 | 83 |
| Oct. | 29 | 62 | 194 | 317 | 95 | 233 | 5 | 127 | 266 | 44 | 176 |
| Nov. | 5 | 158 | 279 | 45 | 193 | 329 | 89 | 216 | 5 | 139 | 259 |
| Nov. | 12 | 242 | 6 | 144 | 291 | 53 | 177 | 316 | 101 | 223 | 347 |
| Nov. | 19 | 328 | 109 | 239 | 15 | 140 | 280 | 50 | 185 | 311 | 91 |
| Nov. | 26 | 70 | 203 | 325 | 105 | 241 | 14 | 135 | 276 | 52 | 185 |
| Dec. | 3 | 168 | 288 | 54 | 203 | 338 | 98 | 224 | 15 | 148 | 268 |
| Dec. | 10 | 251 | 14 | 155 | 299 | 61 | 185 | 327 | 109 | 231 | 356 |
| Dec. | 17 | 338 | 118 | 248 | 23 | 150 | 289 | 59 | 193 | 322 | 99 |
| Dec. | 24 | 78 | 213 | 333 | 115 | 249 | 23 | 143 | 286 | 61 | 194 |
| Dec. | 31 | 176 | 296 | 61 | 213 | 346 | 107 | 232 | 26 | 155 | 277 |

| Month | Date | 1911 | 1912 | 1913 | 1914 | 1915 | 1916 | 1917 | 1918 | 1919 | 1920 |
|---|---|---|---|---|---|---|---|---|---|---|---|
| Jan. | 1 | 289 | 57 | 211 | 337 | 100 | 228 | 23 | 147 | 270 | 39 |
| Jan. | 8 | 20 | 162 | 299 | 61 | 192 | 332 | 110 | 231 | 5 | 143 |
| Jan. | 15 | 122 | 251 | 23 | 158 | 293 | 61 | 193 | 329 | 103 | 231 |
| Jan. | 22 | 214 | 335 | 120 | 256 | 23 | 145 | 290 | 68 | 193 | 316 |
| Jan. | 29 | 298 | 66 | 221 | 345 | 108 | 237 | 32 | 155 | 278 | 49 |
| Feb. | 5 | 31 | 170 | 308 | 69 | 203 | 340 | 118 | 239 | 16 | 150 |
| Feb. | 12 | 130 | 260 | 32 | 167 | 302 | 70 | 203 | 338 | 113 | 239 |
| Feb. | 19 | 222 | 344 | 128 | 266 | 31 | 154 | 298 | 78 | 201 | 325 |
| Feb. | 26 | 306 | 75 | 231 | 353 | 116 | 248 | 41 | 164 | 286 | 60 |
| Mar. | 5 | 42 | 192 | 317 | 77 | 214 | 2 | 127 | 248 | 26 | 172 |
| Mar. | 12 | 140 | 280 | 41 | 176 | 311 | 89 | 212 | 346 | 123 | 259 |
| Mar. | 19 | 230 | 5 | 136 | 276 | 39 | 176 | 308 | 87 | 209 | 346 |
| Mar. | 26 | 314 | 100 | 239 | 2 | 124 | 273 | 49 | 173 | 294 | 85 |
| Apr. | 2 | 52 | 200 | 326 | 86 | 223 | 10 | 135 | 257 | 35 | 181 |
| Apr. | 9 | 150 | 288 | 51 | 184 | 321 | 97 | 222 | 355 | 133 | 267 |
| Apr. | 16 | 238 | 14 | 146 | 286 | 48 | 184 | 318 | 96 | 218 | 355 |
| Apr. | 23 | 322 | 111 | 247 | 11 | 132 | 284 | 57 | 181 | 303 | 96 |
| Apr. | 30 | 61 | 208 | 334 | 96 | 232 | 19 | 143 | 267 | 43 | 190 |
| May | 7 | 160 | 296 | 60 | 192 | 331 | 105 | 231 | 4 | 142 | 275 |
| May | 14 | 246 | 22 | 156 | 294 | 56 | 192 | 329 | 104 | 227 | 3 |
| May | 21 | 331 | 122 | 255 | 20 | 141 | 294 | 66 | 190 | 312 | 105 |
| May | 28 | 69 | 218 | 342 | 106 | 240 | 29 | 151 | 277 | 51 | 200 |
| Jun. | 4 | 170 | 304 | 69 | 202 | 341 | 114 | 240 | 14 | 151 | 284 |
| Jun. | 11 | 255 | 30 | 167 | 302 | 65 | 200 | 340 | 112 | 235 | 11 |
| Jun. | 18 | 340 | 132 | 264 | 28 | 151 | 304 | 74 | 198 | 322 | 114 |
| Jun. | 25 | 78 | 228 | 350 | 115 | 249 | 39 | 159 | 286 | 60 | 209 |
| Jul. | 2 | 179 | 312 | 78 | 212 | 349 | 122 | 248 | 25 | 159 | 293 |
| Jul. | 9 | 264 | 39 | 178 | 310 | 74 | 209 | 350 | 120 | 244 | 20 |
| Jul. | 16 | 349 | 141 | 273 | 36 | 161 | 312 | 84 | 206 | 332 | 123 |
| Jul. | 23 | 87 | 237 | 358 | 125 | 258 | 48 | 168 | 295 | 70 | 218 |
| Jul. | 30 | 187 | 321 | 86 | 223 | 357 | 131 | 256 | 36 | 167 | 302 |
| Aug. | 6 | 272 | 48 | 188 | 319 | 82 | 219 | 360 | 129 | 252 | 31 |
| Aug. | 13 | 359 | 150 | 282 | 44 | 171 | 320 | 93 | 214 | 342 | 131 |
| Aug. | 20 | 96 | 246 | 6 | 133 | 268 | 57 | 177 | 303 | 81 | 226 |
| Aug. | 27 | 195 | 330 | 94 | 234 | 5 | 140 | 265 | 46 | 175 | 310 |
| Sep. | 3 | 281 | 57 | 198 | 328 | 90 | 229 | 9 | 138 | 260 | 41 |
| Sep. | 10 | 9 | 158 | 292 | 52 | 180 | 329 | 102 | 222 | 351 | 140 |
| Sep. | 17 | 107 | 255 | 15 | 141 | 279 | 65 | 186 | 312 | 91 | 234 |
| Sep. | 24 | 203 | 339 | 103 | 244 | 13 | 149 | 274 | 56 | 184 | 319 |
| Oct. | 1 | 288 | 68 | 206 | 337 | 98 | 240 | 17 | 148 | 268 | 52 |
| Oct. | 8 | 18 | 167 | 301 | 61 | 189 | 338 | 111 | 231 | 360 | 150 |
| Oct. | 15 | 118 | 263 | 24 | 149 | 290 | 73 | 195 | 320 | 102 | 242 |
| Oct. | 22 | 212 | 347 | 113 | 254 | 22 | 157 | 284 | 65 | 193 | 326 |
| Oct. | 29 | 296 | 78 | 214 | 346 | 106 | 250 | 25 | 157 | 276 | 61 |
| Nov. | 5 | 26 | 177 | 309 | 70 | 197 | 348 | 119 | 240 | 7 | 161 |
| Nov. | 12 | 129 | 271 | 33 | 158 | 300 | 81 | 203 | 329 | 112 | 250 |
| Nov. | 19 | 221 | 355 | 123 | 262 | 31 | 164 | 295 | 73 | 202 | 334 |
| Nov. | 26 | 305 | 88 | 223 | 355 | 115 | 259 | 34 | 165 | 285 | 70 |
| Dec. | 3 | 34 | 187 | 317 | 79 | 205 | 359 | 127 | 249 | 16 | 171 |
| Dec. | 10 | 138 | 279 | 41 | 168 | 310 | 89 | 211 | 340 | 120 | 259 |
| Dec. | 17 | 230 | 3 | 134 | 270 | 40 | 172 | 305 | 81 | 211 | 343 |
| Dec. | 24 | 313 | 97 | 232 | 3 | 124 | 267 | 44 | 173 | 294 | 78 |
| Dec. | 31 | 42 | 198 | 325 | 87 | 214 | 9 | 135 | 257 | 25 | 181 |

| Month | Date | 1921 | 1922 | 1923 | 1924 | 1925 | 1926 | 1927 | 1928 | 1929 | 1930 |
|-------|------|------|------|------|------|------|------|------|------|------|------|
| Jan. | 1 | 194 | 317 | 80 | 211 | 5 | 127 | 250 | 23 | 176 | 297 |
| Jan. | 8 | 280 | 41 | 177 | 313 | 90 | 211 | 349 | 123 | 260 | 22 |
| Jan. | 15 | 4 | 141 | 275 | 41 | 175 | 312 | 86 | 211 | 346 | 123 |
| Jan. | 22 | 101 | 239 | 3 | 127 | 272 | 51 | 172 | 297 | 83 | 222 |
| Jan. | 29 | 203 | 325 | 88 | 222 | 13 | 135 | 258 | 34 | 184 | 306 |
| Feb. | 5 | 289 | 49 | 188 | 321 | 99 | 220 | 359 | 131 | 269 | 31 |
| Feb. | 12 | 14 | 149 | 284 | 49 | 185 | 320 | 95 | 219 | 356 | 131 |
| Feb. | 19 | 110 | 249 | 11 | 135 | 281 | 60 | 181 | 305 | 93 | 230 |
| Feb. | 26 | 211 | 334 | 96 | 233 | 21 | 144 | 266 | 45 | 191 | 314 |
| Mar. | 5 | 297 | 58 | 197 | 343 | 107 | 230 | 8 | 153 | 276 | 41 |
| Mar. | 12 | 23 | 157 | 294 | 69 | 194 | 328 | 105 | 238 | 6 | 140 |
| Mar. | 19 | 119 | 258 | 19 | 157 | 292 | 68 | 190 | 327 | 104 | 238 |
| Mar. | 26 | 219 | 343 | 104 | 258 | 29 | 153 | 275 | 70 | 200 | 323 |
| Apr. | 2 | 305 | 68 | 205 | 352 | 115 | 240 | 16 | 163 | 284 | 51 |
| Apr. | 9 | 33 | 166 | 304 | 77 | 204 | 337 | 114 | 247 | 14 | 149 |
| Apr. | 16 | 130 | 266 | 28 | 164 | 303 | 76 | 198 | 335 | 115 | 246 |
| Apr. | 23 | 227 | 351 | 114 | 268 | 38 | 161 | 285 | 79 | 208 | 331 |
| Apr. | 30 | 313 | 78 | 214 | 1 | 123 | 250 | 25 | 172 | 292 | 61 |
| May | 7 | 42 | 176 | 313 | 85 | 212 | 348 | 123 | 256 | 23 | 160 |
| May | 14 | 141 | 274 | 37 | 173 | 314 | 84 | 207 | 344 | 125 | 254 |
| May | 21 | 236 | 359 | 123 | 277 | 47 | 169 | 295 | 88 | 217 | 339 |
| May | 28 | 321 | 88 | 222 | 11 | 131 | 259 | 34 | 181 | 301 | 70 |
| Jun. | 4 | 50 | 186 | 321 | 94 | 220 | 358 | 131 | 264 | 31 | 171 |
| Jun. | 11 | 152 | 282 | 45 | 182 | 324 | 93 | 215 | 354 | 135 | 263 |
| Jun. | 18 | 245 | 7 | 134 | 285 | 56 | 177 | 305 | 96 | 226 | 347 |
| Jun. | 25 | 330 | 97 | 232 | 20 | 139 | 268 | 44 | 190 | 310 | 78 |
| Jul. | 2 | 58 | 197 | 329 | 103 | 229 | 9 | 139 | 273 | 40 | 181 |
| Jul. | 9 | 162 | 291 | 54 | 192 | 333 | 101 | 223 | 4 | 144 | 272 |
| Jul. | 16 | 254 | 15 | 144 | 294 | 65 | 185 | 315 | 104 | 236 | 355 |
| Jul. | 23 | 338 | 106 | 242 | 28 | 148 | 276 | 54 | 198 | 319 | 87 |
| Jul. | 30 | 67 | 208 | 337 | 112 | 238 | 20 | 147 | 282 | 49 | 191 |
| Aug. | 6 | 171 | 300 | 62 | 202 | 341 | 110 | 231 | 15 | 152 | 281 |
| Aug. | 13 | 264 | 24 | 153 | 302 | 74 | 194 | 324 | 114 | 244 | 4 |
| Aug. | 20 | 347 | 114 | 253 | 36 | 157 | 285 | 65 | 206 | 328 | 95 |
| Aug. | 27 | 76 | 218 | 346 | 120 | 248 | 29 | 156 | 290 | 59 | 200 |
| Sep. | 3 | 179 | 309 | 70 | 213 | 350 | 119 | 239 | 25 | 161 | 290 |
| Sep. | 10 | 273 | 32 | 162 | 312 | 83 | 203 | 332 | 124 | 252 | 13 |
| Sep. | 17 | 356 | 122 | 264 | 44 | 166 | 293 | 75 | 214 | 337 | 105 |
| Sep. | 24 | 86 | 227 | 354 | 128 | 258 | 38 | 165 | 298 | 70 | 208 |
| Oct. | 1 | 187 | 318 | 78 | 223 | 358 | 128 | 248 | 35 | 169 | 298 |
| Oct. | 8 | 281 | 41 | 170 | 322 | 91 | 212 | 340 | 134 | 260 | 23 |
| Oct. | 15 | 5 | 132 | 274 | 52 | 175 | 303 | 85 | 222 | 345 | 115 |
| Oct. | 22 | 97 | 235 | 3 | 136 | 269 | 46 | 174 | 306 | 81 | 216 |
| Oct. | 29 | 196 | 327 | 87 | 232 | 7 | 137 | 257 | 44 | 179 | 307 |
| Nov. | 5 | 289 | 50 | 178 | 332 | 99 | 221 | 349 | 144 | 268 | 31 |
| Nov. | 12 | 13 | 142 | 283 | 61 | 183 | 313 | 93 | 231 | 353 | 126 |
| Nov. | 19 | 107 | 243 | 12 | 144 | 279 | 54 | 183 | 315 | 91 | 225 |
| Nov. | 26 | 206 | 335 | 96 | 241 | 17 | 145 | 266 | 52 | 189 | 314 |
| Dec. | 3 | 297 | 59 | 187 | 343 | 107 | 230 | 359 | 154 | 276 | 39 |
| Dec. | 10 | 21 | 152 | 291 | 70 | 191 | 324 | 101 | 240 | 1 | 137 |
| Dec. | 17 | 117 | 252 | 21 | 153 | 289 | 63 | 191 | 324 | 99 | 234 |
| Dec. | 24 | 216 | 343 | 105 | 249 | 28 | 152 | 275 | 60 | 199 | 322 |
| Dec. | 31 | 305 | 67 | 197 | 352 | 115 | 237 | 9 | 162 | 285 | 47 |

| Month | Date | 1931 | 1932 | 1933 | 1934 | 1935 | 1936 | 1937 | 1938 | 1939 | 1940 |
|-------|------|------|------|------|------|------|------|------|------|------|------|
| Jan. | 1 | 60 | 196 | 346 | 107 | 231 | 8 | 156 | 277 | 41 | 181 |
| Jan. | 8 | 162 | 294 | 70 | 193 | 333 | 104 | 240 | 4 | 144 | 275 |
| Jan. | 15 | 257 | 20 | 158 | 294 | 68 | 190 | 329 | 104 | 239 | 360 |
| Jan. | 22 | 342 | 108 | 255 | 32 | 152 | 278 | 67 | 202 | 323 | 88 |
| Jan. | 29 | 68 | 207 | 353 | 116 | 239 | 19 | 163 | 286 | 49 | 191 |
| Feb. | 5 | 171 | 302 | 78 | 203 | 342 | 113 | 248 | 14 | 153 | 284 |
| Feb. | 12 | 267 | 28 | 168 | 302 | 78 | 198 | 339 | 113 | 248 | 8 |
| Feb. | 19 | 351 | 116 | 266 | 40 | 161 | 286 | 78 | 210 | 332 | 96 |
| Feb. | 26 | 77 | 217 | 1 | 124 | 248 | 29 | 171 | 294 | 59 | 200 |
| Mar. | 5 | 179 | 324 | 86 | 213 | 350 | 135 | 256 | 25 | 161 | 306 |
| Mar. | 12 | 276 | 48 | 176 | 311 | 86 | 218 | 347 | 123 | 256 | 29 |
| Mar. | 19 | 360 | 137 | 277 | 48 | 170 | 308 | 89 | 218 | 340 | 119 |
| Mar. | 26 | 86 | 241 | 10 | 132 | 258 | 52 | 180 | 302 | 69 | 223 |
| Apr. | 2 | 187 | 334 | 94 | 223 | 358 | 144 | 264 | 34 | 169 | 315 |
| Apr. | 9 | 285 | 57 | 185 | 321 | 95 | 227 | 355 | 133 | 264 | 38 |
| Apr. | 16 | 9 | 146 | 287 | 56 | 178 | 317 | 99 | 226 | 349 | 128 |
| Apr. | 23 | 96 | 250 | 18 | 140 | 268 | 61 | 189 | 310 | 80 | 231 |
| Apr. | 30 | 196 | 343 | 102 | 232 | 7 | 153 | 273 | 43 | 179 | 323 |
| May | 7 | 293 | 66 | 193 | 332 | 103 | 237 | 4 | 144 | 272 | 47 |
| May | 14 | 17 | 155 | 297 | 64 | 187 | 327 | 108 | 235 | 357 | 139 |
| May | 21 | 107 | 258 | 28 | 148 | 278 | 69 | 198 | 318 | 90 | 239 |
| May | 28 | 205 | 351 | 111 | 241 | 17 | 161 | 282 | 51 | 189 | 331 |
| Jun. | 4 | 301 | 75 | 201 | 343 | 111 | 245 | 13 | 154 | 280 | 55 |
| Jun. | 11 | 25 | 165 | 306 | 73 | 195 | 337 | 117 | 244 | 5 | 150 |
| Jun. | 18 | 117 | 267 | 37 | 157 | 288 | 78 | 207 | 327 | 99 | 248 |
| Jun. | 25 | 215 | 360 | 120 | 249 | 28 | 169 | 291 | 60 | 200 | 339 |
| Jul. | 2 | 309 | 84 | 211 | 353 | 119 | 254 | 23 | 164 | 289 | 64 |
| Jul. | 9 | 33 | 176 | 315 | 82 | 203 | 348 | 125 | 253 | 13 | 160 |
| Jul. | 16 | 126 | 276 | 46 | 165 | 297 | 87 | 216 | 336 | 108 | 258 |
| Jul. | 23 | 226 | 8 | 130 | 258 | 38 | 177 | 300 | 69 | 210 | 347 |
| Jul. | 30 | 317 | 92 | 221 | 2 | 128 | 262 | 33 | 173 | 298 | 72 |
| Aug. | 6 | 41 | 187 | 323 | 91 | 211 | 359 | 133 | 261 | 21 | 170 |
| Aug. | 13 | 135 | 285 | 54 | 175 | 305 | 97 | 224 | 346 | 116 | 268 |
| Aug. | 20 | 237 | 16 | 138 | 267 | 49 | 185 | 308 | 78 | 220 | 355 |
| Aug. | 27 | 326 | 100 | 232 | 10 | 136 | 270 | 44 | 181 | 307 | 80 |
| Sep. | 3 | 49 | 197 | 331 | 100 | 220 | 8 | 142 | 270 | 31 | 179 |
| Sep. | 10 | 143 | 295 | 62 | 184 | 314 | 107 | 232 | 355 | 125 | 278 |
| Sep. | 17 | 247 | 24 | 147 | 277 | 58 | 194 | 317 | 89 | 228 | 4 |
| Sep. | 24 | 335 | 108 | 243 | 18 | 145 | 278 | 55 | 189 | 316 | 88 |
| Oct. | 1 | 58 | 206 | 341 | 108 | 229 | 17 | 152 | 278 | 40 | 188 |
| Oct. | 8 | 151 | 306 | 70 | 193 | 322 | 117 | 240 | 4 | 134 | 288 |
| Oct. | 15 | 256 | 32 | 155 | 287 | 66 | 203 | 324 | 100 | 236 | 13 |
| Oct. | 22 | 344 | 116 | 253 | 27 | 154 | 287 | 64 | 198 | 324 | 98 |
| Oct. | 29 | 68 | 214 | 350 | 116 | 239 | 25 | 162 | 286 | 49 | 196 |
| Nov. | 5 | 161 | 316 | 78 | 201 | 332 | 126 | 248 | 12 | 145 | 297 |
| Nov. | 12 | 264 | 41 | 162 | 298 | 74 | 212 | 333 | 111 | 244 | 22 |
| Nov. | 19 | 353 | 125 | 262 | 36 | 162 | 296 | 73 | 207 | 332 | 108 |
| Nov. | 26 | 77 | 222 | 0 | 124 | 248 | 33 | 172 | 294 | 58 | 205 |
| Dec. | 3 | 171 | 325 | 87 | 209 | 343 | 135 | 257 | 19 | 156 | 305 |
| Dec. | 10 | 272 | 50 | 171 | 309 | 82 | 220 | 341 | 120 | 253 | 30 |
| Dec. | 17 | 1 | 135 | 271 | 45 | 170 | 306 | 81 | 217 | 340 | 118 |
| Dec. | 24 | 86 | 231 | 10 | 132 | 256 | 43 | 181 | 302 | 66 | 214 |
| Dec. | 31 | 182 | 333 | 95 | 217 | 354 | 142 | 265 | 27 | 167 | 313 |

| Month | Date | 1941 | 1942 | 1943 | 1944 | 1945 | 1946 | 1947 | 1948 | 1949 | 1950 |
|-------|------|------|------|------|------|------|------|------|------|------|------|
| Jan. | 1 | 325 | 88 | 211 | 353 | 135 | 258 | 22 | 165 | 305 | 68 |
| Jan. | 8 | 50 | 176 | 315 | 85 | 219 | 348 | 126 | 256 | 29 | 160 |
| Jan. | 15 | 141 | 276 | 50 | 169 | 312 | 87 | 220 | 340 | 123 | 258 |
| Jan. | 22 | 239 | 12 | 133 | 258 | 52 | 182 | 303 | 69 | 224 | 352 |
| Jan. | 29 | 333 | 96 | 221 | 2 | 143 | 266 | 32 | 174 | 314 | 75 |
| Feb. | 5 | 57 | 186 | 323 | 95 | 227 | 358 | 134 | 265 | 37 | 170 |
| Feb. | 12 | 150 | 285 | 58 | 178 | 320 | 96 | 228 | 349 | 131 | 268 |
| Feb. | 19 | 250 | 20 | 142 | 267 | 62 | 190 | 312 | 78 | 234 | 359 |
| Feb. | 26 | 342 | 104 | 231 | 11 | 152 | 274 | 43 | 182 | 323 | 83 |
| Mar. | 5 | 65 | 196 | 331 | 116 | 236 | 8 | 142 | 286 | 46 | 179 |
| Mar. | 12 | 158 | 295 | 66 | 199 | 328 | 107 | 236 | 10 | 139 | 279 |
| Mar. | 19 | 261 | 28 | 150 | 290 | 72 | 198 | 320 | 102 | 243 | 8 |
| Mar. | 26 | 351 | 112 | 242 | 34 | 161 | 281 | 53 | 204 | 332 | 91 |
| Apr. | 2 | 74 | 205 | 340 | 125 | 244 | 16 | 152 | 294 | 55 | 187 |
| Apr. | 9 | 166 | 306 | 74 | 208 | 337 | 117 | 244 | 19 | 148 | 289 |
| Apr. | 16 | 270 | 36 | 158 | 300 | 81 | 206 | 328 | 112 | 252 | 17 |
| Apr. | 23 | 360 | 120 | 252 | 42 | 170 | 290 | 63 | 212 | 340 | 100 |
| Apr. | 30 | 83 | 214 | 350 | 133 | 254 | 25 | 162 | 302 | 64 | 195 |
| May | 7 | 174 | 316 | 82 | 217 | 346 | 127 | 252 | 27 | 158 | 299 |
| May | 14 | 279 | 45 | 166 | 311 | 90 | 215 | 336 | 123 | 260 | 26 |
| May | 21 | 9 | 128 | 261 | 50 | 179 | 299 | 72 | 221 | 349 | 110 |
| May | 28 | 92 | 222 | 1 | 141 | 263 | 33 | 173 | 310 | 73 | 204 |
| Jun. | 4 | 184 | 326 | 91 | 226 | 356 | 137 | 261 | 36 | 168 | 307 |
| Jun. | 11 | 287 | 54 | 174 | 322 | 98 | 224 | 344 | 134 | 268 | 34 |
| Jun. | 18 | 17 | 137 | 270 | 60 | 187 | 308 | 81 | 231 | 357 | 119 |
| Jun. | 25 | 102 | 231 | 11 | 149 | 272 | 42 | 183 | 318 | 82 | 213 |
| Jul. | 2 | 194 | 335 | 99 | 234 | 7 | 145 | 269 | 44 | 179 | 316 |
| Jul. | 9 | 296 | 63 | 183 | 332 | 106 | 233 | 353 | 144 | 277 | 43 |
| Jul. | 16 | 25 | 147 | 279 | 70 | 195 | 318 | 89 | 241 | 5 | 129 |
| Jul. | 23 | 110 | 240 | 21 | 157 | 280 | 52 | 192 | 327 | 91 | 224 |
| Jul. | 30 | 205 | 343 | 108 | 242 | 18 | 153 | 278 | 52 | 190 | 324 |
| Aug. | 6 | 304 | 71 | 192 | 341 | 115 | 241 | 3 | 153 | 286 | 51 |
| Aug. | 13 | 33 | 156 | 287 | 80 | 203 | 327 | 98 | 251 | 13 | 138 |
| Aug. | 20 | 119 | 250 | 30 | 165 | 289 | 63 | 201 | 336 | 99 | 235 |
| Aug. | 27 | 216 | 351 | 117 | 250 | 28 | 162 | 287 | 61 | 200 | 332 |
| Sep. | 3 | 314 | 80 | 201 | 350 | 125 | 249 | 13 | 161 | 296 | 59 |
| Sep. | 10 | 41 | 165 | 296 | 90 | 211 | 336 | 108 | 260 | 21 | 146 |
| Sep. | 17 | 127 | 261 | 39 | 174 | 297 | 74 | 209 | 345 | 107 | 246 |
| Sep. | 24 | 226 | 359 | 126 | 259 | 38 | 170 | 295 | 70 | 209 | 341 |
| Oct. | 1 | 323 | 88 | 211 | 358 | 135 | 257 | 22 | 170 | 306 | 67 |
| Oct. | 8 | 49 | 174 | 306 | 99 | 220 | 344 | 118 | 269 | 30 | 154 |
| Oct. | 15 | 135 | 272 | 47 | 183 | 305 | 84 | 217 | 353 | 116 | 256 |
| Oct. | 22 | 236 | 8 | 134 | 269 | 47 | 180 | 303 | 80 | 217 | 351 |
| Oct. | 29 | 333 | 95 | 220 | 7 | 144 | 265 | 31 | 179 | 315 | 75 |
| Nov. | 5 | 58 | 181 | 317 | 107 | 229 | 352 | 129 | 277 | 39 | 162 |
| Nov. | 12 | 143 | 283 | 55 | 192 | 314 | 94 | 225 | 1 | 125 | 265 |
| Nov. | 19 | 244 | 18 | 141 | 279 | 55 | 189 | 311 | 90 | 225 | 0 |
| Nov. | 26 | 343 | 104 | 229 | 16 | 153 | 274 | 39 | 189 | 323 | 84 |
| Dec. | 3 | 67 | 189 | 328 | 115 | 237 | 360 | 140 | 284 | 47 | 171 |
| Dec. | 10 | 153 | 292 | 64 | 200 | 324 | 103 | 234 | 9 | 136 | 274 |
| Dec. | 17 | 252 | 28 | 149 | 289 | 63 | 199 | 319 | 100 | 234 | 9 |
| Dec. | 24 | 351 | 112 | 237 | 27 | 161 | 282 | 47 | 199 | 331 | 93 |
| Dec. | 31 | 76 | 198 | 338 | 123 | 246 | 9 | 150 | 293 | 55 | 180 |

| Month | Date | 1951 | 1952 | 1953 | 1954 | 1955 | 1956 | 1957 | 1958 | 1959 | 1960 |
|---|---|---|---|---|---|---|---|---|---|---|---|
| Jan. | 1 | 194 | 336 | 115 | 238 | 6 | 147 | 285 | 47 | 178 | 317 |
| Jan. | 8 | 297 | 67 | 199 | 331 | 107 | 237 | 9 | 143 | 278 | 47 |
| Jan. | 15 | 30 | 150 | 294 | 70 | 200 | 320 | 104 | 242 | 9 | 131 |
| Jan. | 22 | 114 | 240 | 35 | 161 | 284 | 51 | 207 | 331 | 94 | 223 |
| Jan. | 29 | 204 | 344 | 124 | 245 | 17 | 155 | 294 | 55 | 189 | 325 |
| Feb. | 5 | 305 | 76 | 207 | 341 | 116 | 246 | 18 | 152 | 287 | 56 |
| Feb. | 12 | 38 | 159 | 302 | 80 | 208 | 330 | 112 | 252 | 17 | 140 |
| Feb. | 19 | 122 | 249 | 45 | 169 | 292 | 61 | 216 | 340 | 102 | 233 |
| Feb. | 26 | 215 | 352 | 133 | 253 | 27 | 163 | 303 | 63 | 199 | 333 |
| Mar. | 5 | 314 | 96 | 216 | 350 | 125 | 266 | 27 | 161 | 297 | 75 |
| Mar. | 12 | 46 | 180 | 310 | 91 | 216 | 351 | 121 | 262 | 25 | 161 |
| Mar. | 19 | 130 | 274 | 54 | 178 | 300 | 86 | 224 | 349 | 110 | 259 |
| Mar. | 26 | 225 | 14 | 142 | 262 | 37 | 185 | 312 | 72 | 208 | 356 |
| Apr. | 2 | 324 | 104 | 226 | 358 | 135 | 274 | 37 | 169 | 307 | 83 |
| Apr. | 9 | 54 | 189 | 319 | 100 | 224 | 360 | 131 | 271 | 34 | 170 |
| Apr. | 16 | 138 | 285 | 62 | 187 | 308 | 97 | 232 | 357 | 118 | 269 |
| Apr. | 23 | 235 | 23 | 150 | 271 | 46 | 194 | 320 | 82 | 217 | 5 |
| Apr. | 30 | 334 | 112 | 235 | 6 | 146 | 282 | 48 | 177 | 317 | 91 |
| May | 7 | 62 | 197 | 330 | 109 | 232 | 8 | 142 | 279 | 42 | 177 |
| May | 14 | 146 | 296 | 70 | 196 | 316 | 107 | 240 | 6 | 127 | 279 |
| May | 21 | 243 | 32 | 158 | 280 | 54 | 204 | 328 | 91 | 225 | 15 |
| May | 28 | 344 | 120 | 244 | 15 | 155 | 290 | 55 | 187 | 326 | 100 |
| Jun. | 4 | 71 | 205 | 341 | 117 | 241 | 16 | 153 | 288 | 51 | 186 |
| Jun. | 11 | 155 | 306 | 79 | 204 | 325 | 117 | 249 | 14 | 137 | 288 |
| Jun. | 18 | 252 | 42 | 166 | 290 | 63 | 214 | 336 | 101 | 234 | 25 |
| Jun. | 25 | 354 | 128 | 253 | 26 | 164 | 298 | 63 | 198 | 335 | 109 |
| Jul. | 2 | 80 | 214 | 351 | 125 | 250 | 24 | 164 | 296 | 60 | 195 |
| Jul. | 9 | 164 | 315 | 88 | 212 | 335 | 126 | 259 | 22 | 147 | 297 |
| Jul. | 16 | 260 | 52 | 174 | 299 | 72 | 223 | 344 | 110 | 243 | 34 |
| Jul. | 23 | 3 | 137 | 261 | 37 | 173 | 307 | 71 | 209 | 343 | 118 |
| Jul. | 30 | 89 | 222 | 2 | 134 | 258 | 33 | 174 | 304 | 68 | 205 |
| Aug. | 6 | 174 | 324 | 97 | 220 | 345 | 134 | 268 | 30 | 156 | 305 |
| Aug. | 13 | 270 | 62 | 182 | 308 | 82 | 232 | 353 | 118 | 254 | 42 |
| Aug. | 20 | 11 | 146 | 269 | 48 | 181 | 316 | 79 | 220 | 351 | 126 |
| Aug. | 27 | 97 | 232 | 11 | 143 | 267 | 43 | 183 | 314 | 76 | 215 |
| Sep. | 3 | 184 | 332 | 107 | 228 | 355 | 143 | 278 | 38 | 166 | 314 |
| Sep. | 10 | 280 | 71 | 191 | 316 | 92 | 241 | 2 | 127 | 265 | 50 |
| Sep. | 17 | 19 | 155 | 278 | 58 | 189 | 325 | 88 | 230 | 359 | 135 |
| Sep. | 24 | 105 | 242 | 20 | 152 | 274 | 54 | 191 | 323 | 84 | 225 |
| Oct. | 1 | 193 | 341 | 116 | 237 | 4 | 152 | 287 | 47 | 174 | 324 |
| Oct. | 8 | 291 | 79 | 200 | 324 | 103 | 249 | 11 | 135 | 276 | 58 |
| Oct. | 15 | 27 | 163 | 287 | 68 | 198 | 333 | 98 | 239 | 8 | 143 |
| Oct. | 22 | 113 | 252 | 28 | 162 | 282 | 64 | 199 | 332 | 92 | 235 |
| Oct. | 29 | 201 | 350 | 125 | 245 | 12 | 162 | 295 | 56 | 182 | 334 |
| Nov. | 5 | 302 | 87 | 209 | 333 | 114 | 256 | 19 | 144 | 286 | 66 |
| Nov. | 12 | 36 | 171 | 297 | 76 | 207 | 341 | 109 | 247 | 17 | 150 |
| Nov. | 19 | 121 | 262 | 37 | 171 | 291 | 73 | 208 | 341 | 101 | 244 |
| Nov. | 26 | 209 | 0 | 133 | 254 | 20 | 173 | 303 | 65 | 190 | 345 |
| Dec. | 3 | 312 | 95 | 217 | 342 | 124 | 265 | 27 | 154 | 295 | 75 |
| Dec. | 10 | 45 | 179 | 307 | 84 | 216 | 348 | 119 | 255 | 27 | 158 |
| Dec. | 17 | 129 | 271 | 46 | 180 | 299 | 82 | 218 | 350 | 110 | 252 |
| Dec. | 24 | 217 | 11 | 141 | 263 | 28 | 184 | 311 | 73 | 199 | 355 |
| Dec. | 31 | 321 | 103 | 225 | 352 | 132 | 273 | 35 | 164 | 303 | 84 |

| Month | Date | 1961 | 1962 | 1963 | 1964 | 1965 | 1966 | 1967 | 1968 | 1969 | 1970 |
|---|---|---|---|---|---|---|---|---|---|---|---|
| Jan. | 1 | 96 | 217 | 350 | 128 | 266 | 27 | 163 | 298 | 76 | 197 |
| Jan. | 8 | 179 | 315 | 89 | 217 | 350 | 126 | 260 | 27 | 161 | 297 |
| Jan. | 15 | 275 | 54 | 179 | 302 | 86 | 225 | 349 | 112 | 257 | 36 |
| Jan. | 22 | 18 | 141 | 264 | 35 | 189 | 311 | 74 | 207 | 359 | 122 |
| Jan. | 29 | 105 | 225 | 1 | 136 | 275 | 35 | 173 | 306 | 85 | 206 |
| Feb. | 5 | 188 | 323 | 99 | 225 | 360 | 134 | 270 | 35 | 171 | 305 |
| Feb. | 12 | 284 | 64 | 187 | 310 | 95 | 235 | 357 | 121 | 267 | 45 |
| Feb. | 19 | 26 | 150 | 272 | 46 | 197 | 320 | 81 | 218 | 7 | 130 |
| Feb. | 26 | 113 | 234 | 11 | 144 | 283 | 45 | 182 | 315 | 93 | 216 |
| Mar. | 5 | 198 | 331 | 109 | 245 | 9 | 142 | 280 | 54 | 180 | 313 |
| Mar. | 12 | 293 | 73 | 195 | 332 | 105 | 244 | 5 | 142 | 277 | 54 |
| Mar. | 19 | 34 | 159 | 280 | 71 | 205 | 329 | 90 | 243 | 15 | 139 |
| Mar. | 26 | 122 | 243 | 19 | 167 | 291 | 54 | 190 | 338 | 101 | 226 |
| Apr. | 2 | 208 | 340 | 119 | 253 | 18 | 151 | 290 | 63 | 189 | 323 |
| Apr. | 9 | 303 | 82 | 204 | 340 | 116 | 252 | 14 | 150 | 288 | 62 |
| Apr. | 16 | 42 | 167 | 288 | 81 | 213 | 337 | 99 | 253 | 23 | 147 |
| Apr. | 23 | 130 | 253 | 28 | 176 | 299 | 64 | 198 | 347 | 109 | 235 |
| Apr. | 30 | 216 | 349 | 128 | 261 | 27 | 161 | 298 | 71 | 197 | 333 |
| May | 7 | 314 | 90 | 213 | 348 | 127 | 260 | 23 | 158 | 299 | 70 |
| May | 14 | 51 | 176 | 298 | 91 | 222 | 345 | 109 | 262 | 32 | 155 |
| May | 21 | 137 | 263 | 36 | 186 | 307 | 74 | 207 | 357 | 117 | 245 |
| May | 28 | 225 | 359 | 137 | 270 | 35 | 172 | 307 | 80 | 205 | 344 |
| Jun. | 4 | 325 | 98 | 222 | 357 | 137 | 268 | 31 | 168 | 309 | 78 |
| Jun. | 11 | 60 | 184 | 308 | 99 | 231 | 353 | 119 | 270 | 42 | 163 |
| Jun. | 18 | 146 | 272 | 45 | 195 | 315 | 82 | 217 | 6 | 126 | 253 |
| Jun. | 25 | 233 | 10 | 145 | 279 | 43 | 183 | 315 | 89 | 214 | 355 |
| Jul. | 2 | 336 | 106 | 230 | 6 | 147 | 276 | 40 | 178 | 318 | 87 |
| Jul. | 9 | 70 | 191 | 318 | 108 | 241 | 1 | 129 | 279 | 51 | 171 |
| Jul. | 16 | 154 | 281 | 56 | 204 | 324 | 91 | 227 | 14 | 135 | 261 |
| Jul. | 23 | 241 | 21 | 153 | 288 | 52 | 193 | 323 | 98 | 223 | 5 |
| Jul. | 30 | 345 | 115 | 238 | 16 | 156 | 286 | 47 | 188 | 327 | 97 |
| Aug. | 6 | 79 | 200 | 327 | 116 | 250 | 10 | 138 | 288 | 60 | 180 |
| Aug. | 13 | 163 | 289 | 66 | 212 | 333 | 99 | 238 | 22 | 144 | 270 |
| Aug. | 20 | 250 | 32 | 161 | 296 | 61 | 203 | 331 | 106 | 233 | 14 |
| Aug. | 27 | 353 | 124 | 246 | 27 | 164 | 295 | 55 | 199 | 335 | 106 |
| Sep. | 3 | 88 | 208 | 336 | 126 | 259 | 19 | 147 | 297 | 68 | 189 |
| Sep. | 10 | 172 | 297 | 77 | 220 | 342 | 108 | 249 | 30 | 152 | 279 |
| Sep. | 17 | 260 | 41 | 170 | 304 | 72 | 212 | 340 | 114 | 244 | 23 |
| Sep. | 24 | 1 | 134 | 254 | 37 | 172 | 304 | 64 | 208 | 344 | 115 |
| Oct. | 1 | 97 | 217 | 344 | 136 | 267 | 28 | 155 | 308 | 76 | 198 |
| Oct. | 8 | 180 | 306 | 88 | 228 | 351 | 117 | 259 | 38 | 161 | 289 |
| Oct. | 15 | 270 | 50 | 179 | 312 | 82 | 220 | 350 | 122 | 254 | 31 |
| Oct. | 22 | 10 | 143 | 262 | 47 | 182 | 313 | 73 | 217 | 353 | 123 |
| Oct. | 29 | 105 | 226 | 352 | 146 | 275 | 37 | 163 | 318 | 84 | 207 |
| Nov. | 5 | 189 | 315 | 97 | 237 | 359 | 127 | 268 | 47 | 168 | 299 |
| Nov. | 12 | 281 | 58 | 188 | 320 | 93 | 228 | 359 | 130 | 264 | 39 |
| Nov. | 19 | 19 | 151 | 271 | 55 | 191 | 321 | 82 | 225 | 3 | 131 |
| Nov. | 26 | 113 | 235 | 1 | 157 | 282 | 45 | 172 | 328 | 92 | 215 |
| Dec. | 3 | 197 | 326 | 105 | 245 | 7 | 138 | 276 | 55 | 176 | 310 |
| Dec. | 10 | 291 | 66 | 197 | 328 | 102 | 237 | 7 | 139 | 273 | 48 |
| Dec. | 17 | 30 | 159 | 280 | 63 | 202 | 329 | 91 | 234 | 13 | 139 |
| Dec. | 24 | 121 | 243 | 11 | 167 | 291 | 53 | 183 | 337 | 101 | 223 |
| Dec. | 31 | 204 | 336 | 113 | 254 | 14 | 149 | 284 | 64 | 184 | 320 |

| Month | Date | 1971 | 1972 | 1973 | 1974 | 1975 | 1976 | 1977 | 1978 | 1979 | 1980 |
|-------|------|------|------|------|------|------|------|------|------|------|------|
| Jan. | 1 | 335 | 109 | 246 | 8 | 147 | 279 | 56 | 179 | 318 | 90 |
| Jan. | 8 | 71 | 197 | 332 | 108 | 243 | 6 | 144 | 278 | 54 | 176 |
| Jan. | 15 | 158 | 283 | 69 | 207 | 328 | 93 | 240 | 18 | 139 | 263 |
| Jan. | 22 | 244 | 20 | 169 | 292 | 54 | 192 | 339 | 102 | 224 | 4 |
| Jan. | 29 | 344 | 117 | 255 | 17 | 156 | 288 | 64 | 188 | 327 | 99 |
| Feb. | 5 | 81 | 204 | 342 | 116 | 253 | 14 | 153 | 287 | 63 | 184 |
| Feb. | 12 | 167 | 291 | 79 | 216 | 337 | 101 | 251 | 26 | 147 | 271 |
| Feb. | 19 | 252 | 31 | 177 | 300 | 62 | 203 | 347 | 110 | 233 | 14 |
| Feb. | 26 | 353 | 126 | 263 | 27 | 164 | 297 | 72 | 199 | 334 | 109 |
| Mar. | 5 | 91 | 224 | 351 | 124 | 262 | 34 | 162 | 296 | 72 | 204 |
| Mar. | 12 | 176 | 312 | 90 | 224 | 346 | 122 | 262 | 34 | 156 | 203 |
| Mar. | 19 | 261 | 55 | 185 | 309 | 72 | 226 | 356 | 118 | 243 | 37 |
| Mar. | 26 | 1 | 149 | 270 | 37 | 172 | 320 | 80 | 208 | 343 | 130 |
| Apr. | 2 | 100 | 233 | 360 | 134 | 270 | 43 | 170 | 307 | 80 | 213 |
| Apr. | 9 | 184 | 320 | 101 | 232 | 355 | 131 | 273 | 42 | 164 | 302 |
| Apr. | 16 | 271 | 64 | 194 | 317 | 82 | 235 | 5 | 126 | 254 | 46 |
| Apr. | 23 | 9 | 158 | 278 | 47 | 181 | 329 | 88 | 217 | 352 | 139 |
| Apr. | 30 | 109 | 242 | 8 | 145 | 278 | 52 | 178 | 318 | 88 | 222 |
| May | 7 | 193 | 329 | 111 | 240 | 3 | 141 | 282 | 50 | 173 | 312 |
| May | 14 | 281 | 73 | 203 | 324 | 92 | 243 | 14 | 134 | 264 | 54 |
| May | 21 | 19 | 167 | 287 | 55 | 191 | 337 | 97 | 226 | 3 | 147 |
| May | 28 | 117 | 251 | 16 | 156 | 286 | 61 | 187 | 328 | 96 | 231 |
| Jun. | 4 | 201 | 339 | 120 | 249 | 11 | 151 | 291 | 59 | 180 | 323 |
| Jun. | 11 | 291 | 81 | 213 | 333 | 102 | 252 | 23 | 143 | 273 | 63 |
| Jun. | 18 | 29 | 176 | 296 | 64 | 201 | 346 | 106 | 234 | 13 | 155 |
| Jun. | 25 | 125 | 260 | 25 | 167 | 295 | 69 | 196 | 338 | 105 | 239 |
| Jul. | 2 | 209 | 349 | 129 | 258 | 19 | 162 | 299 | 68 | 188 | 334 |
| Jul. | 9 | 300 | 90 | 222 | 341 | 111 | 261 | 32 | 152 | 282 | 72 |
| Jul. | 16 | 40 | 184 | 305 | 72 | 212 | 354 | 115 | 243 | 24 | 163 |
| Jul. | 23 | 133 | 268 | 35 | 176 | 303 | 78 | 206 | 347 | 114 | 248 |
| Jul. | 30 | 217 | 0 | 137 | 267 | 27 | 172 | 308 | 77 | 197 | 344 |
| Aug. | 6 | 309 | 99 | 230 | 350 | 120 | 271 | 40 | 161 | 290 | 83 |
| Aug. | 13 | 51 | 192 | 314 | 81 | 223 | 2 | 124 | 252 | 34 | 171 |
| Aug. | 20 | 142 | 276 | 45 | 185 | 312 | 86 | 217 | 356 | 123 | 256 |
| Aug. | 27 | 225 | 10 | 146 | 276 | 36 | 182 | 317 | 86 | 206 | 353 |
| Sep. | 3 | 317 | 109 | 238 | 360 | 128 | 281 | 48 | 170 | 299 | 93 |
| Sep. | 10 | 61 | 200 | 322 | 90 | 232 | 10 | 132 | 262 | 43 | 180 |
| Sep. | 17 | 151 | 284 | 56 | 193 | 321 | 94 | 228 | 4 | 132 | 264 |
| Sep. | 24 | 234 | 20 | 155 | 284 | 45 | 191 | 326 | 94 | 215 | 2 |
| Oct. | 1 | 325 | 120 | 246 | 9 | 136 | 291 | 56 | 179 | 308 | 103 |
| Oct. | 8 | 70 | 208 | 330 | 101 | 241 | 19 | 140 | 273 | 51 | 189 |
| Oct. | 15 | 160 | 292 | 66 | 202 | 330 | 102 | 238 | 12 | 140 | 273 |
| Oct. | 22 | 243 | 28 | 165 | 292 | 54 | 199 | 336 | 102 | 225 | 10 |
| Oct. | 29 | 334 | 130 | 254 | 17 | 146 | 301 | 64 | 187 | 318 | 112 |
| Nov. | 5 | 79 | 217 | 338 | 112 | 249 | 27 | 148 | 284 | 59 | 197 |
| Nov. | 12 | 169 | 300 | 76 | 210 | 339 | 111 | 247 | 21 | 148 | 282 |
| Nov. | 19 | 253 | 36 | 175 | 300 | 63 | 207 | 347 | 110 | 234 | 18 |
| Nov. | 26 | 344 | 139 | 262 | 25 | 156 | 310 | 73 | 195 | 329 | 120 |
| Dec. | 3 | 87 | 226 | 346 | 122 | 257 | 36 | 157 | 294 | 67 | 206 |
| Dec. | 10 | 177 | 310 | 84 | 220 | 347 | 121 | 255 | 31 | 156 | 292 |
| Dec. | 17 | 261 | 45 | 185 | 308 | 72 | 216 | 356 | 118 | 242 | 28 |
| Dec. | 24 | 355 | 148 | 271 | 33 | 167 | 318 | 81 | 203 | 340 | 128 |
| Dec. | 31 | 95 | 235 | 355 | 132 | 265 | 44 | 166 | 303 | 76 | 214 |

| Month | Date | 1981 | 1982 | 1983 | 1984 | 1985 | 1986 | 1987 | 1988 | 1989 | 1990 |
|-------|------|------|------|------|------|------|------|------|------|------|------|
| Jan. | 1 | 226 | 350 | 129 | 260 | 36 | 162 | 300 | 71 | 205 | 333 |
| Jan. | 8 | 315 | 89 | 225 | 346 | 126 | 260 | 36 | 156 | 297 | 72 |
| Jan. | 15 | 53 | 188 | 309 | 73 | 225 | 358 | 119 | 243 | 37 | 168 |
| Jan. | 22 | 149 | 272 | 35 | 176 | 319 | 82 | 206 | 348 | 129 | 252 |
| Jan. | 29 | 234 | 0 | 137 | 270 | 43 | 172 | 308 | 81 | 213 | 343 |
| Feb. | 5 | 324 | 98 | 234 | 354 | 135 | 270 | 44 | 164 | 306 | 82 |
| Feb. | 12 | 64 | 196 | 317 | 81 | 236 | 6 | 128 | 252 | 48 | 175 |
| Feb. | 19 | 157 | 280 | 45 | 185 | 328 | 90 | 217 | 356 | 138 | 260 |
| Feb. | 26 | 242 | 10 | 145 | 279 | 51 | 182 | 316 | 90 | 222 | 353 |
| Mar. | 5 | 332 | 108 | 242 | 15 | 143 | 280 | 52 | 185 | 313 | 93 |
| Mar. | 12 | 74 | 204 | 326 | 104 | 246 | 14 | 136 | 275 | 57 | 184 |
| Mar. | 19 | 166 | 288 | 55 | 208 | 337 | 97 | 227 | 19 | 147 | 268 |
| Mar. | 26 | 250 | 20 | 154 | 300 | 60 | 191 | 326 | 111 | 230 | 1 |
| Apr. | 2 | 340 | 119 | 250 | 24 | 151 | 291 | 60 | 194 | 322 | 103 |
| Apr. | 9 | 84 | 212 | 334 | 114 | 255 | 22 | 144 | 286 | 66 | 192 |
| Apr. | 16 | 175 | 296 | 66 | 216 | 346 | 106 | 237 | 27 | 156 | 276 |
| Apr. | 23 | 259 | 28 | 164 | 309 | 69 | 199 | 336 | 119 | 240 | 9 |
| Apr. | 30 | 349 | 130 | 258 | 33 | 160 | 302 | 68 | 203 | 331 | 113 |
| May | 7 | 93 | 221 | 342 | 124 | 264 | 31 | 152 | 297 | 75 | 201 |
| May | 14 | 184 | 304 | 75 | 225 | 355 | 114 | 246 | 36 | 165 | 285 |
| May | 21 | 268 | 36 | 175 | 317 | 78 | 207 | 347 | 127 | 249 | 18 |
| May | 28 | 358 | 140 | 266 | 41 | 170 | 311 | 76 | 211 | 341 | 122 |
| Jun. | 4 | 102 | 230 | 350 | 135 | 272 | 40 | 160 | 307 | 83 | 210 |
| Jun. | 11 | 193 | 313 | 84 | 234 | 3 | 123 | 255 | 45 | 173 | 294 |
| Jun. | 18 | 277 | 45 | 185 | 325 | 87 | 216 | 357 | 135 | 258 | 27 |
| Jun. | 25 | 8 | 149 | 275 | 49 | 180 | 320 | 85 | 219 | 352 | 130 |
| Jul. | 2 | 110 | 239 | 359 | 146 | 281 | 49 | 169 | 317 | 92 | 219 |
| Jul. | 9 | 201 | 322 | 93 | 244 | 11 | 133 | 263 | 55 | 181 | 304 |
| Jul. | 16 | 286 | 54 | 196 | 333 | 96 | 225 | 7 | 143 | 266 | 37 |
| Jul. | 23 | 19 | 158 | 284 | 57 | 191 | 328 | 94 | 227 | 3 | 138 |
| Jul. | 30 | 119 | 248 | 7 | 155 | 290 | 57 | 178 | 327 | 101 | 227 |
| Aug. | 6 | 210 | 331 | 101 | 254 | 19 | 142 | 272 | 66 | 189 | 313 |
| Aug. | 13 | 294 | 64 | 205 | 341 | 104 | 236 | 16 | 152 | 274 | 48 |
| Aug. | 20 | 30 | 166 | 293 | 66 | 202 | 337 | 103 | 236 | 13 | 147 |
| Aug. | 27 | 128 | 256 | 17 | 164 | 299 | 65 | 187 | 335 | 111 | 235 |
| Sep. | 3 | 218 | 340 | 110 | 264 | 27 | 151 | 281 | 75 | 197 | 321 |
| Sep. | 10 | 302 | 75 | 214 | 350 | 112 | 247 | 24 | 160 | 282 | 59 |
| Sep. | 17 | 40 | 174 | 302 | 74 | 212 | 345 | 112 | 245 | 23 | 156 |
| Sep. | 24 | 138 | 264 | 26 | 172 | 309 | 73 | 197 | 343 | 121 | 243 |
| Oct. | 1 | 226 | 349 | 119 | 274 | 36 | 159 | 292 | 84 | 206 | 329 |
| Oct. | 8 | 310 | 86 | 222 | 359 | 120 | 258 | 32 | 169 | 291 | 70 |
| Oct. | 15 | 50 | 183 | 310 | 84 | 220 | 354 | 120 | 255 | 31 | 165 |
| Oct. | 22 | 148 | 272 | 35 | 181 | 319 | 81 | 206 | 352 | 130 | 251 |
| Oct. | 29 | 234 | 357 | 130 | 282 | 44 | 167 | 303 | 92 | 214 | 337 |
| Nov. | 5 | 318 | 96 | 230 | 8 | 129 | 268 | 40 | 178 | 300 | 79 |
| Nov. | 12 | 58 | 193 | 318 | 93 | 229 | 4 | 128 | 265 | 39 | 175 |
| Nov. | 19 | 158 | 280 | 44 | 190 | 329 | 90 | 214 | 2 | 139 | 260 |
| Nov. | 26 | 243 | 5 | 141 | 290 | 53 | 175 | 314 | 100 | 223 | 345 |
| Dec. | 3 | 327 | 106 | 238 | 16 | 139 | 277 | 49 | 185 | 310 | 88 |
| Dec. | 10 | 66 | 203 | 326 | 103 | 237 | 14 | 136 | 274 | 48 | 185 |
| Dec. | 17 | 167 | 288 | 52 | 200 | 337 | 98 | 222 | 12 | 147 | 269 |
| Dec. | 24 | 252 | 13 | 152 | 298 | 62 | 184 | 324 | 108 | 232 | 355 |
| Dec. | 31 | 337 | 114 | 248 | 24 | 149 | 285 | 59 | 193 | 320 | 96 |

| Month | Date | 1991 | 1992 | 1993 | 1994 | 1995 | 1996 | 1997 | 1998 | 1999 | 2000 |
|---|---|---|---|---|---|---|---|---|---|---|---|
| Jan. | 1 | 111 | 242 | 15 | 145 | 281 | 53 | 185 | 317 | 92 | 223 |
| Jan. | 8 | 206 | 326 | 108 | 244 | 16 | 136 | 279 | 56 | 186 | 307 |
| Jan. | 15 | 289 | 54 | 210 | 337 | 99 | 225 | 21 | 147 | 270 | 37 |
| Jan. | 22 | 18 | 158 | 299 | 61 | 190 | 329 | 110 | 231 | 2 | 140 |
| Jan. | 29 | 119 | 252 | 23 | 155 | 290 | 62 | 193 | 326 | 101 | 232 |
| Feb. | 5 | 214 | 335 | 116 | 254 | 24 | 145 | 287 | 66 | 193 | 315 |
| Feb. | 12 | 298 | 63 | 220 | 345 | 108 | 235 | 31 | 155 | 278 | 47 |
| Feb. | 19 | 29 | 166 | 308 | 69 | 201 | 337 | 119 | 239 | 12 | 148 |
| Feb. | 26 | 128 | 260 | 32 | 164 | 299 | 70 | 202 | 335 | 111 | 240 |
| Mar. | 5 | 222 | 356 | 124 | 265 | 32 | 166 | 295 | 76 | 201 | 337 |
| Mar. | 12 | 306 | 87 | 229 | 354 | 116 | 259 | 39 | 164 | 285 | 72 |
| Mar. | 19 | 39 | 189 | 317 | 77 | 211 | 360 | 128 | 248 | 22 | 170 |
| Mar. | 26 | 138 | 280 | 41 | 172 | 310 | 90 | 212 | 343 | 121 | 260 |
| Apr. | 2 | 230 | 5 | 133 | 275 | 40 | 175 | 305 | 86 | 210 | 345 |
| Apr. | 9 | 314 | 98 | 237 | 3 | 123 | 270 | 47 | 173 | 294 | 83 |
| Apr. | 16 | 49 | 198 | 326 | 86 | 220 | 9 | 136 | 257 | 31 | 180 |
| Apr. | 23 | 148 | 288 | 50 | 180 | 320 | 98 | 221 | 351 | 132 | 268 |
| Apr. | 30 | 238 | 13 | 143 | 284 | 48 | 183 | 315 | 95 | 218 | 353 |
| May | 7 | 322 | 109 | 245 | 12 | 132 | 281 | 55 | 182 | 302 | 93 |
| May | 14 | 57 | 207 | 335 | 95 | 228 | 18 | 144 | 267 | 39 | 190 |
| May | 21 | 158 | 296 | 59 | 189 | 330 | 106 | 230 | 1 | 141 | 276 |
| May | 28 | 247 | 21 | 154 | 292 | 57 | 191 | 326 | 103 | 227 | 1 |
| Jun. | 4 | 330 | 119 | 253 | 21 | 141 | 291 | 64 | 190 | 311 | 102 |
| Jun. | 11 | 66 | 217 | 343 | 105 | 236 | 28 | 152 | 276 | 48 | 199 |
| Jun. | 18 | 168 | 304 | 68 | 199 | 340 | 114 | 238 | 11 | 150 | 285 |
| Jun. | 25 | 256 | 29 | 165 | 300 | 66 | 199 | 337 | 111 | 236 | 10 |
| Jul. | 2 | 339 | 129 | 262 | 29 | 150 | 300 | 73 | 198 | 321 | 111 |
| Jul. | 9 | 74 | 227 | 351 | 114 | 245 | 38 | 160 | 285 | 57 | 209 |
| Jul. | 16 | 177 | 313 | 76 | 210 | 348 | 123 | 246 | 22 | 158 | 293 |
| Jul. | 23 | 265 | 38 | 175 | 309 | 75 | 208 | 347 | 120 | 245 | 19 |
| Jul. | 30 | 349 | 137 | 272 | 37 | 160 | 308 | 83 | 206 | 331 | 119 |
| Aug. | 6 | 83 | 237 | 359 | 123 | 255 | 48 | 169 | 293 | 67 | 218 |
| Aug. | 13 | 186 | 322 | 84 | 221 | 356 | 132 | 254 | 33 | 166 | 302 |
| Aug. | 20 | 273 | 47 | 185 | 318 | 83 | 218 | 356 | 129 | 253 | 29 |
| Aug. | 27 | 358 | 146 | 282 | 45 | 169 | 317 | 93 | 214 | 340 | 128 |
| Sep. | 3 | 93 | 246 | 7 | 131 | 265 | 56 | 177 | 301 | 78 | 226 |
| Sep. | 10 | 194 | 331 | 92 | 231 | 4 | 141 | 263 | 43 | 174 | 311 |
| Sep. | 17 | 281 | 56 | 194 | 327 | 91 | 228 | 5 | 138 | 261 | 39 |
| Sep. | 24 | 8 | 154 | 292 | 53 | 178 | 326 | 102 | 223 | 349 | 137 |
| Oct. | 1 | 104 | 254 | 16 | 139 | 276 | 64 | 186 | 310 | 89 | 234 |
| Oct. | 8 | 202 | 339 | 101 | 241 | 13 | 149 | 273 | 53 | 183 | 319 |
| Oct. | 15 | 289 | 66 | 202 | 337 | 99 | 238 | 13 | 148 | 269 | 49 |
| Oct. | 22 | 16 | 164 | 301 | 61 | 187 | 336 | 111 | 231 | 357 | 148 |
| Oct. | 29 | 115 | 262 | 25 | 148 | 287 | 72 | 195 | 318 | 100 | 242 |
| Nov. | 5 | 211 | 347 | 111 | 250 | 22 | 157 | 283 | 61 | 193 | 326 |
| Nov. | 12 | 297 | 76 | 211 | 346 | 107 | 247 | 22 | 157 | 277 | 58 |
| Nov. | 19 | 24 | 174 | 309 | 70 | 194 | 346 | 119 | 240 | 5 | 159 |
| Nov. | 26 | 126 | 270 | 33 | 156 | 297 | 80 | 203 | 328 | 109 | 251 |
| Dec. | 3 | 220 | 355 | 121 | 258 | 31 | 165 | 293 | 69 | 202 | 334 |
| Dec. | 10 | 305 | 85 | 220 | 355 | 115 | 256 | 31 | 165 | 286 | 67 |
| Dec. | 17 | 32 | 185 | 317 | 79 | 203 | 357 | 127 | 249 | 13 | 169 |
| Dec. | 24 | 135 | 278 | 41 | 166 | 306 | 89 | 211 | 338 | 117 | 260 |
| Dec. | 31 | 230 | 3 | 131 | 266 | 41 | 173 | 303 | 78 | 211 | 343 |

| Month | Year | 2001 | 2002 | 2003 | 2004 | 2005 | 2006 | 2007 | 2008 | 2009 | 2010 |
|-------|------|------|------|------|------|------|------|------|------|------|------|
| Jan. | 1 | 355 | 128 | 263 | 33 | 165 | 300 | 74 | 203 | 336 | 111 |
| Jan. | 8 | 89 | 228 | 355 | 117 | 260 | 39 | 165 | 288 | 71 | 211 |
| Jan. | 15 | 193 | 317 | 79 | 209 | 4 | 127 | 249 | 20 | 174 | 297 |
| Jan. | 22 | 280 | 41 | 174 | 310 | 91 | 211 | 346 | 121 | 261 | 21 |
| Jan. | 29 | 4 | 137 | 273 | 42 | 175 | 308 | 84 | 211 | 345 | 119 |
| Feb. | 5 | 97 | 238 | 3 | 126 | 268 | 49 | 173 | 296 | 80 | 221 |
| Feb. | 12 | 202 | 326 | 87 | 219 | 12 | 136 | 257 | 31 | 182 | 306 |
| Feb. | 19 | 289 | 49 | 184 | 319 | 99 | 220 | 356 | 130 | 269 | 31 |
| Feb. | 26 | 13 | 145 | 283 | 49 | 184 | 316 | 94 | 219 | 355 | 127 |
| Mar. | 5 | 106 | 248 | 11 | 147 | 278 | 59 | 181 | 317 | 90 | 229 |
| Mar. | 12 | 210 | 334 | 95 | 244 | 20 | 145 | 265 | 56 | 190 | 315 |
| Mar. | 19 | 298 | 58 | 193 | 342 | 107 | 229 | 4 | 153 | 277 | 40 |
| Mar. | 26 | 23 | 153 | 293 | 69 | 193 | 325 | 104 | 239 | 4 | 136 |
| Apr. | 2 | 116 | 257 | 20 | 155 | 289 | 67 | 190 | 325 | 101 | 237 |
| Apr. | 9 | 218 | 343 | 104 | 255 | 28 | 154 | 274 | 67 | 198 | 323 |
| Apr. | 16 | 306 | 68 | 202 | 351 | 115 | 239 | 12 | 162 | 285 | 50 |
| Apr. | 23 | 32 | 162 | 303 | 77 | 202 | 334 | 114 | 247 | 12 | 146 |
| Apr. | 30 | 127 | 265 | 29 | 163 | 300 | 75 | 199 | 333 | 112 | 245 |
| May | 7 | 226 | 352 | 113 | 264 | 37 | 162 | 284 | 76 | 207 | 331 |
| May | 14 | 314 | 77 | 210 | 1 | 123 | 248 | 21 | 172 | 293 | 59 |
| May | 21 | 40 | 173 | 312 | 86 | 210 | 345 | 122 | 256 | 20 | 157 |
| May | 28 | 138 | 273 | 38 | 171 | 311 | 83 | 207 | 342 | 123 | 254 |
| Jun. | 4 | 235 | 0 | 122 | 273 | 46 | 170 | 294 | 84 | 217 | 339 |
| Jun. | 11 | 322 | 87 | 219 | 11 | 132 | 257 | 30 | 181 | 302 | 68 |
| Jun. | 18 | 48 | 183 | 320 | 95 | 218 | 356 | 130 | 265 | 29 | 168 |
| Jun. | 25 | 149 | 281 | 46 | 181 | 321 | 92 | 216 | 352 | 132 | 262 |
| Jul. | 2 | 245 | 8 | 132 | 281 | 56 | 178 | 304 | 93 | 227 | 347 |
| Jul. | 9 | 330 | 95 | 229 | 20 | 140 | 266 | 41 | 190 | 310 | 76 |
| Jul. | 16 | 56 | 195 | 328 | 104 | 227 | 7 | 138 | 274 | 38 | 179 |
| Jul. | 23 | 158 | 290 | 54 | 191 | 330 | 101 | 224 | 2 | 140 | 272 |
| Jul. | 30 | 254 | 16 | 142 | 290 | 65 | 186 | 313 | 101 | 236 | 356 |
| Aug. | 6 | 339 | 103 | 239 | 28 | 149 | 274 | 52 | 198 | 319 | 84 |
| Aug. | 13 | 65 | 205 | 336 | 112 | 236 | 17 | 147 | 282 | 47 | 188 |
| Aug. | 20 | 167 | 299 | 62 | 201 | 338 | 110 | 232 | 12 | 149 | 281 |
| Aug. | 27 | 264 | 24 | 151 | 299 | 74 | 194 | 321 | 111 | 245 | 5 |
| Sep. | 3 | 348 | 112 | 250 | 36 | 158 | 282 | 63 | 206 | 328 | 93 |
| Sep. | 10 | 74 | 215 | 345 | 120 | 246 | 26 | 156 | 290 | 58 | 197 |
| Sep. | 17 | 176 | 309 | 70 | 211 | 347 | 120 | 240 | 22 | 157 | 290 |
| Sep. | 24 | 273 | 33 | 159 | 309 | 83 | 203 | 330 | 122 | 253 | 14 |
| Oct. | 1 | 356 | 120 | 261 | 44 | 167 | 291 | 73 | 214 | 336 | 103 |
| Oct. | 8 | 84 | 224 | 354 | 128 | 256 | 34 | 165 | 298 | 68 | 205 |
| Oct. | 15 | 184 | 318 | 78 | 220 | 355 | 129 | 248 | 31 | 167 | 299 |
| Oct. | 22 | 281 | 42 | 167 | 320 | 91 | 212 | 338 | 132 | 261 | 23 |
| Oct. | 29 | 5 | 129 | 271 | 52 | 175 | 301 | 82 | 222 | 344 | 113 |
| Nov. | 5 | 95 | 232 | 4 | 136 | 266 | 42 | 174 | 306 | 78 | 213 |
| Nov. | 12 | 193 | 327 | 87 | 229 | 5 | 137 | 257 | 40 | 177 | 307 |
| Nov. | 19 | 289 | 51 | 176 | 331 | 99 | 221 | 346 | 143 | 268 | 31 |
| Nov. | 26 | 13 | 139 | 280 | 61 | 183 | 312 | 91 | 231 | 352 | 123 |
| Dec. | 3 | 105 | 240 | 13 | 144 | 276 | 51 | 183 | 315 | 87 | 223 |
| Dec. | 10 | 203 | 335 | 96 | 237 | 15 | 145 | 267 | 48 | 188 | 315 |
| Dec. | 17 | 297 | 59 | 185 | 341 | 107 | 229 | 356 | 152 | 277 | 39 |
| Dec. | 24 | 21 | 150 | 288 | 70 | 190 | 322 | 98 | 240 | 0 | 134 |
| Dec. | 31 | 114 | 249 | 22 | 153 | 285 | 60 | 191 | 324 | 96 | 232 |

# Dates to Hunt and Fish

| Dates to Hunt or Fish | Qtr. | Sign |
|---|---|---|
| Jan. 6 1:38 am-Jan. 8 12:38 pm | 4th | Cancer |
| Jan. 15 9:33 am-Jan. 17 12:18 pm | 4th | Scorpio |
| Jan. 23 4:29 pm-Jan. 25 10:06 pm | 1st | Pisces |
| Feb. 2 9:03 am-Feb. 4 7:50 pm | 2nd | Cancer |
| Feb. 11 2:58 pm-Feb. 13 6:35 pm | 3rd | Scorpio |
| Feb. 20 2:27 am-Feb. 22 7:45 am | 4th | Pisces |
| Feb. 29 5:12 pm-Mar. 3 4:18 am | 2nd | Cancer |
| Mar. 9 9:03 pm-Mar. 11 11:57 pm | 3rd | Scorpio |
| Mar. 11 11:57 pm-Mar. 14 2:51 am | 3rd | Sagittarius |
| Mar. 18 10:26 am-Mar. 20 4:29 pm | 4th | Pisces |
| Mar. 28 1:23 am-Mar. 30 1:07 pm | 1st | Cancer |
| Apr. 6 6:24 am-Apr. 8 7:50 am | 3rd | Scorpio |
| Apr. 8 7:50 am-Apr. 10 9:33 am | 3rd | Sagittarius |
| Apr. 14 5:24 pm-Apr. 17 12:24 am | 4th | Pisces |
| Apr. 24 9:56 am-Apr. 26 10:14 pm | 1st | Cancer |
| May 3 4:38 pm-May 5 5:08 pm | 2nd | Scorpio |
| May 5 5:08 pm-May 7 5:17 pm | 3rd | Sagittarius |
| May 11 10:52 pm-May 14 6:02 am | 4th | Pisces |
| May 21 4:35 pm-May 24 5:07 am | 1st | Cancer |
| May 31 3:08 am-Jun. 2 3:52 am | 2nd | Scorpio |
| Jun. 2 3:52 am-Jun. 4 3:12 am | 2nd | Sagittarius |
| Jun. 8 5:38 am-Jun. 10 11:49 am | 3rd | Pisces |
| Jun. 17 10:37 pm-Jun. 20 11:05 am | 1st | Cancer |
| Jun. 27 12:13 pm-Jun. 29 2:15 pm | 2nd | Scorpio |
| Jun. 29 2:15 pm-Jul. 1 2:01 pm | 2nd | Sagittarius |
| Jul. 5 2:26 pm-Jul. 7 7:03 pm | 3rd | Pisces |

| | | |
|---|---|---|
| Jul. 7 7:03 pm-Jul. 10 3:51 am | 3rd | Aries |
| Jul. 15 4:40 am-Jul. 17 4:56 pm | 4th | Cancer |
| Jul. 24 7:08 pm-Jul. 26 10:48 pm | 1st | Scorpio |
| Jul. 26 10:48 pm-Jul. 28 11:57 pm | 2nd | Sagittarius |
| Aug. 2 12:34 am-Aug. 4 3:59 am | 3rd | Pisces |
| Aug. 4 3:59 am-Aug. 6 11:26 am | 3rd | Aries |
| Aug. 11 11:20 am-Aug. 13 11:30 pm | 4th | Cancer |
| Aug. 21 12:37 am-Aug. 23 5:08 am | 1st | Scorpio |
| Aug. 29 10:33 am-Aug. 31 1:46 pm | 2nd | Pisces |
| Aug. 31 1:46 pm-Sep. 2 8:16 pm | 3rd | Aries |
| Sep. 7 6:50 pm-Sep. 10 7:06 am | 4th | Cancer |
| Sep. 17 6:25 am-Sep. 19 10:30 am | 1st | Scorpio |
| Sep. 25 6:55 pm-Sep. 27 10:57 pm | 2nd | Pisces |
| Sep. 27 10:57 pm-Sep. 30 5:24 am | 2nd | Aries |
| Oct. 5 2:54 am-Oct. 7 3:23 pm | 3rd | Cancer |
| Oct. 14 2:10 pm-Oct. 16 4:58 pm | 1st | Scorpio |
| Oct. 23 1:13 am-Oct. 25 6:24 am | 2nd | Pisces |
| Oct. 25 6:24 am-Oct. 27 1:37 pm | 2nd | Aries |
| Nov. 1 9:53 am-Nov. 3 10:32 pm | 3rd | Cancer |
| Nov. 10 11:05 pm-Nov. 13 12:56 am | 4th | Scorpio |
| Nov. 19 5:38 am-Nov. 21 11:11 am | 2nd | Pisces |
| Nov. 21 11:11 am-Nov. 23 7:16 pm | 2nd | Aries |
| Nov. 28 5:10 pm-Dec. 1 5:50 am | 3rd | Cancer |
| Dec. 8 9:43 am-Dec. 10 11:54 am | 4th | Scorpio |
| Dec. 16 12:24 pm-Dec. 18 4:52 pm | 1st | Pisces |
| Dec. 18 4:52 pm-Dec. 21 12:52 am | 2nd | Aries |
| Dec. 25 11:38 pm-Dec. 28 12:14 pm | 2nd | Cancer |

Cancer, Scorpio, and Pisces are dates for fishing;
and Aries and Sagittarius are dates for hunting.

# New and Full Moon Cycles
# for 2004

*by Sharon Leah*

The Capitol Building in Washington, D.C., (77W01 38N53) is the location used for all the charts in this article.

The Moon in mundane charts represents the people of the land, and women in particular. It is the natural ruler of the fourth house. It also rules the collective's (general population) attitude toward its female members—as depicted by our instinctive nurturing and caretaking qualities. It also represents popular opinion. The Sun in mundane charts will convey the general nature of the nation, the government (local, state, and national), and our president, governors, and mayors. It often shows the way a nation expresses itself in the world, and our nation's reputation.

The New Moon indicates the end of one cycle and the beginning of another. Of course, everything does not stop and something else start when the Moon is new, but the energy around us changes, moods and opinion change. The Full Moon represents illumination and bringing into the light, but it also symbolizes separation, partnership, and culmination.

Not every person will feel the effect of each New or Full Moon, but to the extent that the changing Moon and other planets interact with your own birth chart, you will notice the energy of the shifting sky. Angular houses and planets in these houses (first, fourth, seventh, tenth) are important because angular houses in a chart represent creating new, initiating action, and forces that bring change.

The forecasts that follow are not meant to be a complete analysis of the New and Full Moons. Please think of them more as thoughts, or meditations, on the energies and patterns that occur as the Moon and Sun meet and separate throughout the year. Pay attention to your own feelings, emotions, thoughts, and actions as the cycles evolve. Look at what is happening in the news, and see if you can identify some events with the Moon's changing faces.

If you think the forecasts sound negative, keep this in mind, mundane astrology—the astrology of groups and nations—works because people tend to think and act according to established patterns. It is more difficult to predict possible outcomes when people challenge themselves to step outside the box with their own thinking and consequent actions.

♋

## January 7 Full Moon in Cancer 10:40 am EST

The fourth house Cancer Moon represents the land, our private homes, and real estate; it also represents the people, especially women. The Moon opposes the Sun in the tenth angular house, indicating the public's opposition to the ruling party. The public may be opposed to actions the government is taking. Keep in mind, that while this chart is generally for the nation, it would also apply to your local and state governments. At this time, emotions and feelings are stronger than logic. There may be a generally somber feeling in the air.

Saturn is also in the fourth house and Mars is in the first angular house. Mars represents the collective's need to have enemies so that aggression can be expressed. (People have to have someone to be mad at!) Mars squaring the Sun, as it does in this chart indicates danger to the head of state; a fall from power; or the overthrow of regimes, often by the military. This often indicates positive change and the start of a better period.

The Sun is in Capricorn and the tenth house. The tenth house represents the ruling class, the reputation of our cities and nation, and our nation's influence in world affairs. Capricorn's energy is stern (the disciplinarian and authority), goal oriented, detached, and driven to achieve. We might expect to see hardship and limitations placed on the people and on agricultural and real estate concerns.

## January 21 New Moon in Aquarius 4:05 pm EST

The New Moon in Aquarius and the seventh house will focus our attention on relationships. The seventh house rules relationships with other societies and countries, all foreign treaties, alliances, and wars. This house often shows what we (citizens) find difficult to see in ourselves. Do we see ourselves standing alone in a foreign camp? Do we see ourselves in a new role as humanitarians (represented by Aquarius)? Or, are we being aloof and cerebral? Countries with Sun in Aquarius include: Iran, Japan, and Mexico; those with Moon in Aquarius include: Afghanistan, China, South Vietnam, and Uganda.

The nation and the people want peace and partnership, and there is a strong collective desire for these things to come about.

The tenth house contains Mars, still in Aries. Mars, is representative of our government and the ruling class, and Mars' energy indicates that their stance is still very aggressive. People see our leaders as aggressors in the world community.

♌

## February 6 Full Moon in Leo 3:47 am EST

The eighth house Leo Full Moon shines a very bright light on finances connected to our partnerships. All international finance and foreign investment are ruled by this house. Leo is a gregarious, generous sign, and the Moon is representing the people. So, what it seems to be showing is that we want to be noticed and appreciated for our generous nature. What have we agreed to that we want to be thanked for?

The Aquarius Sun is in the second house, representing the manner in which our nation produces wealth. The second house includes banks, financial and material resources, the economy and the national product. The Sun is conjunct Neptune here. The political outcome of this conjunction could go in one of two directions: on the one hand, the U.S. government and our rulers could be thinking about humanitarian efforts, universal values, and of the collective needs; but, on the other hand, we might experience this conjunction as a time of unrealistic political expectations, avoiding confrontation, and being devious and subversive in our dealing with others.

We might also see something new and exciting in the world of fashion or the arts, including music and the visual arts.

There are indications that the government will use grain and other agricultural resources to trade or to feed the world. Mars has recently moved into Taurus, the farmer's sign, and Venus (ruler of Taurus) is in a close sextile with Mercury (communications, mental processes). Mercury also rules Virgo. The ninth house represents foreign countries and foreign concerns, and especially shipping. Neptune rules the oceans, and ships would move the grain to foreign ports.

So, we have the nation's resources, political involvement, unknown or undisclosed plans, the oceans, shipping, and agriculture as players. I'm not so sure (based on a Pluto square to Jupiter in Virgo and square Venus in Pisces) that the deals that are being made will be advantageous to Americans. They may result, instead, in extreme losses to the people of this nation.

## February 20 New Moon in Pisces 4:18 am EST

The emphasis stays on our nation's resources at this New Moon, as the Moon-Sun conjunction occurs in the second house (our nation's wealth, resources, economy, and national product). The New Moon is joined by Uranus, Mercury, and Neptune. This "stellium" (concentration of planets) indicates that a lot of activity is going on with regard to our nation's resources and other things under rulership of the second house. Keep an eye on the economic news! We are likely to feel some instability as change occurs and we move in a different direction.

The Moon-Sun conjunction is in a very tight conjunction with Uranus, too. With Uranus thrown in the mix, there could be unexpected, "out-of-the-blue" disruptions, or quick reversals or change in direction by our president.

The people have taken on a very practical, "down-to-earth," persona, as represented by earth signs Capricorn on the Ascendant of the first house and Taurus on the fourth house. The working person, trades, unions, soldiers and armies, public health and public workers are in the forefront of events.

Our leaders, on the other hand, may have reverted to some old behavior patterns that include high-pressure tactics, secrecy, and espionage (Scorpio on the tenth house cusp, ruled by Pluto in the twelfth house of secrets, secret enemies, prisoners, and institutions). Pluto is using Mercury, ruler of communications and transportation, to move information—some secret—to the people in power. There may be a radical political group involved (Uranus) or unusual tactics may be employed.

## March 6 Full Moon in Virgo 6:14 pm EST

The Full Moon is conjunct the Ascendant, and conjunct Jupiter in the twelfth house, which brings added emphasis to the "the people," and popular opinion. Jupiter expands everything. With Jupiter in Virgo and conjunct the Moon, we might feel "more" discerning and critical than usual. It'll be hard to disregard the small imperfections we see in others. Emphasis on the sixth/twelfth house axis indicates political and economic problems and reversals. The people (represented by Virgo) want to take a conservative approach, to be discriminating and fair-minded in our interactions with others. But, the needs of the nation's people will put us at odds (in opposition) with the actions and intention of our leaders—our president and members of the government—especially where our nation's working class and other societies or countries are involved.

The Pisces Sun is conjunct Mercury. This sixth house Sun brings the focus back to the working masses—trades, unions, public workers, soldiers, and armies—indicating that the president and our government may be applying unwelcome pressure on these groups.

Pluto in the fourth house introduces the death-rebirth cycle. This fourth house placement will have a strong effect on the people. Old memories, unconscious fears, and losses will bubble into conscious thought as a result of actions that take place in the sixth (employed classes and their institutions) and twelfth houses (what is hidden, subversive, underground). Pluto represents all things hidden and secretive in a society, and the suffering and loss that occurs before healing can take place. Pluto is square both Moon-Jupiter and Sun-Mercury. Our worries and obsessions are amplified, especially concerning the homeland and our private homes. The power is with the masses in this chart, however.

## March 20 New Moon in Aries 5:41 pm EST

This New Moon occurs at 0 degrees Aries in the seventh house. Our attention will be directed toward our relationships with other societies and countries. Pakistan has an Aries Sun.

The New Moon in Aries is sextile Mars, Aries' ruler. This Moon promises creative thought and action. We are still feeling Pluto's presence—the recycling of memories, traditions, family patterns—due to the conjunction of Pluto to the fourth house cusp in this chart. With the Pluto trine to Mercury (the communicator), a "voice" is available to give expression, perhaps in the form of reminders, to our traditions, beliefs, and values. We may also begin to think about whether or not some of them need to die so new thoughts can be given expression.

## April 5 Full Moon in Libra 7:03 am EST

The Full Moon at 16 degrees Libra in the sixth house, focuses our attention, once again, on the common men and women in our country. Perhaps this Moon is "bringing to light" a situation that needs to be brought into balance. This Moon emphasizes honest communications, partnership, negotiation, and peaceful action. The Sun (representing the rulers) is in Aries and the twelfth house, and considering that Aries is characterized by a state of being "at loggerheads" with its opposition (the workers and common people and their organizations), Libra's objectives might be hard to reach. We have help though. Mars, defender of the people, is supplying assertive energy; a tenth house Neptune indicates support coming from someone or some faction of the party in power (most likely, this group is left of center). Pluto in the eighth house strongly indicates death, which does not necessarily mean a physical death. It could also be the death of a powerful action or law that has oppressed the people.

Saturn in the third house of communications and short-distance travel, including trucks that move produce, grains, milk, and other commodities that keep our economy growing represents some restriction, but Saturn has turned direct in March, meaning that restriction and limitations may be easing.

## April 19 New Moon in Aries 9:11 am EDT

We can hope that this New Moon in Aries is initiating a new cycle, a new line of thought for all concerned, but Mercury is retrograde in this chart, so we might be rethinking some of what we have already done. Resist the temptation to begin new projects related to Mercury at this time; they probably won't work out the way you want them to. The New Moon is in the eleventh house (the House of Representatives, local governments, and civil servants) and trine Jupiter in the fourth house, indicating a turn of events that will benefit our homeland (real-estate holdings, agricultural lands, mining, etc.). Watch for developments from Washington or your local government at this time.

In this chart, Saturn is in the first house, representing our nation as a whole. Saturn represents the amount of freedom we allow or deny ourselves, and it is making beneficial aspects to Jupiter (expansion) and Uranus (unexpected change, new line of thought).

## May 4 Full Moon in Scorpio 4:33 pm EDT

The Full Moon in the second house, opposing the Taurus Sun in the eighth house is accompanied by a lunar eclipse. With the second/eighth house axis activated, our attention is drawn to resources—our nation's and foreign investment—but we may also see or hear about political reversals, losses (particularly financial), death or assassination attempts in the coming days. Saturn is in the tenth house adds to the darker tone of this forecast. Scorpio and Taurus are fixed signs, meaning that people will be trying to "maintain" their own agendas. With the Moon in Scorpio, feelings and emotions are likely to be even more intense than usual. Neptune is the pivot point (square both the Sun and Moon) from the fifth house. Neptune represents collective values, and the left wing; it is also associated with devious, underhanded tactics. I'm not saying that one necessarily goes with the other. Collectively, we can take the high road or the low road. We don't have to sink to the lowest level of thought.

## May 19 New Moon in Taurus 12:52 am EDT

The New Moon at 28 degrees Taurus in the fourth house draws attention to the foundation of our society—our traditions, the land we live on, our homes. We also find opposition to the ruling party, or government (local, state, or national) represented here. Taurus' attitude—how we feel and how we want things to be—is practical, down to earth, persistent, and it can be stubborn. We may be fixated on wanting to maintain what we have, to hold on to our possessions, our money; we may feel that we need to accumulate even more. The ruler of Taurus, retrograde Venus in the fifth house, represents entertainment, pleasure, sports functions, and speculation for gain or loss; in other words—taking risks. Venus is opposed by retrograde Pluto, an aspect that has been influencing women, our rights, our property, and maybe even our freedom, since late April. This indicates trouble and losses have been taking a toll on things ruled by Venus.

## June 3 Full Moon in Sagittarius 12:20 am EDT

The tenth house Moon in Sagittarius and fourth house Sun in Gemini are involved in a grand cross—meaning they are two corners of a square. The other two planets involved in this grand cross are Uranus in the first house and Jupiter in the seventh. This is a fundamentally stressful situation because power and energy are fluctuating between the four planets, and all that they rule, as balance is sought. The planets are in mutable signs, so change, fluxtuation, and a lack of clear direction may be significant influences at this time, but mutability also seeks healing and completion of things. Paying attention to what comes into our awareness at this time—illuminated by the Full Moon—and then trying to be aware of how we can heal or bring complete to something in our own lives could be very meaningful to us at this midpoint of the year.

Pluto and Venus, still both retrograde, are in exact opposition, so the areas of life ruled by Venus continue to experience difficult times. (See page 30 for a partial list of things ruled by Venus.) One benefit of this difficult transit may be that we develop a stronger sense of what we value, and we may see with more clarity how our individual values are different from those of our neighbors.

## June 17 New Moon in Gemini 4:27 pm EDT

This eighth house Moon-Sun conjunction in Gemini opposes Pluto in the second house, activating the second/eighth house axis again, reminding us of the May 4 Full Moon. Think back to that time. What did you see or realize and then respond to with passion and intensity? New Moons are a time for planting seeds for what we want to realize in the future. We may recognize radical or compulsive attitudes that are not necessarily recognized by the individuals themselves, concerning our nation's resources (second house), our collective values, who we hold in high esteem, our economy, and our financial institutions. We can expect our thoughts and feelings to undergo rapid changes for a day or two before we find enough solidarity to feel like it's time to actually proceed with the new plan.

## July 2 Full Moon in Capricorn 7:09 am EDT

The sixth house Capricorn Moon opposes the twelfth house Sun in Cancer, and the Sun is closing in on a conjunction with Saturn (exact on July 8). A week from now, when the Moon squares Saturn on July 9, things could look and feel a lot more difficult. While the aspect is unavoidable, our responses are chosen, so maybe the best thing to say here is: "Be prepared."

Saturn always seeks to establish order and structure, usually through planning and regulations. A strong disciplinarian attitude and intolerance can surface when this planet is active in your individual life, or in the chart for large groups, as this one is. With this energy in the twelfth house, we might see proposals or legislation that impinges on the rights of people in institutions.

The Moon in Capricorn has a tendency to seek detachment, preferring non-emotional responses in most situations. With the Moon in the sixth house (ruling workers and their political institutions, the public servant, and our soldiers), perhaps a detached attitude could be put to good use as individuals "collectively" work to build the kind of life we want, rather than having someone else's vision forced upon us, maybe without our knowledge.

## July 17 New Moon in Cancer 7:24 am EDT

The Cancer New Moon in the twelfth house is conjunct Saturn. In addition, Mars is conjunct the Ascendant in the first house, and Neptune is conjunct the Descendant. A fifth house Pluto is still very much a player in the drama, too. Watch for a big scandal to be exposed at this time.

In her book, *The Astrology of Fate,* Liz Greene describes a dimension of Cancer: the Terrible Mother who seeks to retain control over individuals. This mother would rather do battle and destroy her own children rather than permit them to escape her domination. I can't presume to say how the configuration described in the first paragraph might work itself out in the psyches of Americans, but I'm going to make a couple of guesses. We should be aware that much is occurring behind the scenes that will have a very direct and potent impact on our lives; and, the promise of benefit to the nation will be the carrot that is dangled before us. We should be aware of foggy conditions (Neptune) surrounding what we are being told.

## July 31 Full Moon in Aquarius 2:05 pm EDT

The third house Aquarius Moon opposes a ninth house Leo Sun, and the Moon is conjunct retrograde Neptune. In the third house, the Moon brings attention to communications and trade. This house rules roads, railroads, telephones, schools, postal services, newspapers, and computers. On a local level, we may difficulty communicating with others. Things may not work right, roads may be blocked, equipment may break down—all occurring with some amount of confusion attached. Maybe this is preparation for when Mercury turns retrograde in nine days—in Gemini! My best advice is: back up your systems and plan for detours. Electional astrologers would probably advise against planning events that are Neptune related at this time.

The Leo Sun is vying for attention from long-distance concerns—in particular, shipping. Other areas of life that may receive attention now are our belief systems. What do you consider taboo? Moral? Just? You may find yourself in a conversation about one of these topics, so think ahead, and know what you want to say.

## August 15 New Moon in Leo 9:24 pm EDT

The sixth house is loaded in this chart, with the Moon-Sun conjunction, the Mercury-Mars conjunction, and Jupiter. All of these planets are being impacted by Uranus in the twelfth house, with most of Uranus' influence directed to Mercury and Mars. Uranus is linked to revolution and innovation; Mars is linked to the forces that hold a group (city, state, nation) together, and which give it the ability to be assertive; Mercury is linked to communications between individuals or groups, how messages are delivered, political speeches, and announcements. When we mix these elements together (because the energies interact with and affect each other) we could see some very interesting outcomes.

## August 29 Full Moon in Pisces 10:22 pm EDT

The eleventh house Pisces Full Moon opposes a 5th house Virgo Sun; the Moon is conjunct Uranus and the Sun is conjunct Mars. The fifth/eleventh axis is interesting, as it contrasts the Virgo Sun, which defines itself by how useful it is and how well—and fast—something gets done, to the Pisces Moon, which will have a great deal of trouble defining itself at all. Daydreams, music, creativity, and compassionate love have a strong effect on our emotions and feelings. With the Moon-Uranus conjunction in effect, we might be blessed with some really innovative ideas.

The eleventh house rules the legislature (elected officials in all levels of government); and it reveals something about our long-range hopes, dreams, and ideals. This seems like a perfect opportunity to "see," either because something is exposed to our view, or because we see it in our day and night dreams. We can then make ourselves heard among the elected officials—and they'll have already had some of the same ideas, so maybe they'll be more inclined to make those long-range plans.

## September 14 New Moon in Virgo 10:29 am EDT

As above, so below; or, on Earth, so it is in heaven—however you want to look at it, the New Moon in Virgo and in the eleventh house, where those hopes, dreams, and ideals were exposed two weeks ago, is more than synchronicity. Not only have the Moon and Sun come together in Virgo—a sign well-known for its ability to attend to details and having a passion for doing things well and with economy, but the New Moon is conjunct Mars, and Mars provides the drive to get things done! This New Moon is a real powerhouse, and it provides the perfect opportunity for our elected officials to "plant the seeds" for new growth.

There is a square between the New Moon-Mars conjunction in the eleventh house and Pluto in the second. Pluto represents all that is secretive in a society, our collective shadow side. We might expect to hear from within ourselves and from others in society that we are not adhering to our belief systems with some of these new plans that we are hearing about. It might be said that we are squandering our nation's resources, but it's also true that the old must pass away to make room for what is new.

## September 28 Full Moon in Aries 9:09 am EDT

The sixth house Full Moon in Aries opposes the twelfth house Libra Sun. The events that transpire in the next days will seem to pass quickly, and there is considerably more emphasis on the Sun in this chart than there is on the Moon, because the Sun is accompanied by Mars, Jupiter, and Mercury. These planets are already in the twelfth house, or ready to enter, so we might assume that secret negotiations are taking place in at various levels of government. The newspapers may report on behind closed door meetings, and the reports will cause tempers to flare among the common workers.

## October 13 New Moon in Libra 10:48 pm EDT

This New Moon chart is heavily weighted in the fourth house, with Jupiter, Mars, and Mercury joining the Moon and Sun. Their sign, Libra, is intercepted in the fourth house, meaning that the energy here is not immediately apparent, but seems to be emanating through a slightly different light—namely, Virgo's.

## October 27 Full Moon in Taurus 11:07 pm EDT

The emphasis on the fourth house is still strong, with Mars, Mercury, and the Sun located here. They oppose the tenth house Taurus Moon. The fourth house stellium is squaring Saturn in the first house. People and events may seem more somber than usual. Restrictions may feel oppressive.

## November 12 New Moon in Scorpio 9:27 am EST

The Scorpio New Moon in the eleventh house provides time for introspection as we think about our responsibilities to foreigners. There is support for building relationships but we may be unsettled or unsure about how to pay for the help we might offer. Capricorn's energy in the second house suggests a positive but conservative approach should be taken.

## November 26 Full Moon in Gemini 3:07 pm EST

At the New Moon we might have given some thought about how help others, now it's time to take action. There may be a lot of newspaper space being given to the debate about our economy. Americans want to protect and keep what they have, and we want to secure our countries well being so we feel safe. There are powerful influences active involving foreign investment, though. Jupiter in the sixth is trine Neptune in the tenth, indicating that the left of center group, or individual, in the government is favoring the common worker at this time.

## December 11 New Moon in Sagittarius 8:29 pm EST

The Sagittarius New Moon in the fifth house, is more than ready for a good time, and people will respond to this jovial, generous Moon time. Saturn is in the twelfth house and making a trine to Mars and Venus, which indicates some loosening of limitations that we've all felt this past year. Shoppers will plan to spend, but spending will be along the practical and not frivolous line.

## December 26 Full Moon in Cancer 10:06 am EST

We began the year with the Full Moon in Cancer and the fourth house, and we end 2004 with the Full Moon in Cancer and the fifth house. A lot of attention was placed on the second/eighth house axis—national product vs. international concerns, and on the fourth/tenth house axis—our land, traditions, ideologies vs. the government and their vision for us. National security is still a concern, workers are not faring well, and Americans may be experiencing some unsettling conditions. Pluto, Mercury, and Venus are in the tenth house, so I think we can expect changes from Washington. The change may come in the form of communications—they'll be different—better, perhaps. (I can always be optimistic.) The Neptune—left of center—influence is active, but from behind the scenes.

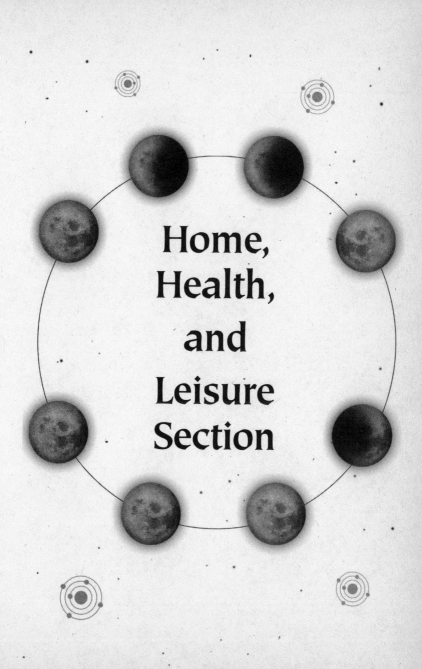

# Home,
# Health,
# and
# Leisure
# Section

# Time to Go on Vacation

### by Maggie Anderson

My definition of a "good vacation" is one that refreshes the mind, body, and spirit. It should not necessarily be memorable because then we would have to include that trip to Yellowstone, when the dog ate the backseat of the van, all the kids broke out with measles, and it rained every day. Ideally, details of a really great vacation will fade with the years, leaving only the warm, fuzzy feelings that we have when flipping through an aging family photo album.

Why are some vacations better than others? There's a heavenly committee in charge of them that can either provide cosmic support or unleash unearthly jokes on travelers. They are the personal planets Mercury, Venus, and Mars. Fortunately, an astrologer can look ahead in his or her trusty ephemeris and see when these three planets will be in a mischievous mood and when they'll help us have a picture-perfect vacation. Mercury, Venus, and Mars become most troublesome when in retrograde motion.

# Revise Your Vacation: Retrograde Planets

Going backward is especially irritating for Mercury, the natural ruler of communications, and he likes to have company on his trips. If you vacation while Mercury is retrograde (see retrograde dates on page 89), it is likely that your luggage will be delivered to a monastery in Sri Lanka and your reservations will mysteriously disappear from the hotel's computer; then, there will be no room at the inn. Otherwise, you'll have a fine time.

Venus retrograde periods are acceptable for travel so long as you don't need money where you are going. Entire industries have been built on replacing the cash of travelers who were foolish enough to take off when the astrological ruler of currency was going in retrograde direction. It may be well to note that Venus also governs love. Vacations with your beloved will bring out the worst in both of you if the vacation starts while Venus is withdrawn from her true purpose—to be loving. This is never a good thing, and it often results in one party being abandoned at a rest stop in southeast Nebraska.

The planet Mars rules physical energy, which can become compromised while Mars is retrograde. Vacations taken during these periods are the most memorable for all the wrong reasons. You'll benefit from the kindness of strangers because they are always helpful to tourists with one foot in a cast limping through their museums. Foreign travel (while Mars is retrograde) is good for international relations, too. While you're quarantined with the locals in their school gymnasium, you'll become more fluent in their language. Once released, you will be able to order bottled water like a native.

Fortunately, once you block out the retrograde periods of Mercury, Venus, and Mars on your calendar, there remain many excellent times to go on your well-deserved holiday. As with other new ventures, the periods

from the New Moon to Full Moon are best for beginning your vacation. These are available at least once a month. Whether you're headed for a world tour or plan to stay at home and paint the porch on your vacation, all start-up activities will have better success when started on the New Moon. Use the time from the Full Moon to the next crescent Moon to plan, make reservations, and get ready for your special time away from your regular routine. Read your Sun Sign below for additional vacation tips.

# Plan According to Your Sun Sign

## Aries (March 20–April 20)

Once you've stuffed your backpack with plenty of sun block, maps, and money, you'll be ready for an Aries-style adventure. This trip involves new destinations, near or far, and preferably alone. It's the exploration of unfamiliar territory that is the most fun for an Aries. Your vacations must include encounters with the unknown, but never make return trips, even to paradise, or you'll be yawning a lot, just like at home. It matters little how you travel because you consider the process of getting there to be half the fun. You're at your best in places where you can participate in outdoor activities. Begin your trip with the Moon or Sun in the sign of Leo or Sagittarius.

## Taurus (April 20–May 21)

Some advanced planning is the key to a successful vacation for you Sun sign Taurus folks. You'll need to make sure that both your travel and room accommodations are comfortable, perhaps even luxurious, so examine travel brochures and videos carefully before committing your time and money. As an earth sign, you'd rather take a road trip than fly. Gastronomical pleasures alone can make your vacation special, so you'll want any destination to have fine local cuisine. The sands of the Sahara won't appeal to you so much as a fine B & B in wine country, surrounded by the fruits of our good green Earth. Begin your vacation with the Moon or Sun in the signs of Virgo or Capricorn.

## Gemini (May 21–June 21)

Leave your large supply of books at home and head for a gathering that is both intellectual and challenging. Youthful and curious Geminis will find vacation fun wherever there are mini-classes and workshops. You consider such vacations to be a holiday because you cherish opportunities to learn something new. A Gemini finds ways to get double the value of his or her

money, or of any experience, so find time between seminars to venture out for a little sightseeing. What you find most refreshing, though, are conversations with bright, stimulating groups of people. Fortunately for your pocketbook, you receive just as much enjoyment from a vacation/learning experience that takes place in your own neighborhood as the one that's far away. Begin your vacation with the Moon or Sun in the signs of Libra or Aquarius.

## Cancer (June 21–July 22)

You specialize in family vacations, so traveling light is not usually an option. Cancers take all the comforts of home along with them wherever they go, even if this means traveling in a large RV. Many of your vacations have a dual purpose: sightseeing, and visiting relatives. No matter how long the airport delays, you want to spend holidays with Grandma or other family members who love you best. After the kids leave home, how-ever, you'll head for the beach to build sandcastles and dine on fresh seafood. Lakefront cabins and condos also hold appeal. Your most luxu-rious vacation will no doubt be an ocean cruise. Begin your vacation with the Moon or Sun in the signs of Scorpio or Pisces.

## Leo (July 22–August 23)

Cut-rate, bargain holidays are not an option for you Leos. Your idea of the perfect getaway includes first-class travel and accommodations in sunny locations. As a vacationing Leo, you wish not so much to view tourist attractions as to be seen by an admiring crowd. Thus, you'll need a new wardrobe before you start out and plenty of money to purchase additional items when you arrive at your vacation destination. Your inner drama coach may nudge you toward the theater district, and your playful nature will draw you to sporting or gaming events. Begin your trip with the Moon or Sun in the signs of Sagittarius or Aries.

## *Virgo (August 23–September 22)*

Virgo vacations are an oxymoron. Working vacations are actually your specialty. Being helpful to others will help you ease into the idea of annual time off. It's perfectly fine with you to spend your vacation putting a new roof on Uncle Henry's lakeside cabin. When you do manage to schedule some real rest and relaxation, you are easily pleased and amused. You'd prefer to stay in a quality B & B than a grand hotel, and travel in a gas-efficient auto rather than experience jet lag. You'll enjoy exploring used bookstores, receiving a healing massage at a good health spa, or visiting the zoo. Begin your trip with the Moon or Sun in the signs of Capricorn or Taurus.

## *Libra (September 22–October 23)*

Libras on vacation want to express their sociability and romantic natures. Trips for two are especially to your liking, you'll book the honeymoon suite for many years after the wedding. It's important for you to have a harmonious interpersonal atmosphere while vacationing, so if you mingle with the crowds, make sure they are happy crowds. See the local sights by day—visit art galleries, take in concerts, explore the studios of local craftspeople—and save your evenings for dining and dancing. Begin your vacation with the Moon or Sun in the signs of Aquarius or Gemini.

## Scorpio (October 23–November 22)

You do not believe in instant intimacy, and your perfect vacation will be one where others respect your privacy and do not invade your personal space. Of course, you'd much rather travel with your partner or a few well-chosen confidants than with a tour group. The only group tour you'd consider would involve a mystery, like the "Death on the Orient Express," a combination theater/train ride across Europe. Scorpions love to uncover secrets. You may happily spend your entire vacation searching for the Lost Dutchman mine, or diving for sunken treasure in the Caribbean. Wherever you go, it's important for you to include some energizing physical activity in your travel plans. Begin your vacation with the Moon or Sun in Pisces or Cancer.

## Sagittarius (November 22–December 21)

You live to travel and may take work that allows you to pile up frequent-flyer miles. Throughout your lifetime, you'll travel often, preferring foreign adventures to vacations closer to home. When you're snowbound in mid-winter, you become an armchair traveler, studying brochures and the journals of other world explorers. You enjoy roughing it in a tent, and you are as happy camping as you are when staying in a four-star hotel. It matters little to you how you get to your destination—canoes or kayaks, pack mule or luxury car, freighter or cruise ship—you want to experience them all. Begin your vacation with the Moon or Sun in the signs of Aries or Leo.

## Capricorn (December 21–January 20)

Of all the signs of the zodiac, Capricorns are most likely to begin a vacation with a detailed itinerary and a firm agenda. You want to gain the most pleasure possible during your vacation, even if this means visiting five museums in one day. Since you're as happy in cold weather as warmer climates, off-season travel bargains are designed for you. Vacation activities that you consider fun may seem like work to other people. Whether taking a walking trip across Montana or playing two 18-hole rounds of golf each day in Hawaii, you manage to see and do more than the average tourist and with less expense. Begin your vacation with the Moon or Sun in the signs of Taurus or Virgo.

## Aquarius (January 20–February 18)

You'd rather stay home than take a vacation alone, Aquarius. Group tours are very appealing to you and your trips are often made with friends and family. You prefer to plan an annual vacation around gatherings of like-minded people, perhaps for a convention, field trip, or political rally that supports a humanitarian cause. Wherever you go, you prefer flying to road travel. Airport delays are just one more opportunity for you to connect with the masses. Once at your vacation destination, you become an eclectic tourist, sampling traditional attractions, and visiting places that are not in the guidebooks, and places that even the locals don't know about. Begin your vacation with the Moon or Sun in the signs of Gemini or Libra.

## Pisces (February 18–March 20)

When the spirit moves them, Pisces have been known to hop on a plane sans luggage or travel funds, and without much preparation. But you'll have as much fun as if you'd been planning the trip for months. It's not necessary for you to take lengthy trips either. Weekends away provide as much pleasure as a month-long world tour. It's the hope of discovery that draws you to a vacation spot. Your life is an art form, and time and space are your canvas. You're attracted to any type of travel that enables you to experience life in a new way. You're most comfortable near water. Begin your vacation with the Moon or Sun in the signs of Cancer or Scorpio.

### About the Author

Maggie is an astrologer, writer, and gardener. She makes her home in the heartland—Mount Vernon, Iowa, where she maintains a full-time astrological practice and teaches classes in astrology. Maggie has two specialties: one involves "all affairs of the heart," which allows her to utilize her experience as a family therapist when counseling astrology clients. Her interest in world affairs is evident in the mundane astrology writings on her website, www.astromaggi.com.

# How Ancient Astrology Viewed the Lunar Cycle

*by Dorian Gieseler Greenbaum*

The ancients were in tune with the Moon in a way that has been lost in our light-polluted, computer-centric world. Many of us don't observe the Moon's position in the sky every night, and our lives in terms of light and dark no longer depend on having moonlight at night. The physical Moon is only a natural curiosity, and the astrological Moon has become symbolic of a physical reality that isn't very present in modern life.

The ancients, with their far more immediate observation of the Moon, could bring this power of observation to their astrological interpretations. The Moon was a living, visible image whose physical characteristics provided instant astrological description. With its cycle of growth and decay, it furnished a clear analogy to life on Earth. The Moon is called "fortune" (something that goes up and down!) by more than one ancient author. It basks in the reflected light of the Sun, and its phases (literally, "appearances" in Greek) are dependent upon its relationship to the Sun.

Many ancient authors discuss the phases of the Moon. In this article, I will be discussing the works of two in particular, Paulus Alexandrinus (C.E. 378) and Olympiodorus (C.E. 564), because they go beyond mere definition of each phase. The material of these writers gives a fascinating picture of how the Hellenistic Greeks viewed the cycle of the Moon. As modern people, we can learn a lot from seeing how these ancient astrologers thought about the Moon as it moved in its circular dance with the Sun.

It isn't always easy to figure out what the ancient writers are saying, but like a crossword puzzle, we can seek out clues from the language used by the Greeks as they describe the appearances of the Moon. Even the simple word *phasis**, which becomes "phase" in English, can give us information. For the Greeks, phases are literal "appearances;" the word *phasis* comes from the verb *phainō*, "to appear." Each appearance heralds a new scene, with new information ready to be given to us by the changing Moon.

What is the Moon saying to us as she makes these different appearances? We can find out in the words the Greeks use to describe each phase. Let's look at each phase and the words used to describe it in detail. Analogies to the birth process are very clear in the first several phases. Though the Greek authors did not carry this birth analogy further than the first crescent phase, I find it productive to continue looking at these phases and the words used to describe them as the cycle of human growth and development. Following a discussion of the phases, I will suggest ways in which we, in the modern world, can use the meaning of each phase in our own lives. In this way we can take the material of the Hellenistic astrologers and apply it in a new way to the present day.

By the way, Paulus and Olympiodorus describe eleven phases of the Moon in their treatises, not the usual eight we are used to. In the discussion that follows, I will refer to the phases by number as well as by the names they used for each phase. You will see that the "extra" phases the Greeks use are, in fact, quite instructive for us in understanding their view of the lunar cycle as a cycle of birth.

## Phase 1—New Moon, Synodos

Our modern term is "conjunction." Astronomically, a synodic cycle goes from New Moon (exact conjunction of Moon and Sun; that is, the Moon and Sun are at the same zodiacal degree) to New Moon. Unlike the word "conjunction," which means "join together," *synodos* actually means "with the path" in Greek. Paulus refers to the synodos as the "coming together" (*sunienai*) of the Moon to the Sun and running along the same path with it.

What path can this be? Maybe Lovers' Lane! Olympiodorus takes Paulus' description of the synodos and elaborates on it, making a play on words by using the verb that means "to bind together" (*sundeō*) and the verb that means "to travel in company with" (*sunodeuō*). He says: "For [the Moon] has been bound (*sundeō*) with the Sun under these circumstances

*Note: All translations of the Greek are the author's.

by travelling along (sunodeuō) with it, whence the astrologers call this phase a concurrent bond (*sunodikos sundesmos*)."

And what is this bond, this joining together of the Sun (certainly an archetypal male principle) with the Moon (female)? It is clearly, as we see from the descriptions of the next two phases, a union that results in birth. Let's call it "conception."

## Phase 2—Coming Forth, Genna

Modern astrologers do not normally acknowledge this phase. It occurs when the Moon has moved to the degree after the exact conjunction, and continues up until it has reached 15 degrees after the conjunction. (Those readers with a knowledge of astronomy know what happens when the Moon moves 15 degrees beyond the Sun: it heliacally rises and has its first visibility to us. This will become significant as we describe the phase following genna.)

*Genna* has a few meanings, among them "begetting," "engendering," "descent," "origin," and "birth." It is related to the verb *gennaō*, which in one form means "to cause to become," and thus "beget." Its translation in the Greek lexicon as a phase of the Moon is given as "Coming Forth." When we combine these two meanings, "begetting" and "coming forth," it is easy to imagine a baby in the process of being born. Let's look at the words of Paulus and Olympiodorus as they describe this phase.

Paulus says, "Coming Forth was so called from the Moon's going out from the Sun, since when she has gone beyond it by one degree, she begins to appear to the Cosmos, though not to us." Olympiodorus again elaborates on the words of Paulus with some stunning imagery: ". . . the phase is said [to be] Coming Forth, since it passes by the bowels of the Sun. And under these circumstances it proceeds from the unseen into the visible, after the manner of fetuses."

The birth imagery is undeniable in this quotation from Olympiodorus. The word "bowels," *koilia* in Greek, refers to the cavities of the body, and can refer to both the bowels and the womb! (Astrologer Rob Hand points out that this word in Greek has the same equivalent meanings as our English word "belly.") So the Moon and Sun come together in the moment of conception (the synodos) and then the Moon moves beyond the bowels, or womb, of the Sun.

We can easily equate this with the portion of the birth process known as labor, when the baby moves down the birth canal but has not yet been born. The Moon, when it moves past the Sun by one degree, is no longer joined but is still invisible. It is "coming forth," but has not yet emerged from the light of the Sun. We will see this happen in the next phase.

## Phase 3—Emergence, Anatolē

When the Moon has moved 15 degrees beyond the Sun, until it reaches 60 degrees, it is called anatolē, "rising." What, you may ask, does "rising" have to do with birth? If we examine the origins of this word, a much more illuminating translation comes to light, one that beautifully shows its connection with the birth process.

Anatolē is a compound verb formed from the preposition *ana*, "up" and the root *tellō*. This root is related to a verb that means "to accomplish, perform or produce," and also has the sense of "come into being." Combining the two, we have "come up into being," or, of stars "rise."

But what does it mean for a star to rise? When stars rise above the horizon, or go far enough past the Sun (beyond 15 degrees) they become visible to us. So rising is associated with visibility to us.

In keeping with the birth analogy, anatolē is the phase where the baby appears to us; it "emerges" from the darkness of the birth canal. Instead of translating anatolē as "rising," I prefer to use the word "emergence." The roots of the Latin-derived "emerge" mean to "come out a sunken condition, come forth, rise up." Paulus says, "Emergence is whenever, having gone past 15 degrees, [the Moon] appears to take on light as a slender line." We now have the appearance of the body in the physical world.

## Phase 4—First Crescent, Mēnoeidēs

This phase corresponds to our waxing crescent Moon. It begins at the waxing sextile (the Moon is 60 degrees ahead of the Sun), when the Moon has grown into its familiar crescent shape. In the Greek name of this phase, we can see an interesting connection between "moon" and "month" (even in English, we can see the semantic similarity). In the ancient world, the month was originally the time elapsed from New Moon to New Moon (or when the first sliver of the Moon was visible), and in Greek the word for "month" (meis, mēnos) can also mean "Moon" (mēnē). At the beginning of the lunar month, the shape of the Moon at first visibility was the crescent, so the word "mēnoeidēs" came to mean the shape of the crescent ("crescent" is Latin, meaning "growing"). In Greek, though, it actually means "moon-form," and Paulus says "it appears to take on the shape like itself,"

Olympiodorus adds: " . . . it receives its familiar form and its own disc, just like a shadow-painting."

The use of the phrase "shadow-painting" is interesting, because it emphasizes the use of light and dark, which in turn accentuates the the gradual illumination of the (dark) disc of the Moon by the light of the Sun. And let's consider the phrase "receives its familiar form." The Moon is now recognizable as the Moon. The word translated as "receive" literally means "to take from another," or "receive what is one's due." Here we have the idea of genetic inheritance, in that the fetus receives what it is ordained to get from its parents. When we consider that the word "familiar" actually means having to do with the family, we can equate this phase with the growth of the baby as it takes on the features of its familial inheritance and becomes recognizable as a member of a certain family. (Every parent and grandparent looks for these familial features! "Oh, look! He has your mother's eyes.") We should also consider that this phase, the waxing sextile, may be the calm before the storm of adolescence (the next phase).

## Phase 5—First Half-Moon, Dichotomos

We are midway between the New Moon and the Whole Moon—90 degrees from both (what moderns call first quarter). The half-Moon occurs when the Moon is in square to the Sun, squares being described by Paulus as "discordant and irregular." This phase is called literally, "cut in two," because the disc of the Moon appears to be cut in half. Olympiodorus says, "Half of the disc appears illuminated and half unlit."

Though Paulus and Olympiodorus do not take this analogy further, isn't this a wonderful description of adolescence? Teenagers know everything, and they know nothing. They are separating from their parents and developing their own character, a portion of which is not yet apparent. This is a time of almost literal dichotomy—sweet one day, ogres the next, full of mood swings and uncertainty.

## Phase 6—First Gibbous, Amphikurtos

This phase occurs when the Moon has moved 120 degrees away from the Sun, forming a trine (triangle) with it. *Amphikurtos* means "humped or swollen on both sides." We are not yet at the Whole Moon, but its shape has moved beyond the half circle. (By the way, "gibbous" comes from Latin *gibbosus*, which means "humped.")

We are beyond the turmoil of adolescence and into young adulthood. We can relate to our parents again in a non-adversarial way (we may even realize they have some wisdom to impart!). We are secure enough in our own sense of self to acknowledge that others will not destroy our identity, but in fact may enhance it. We are ready to embrace what the world has to offer, on the way to filling ourselves up ("rounding out the circle") with the

experiences and knowledge we need to fulfill our life's path. Olympiodorus says that "the Moon begins to fill up its two peaks . . ." The word for "peaks" in Greek is *ta akra*, which means "the heights" (the Acropolis is the high spot in Athens). Young adulthood is usually an exciting time, filled with new experiences and a heady rush of independence, a period of "highs," especially after the angst of adolescence.

## Phase 7—Full Moon, Plēsiselēnos

The Moon is between gibbous and whole; as Olympiodorus says, ". . . a Full Moon . . . since it is neither a full whole Moon, nor gibbous, yet truly both." We are on the edge of maturity here: past the trine but not yet at the opposition, still in the gathering, waxing phase. There is some uncertainty about this phase, too. We can not clearly tell when the exact moment of the Whole Moon is; sometimes when we look quickly at the Moon around wholeness, we can not always see the difference between the very gibbous (full to Paulus and Olympiodorus) and full (whole to Paulus and Olympiodorus). Maturity is like that, too. When do you know you are mature? (Often it's only in hindsight, and we usually see it as a process, not a moment.)

## Phase 8—Whole Moon, Panselēnos

This is 180 degrees from the New Moon (Synodos) and continues until 15 degrees past the exact opposition (matching the description of Anatolē occurring at 15 degrees past the conjunction). Paulus describes it in this way: "Whole Moon because it has been filled with the light from the beams of the Sun, . . . having the whole brightness of the light filled up, whence, when it has become a Whole Moon, it appears itself in the form of a circle like the Sun's."

There are a number of analogies we can make with this phase. Clearly, in the description of the Whole Moon "in the form of a circle like the Sun's" we have another form of union—not conception this time, but marriage. Alternatively, in this phase we come to the realization of life's purpose, and the means to go about achieving it. We are still in process here, for like the Full Moon phase, it is sometimes difficult to tell the exact moment of wholeness. Like the Synodos, we are aware of the moment of opposition only after it has passed. Likewise, we see our maturity only in hindsight.

It is after our realization of the point of opposition that we become aware that the Moon is now waning. Apokrousis, "waning," literally means "beating off" or "driving away," with the sense of repelling or refuting. Does the Sun now begin to drive away the Moon? We are now moving slowly away from the light into the darkness. We have passed from the seventh sign into the eighth, and we become increasingly aware of our mortality.

## Phase 9—Second Gibbous, Second Amphikurtos

This is the waning trine, with the Moon now 120 degrees behind the Sun. We are continuing the completion of our life's work, using the skills and knowledge we have gained, and acquiring the beginning of wisdom. Olympiodorus talks about the waning phases as repeating the same aspects that occurred in the waxing part of the cycle: ". . . it experiences the same figures again." We could make the analogy that the waxing trine was a phase where we were "filling ourselves up" with knowledge, and that the waning trine becomes a period in which we begin to give knowledge away to others.

### Phase 10—Second Half-Moon, Second Dichotomo

The waning square (fourth quarter) again becomes a crisis point, as the waxing square, adolescence, was. The intimations of mortality become more and more clear, so we begin putting together the proofs of our life's work and melding them into the wisdom combined from our learning and experience.

### Phase 11—Second Crescent, Second Mēnoeidēs

The Moon is 60 degrees, or a waning sextile behind the Sun. Now we achieve our swan song, which shows finally the fruits of our purpose to the world. Now we have finished what it was we were meant to do. We are ready now to return without fear to the darkness that gave us birth. Our purpose is complete.

## How Moon Phases Apply to Our Own Lives

Can you see how, metaphorically, the phases of the Moon describe human creation, birth, growth, and development? Now I would like to suggest some ways in which we can use this imagery to help us in our work on ourselves. There are several ways in which this might be accomplished.

First, look at your natal Moon phase. In which phase does your natal Moon fall? (At the end of this article is an easy method for determining your natal Moon phase.) It will give insight into your approach to life in general. For instance, a natal Moon in Coming Forth (Genna), might be concerned with process rather than results, and the knowledge that can be gained from the experiencing the process itself. A person in the First Half-Moon (Dichotomos) phase might be prone to ups and downs, hungry for

information, but maybe inclined to leap before it looks. A Moon in the Second Crescent phase (the last phase before the New Moon) may be searching for knowledge, and only feel in the latter part of life that it can begin to synthesize that knowledge into wisdom to be shared with others. By contrast, people in a New Moon phase (Synodos) may cherish those brilliant moments of inspiration that form the spark of creativity, but may have trouble following up those insights with hard work. A person in the second half Moon phase (third quarter) might feel an underlying sense of crisis, and a need to bring order to that chaos. Those with Moons in the whole Moon (Panselenos) phase may instinctively know that there are two sides to every question, and want to find balance in their lives, integrating rather than separating. Those in Full Moon phase (Plēsiselēnos), however, may feel a certain restlessness and uncertainty about how much they know, and have a need to continuously fill the gaps in their knowledge. A Moon phase in Emergence (Anatolē) might instinctively feel the joy that comes with being alive, and want to share that knowledge of the body in the physical world. First Gibbous phase Moons may want to fill themselves with newfound knowledge and relish their sense of independence, while Second Gibbous phase Moons might want to begin to share that knowledge with others. Those with a first crescent Moon phase in their natal charts may feel very secure in their home and family, and happy in knowing their connections to the past.

Second, look at the transiting Moon as it affects your natal Moon. Pay attention when transiting Moon is in same phase to the Sun as your natal Moon and Sun are to each other—in other words, look at the Emergence phase each month if your natal phase is Emergence. These are times when you may feel particularly "in sync" with the world and your own way of interacting with it—times when you are more easily able to accomplish what you want to do.

If you know more about astrological techniques, you might also find it useful to look at the phase of your progressed Moon, in comparison with the phase of your natal Moon, especially when the progressed Moon mirrors the phase of your natal Moon. Again, this may be a time when you will find it easier to accomplish the work you want to do. Another way to work with these Moon phases is to look at the phase of the Moon in your solar return chart. What phase is it? How might you work with the energy the phase brings in this year of your life?

These are only a few of the ways in which you might interpret the ancient Moon phases. You may also want to do a simple meditation on your particular phase and what it might mean personally to you in your own life path. Utilizing some or all of these techniques can help you to integrate the energy and wisdom of the Moon into your life.

## Finding Your Moon Phase

Take the degree of your Sun as the beginning point in the cycle. Look at the degree of your Moon in relation to this Sun degree. The following descriptions will tell you in what phase your natal Moon falls.

**Phase 1—New Moon.** The Sun and Moon are at the same zodiacal degree. For example, let us put the Sun at 4 degrees of Cancer. A Moon also at 4 degrees of Cancer would be in New Moon Phase.

**Phase 2—Coming Forth.** The Moon is 1–15 degrees ahead of the Sun. Continuing our example of the Sun at 4 degrees of Cancer, a Moon at 17 degrees of Cancer would be in Coming Forth Phase.

**Phase 3—Emergence.** The Moon is 16–59 degrees ahead of the Sun. With Sun at 4 degrees Cancer, the Moon at 4 degrees Leo would be in Emergence phase.

**Phase 4—First Crescent.** The Moon is 60–89 degrees ahead of the Sun. With Sun at 4 degrees Cancer, the Moon at 10 degrees of Virgo would be in First Crescent phase.

**Phase 5—First Half Moon.** The Moon is 90–119 degrees ahead of the Sun. With Sun at 4 degrees Cancer, the Moon at 20 degrees of Libra would be in First Half Moon phase.

**Phase 6—First Gibbous.** The Moon is 120–149 degrees ahead of the Sun. With Sun at 4 degrees Cancer, the Moon at 25 degrees of Scorpio would be in First Gibbous phase.

**Phase 7—Full Moon.** The Moon is 150–179 degrees ahead of the Sun. With Sun at 4 degrees Cancer, the Moon at 29 degrees Sagittarius would be in Full Moon phase.

**Phase 8—Whole Moon.** Moon is 180–121 degrees behind the Sun. (The halfway point in the cycle has now passed.) With Sun at 4 degrees

Cancer, the Moon at 20 degrees Capricorn would be in Whole Moon phase.

**Phase 9—Second Gibbous.** The Moon is 120–91 degrees behind the Sun. With Sun at 4 degrees Cancer, the Moon at 15 degrees Pisces would be in Second Gibbous phase.

**Phase 10—Second Half Moon.** The Moon is 90–61 degrees behind the Sun. With Sun at 4 degrees Cancer, the Moon at 8 degrees Aries would be in Second Half Moon phase.

**Phase 11—Second Crescent.** The Moon is 60–1 degree behind the Sun. With Sun at 4 degrees Cancer, the Moon at 28 degrees Gemini would be in Second Crescent phase.

## About the Author

Dorian Gieseler Greenbaum, M.A., a certified astrologer by the NCGR, has been practicing and teaching astrology for over ten years. She has been a teacher at the Astrology Institute in Lexington, Massachusetts since 1994, and has a private consulting practice. She has a B.A. in classics from Douglass College, Rutgers University, and a masters. in history (Egyptology) from Columbia University. Drawing on her knowledge of ancient Greek and Latin, she is also a translator for Rob Hand's ARHAT, having published *Late Classical Astrology: Paulus Alexandrinus and Olympiodorus* in 2001. Her interest in astrology includes applying the techniques of traditional astrology to modern practice. Most recently, she has been studying the ancient concept of temperament and its application in astrology. She lives in Duxbury, Massachusetts. You can visit her website at www.classicalastrology.org.

## For Further Reading

*Late Classical Astrology: Paulus Alexandrinus and Olympiodorus*, translated by Dorian Gieseler Greenbaum, M.A., ARHAT, 2001

# The Mythology of the Triple Moon Goddess and You

### by Terry Lamb

Demeter . . . Persephone . . . Athene . . . Hecate: These are names we know from mythology, but they were also originally names for the Moon. The mythology of the Moon extends back to earliest human memory. In fact, at the center of our oldest cultures' beliefs are stories containing references to the Moon. Of all the heavenly bodies that the ancient peoples saw, the Moon was the most visible—even more so than the Sun because the Sun was blinding in its brilliance. Understanding the roots of lunar mythology can bring new insights into parts of our own lunar nature lost in the bleaching light of the solar era we are now in. What's more, we can use knowledge of the Moon to get closer to nature.

# The Ancient Role of the Moon

In the time before artificial light, the Moon's light allowed hunters to chase down game that moved nocturnally, and it permitted safe travel at night. The Moon was the first marker of time units longer than a day. As human observers noticed the rhythm of the Moon's motion and light, they began to clock the time it took for the Moon to complete its cycle. They noticed that for three days the Moon is not visible. We refer to this time as the Dark Moon. Then it appeared as a sliver in the west at sunset. We call this the crescent Moon. Evening after evening it grew, until after one week, the half Moon was visible directly overhead. We call this the first quarter Moon. Still the Moon grew in brilliance and size, a little closer to the eastern horizon each evening, until, one week after the half Moon, the Full Moon was visible rising at sunset. After the Full Moon phase, the moonrise occurred later each evening and the Moon began to wane, until one week later it was once again a half Moon visible directly overhead at sunrise. We call this the third quarter Moon. In the final week before the Moon turned dark again, it crept closer and closer to the eastern horizon at dawn, until the barest crescent disappeared and the Moon was dark once again.

These ancient observers determined that the most important points in the Moon's cycle were the Dark Moon, the waxing half Moon, the Full Moon, and the waning half Moon. This came to be called a lunation cycle. It is the foundation of our week. Friday became the day to perform lunation rituals. It is the source of the Sabbath of Judaism and Islam, and both cultures remain rooted in the lunar calendar.

In the earliest times, the month (*moon-th*) was measured from the appearance of one New Moon until the next one. The magi in Babylon read omens at the New Moon and predicted events for the month to come. Both planetary and natural phenomena were read in the prognostications. As the Moon cycles were matched to the yearly solar cycle, the growing agrarian cultures could anticipate what was next in the growing cycle and plan accordingly.

Around the world, the Moon was revered, and in astonishingly similar ways. In most cultures, the Moon was associated with their oldest and most basic concepts. In Basque, a language with no known related tongues, the word for "deity" is also the word for "moon." Throughout the Mediterranean region, the Moon was associated with the Great Mother; this was also true in

Peru. In Gaelic, the Moon's name was *gealach*, whose root is also the source of our word "galaxy," the "mother's milk in the sky."

Around the Mediterranean, the Moon was seen as the triple goddess, one manifestation of the trinity of forces—Creator-Preserver-Destroyer—which the ancients saw flourishing around them. They saw the Moon as an exemplar of the unending cycle of life: The waxing Moon was the Creator, called the maiden or virgin; the Full Moon represented the preserver or mother; and the waning Moon was the Destroyer or Crone–Wise Woman. The triple goddess depiction of the Moon was found throughout the Eurasian continent. The table below gives some of the cultures and the names they used for these Moon goddesses.

| Culture | Triple Goddess | Maiden | Mother | Crone |
| --- | --- | --- | --- | --- |
| Irish | Morgan | Ana | Babd | Macha |
| Greek (Mycenaean) | Moerae | Hebe | Hera | Hecate |
| Greek | Demeter | Kore | Pluto | Persephone |
| Libyan (later, Greek) | Neith | Athene | Metis | Medusa |
| India | Kali | Parvati | Durga | Uma/Kali |
| Pre-Roman | Uni | Juventas | Juno | Minerva |

In Greece, the Moon goddesses were also known as the Moon-spinners, who wove the waxing Moon, then unraveled it as it waned. Libyan Neith, coming from a watery locale, was associated with snakes, no doubt the source of the snake goddess figures found in Minoan Crete.

## The Archetypes Live Within Us

Most of us are curious about how our ancestors lived, but there is another good reason to explore these ancient archetypes: the archetypes live within us. We have heard stories about them since childhood. We see them in movies, television, books, fairy tales, and myths to which we are exposed. These stories form deeply buried constructs that we express through our actions without awareness. By becoming conscious of them, however, we can choose which myths we will fulfill and how we will do so.

If you read myths as they are presented in most literature today, you find them full of death, destruction, and unhappy endings. These late forms of the myths, as they are retold, represent the different values of the conquest-oriented invaders of the Mediterranean region around 1400 B.C., are not very good archetypes to live out. The earliest stories, however, revolve around creation, fertility, motherhood, and the rhythm of the seasons. These earlier stories are also deeply buried in our psyches. The earlier myths were the forums for learning how to be successful in the culture, from coming of age to fostering a family to dying. In those times, the myths reflected a friendlier world. An example of this is Pandora ("Giver of All"), whose vessel was a honey jar. This early Pandora gave out blessings, not the curses (strife, pain, famine, sickness, etc.) that are found in later versions of the myth. It is the same with every story whose genesis is found in the Fertile Crescent—those rich marshlands at the confluence of the Tigris and Euphrates in southern Iraq and Iran.

The story of Demeter is one example. Demeter (also De-Meter or Delta-Mother) was the Great Mother. In modern myths formed in later classical times, Demeter's daughter Persephone is abducted by Pluto—lord of the underworld. However, the oldest version of the myth was the classic Virgin story. In that version, Kore gave birth to the new god Aeon, celebrating the springtime return of vegetation. Festivals dedicated to Demeter celebrated the birth-life-death cycle reflected in the planting and harvesting of grain.

## The Triple Goddess Archetypes

To use them more meaningfully in your life, it is important to understand the various archetypes.

### The Maiden (Creator)

This is the young girl from childhood until maturity. She is in the process of becoming—full of potential not yet realized. She doesn't know yet who she is, and she hasn't been tested by the tides of life. She is innocent of knowledge and experience and approaches life generally with openness and curiosity. In positive form, she is ready to bloom—a flower of life—

and she attracts others to her like bees to honey. She is pure love continually unfolding her potential. Her role is to grow and fulfill her potential. She will discover and reach for her goals in school, and her career is a natural outgrowth of her experiences if she is not impeded in her path. In a less positive manifestation, she may seem shallow or silly, underdeveloped, or be only interested in appearances. In Western culture, she could be prematurely sexualized and lose touch with her inner quest for self. This maiden may struggle with school and career choices because she is distracted by the "eye candy" that the Western world offers to young people in her vulnerable state.

## The Mother (Preserver)

This is the woman from young adulthood to maturity, the latter often measured by menopause. She is fully aware of herself as a woman of childbearing age, even if she cannot or does not plan to have children. At her best, she is in touch with her monthly cycle, allowing it to influence other aspects of her life, from her moods and emotional awareness to her level of physical, mental, and emotional activity. She is aware of her talents and is in the process of manifesting them with increasing skill throughout this period. Her role is to preserve lives—from her children to the family of humanity—in all its forms. Many women will feel drawn to careers that foster healing and improveing the human condition. Tasks or careers that support aggression or activities that do not promote life often repulse them. When expressed less positively, the mother archetype can be clingy and controlling. A person who does not find ways to fully express his or her own potential may seek to do so through his or her children or those under his or her fosterage. They may push their children into a field of study or career path that they unconsciously wish they had followed themselves. If this mother archetype is underexpressed, it is often because the person rejects his or her fertile feminine side. They may neglect those for whose care and nurturing they are responsible, most particularly themselves and their own health and well-being.

## The Crone or Wise Woman (Destroyer)

This is the woman in the peak of her wisdom. She has gained from life's experience and struggled with its obstacles. She was past childbearing age, but that does not make her less vital. She may be sharp of mind and strong in body, even though her age is beginning to show. She has ceased needing to act as the primary caregiver in others' lives, passing that role on to others.

She may be a grandmother who cares for her grandchildren occasionally, or she may be a career woman who has a leadership role in her work community, either through position or because of her experience. No matter what her role in the community, she is often the matriarch who holds the vision of the group(s) of which she finds herself a member—the family, company, department at work, or the membership organization. She represents and deals with death. As she confronts her own life's end, she shows the way to others. She may bury her friends, offer support, or need to take charge when her family is in transition. She may find it necessary at times to represent the harsh lessons of life. Eventually, she must surrender her role as leader and matriarch to those who follow her, even to allowing others to care for her as she returns to the womb of spirit. On the less positive side, the wise woman may become embittered by life and spread this negativity among those who are connected to her. She may refuse to give up her power when it is time and surrender to the demands of age. She may attempt to control others as a way to maintain her power in the face of growing weakness or infirmity. While sometimes these patterns are symptoms of disease and cannot be helped, other times these behaviors are willful and can be avoided through choice.

## What Does This Mean for You?

Each person has all three Moon archetypes in them: maiden, mother, and wise woman. Each of them is expressed in a never-ending series of cycles throughout our lives. Whether we carry out a project at work, build a house, or fulfill our own life cycle, we enter the Creator–Maiden phase during development, the Preserver–Mother phase once something is established, and the Destroyer–Wise Woman stage when it is time to pass beyond that which has been. To accept and embody all of them is to be able to fully express the feminine in all its forms and feel a sense of completeness.

There are many ways that we can move toward this. Start by identifying which archetype(s) you are most comfortable and familiar with. In women, this may be the archetype that you try to become through your style or way of presenting yourself, or perhaps because of your age or stage in life. If you are male, it may be the archetype that you are most drawn to in women. As our culture places the highest value on the maiden, this may be the strongest archetype, especially if you are young.

Then, learn about the other archetypes. Identify people who represent those archetypes to you, both in your personal life and among public figures. In particular, it helps to identify people whose qualities you admire so that you can learn from the way they live those archetypes.

And finally, seek situations where you will be called upon to draw from those archetypal resources in your nature.

## The Moon Phase at Your Birth Time

The phase of the Moon at the time of your birth indicates which of the archetypes you are likely to feel most comfortable in. To determine which role is strongest in your nature, you will need to look at the Sun-Moon relationship at the time of your birth. If you do not have your birth chart or know the signs of your Sun and Moon, you need to get this information before you will be able to figure out your phase. Several ways to do this are suggested below.

If you have your astrological chart, first divide it into thirds starting with the Sun. Then label the thirds starting with the third of the chart below the Sun and moving counterclockwise. Next, locate which of the thirds your Moon is in. The first third is the sector of the maiden; the second the mother; and the third the wise woman.

If you don't have your astrological chart, you can find the sector your Moon is in by counting signs. To do this, you have to know the order of the signs. First, start with the sign the Sun is in. Counting this sign as "1", the first four signs are the sector of the Maiden; the second four the Mother; and the final four the Wise Woman.

Now, find the archetype that fits you. If you find that you want to improve your expression of this archetype, try some of the suggestions below:

To improve your expression of the Maiden archetype, find ways to bring out the childlike innocence in your nature.

- Play and do things spontaneously from time to time.
- Engage in artistic endeavors—anything from painting and drawing to the dramatic arts to design or decorating. Crafts will fulfill this role as long as you experience it as fun.
- Join in sports as an activity rather than a spectator sport, but don't worry about winning.
- Do something that you've never done before.
- Provide the creative juice for a project.
- Get a beauty makeover or buy some new wardrobe items that contribute to your appearance.

- Let others take care of you, and accept their support.

To augment your expression of the Mother archetype find ways to provide support and be of service to others.

- Volunteer to help an organization—the PTA, a professional or political group, in the school classroom or a hospital.
- Take on leadership roles where you have an opportunity to nurture common goals among a group.
- Take care of children.
- Get a pet that interacts with you and requires nurturing—a cat as opposed to a goldfish.
- Engage in healing or health care activities.
- Be a mentor, Big Brother, or Big Sister to someone.
- Teach or tutor through a literacy program.
- Give of your professional skills without direct compensation, through such groups as Doctors Without Borders or a free legal service. (This of course must be in your area of professional expertise.)
- Work within existing systems and programs to improve or sustain them.

To develop the Wise Woman archetype in your nature:

- Develop relationships with senior citizens in your family and community by volunteering at a retirement home or assisted-living facility. Pay attention to their concerns and to what they can teach you about life from their experiences.
- Find things to get rid of; destroy or recycle outdated objects, ideas, and goals.
- Learn about death. Study how various cultures view death, including how death was viewed in ancient times as encoded in myths, stories, and fairy tales. *The Egyptian Book of the Dead* or *The Tibetan Book of Living and Dying* provide enlightening reading.
- Make a journal of your experiences and ponder what you have learned and are learning from them.
- Think about your own senior years. If you are not yet in them, create a vision of what you want for yourself, both in terms of inner qualities and external events. Develop a flexible guideline for how you think you may achieve them.
- Select from among the people around you someone who has

entered the Wise Woman phase. Write down some thoughts about how he or she is fulfilling that stage, what he or she does that is working and what pitfalls you may want to avoid. Ask him or her about life experiences and how he or she feel about this stage.

- Engage in the portion of projects or activities that eliminates or destroys the old and outworn, or act to complete or finalize projects and processes.
- Become a hospice volunteer.

## Applying Them Each Month

These principles are available to us through the natural lunar cycle. From the New Moon to ten days after, we are all in the maiden phase, developing new ideas based on our instincts and inner knowing. From days eleven through twenty, we are in the mother phase, sustaining what we have started so that it will bear fruit and bring us rewards. Days twenty-one through thirty give us a time to integrate what we have done and learned, creating wisdom out of experience.

One of the best ways to get in touch with these parts of our nature is to simply be aware of the Moon in its cycle of light and dark: go out each night and spot the Moon. Get to know its movement and feel its energies, even on cloudy nights. The Moon, though always changing, is constant in her change: she changes the same way month after month, lighting our nights at times, giving us darkness at others. By tapping her energies, we can learn to move with her tides of activity and be replenished in health and fulfillment.

### About the Author

Terry Lamb, M.A. (Linguistics, UCSD), C.A., is a counselor, instructor and healer using a spiritually oriented approach to astrology and subtle-body healing. She specializes in personal counseling to refocus undermining behavior patterns, electional astrology (choosing the right day for an event), as well as family and relationship matters. She is author of *Born To Be Together: Love Relationships, Astrology, and the Soul*. Her forthcoming book, *Zodiacal Healing*, will be published by Llewellyn in 2004.

# Home Is Where the Moon Is

### by Lisa Finander

Imagine yourself in a place that welcomes you as you are today, a place that comforts and nurtures you, a safe haven where you don't feel ashamed, embarrassed, rejected, or guilty for expressing your emotions. This place embraces your struggles, pains, and joys. Just being in this place allows you to see yourself and to know what is important to you. This place does not exist in your mind but in your heart.

This place is your home.

In astrology, the Moon personifies our emotional, unconscious, irrational self; and, it also signifies our home (early environment, nurturing, emotional imprinting, and behaviors that we carry into adulthood). The compatibility and emotional understanding between different people's natal Moon signs greatly affects their ability to live and create a home together, and their emotional styles.

Because the influence of our natal Moon operates just below our waking consciousness, we are seldom aware of its pervasiveness. Becoming attentive to how you live in your home will give you clues to your emotional condition and vice versa. Your home is a picture of your emotional well-being. Your home shows you where you have been, where you are, and where you are going. Home might then be summarized by an acronym "HOME" (health of my emotions). So home is truly where the heart is. You do not have to look far to see how your emotional life and home life are connected. Self-improvement and self-awareness have been and continue to be popular in bookstores, on TV, and in magazines. People are searching to find ways to feel better and to find their purpose in life.

Home improvement information has also grown in popularity. People are spending large amounts of money and time renovating and repairing their homes to reflect who they are and to create comfortable living spaces. A person can learn a lot about her/himself by undertaking a home improvement project.

Consider the rapport you have with your home. What is your reaction when things break down or need renovating? Do you look mainly to others to handle the situation? Do you do it yourself? How much patience do you have? How well do you work with others? What happens when you run into obstacles you cannot resolve on your own? Do you try to: find expert advice, follow directions, or just wing it? Is function or form more important? How much time, energy, and money will you invest? Do you give up and settle for less than you hoped for, or do you persevere until you can realize your vision? Once they are completed, are you proud of your renovations, or do you downplay your efforts? Do you respect the opinions of others more than your own opinions? Your answers to those questions oftentimes apply to your relationship with your emotions. Therefore it is no coincidence that self-improvement and home-improvement are popular simultaneously. They go together naturally, because the more you discover about yourself the more you will want to create a living space that authentically reflects who you are.

It is important then that the environment we call our home, the place we lay our heads down every night, the physical structure that holds our fears, joys, memories, disappointments, shame, achievements, and dreams be compatible and adaptable throughout our lives. From the energy we put into the food we cook to the color we paint (or do not paint) our walls, our homes are filled with our energy and our intentions. Because this is true, our homes can be emotional stockpiles of attachments, unconscious desires, and memories of abandonment and neglect. Our homes then become sources of pain, discomfort, and dread instead of foundations that validate us. Instinctively we struggle to nullify this source of pain.

If we are unclear about the reasons why we try to improve ourselves or our homes, we unconsciously attempt to improve ourselves and our homes for the wrong reasons. The wrong reasons are ones that aspire to impress others. Wanting to impress others, however, makes us dependent on external praise to feel better. This is not connecting with the needs and desires of your natal Moon. Remember, our homes are not meant to be monuments of perfection and status any more than our emotional lives are. They are both works in progress—a mixture of beauty and roughness.

Consider these questions to illuminate your emotional feeling about your home. How would you describe your home? Are you homeless, between homes, living in someone else's home? Do you own, lease, or rent? How did you choose your present home? How easy is it for you to leave your home, to sleep away from home? Whom do you invite into your home? How do you pay your emotional mortgage each month? Do you go in debt, borrow, scrimp, or do you always have enough left emotionally for yourself? How often do you reinvest into your emotional existence? Can emotions pass through your home easily or do they get stuck and stay unresolved? How much emotional space do you need? How do others feel in your home? How do the answers to these questions represent your connection to the world in general?

For the purpose of discovering how your home is a mirror of your emotional life in more detail, I developed the following exercise. All you will need is an open mind, some paper, and something to write with, or if you prefer, you can use a tape recorder to document your responses.

Choose a time when you can move freely throughout your home without being disturbed. Turn off all TVs, telephones, radios, etc. You can start anywhere on the inside or outside of your home. If you live in an apartment building or condominium, explore the environment outside your building. Do not forget hallways, basements, garages, sheds, attics, and unfinished spaces—basically, any areas that are safe and feasible. If possible, do the entire interior and exterior of your home at the same time. But if that is not practical, then do the entire interior or exterior environment at one time. Completing the entire interior or exterior is important; otherwise, the information you gather is fragmented, and you form assumptions about yourself and your home without complete information.

Take a few moments to relax. If your home has a name, say it. You may choose to bless yourself and your home at this time as a way of honoring the process. Remind yourself that this is not a fault-finding process, but an opportunity to understand yourself better and use that information to further enhance your life.

Enter the first space/room of your home. Write or record the name of the space. Close your eyes. Focus on your emotional responses to the space. What feelings arise in this space? What memories, beliefs, and/or sensations does this room retain? Open your eyes and record your impressions. Now look at the space with your eyes open. What do you sense? Are your attitudes about the space attached to objects, colors, textures, smells, and/or the structure of the space? Record your impressions. Now move to a different spot in the same space. Does anything change? Record any additional thoughts. Repeat this process for each space in and around your home.

With the information you have gathered, identify the area(s) where you feel the best, the worst, and neutral. Note as many physical things as you can about each of those areas. Look at your home with your heart's eye. What areas hold love, anger, joy, fear, creativity, safety, and secrets? Begin to make connections about how your home reflects the beliefs you have about yourself. Compare your cur-

rent home to previous ones. What has changed; what has remained constant? How does your current home compare to your childhood home(s)? Have you intentionally or unintentionally created an emotionally happy, healthy home, or have you recreated an environment filled with antiquated dysfunction?

Think about the condition of your home when you moved in. What changes were made to the home before, during, and after you moved in? How did each change reflect your life at the time? How well does your home reflect your needs now?

See if you can give each space both a functional name (living room, dining room, bedroom, hallway, storage room, junk room, etc.) and a feeling name (expressive room, replenishment room, rejuvenation room, releasing way, sentiment room, melancholy room, etc.). Be mindful that this is a representation of where you are now. You may find that the time of day, week, or year will affect how you feel about your home in general. Now that you have all this information about yourself and your home, resist the temptation to create a long to-do list of the things you dislike and want to change about yourself, your home, or both. Allow yourself some time (a few days, a week, more if you need it) to absorb and to contemplate the knowledge you have gathered about yourself before revisiting the information and moving on to the next exercise.

The next exercise is about creating a sense of peace in your home environment. You will be working with only one specific area of your home each time. You can work with each area as long as you want, and the process can be spread over as much time as you need. Your overall mood or feeling that day will determine which area you will work in. If you feel upset, depressed, down, etc., choose an area from the first exercise that you associated upbeat emotions with. Do the opposite when you are in a cheerful mood; find a place that you previously felt unhappy in. Again, you will need something to record your experiences. You may want to draw, paint, or use a different medium to express yourself in this exercise. Find a comfortable spot to be in the space. Stay as long as you want to, and aim for a sense of peace, acceptance, and love. Record your process. What does it require for you to unconditionally accept and love a room that is worn, imperfect, and in need of repair? Can you apply that same compassion to your emotional self? Likewise, how does a room that fosters pleasant emotions affect you when you are feeling down? Continue this process working back and forth at different times and in different areas with your home and yourself. Focus on your emotional needs and what kind of place can best nurture them.

When you are in the homes of your friends and family, notice how you feel. Are their homes similar to yours, or different? What homes do you feel the most comfortable in? Use this information to try to describe your ideal home. Make a collage. Record and explore any dreams you have about homes, houses, and/or rooms, both current ones and ones you remember from your past.

Sometimes it is difficult to change a space because, like our emotional lives, it requires getting rid of the old to make room for the new. Often the reasons for hanging on to things (guilt, fear, shame, emptiness, etc.), are tied to the feelings associated with the people and/or situations that brought the items into our home in the first place. Other times, it is just the opposite. Indecision, apprehensiveness, and evasiveness around what to bring into a space can leave it vacant for years. Practice creating more fluidity in your home by intentionally bringing something into your home that you know you will let go of at a certain time. This will be especially helpful if you are one of the many people who have trouble giving away the presents you originally acquired for other people. Following the Moon phases will allow you to do this on a monthly cycle. When there is a New Moon, bring something new into your home that you will intentionally get rid of in one month's time. During the waxing phase, allow the item to be part of your home. Move it around, use it, whatever feels appropriate. When the Moon is full, release your attachment to it. Use the time when the Moon is waning to decide where its new home will be and bring it there. You can use this same rhythmic process to cleanse your home of emotional debris.

At this stage, if and when you decide to make changes to your home, you will have a clearer understanding of what to do and your reasons for doing it. It is worthwhile to take pictures and notes of the before, during, and after process even if you are just rearranging or cleaning out an area. This will give you a visual reminder of your progress. If you feel unloved or unlovable, create rooms that are more loving. If you are fearful, create spaces that feel safe and protective. If you feel you are giving too much of yourself away, create replenishing spaces.

Remember that your home on Earth is an ever-changing vessel, a place that desires and needs change. Although your home is a constant that reflects your totality at any given moment, it is never static or completely still. Both your emotional self and home require ongoing maintenance to function at their highest potentials. Create a place where you can "feel at home," a foundation, a beginning place that discovers, sustains, and promotes you.

Welcome home!

## About the Author

Lisa Finander shares her home in Minnesota with her husband Brian and their cats Toby, Yule, and Jampers. The inspiration for this article came from Lisa's own home experiences and from numerous conversations with others about their experiences with their homes. She is a writer, teacher, and consultant who works with symbolism, including the symbolism of astrology, tarot, and dreams. The goal of Lisa's work is to assist others in tranquilly living their lives amidst the physical world.

# Your Moon's Intuitive Potential

*by Alice DeVille*

Popular articles about the Moon tend to focus on the timing of important events and planned activity. All matters of business and government benefit from careful scrutiny of the Moon's place. The success of these undertakings depends upon the flow of lunar cycles comprised of waxing and waning periods that take approximately twenty-nine and a half days each month.

Since the Moon spends approximately two and one-half days in each of the twelve houses in your natal chart, you have access to valuable information that helps you plan projects, tend to health and beauty needs, apply for the perfect job, and schedule your dream vacation. These action phases coincide with specific harmonious dates that are exactly right for you. On this personal level, motherhood duties, nurturing self and others, children's interests, career focus, food preparation, housekeeping functions, and identification with emotional factors covering a range of topics interest many readers. Knowing your Moon's sign and location (the house or department of life in which it resides) at birth helps you understand how you communicate and respond to these private areas of your life.

## The Sanctuary

Another aspect of your Moon connects you to your feelings and the world of inner journeys. Reflection is a key quality affiliated with the Moon. By Luna's grace you select the appropriate format to sort through life's mazes using such treasures as meditation, internal searching, and quiet time. When you are able to detach from the daily routine, you tap into your most fruitful spiritual and imaginative journeys. As you go "into the stillness" you develop sacred space within your heart and mind. Fears dissolve and soon you're following the dots that make up the puzzle pieces of your soul's mission. With the constancy of inner peace that flows gently with the Moon's tides you identify more readily with the true meaning of life.

The Moon, one of the key lights in your chart, influences your psyche and spirit and helps you understand life's mysteries. Far too many indi-

viduals deny the presence of their own intuitive faculties and give all the credit to "someone out there" that has those far out gifts. In truth, you have all experienced the higher mind effect that is present from the day you descend upon the earth plane. Think about the number of times you have said you have a feeling in your gut that turns out to be right or felt you were "on to something." The more you use those intuitive and reflective faculties, the more graced by insight you become.

The "sanctuary" property of the Moon helps you play your hunches and stimulates your intuitive faculties. Your impressionable Moon aids your exploration of the metaphysical realm that seems supernatural and dreamy yet holds hidden meanings your "inner knower" decodes in a restful state. Sleep and reflection are essential to the release of information stored in your superconscious mind. Learning takes place while you sleep and your soul travels on the causal plane to receive information from your higher mind. Sometimes you experience spontaneous regression that allows you to visit a fragment of a past life for clues about this one. As in the practice of feng shui the underlying message is balance—use the gifts you have, develop them, and enrich your life. The payoff links you to the truths of the universal mind and puts you in touch with an awesome understanding of why you are here in this lifetime.

Validation of one's existence or authentic self emerges at major transition points. Undergoing a change in your personal or professional circumstances triggers a quest for information and answers. The planets aligned in the heavens influence your natal chart during these times, especially the outer planets Saturn, Uranus, Neptune, and Pluto. As they make aspects to your birth planets you learn lessons, uncover truths, gain wisdom, and experience release.

When your Moon is one of the affected planets, your attitude about life changes and the transformations deeply affect your outlook. Sometimes it is painful since the changes are deeply personal. You can no longer deny the truth of why you are here or which course of action to take. The sacred lunar sanctuary gives your soul the clout it needs to deal with inner realms. The great "ah ha" that comes from within helps you accept the truth about yourself and then its relevance to your spiritual quest. Ignorance may have been bliss, but once you step across the threshold of awareness you enter the Halls of Higher Learning. The path of the Monad opens up and your soul's accelerated journey begins.

# The Soul's Structure

What is the Monad you may ask? In paintings and photos, especially Egyptian in origin, it is depicted as a central Sun from which emanate twelve twiglike arms with two, slightly clawlike fingers at the end of each arm. It looks like the side view of a hand hanging open in profile with only the thumb distinguishable but not the other fingers. (In Soul Mate workshops I have drawn two hearts at the fingertips of each arm to depict the masculine and feminine energies that are within us, a validation that the seed soul splits and allows us to attract our mates time after time.) The terms "twin souls," "twin flames," or "primary soul mates" come from this concept, implying that both our masculine and feminine halves evolve and incarnate for the first time simultaneously. It does not necessarily hold that our twin is on the planet with us in subsequent incarnations as an intimate partner. If it does happen, we have earned it. The persons we bond with come from an abundant pool of partners known as secondary soul mates. As you will learn in the next segment, these prospective partners come from the original body personalities in your soul cluster or from other soul clusters with spiritual missions similar to yours.

The Monad is a minute, ethereal, concentrated mass of energy and intelligence that contains a complete replica of Source or Totality, the divine spark of God in every living thing containing all the attributes of Source. Each Monad contains a soul/intelligence, spirit/energy, and personality. Millions and millions of Monads, or individualized sparks of light, were created spontaneously in our planetary system. Each Monad creates twelve souls and each soul creates twelve soul extensions or incarnated personalities. This grouping makes up a "soul family" of 144 members who take on physical bodies by incarnating and helping each other grow spiritually lifetime after lifetime. Not every soul extension from a particular soul family is in body at the same time. Some are in the spirit world and often serve as guides to other "family" members in body. Although they may have spent numerous lifetimes on the planet in body themselves, they go through a healing phase, enter the Halls of Wisdom for more learning, and reconnect to their spiritual path after death.

The time between incarnations can be considerable in "real time" years, and the soul is under no obligation to hurry back to playground Earth or another planet. Once the brave soul (there is more pain in physical embodiment than there is on the other side) decides to seek another adventure in the galaxy, Master Guides give last-minute counsel and the blessing to return. Simultaneously, the body personality's memory, but not the soul's, is wiped clean of previous life experiences so the new mind has unrestricted opportunity to concentrate on the current lessons.

Before descending on the planet, each of these body personalities has a hand in selecting both a blueprint or map of experiences for this particular lifetime, as well as their parents and other critical contacts. (If there are any members of their core cluster on the planet, they will meet up in this lifetime and recognize each other almost instantly.) The blueprint includes the time, date, and place of birth known as your natal astrology chart.

If you are reading this article you know that you are person in a physical body, also known as a body personality in spiritual terms, on a specially chosen path of development. Your astrology chart contains all the information about your life's potential and the choices you are making to fulfill your destiny. Although each of the planets contains sacred codes related to you, we'll focus more on the Moon's role in developing your intuition. (If you would like to know more about this very detailed work regarding spiritual unfoldment, read the channeled works of Alice A. Bailey that came through the Ascended Master, Djwhal Khul.)

"Do not be dismayed at good-byes. A farewell is necessary before you can meet again. And meeting again, after moments or lifetimes, is certain for those who are friends."

*Illusions* by Richard Bach

## Media Exposure

Fascination with psychic and intuitive phenomena captures the attention of millions of individuals hungry for signs and messages that have particular meaning in their lives. It is not unusual for the wholly mesmerized to ask how an intuitive comes by those faculties. Often seekers want to know what makes the dynamic evolve so they can figure out and practice the pros' techniques. The adventurous can't wait to apply the wisdom for personal advantage. However, a greater majority fear having to use any such gift. They prefer visiting the seers and leaving the predictions to the so-called experts. That's because they have not yet figured out how much ownership they have in the probing and insightful qualities of their natal Moon.

Have you noticed the increasing number of films, TV, and radio shows that have turned their attention to life on the other side, psychic development, astrological insight, and soul journeys? Once hidden from public view, the media has given information seekers around the globe access to metaphysical sciences. Your lunar journey can separate you from all reality. Have you ever thought about what happens when you travel between the worlds? No? Well, by the time you finish this article you'll be doing out-of-body handstands to facilitate your journey.

## Your Lunar Journey

The Moon sends various messages about your psychic and intuitive potential depending upon the house in which it resides. Think of these messages as a range of possibilities. The Moon in any house shows an inclination toward becoming a psychic instrument with the right combination of planets. The house position alone does not mark the intensity of intuitive gifts, as you will learn in the section following this one. Certain houses and signs of the zodiac seem to accelerate the intuitive qualities of your Moon. Esoteric astrologers believe the fourth, eighth and twelfth houses show particular promise for intuitive, out-of-body, or mediumistic experiences. In the natural zodiac, the water signs Cancer, Scorpio, and Pisces rule these houses.

If your Moon is in the fourth house you may be particularly insightful about family and homebase matters. Your feelings are often dead-on and you "see" with your third eye, or reticular activating system (point behind the center of the forehead where the pineal gland meets the pituitary gland). Your brand of intuitiveness could include psychometry, a gift that gives you a sense of people and conditions when you touch objects or look at pictures of the subject in question. If you have highly charged sensory skills, clairsentient observations are your specialty, meaning you perceive information through your stomach area or throughout the entire chakra system of your body. The inner knower is at work and the information comes like a bolt of lightning and not from external sources. Call these phenomena the "chills of truth" because you will find you are dead-on if you experience this flash of insight and information proves valid time after time.

Fourth house lunar types gravitate toward an interest in past life regression and reincarnation related to family members. They are very curious about why they met up with these relatives, especially parents, in this particular lifetime. They look for clues about current tension they have with family by tapping into their past life memory bank especially when trying emotional periods surface. Regression may be either spontaneous whereby they get an instantaneous glimpse of a past traumatic incident, or it may be ignited through hypnotic therapy. The imagery that replays often reveals a parent as a former torturer, antagonist, rapist, or murderer of the subject. The current lifetime allows room for atonement and a balancing out of karma.

Those with Moon in the eighth house travel between the worlds on the astral plane (can be confusing if they run into discarnate spirits) and the causal plane (higher mental plane where thought forms are designed). They have what we call out-of-body experiences and may be soaring through time and space while their bodies remain on the ground. These individuals actually "see" their body in the particular space where they left it while they are "traveling." If they have mastered the technique, they can also take their body to another location through a process called teleportation.

The eighth house relates to rebirth and transformation in the psychological and spiritual realm. Healing at deep levels takes place when individuals let go of fears and get in touch with the psyche. People with eighth house planetary clusters connected to their Moon have the option to practice mediumship by contacting souls who have passed on either individually or in séances. Sometimes the souls contact the mediums because they recognize these particular body vehicles as messengers who will give their loved ones reassurance that there is life on the other side and they are still in touch.

Clairvoyance, or clear vision, means the individual sees into ethereal space without using physical eyesight and brings up a realistic picture of what is occurring, what someone is experiencing, or how he or she is feeling. Certain clairvoyants see words, colors, lights, figures, images or auras. A few can tap right into your body organs with their x-ray vision and see what's going on with your physical health. These symbolic forms arise out of an alpha state and aid the practitioner in interpreting the messages for themselves and others.

When the Moon resides in the twelfth house, individuals are just plain psychic. They have ESP, practice mental telepathy, and use divination to ferret out the truth. Energetic tools may trigger their clairvoyance and include tarot cards, runes, crystal balls, divining rods, or pendants. Yes, you will find the Madam Swami types with placements in this house, yet you will also find those with dead-on insight that peer around the corners of your life with amazing accuracy. By mastering several of the intuitive disciplines, these individuals truly earn the title metaphysician.

While the eighth house psychic healer sees what type of ailments occur in the body, those with twelfth house placements hone in on the cure for their contact's illness. The subject's body may "talk" to the healer by

describing what nutritional and medicinal supplements would cure the problem. The gifted foot reflexologist, for example, not only unblocks the electrical energy in the foot's nerve endings but also tunes in to important data regarding the congested areas in the rest of the individual's body. You will also find this expertise existing in the charts of individuals with strong healing tendencies and planets in the sixth house of health and healing.

Dream interpreters get their energy from placement of the Moon and other planets in the twelfth house. Jungian psychologists use this tool to help troubled patients sort out areas of inner conflict. Other individuals find dreaming is a natural way of identifying their personal truths or those of the world in general. There is nothing like the insight of knowing and dreaming about events that are going to occur ahead of time. The twelfth house lunar seers have a reputation for dreaming prophetically, lucidly, and accurately. Dreams for these individuals are vivid accounts of events to come or answers to problems. They have incredible interpretive skills when you share one of your dreams. If you are a dreamer, be aware that the most insightful time occurs closest to waking. In addition to having profound dream-related skills, the twelfth house Moons are adept at being channelers, mediums, swamis, and casters of spells.

I find in my practice that individuals born with a number of planets placed in these three houses have an acute interest in exploring past lives. Their charts give clues to the particular incarnations where they left unfinished business and have come here to resolve it and move on. The Moon's qualities of retention and recall facilitate the healing process and stimulate the urgency each querent has for discovering the truth. In the next section we look at additional evidence for validating your Moon's intuitive potential.

## Other Power Houses

If you are feeling left out because you don't have the Moon in the fourth, eighth, or twelfth house, rest assured that your lunar toolbox is brimming with insight about other departments of your life. Those with Moon connections in the first house have psychic insight inherited through ancestors, particularly on your mother's side of the family. In fact, some of you may have routine visits from deceased relatives who guide you in a range of activities—while you make important decisions, improve your appearance, or repair your vacuum cleaner. You channel your wisdom efficiently when it comes to taking quick action in emergency situations or understanding the pulse of the people with whom you come in contact. You have the insight to take calculated risks and perform courageous acts knowing on inner levels that you are safe and your judgment is on the mark.

Moon in the second house types make career contacts easily by following hunches that lead them to the perfect jobs. When presented with multiple offers you gravitate toward those with high earning potential and outstanding benefits. Usually you enjoy two or more well-developed careers in a given lifetime and multiple positions. Intuitiveness often focuses around scent when you are picking up vibes about the surrounding environment. You are the ones who talk about smelling bouquets of roses or freshly baked bread affiliated with traits of departed souls or intimate contacts. You also "hear" channeled voices or experience celestial music through the gift of clairaudience.

Third house Moons use mental imagery to access valuable information that aids your productivity, communication techniques, and educational pursuits. You possess mental telepathy and sometimes a photographic memory. What a bonus when it comes to studying new concepts, learning a new language or cramming for exams. With the chakras in your hands in sync with your higher mind, your potential for automatic writing is strong. You have the innate flair for producing amazing literary works. Plus, the high level initiates among you know how to make yourself invisible when you don't want interruptions in your planned routine.

Expressive fifth house Moons follow the heart's direction in looking for their center of compassion that revolves around unconditional love. Once the heart chakra opens, spiritual advancement occurs rapidly and individuals often tap into the akashic records, the storehouse of ethereal attitudes, emotions, concepts, and experiences that occur during each earthly incarnation. Your solar plexus radiates with intuitive energy, especially when you practice the disciplines of yoga, deep breathing, and meditation.

With a sixth house lunar connection, your amazing insight regarding self-healing comes to life. You understand how release of fear cleanses your mind and opens your subconscious to new possibilities. Many of you are natural healers. Perhaps you use a pendulum to diagnose disease or use the clearing force-fields of reiki or seichim (living light energy that flows from the hands of gifted healers; some perform laser surgery without even touching the patient). When you are not taking note of the hot and cold spots in your patient's auric field, you have an interest in the power of numbers. The numerologists among you want to know how the numbers affiliated with birth dates and names influence a person's character and blueprint for a lifetime.

Seventh house Moons, and their planetary contacts, attract balance and harmony through loving relationships. The divine spark that leads to soul mate reunions ignites when you love and accept yourself. Soon after you begin to have precognitive insight through dreams or visualizations that you are going to meet your soul mate or a significant partner. The sense that your partner is just around the corner becomes overwhelming until it occurs. Unusual clues come your way in the form of seeing the future mate's eyes, a glimpse of hair, or even an arm. Conversely, you may be wired in to your higher self-awareness and get the "411" message that it is time to leave the partner when the relationship has run its course. A few of you pick up on the dates and dynamics to release the karma. Then it is up to you to let go with love.

Soul travelers populate the ninth house of spirituality and higher mind. Moons in this house have out-of-body experiences, meaning they have the knack of sailing through the air randomly while in the sleep state to conduct business on the higher planes. Certain individuals know how to do this consciously as well. Disciplined meditation accelerates the spiritual growth cycle and puts them in touch with other world intelligence. UFO sightings and teleportation to other countries or planets are not unusual for highly evolved practitioners with ninth house Moons.

A good number of tenth house Moons resonate to integration of the left brain and right brain hemispheres to give you the best of both worlds operating 24/7. Associations of this house are status and ambition. Use of imagery and imprinting help you get to the top of your career ladder. Sometimes you gravitate toward the martial arts, yoga, and tai chi to open up and clear blocked chakras, and simultaneously clear a rung on the corporate or the spiritual ascension ladder.

When the Moon falls in the eleventh house of associations and groups, you have plenty of company in the world of metaphysical interests. Your friends and associates as well as you enjoy camaraderie and perhaps pool your talent to enhance the quality of life for people on the planet. Talent drips from your toolbox. Among you are amazing graphologists (handwriting experts), innovative astrologers, metaphysicians (those with expertise in three or more intuitive arts disciplines), remote viewers (seeing clairvoyantly what is happening at the present time when the event is out of the range of your physical eyes), and intuitive advisors. Coupled with your altruistic attitude toward humanity, the cosmic intelligence you possess stimulates spiritual depth in contacts from all walks of life.

As you walk your own spiritual path, get to know the Moon in your natal chart. Appreciate its place and you will understand the personality of your soul.

## A Personal Page

I was born intuitive. I walked at nine months old, and I recited nursery rhymes and the ABCs by the time I was a year old. Of course I did not know this was unusual. I assumed everyone knew the same things I knew until I began to get startled looks from adults, especially from my mother and her sister, Lucy. When I walked into a room at a preschool age, I could join in conversations without having been present when they began. I

would "know" what happened in the room before I got there. Or I would get premonitions about events that were going to occur before they actually did. If my mother said there was no more chewing gum left (that meant for me, of course), I could "see" into a high-up cabinet and know there was a stash put away for my older visiting cousin, Ann. I was four years old when Aunt Lucy's husband died. I knew what the message was going to be when the phone rang announcing his death and was not surprised when my mother said we would be traveling to Rochester, New York, for his funeral. The rest of my life has been all about accessing information in a variety of places, but that is another story. For now I share my love for astrology and the wonderful way it serves as a trigger tool for opening the subconscious. May all your journeys be just as fruitful.

## About the Author

Alice DeVille is an internationally known astrologer, writer, and metaphysical consultant. In her busy northern Virginia practice, she specializes in relationships, government affairs, career, and change management, real estate, and spiritual development. She has developed and presented approximately 125 workshops and seminars related to astrological, metaphysical, motivational, and business themes. Alice also writes astrology articles for the StarIQ.com web site. Her interest in the soul's structure has led to development of numerous workshops and an abundance of intuitive experiences. She is also a reiki and seichim master. Contact Alice at DeVilleAA@aol.com.

# Pregnancy and Lunar Rhythms

*by Stephanie Clement Ph.D.*

There have been contraceptive methods for centuries—many of them herbal, and all of them indefinite—and there have been abortion methods—most of them unsafe. It's only in recent years that women were offered means to assure that they will not become pregnant. With IUDs, condoms, and the Pill, women have a variety of choices to avoid pregnancy.

The Catholic church, having proscribed the use of these interventions, reduced the choices to the rhythm method. For most women, this rhythm was connected to the menstrual cycle. Generally, the period of fertility lies in the middle of the normal cycle, when the ovaries release one or more eggs into the system. This method has been refined by using body temperature as an indicator of ovulation, but the rhythm method has proven unreliable in case after case. For one thing, the woman has to keep track of the days since menstruation began. For another, she must abstain at the very time that her body is saying to go for it. Then the male partner has to agree to abstain.

Most of us, separated from nature as we are, have also lost our connection to the lunar cycle. Many women are barely aware of the Moon. However, the Moon is a powerful key to the cycle of fertility. Whether you are seeking to become pregnant, or seeking to avoid it, the Moon provides definite help.

In the 1950s Dr. Eugene Jonas, a Czech psychiatrist, was working with many Catholic patients who practiced the rhythm method of contraception.

Many of these women became pregnant in spite of their best efforts to avoid it. A Roman Catholic, he opposed abortion, which had just been made legal in Hungary, and he wanted to find a way for women to avoid the dangers of abortion as well. So he began his study of birth charts and conception times. Jonas, who understood the basics of astrology, calculated the birth charts of thousands of women, and tracked their pregnancies. He discovered that the failures of the rhythm method, based on the menstrual cycle, were also connected to another cycle, the lunar phase angle. Dr. Jonas stated in a letter in 1997 that he made his discovery on the day celebrating the Assumption of Mary, August 15, 1956. He dedicated all of his work to the Virgin, including his work on the fertility cycle. Dr. Jonas found the clue to this cycle in a Babylonian text that stated "Woman is only fertile during a certain phase of the Moon." The problem was, the ancient text did not clarify which phase of the Moon.

# Lunar Phase Angle

The lunar phase angle is the moment each month when the Moon is the same distance from the Sun as it was in the birth chart. For example, if the Sun is at 0 degrees of Aries and the Moon is at 18 degrees of Taurus, they are 48 degrees apart. Each month the Moon goes through all the signs, and each month there is a moment after the New Moon when the Moon has moved 48 degrees ahead of the Sun in the zodiac. The Sun moves about 1 degree each day, and the Moon moves between 11 and 14 degrees each day. In three days the Sun moves 3 degrees, and the Moon moves between 33 and 42 degrees. In four days the Sun moves 4 degrees, and the Moon moves between 44 and 56 days. For this example we see that the Moon will repeat the birth lunar phase angle some time on the fourth day after the New Moon.

To calculate your own lunar phase angle, you only need a birth chart or an ephemeris. Because the Moon moves so quickly through the zodiac, the accuracy of this system will depend on an accurate birth time. However, even if you don't have a precise birth time, the Moon can only be plus or minus a few degrees from its exact position, based on the ephemeris.

## Example

Suppose you were born on January 22, 1977. Here are the positions of the Sun and Moon for January 22 and January 23 from the ephemeris, which is set for Greenwich in England.

| Date | Sun Position | Moon Position | Difference |
|------|--------------|---------------|------------|
| January 23 | 02 Aquarius 52 | 15 Pisces 34 | 42 degrees 44 min. |
| January 22 | 01 Aquarius 51 | 02 Pisces 29 | 30 degrees 38 min. |

### Daily Movement

| Sun | Moon |
|-----|------|
| 1 degree 1 minute | 13 degrees 5 minutes |

For January 22, the distance between the Sun and Moon is 30 degrees 38 minutes. For January 23, the distance is 42 degrees 42 minutes. So at the outside, the lunar phase is between 30 and 43 degrees. Every month it will be the same. If you know when the New Moon occurs, you can simply count forward to a day when the Moon is 30 to 43 degrees ahead of the Sun. This kind of estimating is not scientifically precise. However, we generally don't know exactly when the egg is fertilized either. Therefore, knowing a two-or three-day period when ovulation is closely aligned with the lunar phase is what is important. If you want more precision, an astrologer can provide a list of dates and times when the lunar phase cycle is exact. Use the method recommended by your physician for determining when ovulation occurs.

## So What?

The lunar phase is only part of this equation. Another part is your personal menstrual cycle. Generally, you are fertile eleven to fourteen days before the onset of menses. This date varies quite a bit, depending on the length of the menstrual cycle. Current technology provides ways to determine when ovulation is occurring, and you can take advantage of these. Once you have determined when you are fertile each month, compare those dates to the dates when your lunar phase angle is repeated. If your cycle is fairly regular, this will be easy. Forecast the dates when your ovulation dates coincide closely with the lunar phase angle returns. These are the most likely times to become pregnant.

## Example

Using the example given above, where the lunar phase is known to be between 30 degrees and 42 degrees, we can help this individual to find out when her biological fertility and her lunar fertility cycles will align. Let's say that her biological cycle is thirty-one days in length, and that she has figured out that she ovulates sixteen days after her menses begin. She began her last menses on January 1, 2004. This means that ovulation will occur on or around January 17; then, every thirty-one days after that. We make a list of those dates.

Then we look at the calendar to determine when the lunar phase will be between 30 and 42 degrees. Remember that the Moon will be in a later sign of the zodiac from the Sun. We make another list of dates, and we compare the lists.

| Ovulation Date | Lunar Phase Date |
|---|---|
| January 16, 2004 | January 23, 2004 |
| February 16 | February 22 |
| March 18 | March 23 |
| April 18 | April 22 |
| **May 19** | **May 21** |
| **June 19** | **June 20** |
| **July 20** | **July 19** |
| August 20 | August 18 |
| September 20 | September 16 |
| October 21 | October 16 |
| November 21 | November 14 |
| December 22 | December 13 |

May, June, and July dates are printed in bold. These are the three months during 2004 when the biological and lunar phase cycles are most closely aligned to each other. If the mother's biological cycle remains consistent, then we know her most likely times for becoming pregnant.

There is an interesting anomaly that researchers have observed. As the cycles come closer to being exact, the biological cycle may adjust to fit with the lunar phase cycle. Most women are aware of times when they have had one or two menstrual cycles that were shorter or longer than usual. These tend to occur when the two cycles are coming into alignment.

*Note:* In this example the cycles were only seven days apart at the beginning of the year. If you start out with a much larger gap—say seventeen days, it will take longer for the two cycles to become aligned. The time span may seem like eternity to the individual who wishes to become pregnant. However, in terms of one's whole life, the extra few months are not so long. The time can be used for financial and emotional planning for the change that a new baby will bring.

If your biological cycle is exactly the length of the lunar cycle, but out of "phase," don't despair. You can consult with your physician about ways to alter your cycle. One way is to change the number of days you take birth control pills, to lengthen your cycle gradually. But don't try something like this without the advice of a doctor, who may have better solutions.

## Will It Be a Boy or a Girl?

This is the third factor many people are concerned about, the first two being conception and contraception. Dr. Jonas found that boys are conceived when the Moon is in so-called masculine signs ( Aries, Gemini, Leo, Libra, Sagittarius, Aquarius) while girls are conceived when the Moon is in a feminine sign (Taurus, Cancer, Virgo, Scorpio, Capricorn, Pisces). As the Sun and Moon are both moving forward through the zodiac, the Moon will reach your peronsal phase angle when it is in both masculine and feminine signs. Assuming that the father has healthy X and Y chromosomes, both male and female conceptions are therefore possible.

The catch: we don't know exactly when the egg will be fertilized. We know when intercourse occurred, but the time lag could be significant. A twenty-four hour time lag may mean that the Moon has transited into the next sign. Therefore, using this method to predict the child's sex is possible, but not infallible.

## What If the Menstrual Cycle Is Irregular?

When the menstrual cycle is irregular, it remains true that the most likely times of conception occur at the lunar phase angle returns. By knowing these cycles, you can maximize your chances of pregnancy (or avoid pregnancy) by tracking the phase angle. There is some anecdotal evidence that by stimulating the body at appropriate times via intercourse, ovulation may be stimulated. We know this is true for other animals, and logic suggests it is likely for humans as well, at least to some extent. This would explain failures of the rhythm method to prevent conception.

## What If Oral Contraception Has Been Used?

Oral contraception forces the body to adhere to a specific cycle—one that may be at odds with the natural cycle. Most doctors recommend a period of abstinence, or using other contraceptive methods, for several months after discontinuing oral contraceptives. This allows the body to readjust to the natural cycle, and it allows time for drugs to leave the body. It may take some time for the menstrual cycle to align itself with the lunar cycle.

## What about Dad's Lunar Phase?

Research in Great Britain, reported on the Internet, suggests that sperm count in a man is increased at the time of his lunar phase angle return. I have been unable to document this research anywhere else at the time of this writing. But, assuming that this is true, and it seems logical, you can align three factors: the woman's menstrual cycle, her lunar phase cycle, and the man's lunar phase cycle. Because the two lunar phase cycles are likely to be different lengths, it is possible that they will come into alignment, even if they are not aligned on a particular date. Because most men have adequate sperm count all the time, considering his phase cycle may not be important. In addition, because of modern medical techniques, his sperm could be harvested and saved until her cycles are propitiously aligned.

## Does the Rest of the Lunar Phase Chart Have an Effect?

Each month, when the lunar phase angle is repeated, you can cast a chart for that moment. As with any other chart, the chart for this moment will have constructive, creative factors, and also factors that are detrimental to conception. For detailed exploration of this potential, you can consult a professional astrologer. For the basics, you can use an astrological calendar or date book that includes an ephemeris. Here are some basic things to look for (these suggestions are paraphrased from "Tutorial for Fertility Cycle," by Marion D. March, http://www.astrologie.ws/mrch.htm):

• Look at the aspects the Moon makes while it is in the sign of the lunar phase angle return. Avoid squares, especially to Mars, Saturn, and Uranus. The reason for this is that squares indicate challenges, and these particular squares are tough challenges. A square to Venus would not be as difficult.

• Avoid Moon opposite Saturn or Uranus.

• Avoid Moon square Pluto, even though Pluto is about birth and rebirth.

• Moon void-of-course—because the phase angle can occur at any point in the Moon's current progress thorough the signs, it may fall when the Moon is void. This does not mean you should abstain. It is less likely to become pregnant then, but not impossible. Marion March points out that after all, the Moon may have moved into the next sign by the time the sperm reaches the egg.

• Sun square Moon in the birth chart—this is a hard combination for pregnancy. There are two times each month when the square occurs—at the waxing quarter and the waning quarter phase. Planning for a phase angle just past the square will give better results.

## About the Pregnancy

Once you are pregnant, you have all sorts of questions about how the pregnancy will unfold. The lunar phase angle chart for the month of conception can tell you a lot about what to expect. The chart for this time is just like any other chart. However, it is NOT a birth chart, and thus will not be read as one. It will be read as an event chart, and can be related to the parents' birth charts, just as any transit chart would be. A complete delineation of a conception lunar phase return chart is beyond the scope of this article, though.

Some important indicators in the lunar phase return chart for the pregnancy include the sign of the Sun and Moon, and how this sign relates to the mother's Sun sign. You don't need any charts to understand this relationship. You already know the mother's Sun sign, and you can determine the current Sun and Moon signs from an astrological calendar. Keep in mind that the distance between the Sun and Moon remains constant in the lunar phase cycle. If you have the Moon 48 degrees ahead of the Sun, it will always be that distance. Forty-eight degrees is just over one and one-half signs. This means that in some months the Moon will be in the sign following the Sun sign, and some months it will be in the second sign ahead. Here's an example of how that works:

| Date | Sun | Moon | Phase Angle |
| --- | --- | --- | --- |
| Jan. 25, 2004 | 4 Aquarius 56 | 22 Pisces 56 | 48 degrees |
| Aug. 19, 2004 | 27 Leo 25 | 15 Libra 25 | 48 degrees |

In the first example, we find Aquarius and Pisces, consecutive signs. In the second example, all of Virgo lies between the Sun and Moon signs. When the phase angle is an exact multiple of 30 degrees, the number of signs between the Sun and Moon will always be the same. Otherwise, there is a chance that they may be different. Therefore it is important to look at the signs of the Sun and Moon each month.

# The Moon Sign Shows the Action

In astrological event charts, and getting pregnant is the event chart in this case, the Sun indicates the nature of the event, while the Moon indicates how the action unfolds. If you know the date for the phase angle, you also know the Sun and Moon signs involved. I have begun with the idea that most pregnancies are normal—that is, they are full term and result in live births. The following descriptions of the Moon signs provide general indications of the primary mental and emotional factors to expect during the pregnancy. By focusing on these general areas during your pregnancy, you make the most of the energy of the lunar phase. Notice how these indications match up to your typical style. You may be surprised by how your approach to life changes with each pregnancy, based on its particular Moon sign!

## Moon in Aries

You're eager for the baby to see the light of day. You have a strong intuitive connection with the fetus, and sense its needs, as well as your own. It is possible that you got into the pregnancy without planning it, as the Moon in Aries can be rash and headstrong. The urge toward a new beginning is very strong in this sign. Given the strength of the Aries Moon, you will want to plan ahead for the eventual birth. You will save up for the appropriate furniture and even buy bright curtains and other decorations for the room. This is appropriate for a baby who will be born in the winter, when the days are shorter. The space will be bright and cheerful, regardless of the winter weather.

## Moon in Taurus

Not so interested in making big changes, you probably will take your pregnancy as it comes, day by day. You may put on a few more pounds than you want to, and should consult with your physician or midwife about dietary changes that can help you to control weight gain. At the same time, you want to enjoy this time in your life, so don't be overly strict with yourself. A few extra pounds will not harm your child. Emotionally, you may find that you really don't want to share your pregnancy with friends and acquaintances. You want it to be your own. Take care of financial matters as you go along. Provide for the future baby's actual needs, without going overboard and buying every darling bootee and blanket you see. This way you will feel secure and confident about the future.

## Moon in Gemini

You are mentally and emotionally mobile. For this pregnancy, you will do well to wait until closer to the due date to make your purchase, as your changing moods early on could result in quite a hodgepodge of furniture, decorations, and toys. Do you want to know the sex of the baby before you buy clothing? Very likely. You may be moving into a new home anyway.

You will still have the energy you need to take care of the basics, and if you have missed something, the baby will survive for a few days until you are able to get out to the store!

## Moon in Cancer

This is a very appropriate Moon sign for the beginning of a pregnancy. First of all, it results in a birth at or near the Spring Equinox, the time of year when everything is beginning to grow (at least in the Northern Hemisphere). Second, the Moon in its own sign promises the fullness of emotional strength, the desire to establish a home, and family matters in general. You will be in the proper mood for having a new face and voice entering your life. You may need to adjust your diet to suit the growing life within you, and to avoid serious digestive upsets.

On the other hand, Daniel Pharr says, "This is not a Moon that can be readily 'used' for your own agenda; it will use you." It demands that you be up-front and honest about your desires—especially be honest with yourself. You have a golden opportunity in this pregnancy to listen to your own inner voice, listen to the voice of your child, and act from the understanding you gain.

## Moon in Leo

You are at your creative best with this Moon, assuming it is compatible with your birth Sun and Moon signs. You can foresee problems in an almost magical way as you prepare for the newest family member to arrive. You are warm and kind to others, and to yourself now. During the pregnancy, you will need to arrange time to rest and relax. During the winter months, you will take advantage of every sunny day, spending time outside if it is not too cold.

While you may have lots of creative ideas at this time, it is easy to overestimate your strength. Keep track of your good ideas by writing them in your journal, and then enlist lots of help in following through on the most important ones. Indulge yourself now, as there may not be much time after the baby arrives.

## Moon in Virgo

Similar to Taurus, the Virgo Moon gives you the desire for comfort and relaxation. You won't be as slow moving as Taurus, but you will want to plan activities so there are few surprises. You are perfectly capable of adapting if you are given advance notice. For the person who is detail-oriented by nature, the Virgo Moon pregnancy could lead to near-obsessive concerns over every tiny physical or emotional change that occurs. One way to handle this tendency is to write down concerns as they arise. You can discuss them with your physician, midwife, or other significant figure in your life. Sometimes just writing them down is enough to stop the worry cycle.

The pregnancy will increase your intuitive powers. Maybe it is that willingness to look at all the details that also helps you to gain insight on another level. Amid the flood of psychic information, you also get simplicity of thought and action. This period of your life may look dull to the outsider, but you are enjoying every minute, getting to know yourself and your unborn child better each day.

## Moon in Libra

The Moon is emotional, nurturing, protective, and receptive by nature. Libra is cooperative, idealistic, and balanced. The combination, then, allows for expression of the feeling nature within the protective nest you are creating for your new child. At first you may be undecided about how you feel—even if you have planned for this child, you may suddenly feel, at times, that you have made a dreadful error. Basic choices elude you and your emotions are all over the place. Don't worry, you will come back into hormonal balance, and your emotions will subside.

The strength of this pregnancy lies in your capacity to engage in social activities with a flair. During the winter holidays you are still able to dress up without feeling huge. You are better able to accept an invitation than to plan a big party, though. You enjoy seeing people, and feel closer to family members.

The unsettled nature of the Moon in Libra could indicate that you change residences before the arrival of the newest family member. Get some help with planning for the baby, as you may not be emotionally grounded enough to remember all the important details.

## Moon in Scorpio

Regardless of how laidback you normally are, this will be an intense nine months for you. Emotions are the name of this game. You are up and down and all over the emotional map. If you are normally quiet and practical, this will seem outrageous, and yet you can't seem to do much about it. If you are emotionally expressive as a general rule, then the exaggerations of this pregnancy will not be all that different for you.

You may find that sexual desire is stronger than ever. That is really not a problem, as sexual activity is safe in most cases, and a good physical relationship can help to stabilize those errant moods.

Just as emotions are enhanced, so are other mental processes. You find that you can delve deep into the study of your favorite subject, and stick to the subject until you learn it thoroughly. Psychic awareness may be heightened, too—you sense what is happening with people around you even before they do. Toward the end of the pregnancy, at the height of summer, your emotions will give way to the desire to rest and relax, taking each day as it comes, and allowing others to wait on you.

## Moon in Sagittarius

Changeable moods mark the Sagittarius pregnancy, too. Here, however, the swings are not as violent. You relish introspection, finding yourself at least as interesting as most of the other people in your life. Self-discovery is wonderful for the expectant mother, as you will be very busy when the baby arrives. You may find that ideals from childhood come back into your life. Imagine, you may even see the world through your mother's eyes!

Your closely held ideas and ideals demand that you control your own life. This could include trying to control your mate and other people, too. There are enough changes going on in your own body—you don't want to do things someone else's way. Still, getting into a ruthless struggle is not helpful for you or the child you carry. The introspection serves you well now, as you can decide which points to cede to others, and which points you must stand firm on. Anticipate a lot of changes, and you won't be disappointed.

## Moon in Capricorn

You may feel surprisingly calm and unemotional, given the stories you have heard from other women about pregnancy. You are a bundle of practical energy, making ambitious plans and carrying them through to completion. Now you get to design and decorate your baby's room, make or purchase clothing, and do all the other essential things you have planned for your future child.

At the same time you may be engaged in a career or new business venture. You are even more interested in your life path than before. If you are a work-from-home person, you find time to rearrange closets, paint a room or two, and generally participate in life to the fullest. These bursts of energy can occasionally alternate with sadness or depression. You find that by keeping active, you overcome these periods.

## Moon in Aquarius

You have more ideas than you know what to do with, and you want to pursue them all! Your mind is working on something every waking moment, and some mornings you are sure it has been at work all night, too. You find yourself observing people, seeking to understand their motivations and actions. You are quite sympathetic to the needs of people around you, and incidentally, you expect some sympathy in return. Not drippy, emotional stuff, just acknowledgement. If you have a favorite charity or humanitarian cause, pregnancy will pose no obstacle to your work. In fact, the nurturing undercurrent suits you. When you are out there with people, you are really into the cause.

When you want to be at home alone, you want privacy. You may have thought you would never want an answering machine or service, but now is a good time to get one. That way, you get the privacy you need now, and you are ready for the time when you need uninterrupted sleep at odd hours of the day. While you need to spend time with others, you require and demand—independence.

## Moon in Pisces

You are wide open to psychic energies around you. This can be a good thing—you soak up feelings and ideas from the air. It can also be quite draining of energy you need to put into the pregnancy. You need to find ways to work with the psychic influences, especially if they were not a noticeable part of your life before you became pregnant. You will find that simply closing yourself off does not work all that well. Spending time alone each day is a good start. By alone, I mean alone. Not at the park with hundreds of people, or the mall with even more. I mean at home, or outdoors, with no other people around.

Now, that may not be easy to accomplish. You need to not answer the phone, not invite people over, or whatever it takes to reserve time for yourself. It's interesting to note that as you begin to withdraw, people will pursue you. You create an energy void, and they rush to fill it. You will need to draw on skills you have learned over a lifetime of social, school, and family activities. It may be helpful to talk about your private time as though it is an important appointment. And it is. Your time for yourself and your unborn child is essential for your physical and emotional health.

# Conclusion

If you have read all twelve Moon signs, you have leaned something about pregnancies that begin in each Moon sign. Because we each have a birth chart that includes all the signs and all the planets, you may find suggestions for other Moon sign pregnancies that resonate with your own. And you may gain fresh understanding about why your pregnancies have been so different! During this pregnancy, you can cultivate the best of each sign, infusing yourself and your unborn child with the richness of emotional support and nurturance.

## About the Author

Stephanie Clement, Ph.D. (Colorado) is an astrologer with thirty years of experience. She's a boardmember of the American Federation of Astrologers and the National Center for Geocosmic Research, and a faculty member of both NORWAC and Kepler College. She has degrees in English literature, humanistic psychology, and transpersonal psychology. Before pursuing astrology full-time, she had a counseling practice in Boulder, and worked with clients on their personal and career issues using astrology, hypnotherapy, and dream work. Stephanie had numerous articles published in astrological magazine, and has written several books: *Charting Your Spiritual Path with Astrology, Dreams: Working Interactive, What Astrology Can Do For You, Meditation for Beginners, Power of the Midheaven*, and her most recent book, *Mapping Your Birthchart*. In addition, Stephanie has given workshops and lectures in Canada, Hawaii, and the continental U.S., and participated in radio and television shows. She is available for radio interviews, writing articles for magazines, workshops, and book signings.

## For Further Reading

Pharr, Daniel. *The Moon and Everyday Living*. (Llewellyn, 2000).

# Lunar Rituals for Better Health

## by Jonathan Keyes

Perhaps on some night you've looked up at the night sky and encountered the Moon in her full radiance—a wonderfully radiant orb. In this Moon moment, something about the way plants keened toward her glow, the way air felt against your face, and the way the moonlight captured your attention, placed a spell on your consciousness. You were entranced.

The Moon has long been associated with mystery, magic, and enchantment. Witches and sorcerers choose particular nights to cast their spells and create magic because they are aware of the Moon's ability to augment their work. Her force pulls at the oceans, drawing forth and releasing the tides in a constant ebb and flow. Her phases imitate the regular turn of the seasons and the cycles of nature.

Since antiquity, we've noticed that the Moon affects human health and behavior. Ancient peoples noticed that plants, animals, and humans developed more energy and intensity as the Full Moon grew close. The word "lunacy" derives from the French word *lune* (which means "Moon"). We say about someone, "He's loony," "crazy," or "eccentric." The Moon seems to increase our emotional sensitivity and heighten our awareness.

## Astrology, Health, and the Moon

Astrologers have noticed that the Moon creates a different mood or ambience depending on the constellation it is passing through. Thus, a Full Moon in the constellation Sagittarius would feel very different from a Full Moon in Scorpio.

In medical astrology, each zodiac sign is associated with a body part. For example, Leo is associated with the heart and Libra with the kidneys. Galen [a famous physician who trained at the medical schools of Alexandria in the middle of second century A.D.] recommended that operations not be done on certain parts of the body when the Moon was in the sign that had rulership over that body part. Thus, one shouldn't have an operation on the kidneys when the Moon is in Libra, or have knee replacement surgery when the Moon is in Capricorn.

We can develop better health by simply understanding the Moon's cycle and transits through the astrological signs. One of the best ways to work with Moon cycles is to simply observe the New and Full Moon—the two most powerful times of the month. Observing these two central times of the cycle puts us in touch with the Moon's energy and creates a good space and time to create rituals and do activities that can help augment our health. Here's a table that explains in what signs the New and Full Moons will fall in 2004.

| January | New Moon Aquarius | Full Moon Cancer |
| February | New Moon Pisces | Full Moon Leo |
| March | New Moon Aries | Full Moon Virgo |
| April | New Moon Aries | Full Moon Libra |
| May | New Moon Taurus | Full Moon Scorpio |
| June | New Moon Gemini | Full Moon Sagittarius |
| July | New Moon Cancer | Full Moon Capricorn |
| August | New Moon Leo | Full Moon Pisces |
| September | New Moon Virgo | Full Moon Aries |
| October | New Moon Libra | Full Moon Taurus |
| November | New Moon Scorpio | Full Moon Gemini |
| December | New Moon Sagittarius | Full Moon Cancer |

The New and Full Moon phases are key times for working on health issues, making prayers, rituals, and transforming our consciousness to help assist the natural healing process. The New Moon is a "seed time," when intentions can be set. Full Moons are times of magic and transformation, when shifts in our health patterns can occur. Each phase of the

Moon in a certain astrological sign carries a particular kind of energy or frequency. We can tap into this frequency and utilize it to augment our health. The New Moon is the seed point, the first quarter Moon (the waxing phase) is the growth process, the Full Moon is the fruition point, the third quarter Moon (the waning phase) is the decay period, and the Dark Moon (or New Moon) is the death and new birth period starting again.

If you have been experiencing pain, distress, or illness in a certain part of your body, you can also choose a Moon time that correlates with that body part to heal on a fundamental level. You don't have to wait for a perfect New or Full Moon, you can choose a phase of the Moon that is transiting the right constellation. Waxing Moons are helpful for augmenting, nourishing, and strengthening our energy. Waning Moons are good times for detoxifying, excreting, and releasing old emotional states.

Knowing the Moon's sign is helpful if you want to develop rituals and create intentions that will help the healing process. For example, if you have been feeling listless, apathetic, and unable to get your creative juices flowing, it can be helpful to conduct a ritual on a fiery Moon (Aries, Leo, Sagittarius). If you have been feeling impatient and too fired up, it can be helpful to pick a watery Moon (Cancer, Scorpio, Pisces) to cool down and relax. Sometimes these emotional circumstances can manifest as physical health problems. If we have been feeling frustrated and angry, a woman may have a difficult time with her men-

strual period, or another may develop a skin rash. A good Moon ritual can help rebalance and reset the system to bring it into balance. Performing a ritual on a good grounding, or earth sign Moon, such as Taurus or Capricorn, could help calm your energy and reduce the "hot" stress that causes the physical disturbance.

## The Moon, Rhythm, and Illness

Being aware of the Moon's cycle as it passes through the zodiac will heighten your ability to tune in your own body's frequency. Disease (which can be thought about as dis-ease) and illness occurs when one aspect of the body is not in rhythmic harmony with the rest of the body. For example, cancer cells multiply fast and are out of sync with the normal bodily rhythms. In liver disease, tissue and cells slow down and die because they cannot keep up with the deluge of toxins coming in. A key step in healing Moon work is to reconnect to the steady healthy rhythms found in nature. By tuning the body to those natural rhythms, the body has a greater chance to heal. One way to do this is to imagine that you are an orchestra playing a symphony. One of your violins is out of tune and playing erratically. This makes the entire orchestra sound bad. The conductor—you—signals the violin player to return to the main tempo, and to tune his instrument. As soon as that happens, the entire orchestra sounds wonderful again.

# Lunar Rituals for Better Health

In this next section I will discuss what areas of the body are ruled by the different constellations, and I suggest ways to harmonize with the influence of each sign. Rituals can be augmented by an altar or ritual space where symbolic tools can be placed. By adding these tools, you set the framework for healing at a deeper level. I also suggest different herbs, stones, and animal totems to work with during a ritual.

Creating a ritual can be very simple. First, bathe and cleanse yourself; then, from the list included here, select your symbolic objects—herbs, stones, animal totems, scents, and so on. I've listed ritual objects that are associated with each sign, but there are many more. Find a quiet space and create a small altar on which you can place your ritual objects to augment the power of the time. Then simply ask for guidance as you state your intentions and your prayers for healing.

## Aries

**Physical body:** Head

**Ritual objects:** Red candles, incense

**Totems:** Ram, shark, eagle, hawk, and wolf

**Stones and metals:** Garnet, iron

**Herbs:** Cayenne, cinnamon, garlic, ginger

**Scents:** Clove, cinnamon, and basil

Rituals done at this Moon time are helpful for strengthening the creative and initiating impulses. This is a great time to do a ritual for those of you who are feeling bogged down or stuck in a rut. Stagnancy can cause phlegm build up and weight gain. An Aries Moon is helpful for menstrual difficulties, when there is an excess of cramping or a lack of flow. Aries Moons are times to get the energy moving, and to open up your creative and passionate channels. It can also be helpful for people who want to start a new project and need to lay down their intentions in a prayerful manner.

## Taurus

**Physical body:** Throat, neck, thyroid gland
**Ritual objects:** Green candles, flowers, gentle music
**Totems:** Cow, bull, boar, bear, wren
**Stones and metals:** Copper, malachite, emerald
**Herbs:** Coltsfoot, sage, slippery elm
**Scents:** Rose, ylang-ylang

Taurus Moon rituals are helpful for grounding energy and getting firmly planted on the ground. When we have spun out of control, feel scattered in a million directions, or spread too thin and feeling incredible stress, Taurus Moon times can help you to find your center, peace, and stability. If you are manifesting nervous system complaints or stomach and intestinal disorders from anxiety and stress, a Taurus Moon ritual will help ground the energy and ease the strain. Taurus Moon phases are helpful if you want to get in touch with your sensual energy. Massage, gardening, lovemaking, cooking, and preparing a delicious meal are all wonderful activities for this phase.

## Gemini

**Physical body:** Arms, hands, lungs, nervous system
**Ritual objects:** Yellow or white candles, chimes, bells
**Totems:** Coyote, fox, butterfly, dragonfly
**Stones:** Agate, topaz
**Herbs:** Mullein, peppermint, vervain
**Scents:** Peppermint, thyme, lavender

When the Moon is in Gemini is a terrific time to increase your social life, and to help you think and speak clearly, with more intent. If you've had difficulty speaking up, or you've used your words and thoughts to be hurtful and destructive toward yourself or others, work with this Moon time to become more mindful of what you think and say. This is a good time to make prayers and set intentions around verbal and mental skills. What we say and think has a large impact on the community around us. Gemini is associated with the image of the messenger, and this is a good time to get in touch with what your essential message in life is.

## Cancer

**Physical body:** Breasts and stomach

**Ritual objects:** Blue candles, bowls of water, ocean pictures

**Totems:** Crab, frog, turtle, duck

**Stones and metals:** Moonstone, silver

**Herbs:** Cleavers, dill, lemon balm, nasturtium, willow

**Scents:** Jasmine, lemon balm

When the Moon is in Cancer is a good time to focus on the family, home, and nourishing yourself and loved ones. One of the best ways to do all of these things is to make a home-cooked meal with close friends and family. Sharing laughter, joy, and intimacy with friends and family around a table is one of the best ways to strengthen relationships and bring peace and happiness to a home. A well-made meal is also wonderfully nourishing to the body. If you feel emotionally stagnant, fearful, or insecure, a healing meal can help to dissolve anxiety. The Cancer Moon is also a good time to work on safety and security issues.

## Leo

**Physical body:** Heart

**Ritual objects:** Red and gold candles

**Totems:** Lion, elk, meadowlark, robin

**Stones and metals:** Amber, citrine, gold, ruby

**Herbs:** Borage, sunflower, St. John's wort, marigold

**Scents:** Amber, neroli

When the Moon is in Leo, take time to honor your inner child. If you have been feeling dull and lifeless, the Leo Moon can help you to harness the energy needed to break through blockages and open the door to a more joyful and playful self. Leo is associated with the child in all of us. It's easy for adults who are bogged down in the minutiae of day-to-day work and responsibilities to forget the child-self. The strong energy of a Leo Moon can remind you to laugh, play, and enjoy the pleasures of the moment—

like children do. Children are intrinsically involved in each moment, and acutely aware of their interactions and experiences. Leo Moons are also times to explore what it means to make a contribution to the world, to share special talents and gifts with others. Through expressing these unique abilities, we come into touch with our core of power and strength. We can channel our gift of making music, managing a business, doing healing work, or writing poetry, when we access the divine within. This light acts as a beacon to lift other people up, and to encourage others to develop their own gifts.

## Virgo

**Physical body:** Intestines, nervous system

**Ritual objects:** Green and dark-blue candles

**Totems:** Mouse, squirrel, bee

**Stones:** Jade, malachite

**Herbs:** Oats, red clover, cascara sagrada

**Scents:** Thyme, rosemary, fennel, sage

When the Moon is in Virgo is a good time to get in touch with three personal qualities: precision, mindfulness, and service. If you have been feeling scattered, and your efforts in the world have been sloppy—without consideration or care—the Virgo Moon can help bring you back into balance. One of Virgo's most important lessons is that, even the smallest detail in life is an essential aspect of a whole life. As much love and care should be devoted to the smallest details as given to the larger aspects of life. Washing dishes, doing laundry, and making a meal are essential to our human path. We can choose to see each action as a chore that we must hurry and finish or we can see each action as a way to develop greater care, compassion, and service in our lives. Small acts—cleaning the house for one's family, cooking a meal for a friend, praising a coworker's skills, or spending time with a child—are Virgo-type acts of service. Ultimately, most actions taken in life have something to do with relationships to others and to the Earth. The Moon in Virgo teaches us to be of service in all aspects of our lives.

## Libra

**Physical body:** Kidneys, lower back, abdomen

**Ritual objects:** White, light blue and yellow candles, feathers

**Totems:** Deer, rabbit, dove, swallow, swan

**Stones:** Rose quartz, jade

**Herbs:** Parsley, rose, licorice

**Scents:** Rose, raspberry

Libra is symbolic of balance. Balance is an important theme in all aspects of our life: relationships, work, family, and personal creative pursuits. Perhaps we have been focusing on one area of our lives at the expense of others. When the Moon is in Libra is a great time to work on balancing. This is a wonderful time to make prayers and intentions for the creation of new priorities that honor balance in all areas of your life. Libra Moons are also wonderful times to focus on partnerships—especially romantic partnerships. The Libra Moon provides a time to stoke up affection by honoring your partner's gifts and the qualities that made you love and admire them.

## Scorpio

**Physical body:** Sex and reproductive organs, colon, prostate, rectum

**Ritual objects:** Black and maroon candles, pictures of ancestors

**Totems:** Bat, crocodile, lizard, snake, owl

**Stones:** Obsidian, smoky quartz

**Herbs:** Basil, raspberry, sarsaparilla, garlic

**Scents:** Sage and patchouli

The Scorpio Moon is perhaps the most magical and transformative Moon. We can often feel things on a deep, intense level during these times. Scorpio Moons are times when we can acknowledge some of the darker aspects of our emotional life, the places of self-hatred and fear, but it is also a time when we can acknowledge our essential gifts and beauty, transforming the negative emotions with healing and love. This is a good time to release stuck emotional energy, and to connect to hidden and unseen realms. Spiritual and magical work is heightened tremendously at this time. Finally, the Scorpio Moon is associated with death and dying, making this is a good time to honor ancestors and give them thanks for their teachings and wisdom.

## Sagittarius

**Physical body:** Liver, hips, thighs, sciatic nerve

**Ritual objects:** Red and purple candles

**Totems:** Dog, elephant, horse

**Stones:** Amethyst, carnelian

**Herbs:** Echinacea, elder, chicory, dandelion

**Scents:** Sandalwood, juniper, cedar

When the Moon is in fire sign Sagittarius—a sign well-known for enjoying the rich life—there may be a deep desire to play, party, stay up late, eat rich food, and have a few drinks. It is good for us to really enjoy the pleasures of life, but we need to be careful about not overdoing it. This Moon time is also a good time to be an adventurer and explore life. If we have been too involved in the mundane details, this Moon can help us to open up and expand. The Sagittarius Moon can also have the quality of lighting one's social and creative fires. For those who are feeling a little lethargic, fatigued and have low energy, this could be a good time to get renewed and reinvigorated.

## Capricorn

**Physical body:** Skin, bones, teeth, knees

**Ritual objects:** Dark green and maroon candles

**Totems:** Beaver, mountain goat, crow, woodpecker

**Stones and metals:** Diamond, lead, onyx

**Herbs:** Comfrey, pine, plantain, horsetail, oak

**Scents:** Cedar and sage

The Capricorn Moon is a time for creating solid foundations and developing projects in our lives. If you have a hard time getting motivated and often procrastinate, the Capricorn Moon can help you develop the will power, ambition, and ability to move forward in life. Capricorn Moons are also times to tend to your physical, emotional, and spiritual foundations. If you do not have a firm footing, one based on authentic intentions, you can take a path in life that is not healthy. Examining foundations means looking at how we are setting up our lives on a fundamental level. The Capricorn Moon is a good time to adjust yourself so that your foundations are properly set.

## Aquarius

**Physical body:** Ankles, circulation, nervous system

**Ritual objects:** Light-blue or white candles, feathers, bells

**Totems:** Dolphin, hummingbird

**Stones:** Garnet, peridot

**Herbs:** Lavender, lobelia, skullcap

**Scents:** Eucalyptus, cinnamon, clove

The Aquarius Moon is a time to open up to revolutionary, progressive, and unusual ways of acting and thinking about life. Aquarius is associated with the divine spark of intelligence and enlightenment. This is a time to focus on group concerns. You can make intentions at this time to develop stronger bonds with your community, and to draw different diverse groups of people together. This is a time to examine how you use caffeine, sugar, and electronic stimulation, and how they are affecting your nervous system. If you are over-dosing on these things, it can be a time to find greater balance.

## Pisces

**Physical body:** Feet, immune system

**Ritual objects:** Blue and blue-green candles

**Totems:** Otter, salmon, seal, whale, great blue heron

**Stones:** Coral, opal, labradorite

**Herbs:** Kelp, horsetail, sage

**Scents:** Lotus, frankincense, sage

The Pisces Moon is associated with how we find transcendence in our lives. For some it comes through music and art. For others it comes from zen meditation, and for others it comes through a whiskey bottle. There are healthy and unhealthy ways to find transcendence. One of the best ways to work with the Pisces Moon is to explore your dreams. Examining dreams is an exploration of your unconscious, and it opens you up to important messages that are symbolically expressed through nighttime images. This is a time to see life from different perspectives. A Pisces Moon will help to open you up emotionally if you have been feeling shut down and cold. We are often more permeable to outside influences during this time, which makes it important to stay protected and grounded so you are not overwhelmed by outside influences.

### About the Author

Jonathan Keyes is an astrologer, herbalist, and writer living in Portland, Oregon. Recently, Jon's book *Guide to Natural Health: Using the Horoscope as a Key to Ancient Healing Practices* (Llewellyn, 2002) offers techniques for balancing and nourishing oneself optimally according to one's astrological birth chart. Jon also writes a regular New and Full Moon health column for StarIQ.com; and he has been published in the *Mountain Astrologer* and numerous Llewellyn almanacs. He has just finished a book titled *A Traditional Herbal,* which is due out the summer of 2004. This book is a practical guide to using medicinal herbs according to traditional European healing methods. Jon also enjoys digging around in his backyard, growing a medicinal herb garden, and playing with his cat.

# Timing Home Repairs and Improvements

## by Bruce Scofield

Home improvement has become an integral part of the American psyche. For many years now television shows have glamorized the methods and materials of what is a major hobby for many homeowners. What we see on television and in printed ads are happy people with the latest tools, top-quality working materials and products, and more importantly, a beautiful conclusion to their work. We see the home improvement projects in various stages of completion, mostly moving along like clockwork. What we don't see is what often happens to the rest of us when we take on a home repair or improvement ourselves—or when we hire a contractor to do the work for us. It just ain't that easy most of the time.

Before we get too far into our subject material, let's review a few astrological basics. The Moon itself symbolizes the home, the nest (the bedroom), and the family. It is probably the single most important factor in any astrological analysis of home improvement or repair. The Sun represents the center of the home, perhaps the fireplace or family hearth. In today's world this might be the family room or living room. Mars symbolizes the actual work that needs to be done—the banging, sawing, cutting, etc. Venus symbolizes the form and pattern of the work, which we always hope is aesthetically pleasing. Mercury symbolizes passageways, doors, and windows. Jupiter symbolizes largeness (even excessiveness) and the biggest rooms in the house. It's also the back yard deck. Saturn is the foundation, the cement pad that the house sits on, and the concrete or stone walls that maintain the integrity of the house. Uranus is electrical work, and Pluto is the plumbing. Neptune rules floors, walls, roofs, and ceilings, and is also about finishing things.

# Some General Advice

So you want to improve your home? You can do it yourself or hire a contractor. If you opt for someone else to do the work, it's important to begin with the right mindset. Having been a contractor myself, I can report that when work comes, it comes from everywhere. You can go a few weeks without a job and then Mars enters your Moon or Sun sign and suddenly you get calls from ten people who all want their decks and bathrooms done immediately. You've got to make a living, so you take all the jobs. Then comes the juggling part where you start one, go to the next, and start that, then another, then go back to the first, etc. If you're lucky you've got some helpers that will stay on a few of the jobs to make it look like something is happening. But if you're not, it can become like a silent film comedy. You will need to be in three or more places at once and you will need many excuses.

Now, if you're the customer and you've hired a contractor, what do you do when he fails to show up for three days; and then he spends two hours on your job, only to disappear again? You are at their mercy folks, and here's one bit of advice: *don't pay too much in advance*. A small deposit first, then payments as work is completed. But even better, don't hire somebody to work on your house when you've got planet trouble (see below) in your chart. The results could be messy.

## Pay Attention to the Planets and Moon

The same goes for the home handyman. Don't even start a project under threatening stars. You'll spend more time going back over what you did wrong than you'd care to admit. It will make you seem incompetent. Here's an example. You start a bathroom remodeling project on the day Mercury turns retrograde in your Moon sign (the sign the Moon was in when you were born). You try taking out the toilet, but one of the two bolts that holds it down is corroded and the nut is stuck. You pry it off, but you break the toilet in the process. This means you can't use that toilet ever again because it will leak. So you go down to the plumbing supply and find that the toilet you want has just gone out of stock and it will take four weeks to get another one. So what do you do? Buy a cheap toilet and use it until the good one comes in when Mercury finally turns direct?

Share the other toilet in the house with the other five people you live with? Use the backyard? This is a no-win situation and it began on the day Mercury turned retrograde in your Moon sign.

Not all Mercury retrograde periods are this frustrating, only the ones that connect with your chart in some way. But most of them will soon be revealed in the home improvement process because along the way you have to deal with other people. Take the building inspector, for example. You want to put a bedroom in your basement and you want to have it done by Labor Day so you can rent it to a college student. Mercury turns retrograde and then you call the inspector only to find out he's on an extended vacation and there's nothing you can do except wait. Or suppose you ask a friend to help you put up a deck. At the last minute he's got a problem somewhere and is not available that day—but he will be right there to help you in three weeks!

Three weeks later is when Mercury turns direct again, and it's often that long before all the snafus get worked out. My advice for those of you who happen to stupidly start a job within a day or two of Mercury turning retrograde is two-fold.

First, only do something you've either already started or want to do over again. If you started putting in a closet six months ago but smashed your finger with a hammer and couldn't finish the job, this might be a good time to have another go at it. Finish that closet while Mercury is running backward. If you remodeled your kitchen fifteen years ago and want to redo it, then great, the job will probably work out fine.

The second bit of advice I'd give to anyone who starts a job with Mercury turning retrograde is to stop immediately when you hit a wall (so to speak) and go onto something else, like having a beer and watching *The Red Green Show*. Wait a few weeks, then get back into the job again. You won't waste any time, and you'll be a better person for it. The only problem that may come up is having to explain your astrologic to other people, like your spouse who is skeptical of astrology. I suggest giving them a copy of this article. I'll go to bat for you.

One of the characteristics of a void-of-course Moon is actually not knowing exactly how things would turn out. One day I was sitting in my office talking to people on the telephone when I heard a loud crash from the other side of the house. Then another crash, and another. I ran to see what was happening and found my now ex-wife bashing the wall between the bedroom and the living room with a ten-pound sledgehammer. I said

"What the ___ are you doing?" She said, "I'm changing the floor plan of this house around and I'm not waiting for you to do it." Taking that to be an indication that she wanted to do it herself, I went back to my office and checked the ephemeris. The Moon was void-of-course. So I just sat back and let things go as they would. I wasn't about to take charge of that job, and I really didn't want to know anything about it either. It's good void-of-course Moon policy to have no expectations, and at that moment I don't think she did either. It all turned out fine in the end. I got on board the next day or so. The dangling wires were a bit of a problem, but we got around that. This was spontaneous void-of-course Moon home improvement. Just let it rip and see what happens.

People who start major home repair projects under a void-of-course Moon, and do have a definite vision of how things will turn out, are often deeply troubled by the final product. You might expect to have a fully functional kitchen, only to find out the refrigerator doesn't fit in its slot and you can't fully open two of the cabinets. Maybe some of this could be ascribed to poor planning and design, but I've seen many cases where void-of-course actions were exactly that—they drifted in some strange direction and consequently missed the mark. One of my clients decided to remodel her bathroom and kitchen and told the contractors to start on Tuesday at nine o'clock, when the Moon was direct and applying to a trine to Mars. Now, these are good astrological indicators of a job that gets done. Keeping the reputation of home improvement contractors intact, the guys showed up at eleven o'clock, when the Moon had gone void-of-course. So things got out of hand in a matter of days. The wrong floor was put in and

had to be torn up. The new fixtures required massive remodeling. The job went on for month after month. Now some of this could be ascribed to poor planning and unrealistic demands on the existing construction, but I think it was made worse by the general lack of focus that the contractors had about the job. At every point along the way nobody seemed to know what to do next. So think about the void-of-course Moon after you know when Mercury is going retrograde.

Here's another astrological challenge for home repairs and improvements: transiting Neptune. When this planet gets going, nobody knows what's happening. I can't tell you how many people I know who have found home repair or improvement to become incredibly complicated when it is begun under the influence of this planet. Here's the rule: if transiting Neptune is making a hard aspect (square, opposition, quincunx, etc.) to your Sun or Moon, it's time for a time-out. This is a signal to rethink what you want to do. Do not go headfirst into something you don't understand. Usually, Neptune problems have to do with leaks. Bathrooms and kitchens are places where leaks are waiting to happen. There's not only water leaks, but if you use gas to cook there could be problems there as well. What to do? Well, first keep calm and realized that you are really having a vision crisis of some sort. Maybe you really don't know what you want, or maybe you know exactly what you want but you can't get it. Don't frustrate yourself. Be patient, be sure you have made good closure with your past and move along at a slow pace. You'll get there, and with less wear and tear than if you try to force your half-baked or rigid visions over an unwilling kitchen or bath.

By now you must be saying to yourself, "Home improvement and repair is a problem waiting to happen. Get me out of here." Don't be discouraged. I've got a remedy that requires only that you look at your house, and maybe your car, too, as an extension of who you are. Think about your kitchen and bath as your deeper psychological self. These areas of the house have pipes that are connected to places you don't want to go—but then sometimes you have to. When you remodel or repair your bathroom, you are symbolically digging into a part of your brain, a part that needs to be ventilated perhaps, or maybe exorcised. When you paint your bedroom you are trying to change and improve your deep sense of feeling safe and secure. Bedrooms are very lunar—all about nesting and nurturing. Living rooms are about getting along with people. Additions are obviously indications of a need to grow. All the rooms and parts of a house have a symbolic meaning, and each has its own unique set of challenges, and there are a few astrological pointers that can lead to success in home repairs and decoration.

## Find Jupiter, Saturn, Uranus, Neptune, and Pluto

First, consider where Jupiter is. When Jupiter transits your Moon sign, it may a good time for an expansion of some sort in your home. Maybe you need an addition, or maybe you need to move somewhere else, to a larger space, and then improve it. The same kind of urges may arise when Jupiter passes through your Sun sign. When Saturn transits your Moon or Sun sign, conditions are reversed. These are times for repairs and even for making things tighter, smaller, and more efficient. Get practical about what you want to do under Saturn. Maybe routine maintenance is the right thing for this planet. If Pluto is transiting near the degree of your Moon or Sun sign, it could indicate the need for a renovation, or perhaps fixing up the basement and replacing old pipes. Uranus brings strange, often unexpected, improvisatory, and electrical home repair themes into prominence.

One of the problems with using astrology to time your repairs and improvements is that weather is often a factor that doesn't cooperate with your careful plans. I should also add that this is a major factor if you happen to live in New England where weather patterns are unstable. You decide to start a back yard deck on a day when the Moon is making great aspects to the other planets, it's not void-of-course, and Mercury is moving direct. However, on that day it's raining steadily, and rain continues for the next three days. You've lost your window of opportunity and your spouse is laughing at you. What do you do? Short of learning how to do astrometeorology, I'd say you should always have some back-up dates on hand. Don't pick a single day for an outside job (unless you live in California). Be ready to strike when the Moon is right, but know when that will be for the next two weeks.

Here's another angle on using the Moon. If you've got a bathroom or kitchen to fix, start it when the Moon is in a water sign. If you want to work on your living room, or any room in which you entertain people or are active in, start it when the Moon is in a fire sign. If you need to work on your yard, garden, or landscaping, do it when the Moon is in an earth signs. And when the Moon is in an air sign, work on your phone system, your sound system, your sidewalk, and your driveway.

The astrological timing of a home improvement is something worth considering. The cost of materials and labor, or your own valuable time, can be quite high for many projects. Take your time in preparing for any work on your house. Make sure your plans make good sense and then pick a few possible start dates based on the above information. As for home repairs, these often come at inopportune times—its just the way things are. Breakdowns occur under stressful transits, and there you are having to do the repair under these same stressful transits. If you can wait until a more favorable time arises, great, but if not proceed slowly and don't be afraid to ask for advice. In either case, try to enjoy the process of pulling your home together and making it a better environment for you to live in.

## About the Author

Bruce Scofield, C.A. NCGR, is a professional astrological consultant who works with clients in the U.S. and abroad. He has a master's degree in history and level four certification from NCGR. As a consulting astrologer, he specializes in both psychological astrology and electional astrology. His special interest is the astrology of ancient civilizations, especially those of the Maya and Aztec civilzations. He is the author of thirteen books and numerous magazine and journal articles, and is on the faculty of Kepler College.

# How Not to Buy a House

*by Marlene Utescher*

This is the story of a lady who was looking to purchase a house. She was doing her homework by checking the real-estate ads in the newspapers and going to open houses. In July 2001, while she was out doing errands one day she saw a "For Sale" sign on a little ranch-style house, which is what she had been hoping to find. She called the number listed on the sign and found out the asking price was more than she could afford. In December, she happened to go down the same street again, and there was the house, still for sale, so she called the number again. The price had come down and she felt it might be negotiable, so she made an appointment to see the house on December 9, 2001. The agent for the house, who was leaving on a six-week vacation, told the lady that she would have to come to the office to sign the paperwork and write a check for the earnest money on the same afternoon if she was interested in it.

The woman walked through the house and liked it. The yard was fenced and the basement was finished, including a small second kitchen. It was perfect! She went back to the office with the agent, signed the paperwork and wrote an earnest money check for $10,000.

The agent returned from vacation one day before the closing, which was set for January 28, 2002. The woman buying the house had one hour to do her walk-through and inspection before the closing. What they found when they arrived at the house was, in short, a disaster. The old owners had shut off the heat in the house sometime after December 9 and the water pipes had frozen and broke. Upon inspecting the exterior of the house they found the gutters on one side of the house had broken away from the edge of the roof and were hanging down. Once inside, they found a place where the roof had leaked, leaving a huge water mark on the living room ceiling. When the buyer and agent went into the basement, they found that neither the washer nor dryer worked. The agent's husband, a retired gas company employee, had accompanied them. He was unable to find where the furnace air filter would go. The buyer also wondered why the basement windows were covered with a heavy plastic held in place with duct tape. They removed the tape on one window and discovered there were no window frames. Apparently, when the owners paneled the basement they simply left an open hole in the wall where the window should have been. All the basement windows were treated the same way.

The buyer decided not to go through with the closing, but the attorney said the contract was "tied up," and she would not be able to get her earnest money returned. She would either have to forfeit the $10,000 or be sued by the previous owners. This was a disaster for the woman, a senior citizen, who had saved money for years to buy a house. But the reality of having to do so much repair work was too much and she forfeited the earnest money. This was a terrible experience, and as a result, the woman lost not only her money but her health, too.

## What Does the Astrology Have to Say?

The chart of the "Appointment to See the House" could have helped the woman to make decisions during the buying process. At the very top of the chart is the planet Neptune (illusion, cheaters, camouflage, dreamers, floods, secrets). This indicates that the buyer was looking through "rose-colored glasses," and seeing what she wanted to see. The house was everything she had hoped and wished it would be. With the Moon trine Uranus, and the time pressures of the agent's vacation being a factor, the woman impulsively signed the paperwork and wrote the check for the earnest money.

The Taurus Ascendant tells us that circumstances were changing, as was born out by the seller shutting off the heat and the water pipes breaking. Also, with such a late degree on the Ascendant we know the situation was already over before it had even begun. In addition, this degree of Taurus is associated with blindness (literally, not seeing), and the defects in the house were not seen by the buyer.

The planet Saturn in Gemini is "hidden" (below) the Ascendant in Taurus. The house had been on the market for eight months, too long of a time. This Saturn forms powerful opposition aspects with Venus, Pluto, the Sun, and Mercury in the seventh house. In contracts such as this, the first house would represent the seller. It turned out that this house had a history of contractual problems. Three buyers were unable to qualify financially. One buyer had already lost $1,000 earnest money, and one buyer had simply walked away. Saturn in the first house shows the hidden responsibilities the buyer would need to assume if she purchased the property. Saturn opposing Venus, Pluto, and the Sun show it would be extremely expensive to perform the repairs.

The chart for the "Closing of the House" was not much better. The tenth house cusp represents the value of the property. With Saturn as the ruler of Capricorn in the tenth, it is clear the house was worth much less than it would at first seem to be. And with Saturn retrograde in the second house, it shows additional costs and a lot of work to bring the house into proper condition.

We see the first degree of Taurus on the Ascendant, indicating a "new" course of action the buyer took. The Moon (ruler of Cancer) is powerfully placed in its home house (fourth), but it's not in its home sign, which is Cancer. The Moon forms a tight opposition to Mercury (walking away), the Sun (the deal), and Neptune (water damage and extreme emotions). The hidden factors are also represented by the Sun-Neptune conjunction.

Finally, the loss of the earnest money is indicated by the sign of Gemini on the cusp of the second house. Saturn is placed close to the cusp here, and forms a powerful opposition to Pluto in the eighth house. Add to this the fact that the ruler of the second house (Mercury) is retrograde, and it is clear that any money involved will be lost.

This is a situation where the appearance seemed perfect, but when something seems too good to be true, it usually is. Astrology could have helped this woman. If she had scheduled the first appointment with more favorable aspects, perhaps the problems would have been revealed before she signed the papers. This is an example of how astrology can be helpful, especially when one needs to make significant life decisions.

### About the Author

Marlene Utescher lives in Chicago, Illinois, where she is an active member of Friends of Astrology, the oldest astrological association in Chicago.

# Business
# and
# Legal
# Section

# Economic Watch 2004

### by Dorothy J. Kovach

Reality has cast a long shadow over Wall Street, and we are forced to face reality: the stock market is not a slot machine that pays out at steady intervals. Instead, it is a place of risk—big risk. If you think the government, banks, or venture capitalists control the ebb and flow of business cycles, it's not true. Our business cycles are controlled by the celestial entities, especially Jupiter and Saturn. Together, these two titans of business determine what investments go up and when they will come down. Jupiter represents irrational exuberance, while Saturn signifies the corrections that force the market down to reality. Knowing where these two last met is important, and their last meeting took place in the sign of Taurus in May 2000. Knowing the sign they met in is important because it is the basis for what consumers will buy, as well as what will be shunned for the next fourteen years. (In December 2013, retrograde Jupiter in Cancer will make a square to Saturn in Scorpio, thereby changing the cycle.) One way we will experience the influence of Taurus is by demanding value for money spent. In a nutshell, tech is out and manufacturing is in.

The wise investor will take a critical inventory of his or her assets. If your portfolio possesses even a few non-performing network or technology-driven issues, get rid of them. This is not the time to be sentimental. Only the bluest of technology stocks are recommended and then only those companies with substantial cash on hand and little or no debt. Again, Microsoft comes to mind. Stocks should be bought for the long haul.

The airline industry will continue its losing ways, because of it connection to the air element, but like their computing cousins there will always be winners in losing sectors. Even if people fly less often, they will not give up flying altogether.

Knowing what to do in a bear economy can spell the difference between security and disaster. Basically, 70 percent of stocks move with the market regardless of their virtues. This is great in a bull market, because the rich get richer (or think they do). However, no matter what spin your broker puts on it, we are firmly entrenched in a bear market, so that trend is reversed. During a bear market, securities become undervalued. Just as the dollar value of tech stocks were outrageously overvalued during the bullish climate of 1980s and 90s, stock in solid companies may well be undervalued during a bear market.

---

Market Tip: Look to the best-run airlines when investing. Southwest Airlines comes to mind.

---

Since the general direction of money trends upward, the wise investor can find bargains, but only if you buy company stocks at their real value, not book value. For instance, if the market crashed tomorrow, the odds are high that companies like General Motors and Proctor Gamble will still be here. We must know the difference between the trading price and the underlying value of the company in order to make wise investing decisions. Buying company stock with the idea of holding it for the long term is suggested, but do your homework. The climate is extremely risky.

---

Market Tip: Review the contents of your portfolio on a quarterly basis, with an eye to getting rid of non-performers at each upswing. It is recommended to put a larger percentage of assets in more stable investments, like real estate, bonds, metals (gold and silver), and of course, that favorite of Taurus—CASH.

---

## Jupiter in Virgo

### Overview

Where Jupiter is by sign will give some indication about which industries will do well in the upcoming year. Jupiter is in Virgo, having entered that sign on August 28, 2003. When Jupiter stations, we should expect the market to change course. The market tends to go up when Jupiter is in direct motion, and turn downward when it retrogrades. Jupiter will turn retrograde on January 3, 2004, at 18 degrees Virgo, and it will turn direct on May 5, 2004, at 9 degrees Virgo.

People looking for jobs in an ever-shrinking economy may find success in the health care industry (associated with Virgo). Many workers abandoned the health professions in the 90s with the advent of the HMO. Now, there is a shortage of medical professionals to meet the demands due to our population of graying baby boomers. Coverage is expensive. Many, especially the self-employed, still go without insurance. With hospitals closing in record numbers over the past twenty years, there are fewer and fewer beds in a country with an aging population.

The smart politician will not lose sight of this most important of issues, during this election year. The last time Jupiter was in Virgo, Bill Clinton

> Market Tip: Invest in businesses that will help an aging population.

got elected on the issue of health care reforms. Smart candidates will have some sort of workable solution to this thorny crisis. Health maintenance organizations will continue to be big winners in 2004. With more people desiring to be fit, businesses from gyms to health care professionals will see a lot of business in 2004.

Above all, when Jupiter is in Virgo (symbolized by the Virgin), purity will be an obsession. The threat of getting cancer from chemicals and pesticides in our food and environment is real. We want to know that our food is healthy. We are less trusting than ever of chemical additives in food and bioengineered foods on the market. Many of us are willing to spend the extra money for organic produce, range-fed organic meat and dairy products to avoid medical problems later in life. Organic is no longer the provenance of peculiar "health nuts." People are putting their money where their mouth is. Agribusiness is finally realizing that they will see higher profits by devoting more acreage to growing organic products, rather than using expensive chemicals that people will shun.

## Jupiter in Libra

### Overview

Jupiter enters Libra on September 26, 2004, but it will not station in Libra until February 2005. The goddess of beauty, Venus, rules Libra. So, we can expect anybody who designs, paints, decorates, or otherwise makes life more pleasant for us to do well in 2004. This is an excellent placement for companies that produce make up and perfumes.

### What it All Means

Weddings will provide a good business boost. People like to tie the knot under this influence, and the bridal industry will benefit from a higher than average number of marriages beyond June 2005.

The image of Libra has changed over the centuries. Libra is very much a human sign, and as such it is connected to the idea of human rights. Libra's symbol, the scale, is indicative of the scales of justice held in the hands of man. Libra is intrinsically tied to fairness, making democracy an issue synonymous with Libra. Expect to see human rights become an important issue in the 2004 election campaign as we seek answers to the question about how much right to privacy we are entitled to during a war on terrorism.

Some astrologers say that because the Democratic Party is the older of the two parties that Saturn is its ruler. That leaves Jupiter to rule the Repub-

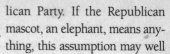

lican Party. If the Republican mascot, an elephant, means anything, this assumption may well be true. So, Jupiter leaving Virgo (where it is considered debilitated) and transiting into the air sign Libra (where it is thought to be stronger) may well be a good omen for the Republicans.

In practical-loving Virgo, Jupiter is not comfortable because that energy is the opposite of Jupiter's "fat cat" temperament. This may give the Republicans an edge at the polls. Since Jupiter has to do with upward movement in the markets, Jupiter's ingress into Libra should be an improvement for the stock market. No, it will not bring back the boom days we enjoyed in the 1990s, but it does give hope for a financial future that is not quite as painful as in our recent past.

## Saturn in Cancer

*Whiskey is for drinking, water is for fighting over.*—Mark Twain

### Overview

Saturn entered Cancer in June 2003, and it will stay in Cancer until August 2005. Saturn rules business, and Saturn stations mark market downturns. Saturn turns retrograde on October 24, 2003. It will be in retrograde motion until March 7, 2004, when it again turns direct. The times surrounding these stations is critical for business markets and people everywhere.

### What it All Means

Saturn is sitting in the spot of the nation's chart that traditionally is associated with our earnings—the second house. What this means is that there will be fewer resources to go around, and we need to squirrel away as much money as we can in safe places. Worrying about debts can cause ulcers. This is especially true when Saturn is in Cancer (ruler of the stomach), and why it is more important than ever, with interest rates low, to

---

Market Tip: Bounty will be found in the business of beauty.

---

pay off credit card debt. Many credit cards carry with them high interest rates. In a time of less money to go around, cutting interest payments is one of the easiest ways to cut costs and save for a rainy day.

With Saturn in Cancer—the sign of oceans, lakes, and streams—water becomes a precious commodity. You should be aware that some in the business world have plans for your water. Schemes run the gamut from gaining water rights to bagging excess water as it flows from rivers into the ocean. The bagged water would be sent to thirsty desert metropolises like Los Angeles and San Diego.

In the east, years of drought and overfishing have left the fish population in trouble, and forced fishermen to find other means of earning a living. Continued unrest at our nation's ocean ports—longshoremen grappling with new technology and ship owners eyeing a large non-union population waiting in the wings—remains a problem, too. With Saturn in Cancer, problems will linger on the oceans. Everything from oil spills to potential terrorism will threaten until Saturn's trek through Cancer is over in August 2005.

When it comes to the stock market, only investors with strong stomachs need apply. We must separate thinking from emotions (Saturn in Cancer) if we are to have success in 2004. Saturn will continue to be our leading economic indicator, and because of this fear—an emotion linked

to Saturn in Cancer—will permeate the markets. Domestic life suffers as worries about security intensify.

While Saturn is in the sign of our nation's Sun—Cancer, and with less money to spend and uncertainty about conditions abroad persisting—people will be more introspective than in years past. We are sure to see a rise in depression, resulting in people seeking relief in prescription drugs. Expect the sales of antidepressants to continue growing.

Cancer also represents those things maternal in our lives, and mothers may be especially hard hit by this transit of Saturn through Cancer. Saturn's last station in this sign marked the height of the antiwar protest in the early 1970s.

When the stock market turned down a few years back, many of us decided to invest in more stable issues like real estate. As we know, demand drives prices, and housing prices have gone through the roof.

When any sector goes up quickly, there is the chance of a bubble occurring. A bubble takes place when demand followed by large influxes of money cause a given sector to grow at a far faster rate than the actual worth of a product or sector. The sector is said to be "on fire." Eventually, the price gets so high that it is out of reach, and like a bubble it bursts.

The best example of a bubble in recent history was the tech boom of the late 90s, when the computer-laden NASDAQ was bursting at 5,000. Some Internet companies that were trading for over a $100 a share never even turned a profit. There was only one way to go: down. Likewise, some houses that were selling for half a million dollars are not worth that in real value. Saturn always bursts bubbles, and Saturn transits through Cancer can feel especially harsh.

What happened to the tech sector could easily happen to the real-estate market because many of the high-paying jobs generated by the stock market are gone. In order to keep real estate prices up, those jobs will have to be replaced by new jobs. This cannot happen unless the stock market goes up. Knowing that the stock market is not going to return to its pre-2000 value may have a sobering effect on real estate. This may be especially true in cities that were either highly dependent on the stock market, like New York, or places that housed tech industries, like the San Francisco Bay area and Silicon Valley.

There is good news, though. Prices that have been ridiculously high are coming down, and in some places housing is becoming more affordable.

However, in places where the economy does not recover, a brisk business in home foreclosures might be expected.

With Saturn in Cancer and Jupiter in Virgo, we will need to be especially careful against outbreaks of disease. The threat of bioterrorism is very real under this combination. The great influenza outbreak after World War I took place when Jupiter and Saturn echoed their present locations—Jupiter in Virgo and Saturn in Cancer—so take precautions.

If you're not thinking about the Social Security fund, you ought to be. As of this writing, a projected 5.6-trillion-dollar budget surplus has vanished. The projected surplus was based in part on the idea that we would be reaping more due to a reduction in defense spending. But with the war on terrorism heating up, defense spending is way up while tax cuts from the Bush administration has meant less money going into the government. Lower taxes and higher spending means that more money is going out than is coming in, making the dollar go down in value. We can buy less, and one does not have to be an accountant to see that this does not add up.

Two thousand and four is an election year. Wise voters will insist that their candidates have a workable plan regarding Social Security that does not involve the stock market!

> Market Tip: We can expect companies that make drugs to soothe our tummies to do well in 2004. However, Astra Zeneca (AZNCF), maker of Prilosec, whose "little purple pill" has done so well in recent years, may see a downturn in late March.

# The President and the Inauguration Chart

*There is no truth more thoroughly established than that there exists in the economy and course of nature an indissoluble union between virtue and happiness, between duty and advantage.*

George Washington
(From his inaugural speech, 30 April 1789)

The ancients believed that a country was subject to the chart of its ruler. They also believed that subjectivity began at the moment the man took his first breath as ruler. The same theory applies today. To know what lies in our economic future, we need to know about President Bush's fortunes. To know our weaknesses, we need only look to Bush's weaknesses. (George W. Bush, born 06 July 1946, 7:26 am Eastern Daylight Time, New Haven, Connecticut.)

George Walker Bush has Leo rising in his natal chart, which means that the Sun rules his chart. According to astrological rulership, the Sun rules gold as well as many other things. It's of interest that in the years since George W. Bush became our president we have seen the price of gold rise.

Bush has the North Node, also known as the Dragon's Tail, placed in the fifth house of speculation. The Dragon's Tail is known for symbolically "draining" whatever it touches. We need look no further than the stock market to know that the Bush presidency has been terrible for all types of speculation. But, while Bush may be bad for stocks, he is great for real estate. Bush's chart possesses a Moon-Jupiter conjunction right on the sector of the chart that has to do with our homes and families, the fourth house. In a sense, as long as George Bush is president, the real-estate market will be somewhat protected. For most Americans, the single greatest investment is not in the stock market, but in their home, so we are all fortunate that he has this placement. It acts, to a certain extent, as a counter-balance to Saturn.

Incumbent presidents who are engaged in war almost always have a natural edge in political races, and this is especially true for Bush after his birthday in 2004. According to the astrological premise that no event is stagnant but continues to grow and change (as reflected in progressed astrological charts), the inauguration chart is not a stagnant event, either. That chart, like the presidency, changes with the times.

If we wish to know what 2004 will bring, we need only look at Bush's inauguration solar return—the date, one year later, when the Sun returns to the exact degree it was in when the event took place—to see the highlights of the coming year. (Solar return for Bush's inauguration is 21 January 2004, 10:27 am EST, 77W00, 38N53, Ascendant 29 Sagittarius.)

The original Bush inauguration chart (20 January 2001, 12:01 pm, EST), with its Taurus Ascendant, echoes Bush's practical and traditional, though, "down home" values. In hindsight, we can also see the horror that was 9/11 in Bush's inauguration chart. The Moon and Pluto sit on either side of that chart's eighth house of endings, death, taxation, and inheritance.

With the last degree of Sagittarius rising, Americans should use utmost caution when traveling abroad as anti-American sentiment is at an all time high. Pluto tied to the Part of Fortune in the twelfth house implies that terrorists may be operating behind the scenes. It also implies that American interests are once again vulnerable to subtle attack. Government surveillance will be working overtime with this aspect operative. Uncertainty continues to be the watchword of the year ahead.

Another problem in 2004 will come to President Bush's closest adviser in 2004. This implies that Vice President Cheney should take every measure to protect his health. If he does not, he could be in severe jeopardy during the first half of the year.

The bleak economic picture does have a silver lining, though. Saturn, the ruler of our nation's money, is in a perfect trine to Venus in Bush's solar return chart. Venus and Saturn might represent stock in companies that keep an aging population youthful. We all want to look younger, and we could see modern medicine come up with new methods to bring this about.

There is a quiet revolution going on in our oceans as great discoveries are rising from our ocean floors. Major innovations in the way oil is drilled will allow us to tap the wealth buried deep within the oceans. We are poised to see the harvesting of vast new oil deposits, which are buried deep in the ocean near places like Indonesia and Russia, begin soon. New drilling techniques will help to lessen our dependence upon oil from the Middle East. We might also see the price of oil and gas come down toward the end of the year. We might also see great innovations in the search for underwater treasure. New methods for remaining stable on top of the ocean will be utilized. This will aid in all oceanic operations, such as the surveying ships and in the cleanup of those unfortunate toxic spills. All these changes may be due to a grand trine in the inauguration chart in the water signs, between the North Node, Saturn, and Uranus.

I have a final note about Bush's solar return chart. With the Moon in the seventh house of his 2004 solar return chart, Bush is advised to never underestimate the power of women.

---

Market Tip: Companies in the business of surveillance—from private investigators to hidden camera companies—will do well in this climate; and plastic surgery and companies that work with technology to trick the hand of time are slated to make gains in 2004.

---

## Winter Solstice: 22 December 2003

### Overview

One technique the ancients used to forecast for the year to come was to draw a chart for the exact moment the seasons changed. Our business year begins January 1, so we will begin with the season change closest to that date, the Winter Equinox. That is when the Sun enters 0 degrees Capricorn in 2003.

### What it all Means

There is no place like home for the holidays. With Venus in the sector of the chart representing "home sweet home," and Saturn in the ninth house of far away places, this may well be the year to stay home instead of traveling. We can expect trouble on our oceans, waterways, and roads, but especially those places by the sea. This is due to the Moon's very close relationship to Pluto in the third house of the chart for the Winter Solstice. This Moon-Pluto conjunction indicates problems for any kind of travel—long distance or short. Due to the placement, my sense is that the conjunction in the third house of travel and communication spells trouble, especially for truckers and other highway travelers.

The Moon is very important in a seasonal chart because it represents the people. It is worrisome, then, when the people's representative is tied to Pluto, god of the underworld, because lives may be lost where these two meet.

In this chart, they meet close to the third house of local highways and railroads. Add all this together, and the potential for

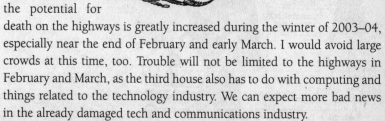

death on the highways is greatly increased during the winter of 2003–04, especially near the end of February and early March. I would avoid large crowds at this time, too. Trouble will not be limited to the highways in February and March, as the third house also has to do with computing and things related to the technology industry. We can expect more bad news in the already damaged tech and communications industry.

The air sign Libra is on the Ascendant of the 2003 Winter Solstice chart. This means, among other things, that Americans will be forced to balance their books. Consumers will finally stop fueling an economy gone sour. Dismal sales and a stock market heading for the floor make this winter season anything but jolly. Our incomes are just not what they used to be, and we must adjust to leaner times. The Dragon's Tail (North Node) in the eighth house of this chart is a distinct signal that money will continue to go down the drain.

The South Node (directly opposite the North Node) is in the very sign—Scorpio—that it was in during the crash of 1929. This is not a good omen for Wall Street. In fact, it is yet another sign of strain on the market and an indication that we may not have seen the bottom yet. The value of the dollar might be quite low as capital flees the market. With the Node placed in Scorpio, and with Saturn in the ninth (foreign interests), we will be keeping one eye open as we worry about our family and comrades abroad.

There is good news, though. Credit is still rather easy to come by, as indicated by the North Node's placement in the eighth house. This is a great time to pay down our credit card debts.

## Spring Equinox: 20 March 2004

### Overview

The chart for the Spring Equinox is an indicator of general trends during the next three months. It will be important to ask ourselves: at what price does security come? Can we afford an isolationist stance? Will we allow the government's spying to cut into our freedoms? We will have to ask ourselves these questions with Pluto and the Part of Fortune sharing the same place in the twelfth house. We may also be dealing with circumstances left over from last winter.

## What It All Means

The focus this spring will be on making do with less. Saturn is the natural ruler of diminishing returns, and in the Spring Equinox chart Saturn rules the nation's collective income. This is not a good sign for business. Business lags when Saturn is in Cancer. The lag is even more pronounced when Cancer and Saturn are placed in the seventh house. It is like, what little money we do have (restriction from Saturn) is being spent elsewhere (seventh house is "others"). This placement indicates that our deficit will mount as we spend money overseas.

The saying, "What the market hates is uncertainty" is true. The markets certainly will be hateful this spring. Bad news in the second quarter threatens to bring an already flattened economy to a stand still. Stocks that promised to rebound years ago continue to slump. Meanwhile, the dual threat of biological and nuclear war continues to weigh heavily on the stock market.

As a nation, we may be very intent on what is happening in the war on terrorism, remaining resolute, though worried. International admonitions will continue, directed at what some consider meddling in affairs that do not concern us.

The first house has to do with the people of this nation, while the seventh house has to do with people elsewhere, especially those who are our known enemies. As in recent years, we will be spending more time engaging other nations, and this involvement will surely cost us. But more than this, it is precarious for a nation that is represented by the Sun in Cancer to be positioned in the seventh house because it is as if we are on enemy territory.

## Summer Solstice: 21 June 2004

Business, or rather, the lack of it, remains on all of our minds with the sign of Capricorn perched at the Ascendant of yet another seasonal chart. This is an indication that we will be dealing with many of the same issues that we dealt with in the spring—job losses and a general uncertainty regarding our future as a nation. Saturn so placed in the sign opposite its home sign of Capricorn may create in us the feeling of being more vulnerable than usual. The American public is aging rapidly. Social security, health care, and effects of the war on terrorism will be very much on our minds.

Fiscally, the American public may be feeling a stretched and insecure. America's policies will continue to be highly controversial, and like last season, Americans who live in foreign countries should use extra care. The

American public will have to make do with less, as our collective income seems to vanish as fast as it comes in. Much of the goods that we rely on for our day to day life, are manufactured on foreign shores.

With the war on terrorism being fought on multiple fronts, our dollars can only continue to lose value against other currencies. The slumping economy will not help President Bush this season, as indicated by the South Node placed in the tenth house, which represents the executive branch of government. Democratic candidates who focus on the weakness in the economy may move ahead in the polls during the summer months.

All is not bleak, however. The health and beauty sectors may be the first glimmer of light to a dark and battered market place. (Venus trines both the Part of Fortune and Neptune in the nation's 2nd house.) We cannot expect this to carry an entire sagging economy, though.

## Fall Equinox: 22 September 2004

As autumn leaves fall, we become less preoccupied with the economy and more concerned with religious extremists. With Sagittarius on the Ascendant and Pluto in the first house, some of us may find ourselves grappling with questions about whether the cost of security is worth the loss of freedom. We may hear of some good news in the overseas war as Pluto receives a trine from Venus in the ninth house of faraway places. We also might see a pickup in war-related contractors, especially after Thanksgiving, when North Node moves into war-loving Aries on November 30.

> Market Tip: Look for disruption in the weeks before Easter to bring the markets down.

Finally, some positive earnings numbers spell relief, and the economy gets good news in the form of a nice trine from the nation's second house of money, where the Moon sends a trine to Mercury. We might see the tech sector pick up a bit as orders for new equipment come in. Be advised that while the trine between the Moon and Mercury is good, it is most assuredly not a return to the good old days of the late 90s. The fundamentals are still not solid, but there is reason to be encouraged. (The ruler of the chart, optimistic Jupiter, is just about to change into a sign more of his liking—Libra—which has been historically good for the computing issues.) However, again, it is important to remember that this is an up period in a larger bear cycle, so we will still have to be very cautious with our money. Those who have sidelined some cash might begin to get their feet wet again by investing in well-run companies with solid track records that are trading well below their real value. However, buying stocks is tricky at any time and one should only do so with the utmost of care.

# The Market Month by Month

## January 2004

Markets are volatile. The Moon is very influential this season and markets will see much fluctuation. Home product and products for women are highlighted. Market turns positive around the 15th, downward on 21st, and up again on the 26th.

## February 2004

Markets are pessimistic until the 24th, when good news in the ailing computing industry is finally here. Markets turn skittish at the end of the month.

## March 2004

Markets are mixed but some good news around the 9th spurs the markets upward until around the 20th. Threats of terrorism are high toward the end of the month. This keeps the market down. Sales of pharmaceuticals is favored.

## April 2004

Nerves are tattered on Wall Street at the beginning of the month, but investors are less worried by the second week, only to continue their volatility on the 14th. Good news from government contractors brings market up around the 17th, but down again near the end of the month.

## May 2004

First few days are worrisome, but the market begins to turn around on 5th only to fall back to fear around the 10th, when bad news sends markets into a spin. From the 11th until the 21st, gold is favored. Markets finally have a solid rally the last week.

## June 2004

June opens on an optimistic note and for once remains so for much of the month. Stocks are bullish until the 6th, again on the 13th, and with some fluctuation on the 19th, when some profits are taken. War-related stocks are favored.

## July 2004

This month opens on a more worrisome note but a good rally occurs around the 8th and the market bounces back, only to turn downward around the 12th when bad news turns markets sour.

## August 2004

August opens down, but optimism returns to the market about the 5th. Some bad news around the 8th takes the wind from her sails, but optimism returns near the 16th only to vanish between the 23rd and the 26th.

## September 2004

Worry plagues the market place in the initial weeks of September. They ease after the third anniversary of 9/11, and the market turns positive until around the 28th, when fear returns. Gold is bullish for the rest of the month.

## October 2004

Markets are especially volatile from the 6th onward. Ripples are sent through the market place around the 18th, and there's a little upswing around the 27th, but much rumbling will be heard at this time.

## November 2004

Markets are solemn around Election Day, turning upward on the 14th, but bad news on the 22nd sends jitters through the market turning them pensive for the remainder of the month.

## December 2004

Dismal holiday sales send markets downward until the 13th when they recover nicely after the solstice. At last, some positive economic indicators turn the market merrier this holiday season.

## About the Author

Dorothy J. Kovach is a full-time astrologer, trends and timing expert based in northern California. She acts as a consultant to both businesses and persons interested in finding the very best time to start projects for successful outcomes, from surgery, starting new businesses, to saying "I do." Her specialty is in the field of answering direct questions, known as horary astrology. For the past decade, she has been successfully applying the ancient methods to predict the financial markets. She is best known for having called the end of the bull market to the month, some five years in advance, and in March of 2001, the wise to divest their holdings on the NASDAQ by the fall of 2001. She was a regular contributor to the *Horary Practitioner*, and her articles have appeared in media such as the *Astrological Association*, *The Traditional Astrologer*, and www.stariq.com. She wrote the economic forecast for Llewellyn's *2003 Moon Sign Book*.

You may reach her by e-mail at Dorothy@worldastrology.net, or at her website: www.worldastrology.net.

## References:

*Christian Astrology* by William Lilly

*Prophetical Merlin* by William Lilly

*Dark Year* by William Lilly

*Introduction to Astrology* by Kusyar Ibn Labban, edited by Michio Yano

# Great Salesmanship with Your Moon

## by Leeda Alleyn Pacotti

Selling may appear to be the solitary province of business or commercialism, but, like the Moon, it reaches deeply into the human psyche. Selling requires an understanding, finding a common basis, or sharing an inner motivation to produce satisfaction for both seller and customer. Although this understanding may be short-lived, it flows from a specific inner need, successfully propelled by the seller.

Such successful sellers have some common attributes. They interact by listening; they discover the real desires of customers; and they know satisfaction over a purchase resolves their need to sell with their customers' desires to acquire.

Although we think of selling as work, we do it every day. A woman persuades her husband to help with chores. A child barters her homemade sandwich against her schoolmate's apple pie. An employee presents a compelling point to an employer to gain a desirable promotion or pay increase. What all these people do is to communicate a deep need or belief, probing for a mutual desire, which validates that need or belief.

The long and short of selling is that it is a practical, proven method of self-validation, making us feel comfortable about ourselves. For this reason, selling is neither advertising or marketing, which serve only as attractions for potential buyers or those interested in agreement. These techniques neither produce the hearty handshake of agreement, the smooth flow of ink on the dotted line of a contract, nor the delightful coolness of paper money and the weight of coins in the hand.

## Persuasion and Propaganda

For a seller, the Moon plays a dynamic role. Through the Moon, we encounter our deepest needs, especially those representing fundamentals of personal survival. Aside from physical survival needs of food, water, and air, individual needs for personal survival, or an acceptable condition for continued life, are widely divergent. Some persons have few demands beyond basic sustenance. Others cannot live without a creative expression. Certain people must have status, wealth, or acquisitions.

When we confront a lack of fulfillment about our needs, we are compelled to find a solution. Fortunately for the rest of us, some people discover interesting methods or things that produce deep, lasting satisfaction. Rather than giving in to a gnawing specter of threat or lack, they let the Moon lead them to intensely personal nurturing to fulfill their innermost longings. These people gain not only survival but an abiding faith in the solution. Faith that the solution works continues to integrate into the person's beliefs about life enhancement. They are able to speak assuredly about the solution and develop a genuine integrity toward it. Having reconciled lunar survival needs, the Moon bestows on these people the most powerful of selling traits—self-assurance.

Born from fulfillment, self-assurance in selling marks the difference between the verbal techniques of persuasion and propaganda. While both communication methods provide information, they differ in the decision-making process of the customer. Roughly, persuasion and propaganda parallel to soft-sell and hard-sell. Persuasion, or soft-sell, gives the customer verifiable information, offers suggestions about how the product or service enhances or changes the customer's situation, and allows the customer to make a considered decision. On the other hand, propaganda, or hard-sell, requires that information be taken as a truth, coerces a belief that the product or service is necessary for an enriched existence, and it demands an immediate agreement. The hard-sell often projects the "thrill of the hunt," alienating buyer from seller and effectively eliminating a very important consideration in selling—relating.

This idea of relating to the customer reflects the fluid sensitivities of the Moon. Although not all salespeople are Cancers, or are born with a prominent Moon, the successful ones mold their personal image, verbiage, and presentation to the individual needs and desires expressed by potential customers. Consequently, the good salesperson manifests the shape-shifting variability of the Moon. Much like water assuming the shape of its container, considerate sellers mimic the intellectual, emotional, and sometimes physical postures of their customers to create a comfortable interchange.

## The Moon and the Buying Public

Of course, the ability to sell means nothing if we cannot put ourselves together with receptive people. The Moon gives us a wide and varied field of potentials as we seek the reflection of our innermost beliefs among the desires of customers.

In mundane and political astrology, the Moon represents the public and its aggregate opinions. In the natal horoscope, the Moon still indicates the public, but more specifically, it shows the public's receptivity toward you, or a willingness to agree with your beliefs, perspective, and persuasion. However, the highly adaptable Moon creates a two-way influence, showing your best sales approach toward the public for developing and sustaining sales. Because the Moon thrives in situations of similarity, its descriptions of your personal foundations of comfort and security echo in specific segments of the public, allowing you to assess and target viable clients and customers. Further, the natal Moon delineates the particular types of goods and services you feel comfortable promoting and that symbolize your personal nurture and security.

This wealth of information derives from the placement of the Moon by sign and house in your natal horoscope. Strengthened with lunar motivation, your ability to sell can produce amazing commercial success. Listed below are the general descriptions of the Moon's position to help you discover your best salesmanship.

## Moon in Aries or First House

Your sales approach is out front and in the face of every person who walks through the door. You have to be the first to greet customers. It's your aggressiveness you need to rein in. Take time to let the customer reveal through words and actions whether or not he or she is a quick, decisive sale.

The deliberative, chew-the-fat customer is just not your bag. You thrive on people who know what they want, and you categorize them as "impulse buyers," but they only seem impulsive because they already know the advantages of the product or service. After a sale, your best customers need little service or direction. Consequently, you do best with entrepreneurs and others who want to think for themselves.

Goods and services reflect the Aries temperament for fire, newness, and precision. To satisfy your fire dynamic, you are comfortable with fire engines, fireplaces, forges, furnaces, guns, ovens, rubies, pungent herbs and seasonings, and coffee, of course. Realty in new land tracts, virgin pastures, and hilly grounds for spirited freethinkers and nudists mirror your preferences for newness and originality, as do baby goods and furnishings. When it comes to precision, it's either rhythm or sharp edges. Entertain sales of axes, engineering tools, motorized equipment, percussive musical instruments, sharp instruments for surgeries or slaughterhouses, steam engines, swords, and weaponry along with the attendant military apparel and paraphernalia. If you gravitate to sports, consider adventure vacations, arenas, gymnasiums, kennels, prizefighting, and sporting equipment.

## Moon in Taurus or Second House

You appreciate anyone who takes time and carefully expends effort. Although you make first contact, you allow customers to appraise and evaluate before making up their minds. What you want is the sure sale. Goods and services must have an innate, recognizable value, which continues to appreciate or show gain, if resold. Gently applied persistence and strong knowledge create a bond of trust, which yields you many referrals.

To some extent, your clients and customers want display or trappings that announce success. Although exterior beauty is important, intrinsic worth must shine through. Expect your clients to be well heeled, genteel, and understated, people who give themselves rewards on a large or small scale.

The goods of the earth, earthly delights, physical comfort, and accruable tangible assets demonstrate your need for proven security. Realty is a winner for Taurus, and you do well selling or reselling barber shops, beauty salons, cultivated pasture land, outdoor cafes, and restaurants. Those earthly delights are either a feast for the eyes or tummy. Sell any product for exterior beautification, such as bronze, delicate herbs, garden flowers, landscaping, statuary, tiles, trailing plants, and vines. For tummy feasts, it's candy all the way. Personal physical comforts soothe and reflect ease of living, but satisfy the tactile sense. Objects you can stroke, including small pets, smooth-furred cats, and rabbits. A combination of comfort, security, and display demands luxury furnishings, with plump cushions and enameled woods, good jewelry without ostentation, or personal apparel adorned with silks, laces, and ribbons, particularly the bridal trousseau. Services in tangible assets comprise investments, securities, and secure storerooms.

## Moon in Gemini or Third House

Talking and communication sum up your best sales approach. You thrive on high variety. Knowledgeable and informative, you shine in dealing with chatty groups where an initial presentation generates enthusiasm for a tougher seller to take over. With that need for variety, you also do well with products or services developed by route that puts you in constant contact with different people. Although personable, you tend to be less personal with your clients, making you an excellent advance person for presentations at public events and rallies.

Target business-to-business services, where your clients will use your service to enhance their own business prospects. Look for your customers among people who understand concepts but manipulate ideas to their own needs.

The Gemini influence contributes a breezy mentality, communication, and short travels to your salesmanship. To satisfy the dabbling mind, you aren't compelled by the complexity of prolonged education. Consider products and services for places of short-term learning, such as grade schools, high schools, and continuing education. In the field of communication, advertising stands out, but you also are comfortable with art supplies, billboards, direction signs, messenger services, newspapers, postal services, printing, book publishing, signaling equipment, traffic lights, weather vanes, and writing instruments. Constantly on the go, you appreciate the ways to arrive at your destination; those small personal conveyances: bicycles, elevators, escalators, rollerskates, skateboards, and sleds. Your love of novelty and variety suggest costume jewelry, grafted trees bearing several kinds of fruit, talking birds, and wind instruments.

## Moon in Cancer or Fourth House

Although Cancer is the most versatile and personal of signs, you maneuver best with the buffer of a support team or the seclusion of a home office. Cancer needs shelter and withdrawal, whether it's from a physical structure or within a group. You don't have to be babied; you simply derive a sense of confidence from enclosure. On the plus side, when you feel strengthened, you gladly bolster your sales colleagues. The Moon goes through phases, causing Cancer's sales products and services to go through many hands. You may find yourself more comfortable as a wholesaler, reseller, agent, or secondhand retailer.

Your target clients purchase for personal security, whether it's a sheltering residence or a sanctum sanctorum. For them, the best products remain within easy reach, and the best services, closely accessible. Your clients appear pastoral, withdrawn, and reclusive; however, they have varied and lively inner landscapes, demonstrating Cancer's diversity.

Your preferred goods and services for Cancer show water, domesticity, nurture, and sentimentality. Water is your strong suit; use it for goods and services relating to boats, docks, fountains, houseboats, piers, plumbing, ships, waterways, and wharves. Domesticity in realty helps you sell or resell farms, homes, hotels, lodges, motels, multifamily complexes, and other improved properties. The domestic front broadens when you turn your attention to cultivation, nurture, and care-tending. Consider beer, cattle, china, everyday clothing, fish, mild herbs, home furnishings, kitchenware, linen, milk and dairy products, night birds and flowers,

domestic poultry, sheep, turtles, vegetables, and water plants. Previous ownership confers a sentimentality, which reverberates in antiques, collectibles, pearls, silver, and secondhand items of all sorts.

## Moon in Leo or Fifth House

Wherever the Leo influence is present, expect flair, style, and the desire to be the center of attention. All these qualities help you grab and hold the attention of customers. You're no ball of fluff; you've got a powerful mind filled with facts and persuasive reasoning. With innate poise and presence, you'll stumble only if you try to sell goods or services that are below the caliber of your pride and self-image. Ever the actor, your range of presentation goes from the understated to the dramatic.

Your fine eye for increasing assets provides the same for your customers. Frivolity is unbefitting your clientele—those with high expendable incomes, the independently wealthy, vanity buyers, and high-ticket customers. Don't waste time on anyone who considers you extravagant. You do best with owners rather than renters or lessees.

Leo bestows radiant fire, largess, love of recreation, and an appreciation for rarity. The fire of Leo glows from within and accepts only two products: diamonds and coal. Your presentation fits well with items larger than life, such as large, showy buildings, casinos, mansions, palaces, resorts, and theaters, especially if these are located on overhanging cliffs. With an eye for the impressive, you easily promote and sell luxury cars, designer clothing, rich furniture, furs, and fine wines. Pastimes are your favorite diversions; consider sales in pedigreed animals, exotic animals, racehorses, recreational equipment, and toys and games, as well as pregnancy apparel. Your clients appreciate the singularity of rare plant specimens and one-of-a-kind objects, such as old-masters' artworks.

## Moon in Virgo or Sixth House

Virgo emphasizes dexterity, acquired expertise, and a mind like a reference library. You understand intricacy and appreciate structured integrity in components, products, and services. Ever busy, you delay rest until a project or process to completion. Although you don't dismiss success, usually completion signals another beginning. You do well with territorial sales.

Your best clients and customers are people of accomplishment, with an eye for excellence. They appreciate your fastidiousness, encyclopedic mind, and unwavering respect for appropriate steps taken at the appropriate time. Consequently, your best attention is paid to business people and professionals whose livelihood rests on attention to detail or careful manipulations.

Unswerving attention, business, busy-ness, health, and practicality are the hallmarks of Virgo. As mentioned, business is a paramount issue, and you well serve all places of business and home offices, understanding how to ease workloads with the appropriate, practical office supplies, furniture, and compartmentalized accouterments, such as briefcases, filing cabinets, luggage, enclosed shelving, and storage units. The foundational, practical needs of dextrous, independent professionals benefit from sales of keys, sewing machines, sewing notions, spinning wheels, surveyor's equipment, and weaving looms and supplies. Health equipment and medicines fulfill your sense of wholeness, but so do the special needs and services of conventions and public events, where masses of people congregate. When it comes to staying busy, consider selling proliferating products, such as bees and beekeeping equipment, dogs, houseplants, monkeys, and wild flowers.

## Moon in Libra or Seventh House

The most cerebral of signs, Libra enjoys complex and theoretical thought. Idealistically motivated, you gravitate to wide open spaces and light-filled rooms. You prefer rendering a service and selling a concept, because products are too down-to-earth to keep your mind sharp. Nonetheless, you have an eye for gain, and anything you sell brings a sizeable return.

Your clients often are people with whom you socialize. Even if they don't share the same ideas, they appreciate intrinsic value and a gentle approach. These people enjoy your calm, relaxed approach, your thorough discussion of pros and cons, and an invitation to take their time to reach a decision. Your sense of "no rush" clinches the deal.

Libra's traits confer openness, sociability, refinement, and deliberation, all of which appear as themes behind the goods or services you sell. Openness is reflected by open airiness, such as grassy areas, hanging plants, hunting areas, mountainous open spaces, and trees. Your social side releases with ballrooms, doves, flower bouquets and arrangements, garden furniture, public gardens, social centers, songbirds, swans, teas, and light, sweet wines. Display your refined tastes with copper, dressing rooms, fine embroideries, evening clothes, paintings, perfumes, stringed instruments, wardrobes, and wedding apparel, and beautiful but useful items, such as rugs, carpets, purses, and gloves. Your fine mind is usefully exercised in campaign coordination, international negotiations and treaties, legal services, management analysis, and speechwriting.

## Moon in Scorpio or Eighth House

Unlike your Aries counterpart, you are assertive, rather than aggressive. Instead of blowing off steam, you are certain of what you need and determined to get it. You are not a scattershot seller, but if your sales include a high volume of customers, it is more likely that you are the sales manager with a percentage of sales from those under you. Excellent at negotiation, you gravitate to high-priced good and services.

Expect your customers to be event or one-time purchasers, motivated by the rare momentous times in life, such as birth, death, or war. Some are strategically minded, like you, seeking to create a one-time, but enduring, advantage.

Scorpio understands death or removal as a means to preserve life. You do well in sales involving bathroom safety items, chemicals, laboratory equipment, medicines, operating rooms, surgical and x-ray equipment. This powerful, withstanding sign plumbs the depths, giving you the forbearance to deal in crude oil, drilling and dredging equipment, explosives, liquors, mining equipment, and nuclear materials. Never without financial resources, consider services that recoup from disastrous circumstances, such as redevelopment of devastated areas, catastrophic insurance against improbable circumstances, legal dissolutions, mutual funds, mutual trusts, and salvage operations. Your lack of fear allows you to deal in birds of prey, flesh-eating plants, odorous plants, and snakes.

## Moon in Sagittarius or Ninth House

Others may think you're happy-go-lucky, but what you have is enthusiasm! Mental buoyancy lets you move on and feel positive, after a fruitless or disastrous encounter. You know your sales subject very well, adding conversational flourishes to heighten the imagination of your customer. However, your aim is not just to make a sale, but to develop an honorable exchange that raises the esteem of your client.

Depending on the goods or services, your customers are high-ticket, or as high a spender as possible within a given economic range. What they all desire, besides an equitable arrangement, is an enhancement of dignity and respect afterward. Those with high incomes usually seek items and services that give a superior advantage or create high regard in others.

Sagittarius loves the great outdoors, travel, abundance, and high aims. You raise your eyes to the heavens, and others do, too, when you deal in goods or services for banks, bibles, cathedrals, churches and furnishings,

courtrooms, crown jewels, estates, great libraries, holy objects, judicial buildings, publishing empires, religious items, universities and furnishings, velvets, wigs, and any realty offering high, visible grounds or acreage. To satisfy your outdoor fervor, trade in ammunition depots, large animals to ride (such as camels, elephants), and ostriches, barracks, berries, forests, valuable furs, horse stables, pleasure horses, orchards, large shrubs, shade trees, and vineyards. Abundance flourishes with barter exchanges, fruits, fruit woods, gambling equipment, sweet herbs, honey, monetary exchanges, olive oil, turkeys, and sweet, heavy wines. You are very comfortable with long-distance travel involving buses, foreign enterprises, imports, exports, and trains.

## Moon in Capricorn or Tenth House

In the outer world, Capricorn's goat reaches the highest pinnacle from the lowest point. You are the most hopeful of signs, seeing the best and willing to work to bring it out, no matter how dire the circumstances. Reserved and self-controlled, you apply thought toward everything and readily understand how to reinvigorate a forgotten asset.

Many of your clients share your natural reserve and perhaps your reclusive nature. Often, they desire isolation or remoteness, giving themselves important time to think, assess, and develop their aims. Expect them to be hands-on people, as agriculturalists, agronomists, or manual laborers. All of them have a deep understanding of how to make a little money do a lot.

Capricorn tends to ponderous effort, conservation, rejuvenation, and redevelopment of resources. You truly understand labor and its needs. All goods or services that improve the condition of the common laborer suit you. Consider supplies and enduring clothes for tradesmen in graveyards, leatherwork, masonry, mines, pottery, steel, stone quarries, steel, trucking, weights and measures, and wells. Care and conservation of the land is shown by desert xerothermic landscape, farming equipment, fences, forest preserves, mountains, and stable equipment. You know how to breathe life into depletion and can sell beasts of burden, such as mules, fallow fields, neglected farms, bitter herbs, and dry wines. Finding new uses for old resources makes you a natural for providing credit and recapture of treasure.

## Moon in Aquarius or Eleventh House

You are comfortable standing alone; after all, your thinking is hardly herd-like. Intelligent and friendly, you attract people to you who are astounded by your incredible mind. When it comes to sales, you do very well in presentations to large groups, especially if you have the opportunity to impart new scientific developments.

Expect your clients to share your love of science. These people enjoy rearranging the known to create an improvement, and money is not usually an object. You sell them on the possibilities of practical application, sparking their own creativity.

Aquarius loves invention, innovation, science, and public display. Anything that can be labeled "newfangled" satisfies your needs for progress and inventiveness. You can sell computers, convenience equipment, electricity, nuclear energy, portables, and software. Readily understanding the complexities of established science, consider airplanes, automobiles, extraterrestrial domiciles and vehicles, helicopters, jets, racing cars, radio, rockets, scientific equipment, television, and telephones. Recombining the known into something new draws you to hybrid animals and plants. You believe in the public domain, and find success with architectural projects, fundraising, and lobbying.

## Moon in Pisces or Twelfth House

Your sympathy toward others often forces you to remove yourself from the strongly magnetic influences of their emotions. You are very adaptable and humane, creating an instant understanding with a customer. Easily blended with others, you need to separate yourself to avoid a sales presentation that appears sycophantic.

Sharing your love of elegance and luxury, your customers and clients seek goods and services that project an assumption of value. However, their pockets may not be deep. You gain trust by considerately eliminating embarrassment and suggesting practical alternatives with a glamorous face.

Impression and reclusiveness define watery Pisces. Goods or services reminiscent of water are successful, such as beachfront property, lake property, transparent fabrics, iridescent glass, medicinal plants, natural gas, refined oil, porcelain, shellfish, and succulent plants. The need to remove yourself from others causes you to provide for meditation rooms, religious sanctuaries, retirement complexes, and retreats. You can help create an impression beyond known reality by selling cameras, cinematic ventures, filming equipment and supplies, imitation furs, dwarf plants and trees, photography supplies, plastics, prosthetic devices, and tobacco.

# Timing Sales with a Electional Astrology

Once you know what to sell, set a preferred time for your sale. Electional astrology, a cousin of horary astrology, provides answers. Although both branches of astrology are based on an event, electional astrology lets you choose a future time, rather than relying on the time of an actual occurrence.

The election chart is based on the stronger of either your natal horoscope's Ascendant or Midheaven. This strength is determined by the least number of afflicting aspects (conjunctions, squares, or oppositions) from planets that create difficulties or complications, specifically Mars, Saturn, Uranus, Neptune, and Pluto.

If the Ascendant is strong, look for the natal house where the transiting Sun will reside on the preferred date. If the Midheaven is stronger, turn the natal horoscope so that the Midheaven becomes the new ascendant. With the Midheaven as the first house, look for the house where the Sun will transit on the desired date.

The Ascendant line divides night and day, with the upper half of the horoscope representing the daytime hours, generally 6:00 am to 6:00 pm, and the lower half of the chart representing 6:00 pm to 6:00 am. Each house, moving clockwise from the Ascendant covers about two hours; for example, the 9th house is 12:00 noon to 2:00 pm.

Success in selling is greater if the Sun falls in the house ruling the goods or services you want to sell. If the time of day is practical, an election chart is calculated for that day and time. If the time is impractical for selling, select a different day or an earlier or later hour. If this method produces no advantage, create an election chart with the Sun in either the tenth or eleventh house.

After the chart is calculated for your advantageous time, examine whether the Moon makes only a sextile or trine to the Sun. If the Moon has a conjunction to the Sun, choose the succeeding day so that the Moon is at least 14 degrees past the Sun, especially if other aspects to the Sun are very good.

Check whether Venus and Jupiter are in the same house as the elected Sun, or in an angle (first, fourth, seventh, or tenth house). If neither of these conditions apply to Venus and Jupiter, see if they are in mutual reception, that is, in each other's signs. Finally, the Ascendant of the election chart must not contain Saturn or have an afflicting aspect by square or opposition from Saturn. If your chart achieves these conditions, the election chart is good.

In the election chart, if the Moon is increasing in light, or between the New Moon and Full Moon phases, your sale comes to fruition, which means money changes hands. To increase profitability, the Moon needs a trine or sextile to Venus, Jupiter, the Part of Fortune, the ruler of the second house of the election chart, or the ruler of the second house of your natal chart. Those second house rulers are important, because they represent earnings you stimulate.

If you typically resell goods and services, watch the following rules closely. When the Moon in the election chart is between 0 Cancer and 30 Sagittarius, you pay less but sell for more, creating a high profit margin. If the election Moon is between 0 Capricorn and 30 Gemini, you pay more but sell for less, causing either a low profit margin or a loss.

## About the Author

Leeda Alleyn Pacotti practices as a naturopathic physician, nutritional counselor, and master herbalist, specializing in dream language, health astrology, and mind-body communication. A former legal analyst in antitrust and international law, with judicial and executive governmental experience, she enjoys poking a finger in political machinations of all sorts.

## For Further Reading

Louis, Anthony. *Horary Astrology Plain & Simple* (Llewellyn, 1998).

Goldstein-Jacobson, Ivy M. *Simplified Horary Astrology.* (Ivy M. Goldstein-Jacobson, 1960).

# Women in Politics 2004

*by Madalyn Hillis-Dineen*

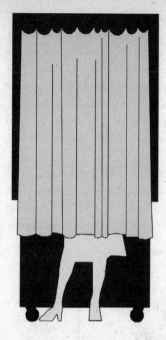

You've come a long way, baby! Those of us who are of a certain age remember those words not only as a clever slogan for a cigarette brand but as a battle cry for the new freedom of the women's liberation movement. No longer would women have to stay in the kitchen and bedroom. We could take our rightful place in the boardroom.

In the early 1970s, a popular T-shirt exclaimed, "A Woman's Place is in the House—and in the Senate!" But, as we near the halfway mark of the first decade of the twenty-first century, a question remains. Baby, have you come far enough to take up residency in that elusive address: 1600 Pennsylvania Avenue?

While a woman president would represent a great symbolic milestone for women, a more basic issue for millions of American families remains the question of equal pay for equal work. The Equal Rights Amendment, first introduced in 1923, still has not passed and women are still not guaranteed equal protection under the Constitution of the United States. Perhaps astrology may offer clues for the future of women in U.S. politics.

## The State of Women in the U.S. Horoscope

To assess the state of women in the horoscope of the United States, we look to the Moon, which symbolizes women and the feminine archetype. While there is a great deal of controversy over which chart to use for the U.S., most people agree that July 4, 1776, is the psychological birthday of the U.S., if not the legal one. The matter of what time on that date the U.S. was "born" is a matter of considerable debate, one that is far beyond the scope of this article.

On July 4, 1776, the U.S. was blessed with Moon in Aquarius, a hall-mark of freedom and democracy. The Moon in Aquarius is associated with progressive and original thought, but since Aquarius is a fixed sign it is often difficult to see another's point of view. Feelings may take a back seat to the rational mind; and, while there is an inherent respect for the rights of the individual, there is, as well, a strong attachment to the principle of social order. Therefore, while fairness and justice for all might be an ideal our country aspires to, as a practical matter, the idea of equality is meas-ured against the good of society as a whole.

So, when the ownership of slaves was considered to be in the economic interest of the nation, the principal of individual freedom was outweighed by the greater benefits that slavery held for society as a whole. Likewise, the right of women to work outside the home had to be measured against

the preservation of the family unit and the impact working moms would have on their children.

Eventually, business leaders realized that women, who were usually immigrants or single women, provided cheap labor for our increasingly industrialized society. This need was counterbalanced against the more idealistic desire to protect the family. Despite a brief respite, when women were needed to "man" the factories during World War II, the role of women in the United States was largely confined to that of wives and mothers.

## Family Values

With the Sun, along with Venus, the planet of femininity; Mercury, the planet of communication; and Jupiter, the planet of luck and overall well being, all in the sign of Cancer, family and family values, patriotism, and tradition are highly valued in the U.S. With all of this emphasis in the sign of Cancer, is it any wonder we use the phrase "It's as American as mom and apple pie" to describe those things that are quintessentially American? And, as a further reflection of Cancer's influence, the concept of "mom" holds an exalted place in our society—a concept that must be protected. Yet, the fact that many moms must join dads in the workplace in order to make ends meet seems lost on the many men and women who oppose initiatives like the Equal Rights Amendment and the Equal Pay Act.

## Equal Rights and Equal Pay

A woman's right to equal pay is fundamentally a family issue, not a feminist one. The fact that women earned seventy-three cents for every dollar earned by a man (in 2000) impacts, in the short run, the ability of American families to survive on a weekly basis and, in the long run, a woman's retirement income in the years ahead.

Clearly, the framers of the Constitution did not consider women as equal to men. Women were not given the right to vote nor were they provided with any of the other inalienable rights afforded to men. In July 1848, 300 men and women met in Seneca Falls, New York, to take up the cause of justice and equality for women. Not coincidentally, most of these people were abolitionists who saw the cause of women's rights as a natural outgrowth of that movement.

At the first Women's Rights Convention, twelve resolutions were adopted, including the right of women to vote. Women's suffrage was considered the one right that would secure the other rights women so desperately needed. At that time, the progressed Moon of the U. S. was in the sign Libra, which represents equality, balance, justice, and fairness. The progressed Moon in the sign Libra also makes a difficult and stressful aspect to the four planets in Cancer in the U.S. birth chart. Though few took their pronouncements seriously, the women and men who met in Seneca Falls were daring to challenge the very fabric of American society.

## Seventy-two Years Later

It took seventy-two years for the 19th Amendment, granting women the right to vote, to be enacted on August 26, 1920. On that date, the progressed Moon of the U.S. was in Gemini, in conjunction with Uranus, the planet of freedom. The progressed Sun of the U.S. birth chart was in Sagittarius, in an opposition to Uranus, illustrating that the victory of women's suffrage movement had a great deal of resistance. In fact, passage of the amendment hinged on the vote of a twenty-four-year-old legislator Harry Burn from Tennessee, who was urged to change his vote from no to yes by his mother.

In 1923, on the seventy-fifth anniversary of the Seneca Falls Women's Rights Convention, Alice Paul first introduced the Equal Rights Amendment that would constitutionally guarantee American women equal protection under the law. The U.S. progressed Moon had moved to the sign Cancer and was close to a conjunction with progressed Jupiter, the planet of law, philosophy, and justice. The transiting Sun and Mercury were also in Cancer, activating the significant progression. This amendment was introduced in Congress every year from 1923 until March 22, 1972, when the Alice Paul Equal Rights Amendment to the Constitution was finally sent to the states for ratification. Interestingly enough, the push for women's rights closely followed the drive for civil rights, just as women's suffrage grew out of the abolitionist movement.

In 1972, the U.S. progressed Moon was in Aries and the progressed Sun was in Capricorn, again challenging the natal U.S. Cancer placements, and activating the progressions that were in effect when Alice Paul first introduced her amendment. Though the amendment itself did not impose a time limit for ratification, Congress placed a seven-year limit on ratification by the needed thirty-eight states. In the first year, twenty-two of the needed thirty-eight states ratified the amendment. But the ratification process slowed, and by the deadline in 1979 only thirty-five states had ratified the amendment. More time was needed.

Congress granted a three-year extension on the deadline. Though organized labor was finally behind the concept of recognizing the rights of women as citizens, opposition from social conservatives was strong and, in the end, the amendment failed to gain ratification. Ardent supporters of women's rights continue to introduce the amendment each year though many people fail to see the need for it any longer. After all, the Equal Pay Act and dozens of other laws are designed to protect women. Women have made great strides in every sector of society, however, proponents of the ERA point out that laws may be repealed and that the only true protection of women's rights lies in the U.S. Constitution.

In 2004, the progressed Moon of the U.S. is once again in Cancer, just as it was in 1923. Perhaps, Alice Paul's vision will finally become a reality during the movement of the U.S. progressed Moon through Cancer from 2004–2006.

## Women Have Come a Long Way

Women certainly have come a long way in the arena of politics. After the 2000 election, there were thirteen women in the Senate. And, more importantly, in 2002, there were no less than ten women running for governor in nine states. While this may not seem like a staggering number, contrast it with the fact that up until 2002, only twelve women had ever been elected governor in the history of the U.S., and only seven more had served, completing the unexpired terms of male governors who had resigned or died.

Many believe that this focus on the corner office in the fifty state houses is a concerted effort on the part of women to finally be ready for a presidential run. After all, executive experience seems a likely prerequisite for the commander-in-chief, and four of the last five presidents were all state governors before winning the presidency. While senators, like Hillary Clinton and Kay Bailey Hutchinson, are often mentioned when discussing female presidential hopefuls, the movement dedicated to electing a woman president clearly believes that the best candidate will likely come from one of the state governments.

## Job Qualifications

The ideal candidate will have strong managerial skills and be able to make tough decisions. She needs to show herself, not as a soft and conciliatory female, but as a hard-nosed leader, able to steer the nation through difficult times. And, the state government seems like a logical proving ground from which just this type of woman leader may emerge. So, this brings us to the million-dollar question: is the U.S. astrologically ready for a woman president?

To help answer that question, perhaps we should look at another chart—that of the presidency cast for the moment of the inauguration of our first president, George Washington, on April 30, 1789. We will call this chart POTUS (president of the U.S.). The Moon is in Cancer in that chart, too, and there is a preponderance of planets in feminine signs. The Moon is conjunct Jupiter, and echoes the Cancer stellium of the U.S. birth chart.

# Woman Candidates: Past and Future

The first woman to run for president of the U.S. was Victoria Woodhull. She announced her candidacy in 1870, just as the POTUS progressed Moon touched Venus, another symbol of women. In 1964, Republican Senator Margaret Chase Smith became the first woman to attempt to become the presidential nominee of a major political party. At that time, the POTUS progressed Moon was in Sagittarius, making a favorable aspect to Mars, the planet of competition and action, in the POTUS chart. In 1984, Geraldine Ferraro became the Democratic nominee for vice president, the first woman ever to run for that office on a major party ticket. The POTUS progressed Moon was making an aspect of opportunity with the POTUS natal Moon. But, it was also in a stressful aspect with the natal POTUS Saturn, planet of restrictions and limitations. Ferraro didn't win but she still holds the distinction of being the only woman ever to be on the major party ticket for national office.

The outlook for 2004 suggests that the time may again be right for a woman to be on the ticket as a vice presidential candidate for a major party. At that time, transiting Saturn conjoins the POTUS Moon, indicating responsibility and achievement; and, the progressed U.S. Moon is in Cancer, activating much of the U.S. natal chart during 2004. While it may not be in the immediate future, there is no doubt that the U.S. will eventually have a woman president—it is just a matter of time.

## About the Author

Madalyn Hillis-Dineen, a well-known Uranian astrologer, teacher, author and lecturer, holds a Consulting Astrologer certificate from the National Council for Geocosmic Research (NCGR) and is also a certified Astro*Carto*Graphy interpreter. She is the director of marketing for Astrolabe, Inc., an astrological software developer. Madalyn's articles have appeared in a variety of astrological and non-astrological magazines, and she is a contributor to the 1996 Llewellyn anthology, *Astrology for Women: Roles and Relationships*. An active member in a number of astrological organizations, she is the winner of the 1995 United Astrology Congress Regulus Award for Community Service. She currently serves as the Clerk and Parliamentarian of the NCGR National Board of Directors and has served two terms on the steering committee of the Association for Astrological Networking. Madalyn takes a compassionate yet practical approach to her consultations. She is a faith-based astrologer, conversant in Twelve-Step recovery and other methods for personal growth. You can reach her by writing to madalyn@alabe.com.

# Beyond September 11

*by Robin Antepara*

This piece was written in the emotional weeks after 9/11. Since that time the U.S. has launched a shadowy war on terrorism in which it has often found itself swimming against a tide of criticism from overseas. As events in the Middle East continue to unfold, one facet of the U.S. chart becomes more and more salient: the grand trine in air, a configuration that indicates intellectual self sufficiency and, in its extreme form, arrogance.

This intellectual self-sufficiency extends beyond the perimeters of the fight against terrorism. In the years since the terrorist attacks, the U.S. has thumbed its nose at one international treaty after another. This could be seen in Washington's opposition to the Kyoto treaty on global warming, then, later in its demand to be exempted from the reach of the new International Criminal Court, and, despite surface gestures toward teamwork, the U.S. government continues to call the shots in Iraq, riding roughshod over the objections of long-time allies in Europe and beyond.

As our alliances with previously friendly countries reach near-crisis proportions, the American people must ponder anew the increasingly inflexible stance the U.S. is taking on the world stage. Columnist W. Pfaff summed up the situation quite nicely when writing in the *International Herald Tribune*: "The administrations' implicit demand is for a totally free hand in acting internationally. To put it in other language, it wants a grant of unaccountable power. No one is going to agree to that."

Washington's demand for a grant of "unaccountable power"—and the logic that underpins it—is the grand trine in air talking. The question is how long will Americans agree to implicitly or explicitly support such a demand? The following article was written in the hope that we can wake up to the shadow side of that grand trine and find more constructive avenues of expression.

☽

Two weeks after the 9/11 attack on America, Ira Glass, the normally unemotional host of National Public Radio's "This American Life" took to the airwaves and voiced a sentiment haunting millions of Americans: "Why does the world hate our guts?"

Indeed, for many Americans the animosity that erupted in the wake of the attacks (not to mention the ferocity of the attacks themselves) was truly stunning. From demonstrations in Indonesia where people burned down a KFC restaurants, to protests in Pakistan, to the infamous images of Palestinians dancing in the streets, the intensity of anger and hatred directed at the U.S. was something that many Americans simply could not comprehend.

Much of the animosity poured out of the world's Muslim countries, and in a way that was understandable: people were angry about U.S. policy in the Middle East, about the government's bombing of Iraq, and about the bombing of a pharmaceutical factory in Sudan, among other things. I, for one, stand firmly in the camp that believes America has much self-reflection and learning to do about its policies and actions abroad.

Even more bewildering than the Islamic outrage, however, was the self-righteous anger and condescension that emanated from supposedly neutral and even friendly countries. Consider, for example, the comments of former Conservative Party member Matthew Parris in Britain. Upon hearing of the collapse of the Twin Towers, Parris blithely remarked: "The bigger they come, the harder they fall."

Or the comments of Dario Fo, the Italian playwright and satirist who won the Nobel Prize for literature in 1997, stated in a widely circulated e-mail: "The great speculators wallow in an economy that every year kills tens of millions of people with poverty—so what is it to them that 20,000 are dead in New York? . . . this violence is the legitimate daughter of the culture of violence, hunger, and inhumane exploitation."

I was affected by this outpouring of hostility in a very personal way. After hearing the news of the attacks, I dragged myself to work at the university in Tokyo, Japan, where I teach. The first person I saw was a Canadian man who worked in the same department. The topic of the attacks immediately arose, and I mentioned that my sister narrowly missed being in the World Trade Center at the time the planes hit. His response? "Well, Americans are racists. This is what they deserve." After several moments of silence he added, as an afterthought: "Oh, how is your sister?" I was too stunned to answer, and instead excused myself and left the table where I'd been sitting.

Why does the world hate us so much? What would account for the venom and hyperbole of these criticisms? Surely Fo understands that a handful of speculators on Wall Street does not equal the 5,000 people killed in the World Trade Center, let alone the 260 million living in the U.S. And while American culture has its violent aspects, does he really mean to say that all Americans contribute to the culture of violence, hunger, and inhumane exploitation that he cites?

Sure, some Americans are racist. Some Canadians are racist. Some Japanese, Germans, French—you name the country—are racist. But to brand an entire nation racist? The Canadian man cited attacks on Arab Americans that had been made during one of the last oil crises, and alluded to others certain to occur in the wake of the terrorist attacks (which they of course did.) But just as we know that all Muslims are not killers, neither are all Americans bigots. According to a NPR report, for every threatening phone call received by Islamic centers and mosques in the U.S. in the wake of 9/11, there were two or three people calling to express their support. My colleague condemns the prejudice that brands all Muslims killers, while condoning that which pigeonholes Americans as racists.

What is fueling the virulence and exaggeration of these, and countless other, statements? What does astrology have to tell us about this question? Specifically, what does the natal chart of the U.S. have to say? In this article, I focus on America's Sun and Moon signs, and on a prominent aspect configuration as I attempt a response.

## The Natal Chart of the United States

In the natal chart for the U.S., July 4, 1776, at 3:10 am, the Sun is at 12 degrees of Cancer. A water sign ruled by the Moon, Cancer is known for its empathetic, nurturing nature. Here the Cancer energy is particularly strong because Venus, Jupiter, and Mercury are all in the sign of the crab as well. Those of us ruled by lunar Cancer are adept at tuning into how people are feeling and (given supporting aspects in the rest of the chart) and adept at responding to what we sense in others. Some famous Cancer people are Princess Diana, the Dalai Lama, and Elizabeth Küebler-Ross. All are known for their nurturing abilities.

America's need to be seen as a nurturer and caretaker, or, as some would put it, the "world's policeman" is well-known. From the 1947 Marshall Plan, which helped rebuild a devastated Europe after World War II, to peace initiatives and accords in Ireland and the Middle East, to the birth of the Peace Corps in the 1960s, to the billions of dollars in aid it extends every year, the U.S. is clearly a country that sees beyond its borders.

But it is precisely around these issues of nurturing that our analysis gets sticky. Where does nurturing end and imperial overreach begin? How do we tell when caretaking becomes an arrogant insistence that our way is the only way? America's adversaries argue that if the only thing at issue were questions of nurturing then the U.S. would not have engendered the ferocious backlash that arose in the wake of the terrorist attacks. Had the U.S. government only been concerned with administering no-strings-attached aid after natural disasters, had it been content to support true democracies, as opposed to corrupt regimes in Saudi Arabia, Kuwait, and other countries that maintain harrowing differences between rich and poor, perhaps we would not be in the position we find ourselves in today.

But alas, that is not the case. The exquisitely attuned feelings indicated by the Cancer Sun are offset by the Moon's placement in Aquarius. Here we have fixed air and, in contrast to the empathy of Cancer, we have intellectualism and detachment. The Moon in Aquarius values ideas but not feelings. It responds individualistically and has a need for total independence. True, there is a humanitarian urge to the Aquarian Moon that mirrors the mothering instincts of Cancer, but it is a much more abstract, generic need to help society as a whole. And because Aquarius is a fixed sign, there is a crusading quality to this Moon, which can incline it toward proselytizing and imposing its values on others.

Tommy Koh, a former Singaporean ambassador to the U.S., wrote a perceptive essay about America several weeks before the 9/11 attacks that speaks directly to issues relating to the Aquarian Moon. "In the Cold War," Koh said, "the Soviet Union was the most ideological country in the world. With the end of the Cold War, the U.S. has succeeded the Soviet Union as the most ideological country in the world. It has elevated democracy, human rights, and capitalism to the status of dogmas, and any deviation is condemned. The U.S. mind-set is very ideological."

To explain more fully, Koh goes on to note the differing "cultural boxes" Asian and Americans inhabit.

"For reasons of history, many Asians fear chaos. Asians therefore attach great value to public order and social harmony. When confronted with a choice between individual liberty and order and harmony, many Asians choose public order over personal freedom. This choice can be understood only in the context of the history of Asia, which has experienced so many tragedies and disasters resulting from war, conflict, revolution and anarchy. When confronted with the same choice, most Americans would choose individual liberty. Such a choice makes good sense in the American cultural box because the U.S. was founded by European settlers who fled persecution and oppression. Given this historical background, it is not surprising that the liberty of the individual is paramount. The government is viewed as a necessary evil who should be kept small and constrained by an elaborate system of checks and balances."

The Aquarian Moon is an able administrator of these checks and balances, as well as a powerful advocate for the individual liberties of which Koh so eloquently speaks. But as we know, this is quite a departure from the needs of the Cancer Sun, which values intimacy and connection over liberty any day of the week. Aquarius is an uneasy sign for the Moon. For this same reason, its relationship with the lunar-ruled Cancer Sun is uneasy. In short, there's a conflict between the emotional impulses of the Sun and the intellectual inclinations of the Moon.

There are several other complicating factors in the U.S. natal chart. First, there is no fire. This is probably quite difficult for a lot of Americans—and even more of America's adversaries—to believe. Our image in the world is of a blundering, bludgeoning bully: the cowboy roaring out of the saloon with guns blasting, the military superpower that drops bombs without a moment's hesitation—the very essence of fire. Fighting fire with fire, a well-known Western aphorism, could be said to be the mantra of the U.S. Department of Defense: with a military budget of $310 billion, and an arsenal of 7,000 land-, air-, and sea-based offensive nuclear weapons, our military preparedness far exceeds that of any other country in the world.

And all this in a chart with no fire and, moreover, with a marked water component! What could explain the American preoccupation—even obsession—with self-defense and instruments of destruction? I suggest it is compensation, or more accurately, overcompensation: a child's desperate efforts to make up for talents and abilities he lacks and thinks he must have. It's as if we were looking at the profile of a deeply sensitive and caring young man whose father insists he assume a macho, aggressive role, one utterly contrary to his nature. As a result, the youth overdoes it, throwing his weight around, trying to prove himself, insecure about his sensitive Cancer nature. Interestingly, the U.S. Sun is squaring Saturn, one of the archetypal "father" figures of the zodiac. In addition, Mars, indicative of masculine, yang energies, is in a tight square to Neptune—yet more fears about masculinity.

There's one final thing we need to consider to understand this picture: America's grand trine in air. A grand trine is comprised of three 120-degree aspects: easy, flowing connections between planets that link their energies in a harmonious way. Grand trines always suggest closed units of self-sufficiency. When the configuration is in air, a closed circuit of intellectual self-sufficiency is indicated. In the U.S. chart, we see the aforementioned Moon in Aquarius, trining Mars in Gemini (conjuncting the Ascendant, a powerful proponent of diversity), and Saturn in Libra—an upholder of democratic traditions. In the U.S. chart, this grand trine functions in two ways: (1) to bolster and amplify the Aquarian Moon's drive for human rights and individual freedoms; and (2) to effectively rule out the possibility of other countries dialoguing with us on these points. "What need is there of dialogue?" asks the grand trine in air. "We have the whole thing figured out already. We already have all the answers. There's really nothing more to discuss."

Unfortunately, this intellectual self-sufficiency—even hubris—is not something most people in the U.S. government and diplomatic corp are very aware of. If asked, most Americans would say their country by its nature is open to new ideas and receptive to people and trends from different cultures. And on many levels this is true. However, in our myriad efforts to play world caretaker/policeman, there's been precious little consideration for value systems other than our own. One of the most recent examples of this that comes to mind is President George W. Bush's refusal, in 2001, to abide by the decisions of the Kyoto Protocol—a stand that infuriated other world leaders. In another context, the members of various antiglobalization movements rightly cite America's prominent role in forcing corporate culture on Third World and developing nations.

Yet this lack of team spiritedness is not how most Americans view themselves. As the *New York Times* put it, there is a "broad chasm between the way Americans see themselves and the way they are seen." In this lack of awareness, we have the textbook definition of what psychologist Carl Jung called the shadow—an element of psyche that "contradicts who we would like to see ourselves as, who we would like to seem to be in the eyes of others." Our ego "senses its authority challenged by this shadow and feels the shadow's closeness as a threat continually at our heels, awkward, nettling, anxiety-provoking, shameful."

For this reason, the shadow often falls into unconsciousness and may even be "actively, ruthlessly suppressed to maintain the sanctimonious sweetness of our illusory perfection."[2] Thus, we see American's collective inability to see past the best intentions of the Cancer Sun, and the more humanitarian impulses of the Aquarian Moon, to the more self-serving aspects in the U.S. natal chart as a whole.

When this happens, the rest of the world responds with understandable anger. Speaking about the shadow aspect of the American psyche, John Brandon, a Southeast Asia specialist, notes: "The knowledge of most Americans about the rest of the world is still woefully inadequate. The U.S. presence is strongly felt—politically, economically, culturally and militarily—in all corners of the globe. Yet Americans treat their preeminence with indifference, exhibiting little interest in foreign affairs, much as they did before the bombing of Pearl Harbor. The rest of the world senses U.S. indifference, construes it as arrogance and resents it greatly." It is the resentment, in short, of people locked out of our formidable grand trine in air.

Is there any hope to be seen in this discouraging picture? Indeed there is, and we see it all around us, every day. We see it when ordinary citizens contact local mosques and Islamic groups to arrange community meetings and conflict resolution sessions; we see it in the books that have topped the bestseller's lists over the past year: books on Islam, on the culture and history of the Middle East, on Osama bin Laden, and the roots of terrorism. In essence, the air grand trine is seeking to extend itself, to broaden its horizons, to take in more than what it took in before. It is an axiom of many religious and depth psychological traditions that the solution to our problems lies within the very thing that most disturbs and upsets us. If the grand trine is part of what got us into this fix (with the stubborn, crusading nature Aquarian Moon acting as lead batter), then it just might be the grand trine in air that gets us out. The Gemini Mars' drive for diversity, and Saturn in Libra's love for harmony and democracy can greatly boost the process. The work that remains—and it is considerable—is for us to reacquaint ourselves with the deeper, truer impulses of the Sun-Venus-Jupiter placement in Cancer. It's time for Americans to realize that the role of fiery watchdog we've been playing is contrary to our deeper nature. Only then can we discover a way to truly look beyond our borders and work towards a greater goal: not merely the economic prosperity of the U.S. of America but for the welfare of the Earth.

## About the Author

Robin Antepara, M.A., is an astrologer who divides her time between Tokyo, Los Angeles, and Brattleboro, Vermont. She is currently working on a Ph.D. in depth psychology at Pacifica Graduate Institute.

## References:

Billington, R.A. *The United States*. New York: Rinehart and Co. Inc., 1947.

Hopcke, R. *A Guided Tour of the Collected Works of C.G. Jung*. Boston: Shambhala, 1989.

# Moon Signs While You Work

### by *Sally Cragin*

Tanya was vexed. Worse than vexed, she was resentful. Here she was, the most responsible Virgo in the world, who'd volunteered out of the goodness of her heart to take charge of the product auction at her business convention, and not one person in her profession, which is a specialized health-care service provider, was willing to ante up money or a product.

I happened to call her right in the middle of these woes, and it was clear something was wrong. "I just hate this," she fumed. "I've made forty calls and been turned down forty times!"

"Whoa," I said. "Those are pretty damning statistics."

She agreed, and told me more. I had to agree with her. Yes, it's tough being a Virgo in business. Especially if you're on your own and don't have a helpful air or fire sign person to say, "Lighten up . . . take the day off . . . don't take it personally."

To be fair, one of the most successful non-profit fundraisers I know is a man who helped build a large regional museum. His Virgo Sun is right on the cusp of enthusiastic, persuasive Leo, though. Virgos prefer others to be as logical and methodical as they are. Somewhere in her heart Tanya was hoping colleagues would make a leap of logic and altruism and say, "Gee, I should do something generous because it will be good for all of us in the profession."

"When did you make your calls?" I asked, looking up at my *Moon Signs* calendar.

"Last week," she said.

The Moon had been waning that week, which meant her situation could be a very easy fix. She still had a couple of weeks to get this package together, so I advised her to take time off until after the New Moon. "Just don't think about what you need to do and when it needs to be done until the Moon starts waxing again," I suggested. "Give yourself a brief vacation from this project because when you get back to it, you'll actually feel like doing it." Next, I checked the lunar calendar, and crossed off the days when the Moon would be squaring her Sun. For some signs, a Moon square Sun time can be invigorating, but she didn't need more stress. Since Gemini and Sagittarius both square Virgo, there were five days that she was excused from making any effort. That left at least two days a week that would be more propitious times for making the calls.

A few weeks later, I caught up with Tanya, who was, to coin a phrase, "over the Moon." She excitedly told me the auction had been a huge triumph. "I circled those dates on my *Moon Signs* calendar and when I called, every single person offered to donate. So the auction was successful after all, thanks to the waxing Moon."

My husband Chuck (Scorpio Sun, Taurus Ascendent, Aquarius Moon) runs a record label, hyped2death.com. He puts out compilation CDs of rare bands and has begun doing reissues of defunct bands. (*Spin* has called his company "the Smithsonian folkways of Punk"—just so you know we're not dealing with mainstream material, although the business is typical of any small entrepreneurial endeavor.) Last fall, he put out a new CD by a Milwaukee band called the Shivvers, which had some irresistibly catchy pop tunes. Announcements were sent out in September, when the Moon was in Gemini. Exactly one month later (Moon in Gemini), the final version of the Shivvers CDs (and some others) were announced. Between October 15 and November 10, sales were unusually heavy to individuals overseas. The

first Japanese query came when the waxing Moon was in Virgo. Then the CD started taking off, mostly between the New Moon on November 4 and the middle of November. I asked Chuck to give me a detailed breakdown of the most significant ordering patterns, and guess what elements were overwhelmingly involved? That's an easy call—air signs and fire signs. Virtually all the dates where there were heavy requests were when the Moon was in Sagittarius or Libra, although the largest Japanese order came when the Moon was in Capricorn.

"Interestingly, the distributors, save one, have all been slow and unwilling to order in their usual quantities," says Chuck. "Distributor sales are usually 50 percent of the total, but for this product, they're no more than 20 percent." For the most part, a combination of a number of factors, not discounting word-of-mouth on what happens to be a completely delightful record, has made for some interesting data. Looking at these dates, especially as they built toward the Full Moon on November 20, suggest that air and fire signs are when things happen.

I write a Moon-based astrology column, moonsigns.net, which can be found in various newspapers. On the web, there's also an advice column (I'm "Symboline Dai" for that). Over and over, I notice that clients who write about love problems invariably write me when the Moon is squaring their Sun sign. What does this have to do with work? They write me *from* work, as I can tell by the return-address e-mail. Plus, the weekday and time the letter was sent indicate that they're probably sitting in an office, or in "work mode."

Ferris is a client who goes *waaay* back. When we started, he had just finished a master's degree in the humanities and was beginning preliminary doctorate work. Now he's tidying up his thesis. He's a happy guy who loves his life, and what could be a better fit than a Gemini pursuing specialized studies in literature and philosophy? Recently, he wrote me:

"As for lunar cycles, I find Moon in Pisces to be particularly dreadful, often for no obvious reason, and sometimes (like this month) this feeling even continues into Aries. (Moon in Cancer have a tendency to be 'downtime' days,' when things shift into a lower gear for a bit; but this is less pronounced and can usually be attributed to lots of activity in the days before.) Basically, with Luna in Pisces I tend to feel aimless and unsatisfied with my general situation. Your chart for me notes that here the Moon squares my Sun, Jupiter, and Neptune. Question: Is there something that I should be doing or not doing during this time? Is there something I've missed?"

Now, here's someone clearly capable of doing a close textual reading! I responded:

"People who think quickly who are also air signs like you will ALWAYS be more available because you can ALWAYS squeeze more into a day than everyone else. As for lunar cycles, Moon in Pisces is squaring your Sun, and followed by Aries, so sometimes you probably get depression, then mania. Moon in Pisces is not the time to reflect on the 'Big Picture' of your life, though sometimes it's inevitable and irresistible. I'm not surprised to hear about Moon in Cancer being downtime, because it's just after the Moon is in your Sun sign, you're ready for a rest."

Knowing that Ferris is available—sometimes too available—to his family, his friends, and his students, taking that Cancer Moon phase for himself is probably a very wise move. Indeed, a follow-up letter from Ferris confirmed that he'd found his own way through the lunar pattern.

"Generally in teaching I'm better at using the (for me) 'up' days (usually moon in air or fire signs) than the down days (especially moon in water signs). I think I need more advance thinking to figure out what to do with the latter (and maybe loading the lunar phases into some better calendar software would help); typically I don't look too much further ahead than a week to ten days. If I'm going to really be challenging my students and trying to get some discussion/interaction going, I try to make sure the moon is with me."

# Using the Moon as a Tool in Your Work

Obviously, different professions have different activities, and the "hunter-gatherer" image is still useful, though we are well past the Neolithic times. These days, we're basically a little bit of both all the time. When we spend time in meetings, we're gatherers. When we're looking for information, products, clients, connections, we're hunters. Are you a teacher? You're a hunter when you're in the classroom, and a gatherer when you prepare the work. Are you an accountant? You're a gatherer of information, but a hunter of precision. And yes, this does have bearing on the Moon. Do you think some hunters were more successful by the light of the Full Moon? Absolutely.

So, understanding some basics about the waxing and waning phases can save you all kinds of time in terms of your expectations of success. You don't have to know anything about astrology, beyond the fact that you, as a Sun sign Leo, say, need a lot of acclaim or, at least, acknowledgement from others (even if you hate admitting this!). Or that you, as a Capricorn, need to be respected in your approach to work, which means no one makes comments about the state of your desk.

Even if you close this volume now, and let all this astrological jargon drift into the void, practice this simple mantra when thinking about how to use the Moon: waxing Moon is building and growing; waning Moon is retreating or concluding. New Moons begin and end matters and anything can happen in the Full Moon. The first quarter and the last quarter are turning points in a matter, so speed accelerates or sharply brakes, depending on other factors.

I had a friend who was a licensed practical nurse. She worked in a nursing home and spent time on the floor that specialized in Alzheimers patients. Her theory about the effects of the Full and New Moon is interesting. She found that both are distinct but separate. Both phases cause agitation in the residents, who clearly had cognitive deficits, but differed in diagnostics. "The people who aren't affected by the Full Moon act up during the New Moon," she says. "And the people who act up during the Full Moon aren't bothered during the New Moon."

# The Moon Through the Twelve Signs

This section offers a generalized overview of the effects of each lunar phase, followed by specific comments for some of the signs.

## Moon in Aries

This is the classic "fresh beginning" lunar phase. Your impulse is to start projects, regardless of what you think the outcome will be. Aries Moons are great times to have meetings to talk about future goals, but they aren't so good for assessing previous performance. People who generally function well during an Aries Moon (if there aren't mitigating factors) are either a Leo, Sagittarius, Aquarius, or Gemini. Aries can be at their best during this Moon, but the impulse will be to push it in too many directions at once is strong. An Aries is not likely to use his or her "listening skills" during this phase. Those who might find they're more irritable with the flightiness of others during this phase are Capricorn and Cancer. Libra people might find they're trying too hard.

## Moon in Taurus

Forget work, let's shop—seriously, however. Taurus Moons are useful for activities requiring dogged concentration and perseverance. Others might be very set in their ways during this lunar phase, however, so you should be hesitant about coming in with the great new idea. Activities requiring repetition or attention to detail can be strangely comforting during this phase. People are less picky here than when the Moon is in Virgo. If you apply for a job during the phase, and the stars are with you, you can be perceived as tremendously responsible, but do let the interviewer proceed at his or her own pace. People who can function well during this Moon are Cancer, Pisces, Virgo, and Capricorn. Leo and Aquarius people won't be at their best, and quick with a defensive response. Taurus people can be emotional (which they'll deny), but also more prone to play the martyr. Don't call them on it now, though, Scorpio can be even more mysterious than usual.

## Moon in Gemini

A great time to return phone calls and make new ones. If you're in a job that's all about explaining matters to others, it's very good for writing. Not so great for editing or revising. Meetings that happen during Gemini Moons can be all over the place; not undisciplined so much as "Well, if we did this, would X or Y happen?" Conjecture gets stirred up. If you're planning a convention or some kind of seminar, try to schedule this on a Moon in Gemini day or weekend. One-on-one relations aren't as satisfying as relations with a group—unless you're working with your comedy-writing partner on a new spec script. Then, having a short attention span can be a boon. People who can function well during this Moon are Leo, Aries, Aquarius, and Libra. Virgo and Pisces could be anxious or quick to judge during this Moon, and Sagittarius could get talked into something that's definitely the wrong thing to do. Gemini can be at their best, or their worst, but consistency is not the story during these two or three days.

## Moon in Cancer

A great time to be hospitable to others, to train someone, or perform some sort of nurturing job. However, it is a time when people may need to be helped emotionally rather than intellectually, so listening skills are key right now. One on one can be more rewarding than working with a group. Working with people you're comfortable with could be preferable to strangers. What's great about Moon in Cancer is that you can get down to the bottom of things without trying. People who can function well during this Moon are Taurus, Virgo, Pisces, and Scorpio. Libra and Aries people might not be at their best, and too quick to respond defensively. Capricorn can be aimless and anxious, alternately needy and sulky. Cancer can actually be very useful and powerful, but too easily exhausted. Learning how to expend energy during this time is the crab's big challenge.

## Moon in Leo

This is the classic sales position. A Moon in Leo can be an energetic time, even when the Moon is waning, as it is during the winter months. A good time for meetings or job applications or "Everything must go" and "90 percent off" sales. It's a great time for business parties. If you're in charge of setting up social-izing events for your workplace, for heck's sake, make them happen on this Moon. Okay, Artie and Andrea in accounts receivable might drink too much, and Raylene and Raymond might flirt too much, but isn't the point of the event *social*? People who can function well during this Moon are Gemini,

Libra, Aries, and Sagittarius. This won't be the best time to negotiate with Taurus or Scorpio people, and don't think you can count on Aquarius, either. But Leo could be invincible, funny, humorous, loud, and compelling. Just don't overdo it, guys, and remember that the other person needs to feel good, too!

## Moon in Virgo

Here is a great time for the office grinch to get snippy about the scraps next to the paper-cutter, or the crumbs by the coffee machine. If you have an office door, keep it closed during this lunar phase, because the kind of concentration you can maintain is titanic. People who function well during this Moon are Scorpio, Cancer, Taurus, and Capricorn, though Capricorn's tendency might be to over manage. People who should give themselves a break from being high function are Sagittarius and Gemini, who might feel other people want them to be perfect, and (sniff), that's just not how they function (whimper). Pisces, especially, should be wary during this phase. You may feel like you need approval, but then engage in some self-sabotage behavior. Your usually sharp antenna gets covered with mutable earth during this phase. Virgo, I'll leave it up to you to decide how to play it. Getting mired in nostalgia comes too easily, as well as self-blame. More useful in business is for you to use this time to reach out to others, and use your (not inconsiderable) charm and humor.

## Moon in Libra

As a Sun sign Libra myself, I can assure you this is the one time of the month where I feel very confident about making snap decisions. Most of the time. Well, at least half of the time. However, I have noticed in my various workplaces that Moon in Libra is a time when the general mood gets very wishy-washy. It's not a good time for purchasing office furniture, though you could have surprising energy for turning pages and marking desired items with Post-its. However, meetings in general (as is true during air and fire sign days) can be dynamic, and civility could be a premium. Cancer and Capricorn people can find this Moon troubling because their instincts get dulled. Capricorn thinks people aren't being straightforward whereas Cancer may find folks aren't being "honest." Leo and Sagittarius could shine during this lunar phase, but Aries could be in "people-pleasing" mode and resenting it.

## Moon in Scorpio

Cut to the chase. Do it for less. Make it happen faster. That's Moon in Scorpio, and it isn't for the faint-at-heart. It's a splendid time for covert operations or any business that has to do with budget cutting. Put off figuring out how to do those cuts for a Moon in Scorpio (or Capricorn) interlude. Water sign people could be at their best during this Moon, if they could get past their emotions. Virgo and Capricorn could also be high-functioning, even without a to-do list. Leo and Aquarius need to lie low. Don't ask for attention or favors and let others say their piece first. Scorpio, if you're applying for a job at the Department of Defense, a non-profit arts agency, a hospital, or medical institution, you could seem at your most competent and appealing during this phase. However, the downside is that you might not want to share all your charisma with others. It's a "go-to-ground" time for your sign. Taurus, feelings of vulnerability could be strong, so you may be self-conscious if you don't have it *all* figured out. Give yourself a break.

## Moon in Sagittarius

Meetings held during this phase can be entertaining, but drag on a too long. At the non-profit arts institution where I work, meetings happened to

sync up with mutable signs one month. The Sagittarius meeting day seemed to last two hours, and there was much in the way of distraction and digression—most of it amusing. The classic prescription for this Moon phase is to plan travel or educational pursuits, or at least entertain myriad possibilities of same. Fire sign people could be at their best, though a little over-the-top in terms of forcefulness. Watch the pitch of your voice. Virgo and Pisces do not want to take chances during this phase, whether it's moving forward on business that hasn't received committee approval or presuming the worst of others. Your perceptions will definitely be skewed toward the dramatic. Sagittarius, slowing down won't be an option here, so you may as well go for broke, say what you think, and be as generous as you can. Gemini could be incredibly amusing to others, as well as in a go for broke mode, but be careful you don't "overpromise" either with deadlines or what you can do during this lunar phase.

## Moon in Capricorn

Capricorn is all about work, so if you put your nose to the grindstone, you'll be lucky if you have a skull left by the end of the day. Not good for dealing with others, for the most part, but very good for taking apart a system or code, or doing some god-awful job you've been putting off. Unless, that is, you've got a Sun sign Capricorn to do that for you when the Moon was in the other two earth signs! This can be a good phase for Pisces and Scorpio, especially if they need an excuse to get organized, but seclusion is key. Moon in Capricorn is not particularly social. Aries and Libra also need to be very structured in their worklife. Don't leave things to chance during this Moon, and try not to "do it all yourself." This is the Moon of the maverick, and some signs just function better in partnership. Capricorn, this could be both useful and pleasant for you, but you may seem stiff and ungracious to others. Watch the tendency toward sarcasm, especially when you're around those innocents who think irony is something you do to wrinkled clothes. Cancer, this is a great day for you to set limits on others. Even if it gives you a stomach ache.

## Moon in Aquarius

A great Moon for work if you can do the following: stay on task, stay disciplined, and keep your wandering attention span from seizing on trifles. For example, you start an e-mail letter, and then realize it leads to a letter you need to write to X, which reminds you of the information that A, B, and C need to receive. As Aquarius is all about new technology and mass-communications, this can be a useful phase for sending out announcements or marketing product. Libra and Gemini could be cruising at very high altitudes during this Moon—so high, that others ask you, "Can you explain what you're doing?" Keep your temper, air signs, and you may be able to drag colleagues into the twenty-first century. Taurus and Scorpio may find they're touchy during this phase—is it that more is presumed of you than you can provide? Or that you're making assumptions without having all the facts. Leo—avoid putting yourself in a vulnerable position during this Moon—if you're in a job that requires endless, boundless confidence, this could be a low couple of days. And Aquarius—you should plan for this Moon every month. This is the time you do presentations, speeches, pitches, and so forth. Just be on time.

## Moon in Pisces

Very, very interesting. Excellent for finishing projects, even if you hadn't planned to. As Pisces can be a mystical, scattered sort of sign, figure that people might be guilty of unexplained absence or working behind the scenes. It's a great day for working on artwork for posters or flyers or newsletters. It's not so good for exit interviews (too painful), and can be low energy for applying for a job (unless you're a water sign seeking work in the healing, helping, or teaching professions). Scorpio and Cancer could have remarkable insight into others' motives during this phase. If the previously mentioned suggestions don't appeal to you, then consider this a day for research. Gemini and Sagittarius could be unduly emotional and prone to take slights personally during this phase. Virgo could feel overwhelmed— too much to do, too little time to do it. And Pisces could be at a peak in terms of appeal, and the ability to be a masochist. Let others love you (or help you) during this phase.

# Void-of-Course Moon

When the Moon changes Sun sign, as it does every 2.5 days or so, there is invariably a time when it ceases making major angles to other planets. These interludes are called "void-of-course," and can last anywhere from minutes to many hours. The shorthand on this "astrological freefall" is this: avoid making a million copies, because you'll find the work wasn't done to your specifications. Avoid asking others to do specific tasks relating to bookkeeping, records, correspondence, and so on. This is the kind of day where you send out three separate e-mails to an important business colleague—all of them including corrections and updates on material you sent before. This isn't a good time to initiate phone calls or for calls that relate to new business to have a good outcome. Business calls that come in during the void-of-course period seldom pan out.

Here's one example. Some time ago, I got a call from a small newspaper in the Midwest hoping to carry my column. I had a bad feeling about these folks—they didn't seem focused or realistic in their aspirations or businesslike in their manner. But what the heck, a new client is a new client. Of course, when I looked at my lunar calendar, I saw the initial call came in during the void-of-course Moon, and that many subsequent calls were made by them when the Moon was void-of-course. They seemed to get energized when the lunar energy meant things would mess up, and my subsequent dealings with them revealed some disturbing textbook examples of how *not* to run a business.

No one seemed clear about what his or her duties were. The three personalities I dealt with on the phone were constantly shifting responsibility. Though native speakers, no one seemed to have a grasp on the English language, and their tendency was to mangle sentences that were brief and grammatical. The result was labyrinthine and tortured syntax. I yearned for the end as much as I yearned for my overdue check. Both weren't long in coming, and I cashed the check immediately (when the Moon wasn't void-of-course, by the way!). The happy ending is that the newspaper and these folks went away very quickly. The best part of the experience was seeing the void-of-course Moon in action. Beware of folks who always call during that time, or who are more present than usual in your life during then—unless you've got a taste for chaos!

Finally, using the Moon as a short-term tool for determining conditions and possible outcomes is actually really enjoyable, and easier, if you know the birthdays of the people you work with. Try and take some notes when the Moon is in certain signs and see if there's a trend. Everyone will adapt the previous explanations to suit their own needs.

## About the Author

Sally Cragin writes "Moon Signs" for the *Phoenix* newspapers in New England and the *San Francisco Bay Guardian*. Look for her at www.moon-signs.net.

Farm,
Garden,
and
Weather
Section

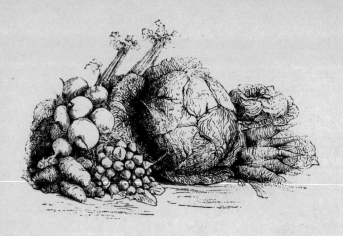

# Gardening by the Moon

Today, people often reject the notion of gardening according to the Moon's phase and sign. The usual nonbeliever is not a scientist but the city dweller who has never had any real contact with nature and little experience of natural rhythms.

Camille Flammarian, the French astronomer, testifies to the success of Moon planting, though:

"Cucumbers increase at Full Moon, as well as radishes, turnips, leeks, lilies, horseradish, and saffron; onions, on the contrary, are much larger and better nourished during the decline and old age of the Moon than at its increase, during its youth and fullness, which is the reason the Egyptians abstained from onions, on account of their antipathy to the Moon. Herbs gathered while the Moon increases are of great efficiency. If the vines are trimmed at night when the Moon is in the sign of the Lion, Sagittarius, the Scorpion, or the Bull, it will save them from field rats, moles, snails, flies, and other animals."

Dr. Clark Timmins is one of the few modern scientists to have conducted tests in Moon planting. Following is a summary of his experiments:

*Beets:* When sown with the Moon in Scorpio, the germination rate was 71 percent; when sown in Sagittarius, the germination rate was 58 percent.

*Scotch marigold:* When sown with the Moon in Cancer, the germination rate was 90 percent; when sown in

Leo, the rate was 32 percent.

*Carrots:* When sown with the Moon in Scorpio, the germination rate was 64 percent; when sown in Sagittarius, the germination rate was 47 percent.

*Tomatoes:* When sown with the Moon in Cancer, the germination rate was 90 percent; but when sown with the Moon in Leo, the germination rate was 58 percent.

Two things should be emphasized. First, remember that this is only a summary of the results of the experiments; the experiments themselves were conducted in a scientific manner to eliminate any variation in soil, temperature, moisture, and so on, so that only the Moon sign is varied. Second, note that these astonishing results were obtained without regard to the phase of the Moon—the other factor we use in Moon planting, and which presumably would have increased the differential in germination rates.

Dr. Timmins also tried transplanting Cancer- and Leo-planted tomato seedlings while the Cancer Moon was waxing. The result was 100 percent survival. When transplanting was done with the waning Sagittarius Moon, there was 0 percent survival. Dr. Timmins' tests show that the Cancer-planted tomatoes had blossoms twelve days earlier than those planted under Leo;

the Cancer-planted tomatoes had an average height of twenty inches at that time compared to fifteen inches for the Leo-planted; the first ripe tomatoes were gathered from the Cancer plantings eleven days ahead of the Leo plantings; and a count of the hanging fruit and its size and weight shows an advantage to the Cancer plants over the Leo plants of 45 percent.

Dr. Timmins also observed that there have been similar tests that did not indicate results favorable to the Moon planting theory. As a scientist, he asked why one set of experiments indicated a positive verification of Moon planting, and others did not. He checked these other tests and found that the experimenters had not followed the geocentric system for determining the Moon sign positions, but the heliocentric. When the times used in these other tests were converted to the geocentric system, the dates chosen often were found to be in barren, rather than fertile, signs. Without going into a technical explanation, it is sufficient to point out that geocentric and heliocentric positions often vary by as much as four days. This is a large enough differential to place the Moon in Cancer, for example, in the heliocentric system, and at the same time in Leo by the geocentric system.

Most almanacs and calendars show the Moon's signs heliocentrically—and thus incorrectly for Moon planting—while the *Moon Sign Book* is calculated correctly for planting purposes, using the geocentric system. Some readers are confused because the *Moon Sign Book* talks about first, second, third, and fourth quarters, while other almanacs refer to these same divisions as New Moon, first quarter, Full Moon, and fourth quarter. Thus the almanacs say first quarter when the *Moon Sign Book* says second quarter.

There is nothing complicated about using astrology in agriculture and horticulture in order to increase both pleasure and profit, but there is one very important rule that is often neglected—use common sense! Of course this is one rule that should be remembered in every activity we undertake, but in the case of gardening and farming by the Moon if it is not possible to use the best dates for planting or harvesting, we must select the next best and just try to do the best we can.

This brings up the matter of the other factors to consider in your gardening work. The dates we give as best for a certain activity apply to the entire country (with slight time correction), but in your section of the country you may be buried under three feet of snow on a date we say is good to plant your flowers.

So we have factors of weather, season, temperature and moisture variations, soil conditions, your own available time and opportunity, and so forth. Some astrologers like to think it is all a matter of science, but gardening is also an art. In art, you develop an instinctive identification with your work and influence it with your feelings and wishes.

The *Moon Sign Book* gives you the place of the Moon for every day of the year so that you can select the best times once you have become familiar with the rules and practices of lunar agriculture. We give you specific, easy-to-follow directions so that you can get right down to work.

We give you the best dates for planting, and also for various related activities, including cultivation, fertilizing, harvesting, irrigation, and getting rid of weeds and pests. But we cannot tell you exactly when it's good to plant. Many of these rules were learned by observation and experience; as the body of experience grew we could see various patterns emerging that allowed us to make judgments about new things. That's what you should do, too. After you have worked with lunar agriculture for a while and have gained a working knowledge, you will probably begin to try new things—and we hope you will share your experiments and findings with us. That's how the science grows.

Here's an example of what we mean. Years ago, Llewellyn George suggested that we try to combine our bits of knowledge about what to expect in planting under each of the Moon signs in order to gain benefit from several lunar factors in one plant. From this came our rule for developing "thoroughbred seed." To develop thoroughbred seed, save the seed for three successive years from plants grown by the correct Moon sign and phase. You can plant in the first quarter phase and in the sign of Cancer for fruitfulness; the second year, plant seeds from the first year plants in Libra for beauty; and in the third year, plant the seeds from the second year plants in Taurus to produce hardiness. In a similar manner you can combine the fruitfulness of Cancer, the good root growth of Pisces, and the sturdiness and good vine growth of Scorpio. And don't forget the characteristics of Capricorn: hardy like Taurus, but drier and perhaps more resistant to drought and disease.

Unlike common almanacs, we consider both the Moon's phase and the Moon's sign in making our calculations for the proper timing of our work. It is perhaps a little easier to understand this if we remind you that we are all living in the center of a vast electromagnetic field that is the Earth and its environment in space. Everything that occurs within this electromagnetic field has an effect on everything else within the field. The Moon and the Sun are the most important of the factors affecting the life of the Earth, and it is their relative positions to the Earth that we project for each day of the year.

Many people claim that not only do they achieve larger crops gardening by the Moon, but that their fruits and vegetables are much tastier. A number of organic gardeners have also become lunar gardeners using the natural rhythm of life forces that we experience through the relative movements of the Sun and Moon. We provide a few basic rules and then give you day-by-day guidance for your gardening work. You will be able to choose the best dates to meet your own needs and opportunities.

## Planting by the Moon's Phases

During the increasing or waxing light—from New Moon to Full Moon—plant annuals that produce their yield above the ground. An annual is a plant that completes its entire life cycle within one growing season and has to be seeded each year. During the decreasing or waning light—from Full Moon to New Moon—plant biennials, perennials, and bulb and root plants. Biennials include crops that are

## First Quarter

Plant annuals producing their yield above the ground, which are generally of the leafy kind that produce their seed outside the fruit. Some examples are asparagus, broccoli, Brussels sprouts, cabbage, cauliflower, celery, cress, endive, kohlrabi, lettuce, parsley, and spinach. Cucumbers are an exception, as they do best in the first quarter rather than the second, even though the seeds are inside the fruit. Also plant cereals and grains.

## Second Quarter

Plant annuals producing their yield above the ground, which are generally of the viney kind that produce their seed inside the fruit. Some examples include beans, eggplant, melons, peas, peppers, pumpkins, squash, tomatoes, etc. These are not hard-and-fast divisions. If you can't plant during the first quarter, plant during the second, and vice versa. There are many plants that seem to do equally well planted in either quarter, such as watermelon, hay, and cereals and grains.

## Third Quarter

Plant biennials, perennials, bulbs, root plants, trees, shrubs, berries, grapes, strawberries, beets, carrots, onions, parsnips, rutabagas, potatoes, radishes, peanuts, rhubarb, turnips, winter wheat, etc.

planted one season to winter over and produce crops the next, such as winter wheat. Perennials and bulb and root plants include all plants that grow from the same root each year.

A simpler, less-accurate rule is to plant crops that produce above the ground during the waxing Moon, and to plant crops that produce below the ground during the waning Moon. Thus the old adage "Plant potatoes during the dark of the Moon." Llewellyn George's system divided the lunar month into quarters. The first two from New Moon to Full Moon are the first and second quarters, and the last two from Full Moon to New Moon the third and fourth quarters. Using these divisions, we can increase our accuracy in timing our efforts to coincide with natural forces.

## Fourth Quarter

This is the best time to cultivate, turn sod, pull weeds, and destroy pests of all kinds, especially when the Moon is in the barren signs of Aries, Leo, Virgo, Gemini, Aquarius, and Sagittarius.

## Moon in Aries

Barren, dry, fiery, and masculine sign used for destroying noxious weeds.

## Moon in Taurus

Productive, moist, earthy, and feminine sign used for planting many crops when hardiness is important, particularly root crops. Also used for lettuce, cabbage, and similar leafy vegetables.

## Moon in Gemini

Barren and dry, airy and masculine sign used for destroying noxious growths, weeds, and pests, and for cultivation.

## Moon in Cancer

Fruitful, moist, feminine sign used extensively for planting and irrigation.

## Moon in Leo

Barren, dry, fiery, masculine sign used only for killing weeds or cultivation.

## Moon in Virgo

Barren, moist, earthy, and feminine sign used for cultivation and destroying weeds and pests.

## Moon in Libra

Semi-fruitful, moist, and airy, this sign is used for planting many crops, and producing good pulp growth and roots. A very good sign for flowers and vines. Also used for seeding hay, corn fodder, and the like.

## Moon in Scorpio

Very fruitful and moist, watery and feminine. Nearly as productive as Cancer; used for the same purposes. Especially good for vine growth and sturdiness.

## Moon in Sagittarius

Barren and dry, fiery and masculine. Used for planting onions, seeding hay, and for cultivation.

## Moon in Capricorn

Productive and dry, earthy and feminine. Used for planting potatoes and other tubers.

## Moon in Aquarius

Barren, dry, airy, and masculine sign used for cultivation and destroying noxious growths and pests.

## Moon in Pisces

Very fruitful, moist, watery, and feminine sign especially good for root growth.

# A Guide to Planting

Using Phase & Sign Rulerships

| Plant | Phase/Quarter | Sign |
|-------|---------------|------|
| Annuals | 1st or 2nd | |
| Apple tree | 2nd or 3rd | Cancer, Pisces, Taurus, Virgo |
| Artichoke | 1st | Cancer, Pisces |
| Asparagus | 1st | Cancer, Scorpio, Pisces |
| Aster | 1st or 2nd | Virgo, Libra |
| Barley | 1st or 2nd | Cancer, Pisces, Libra, Capricorn, Virgo |
| Beans (bush & pole) | 2nd | Cancer, Taurus, Pisces, Libra |
| Beans (kidney, white, & navy) | 1st or 2nd | Cancer, Pisces |
| Beech tree | 2nd or 3rd | Virgo, Taurus |
| Beet | 3rd | Cancer, Capricorn, Pisces, Libra |
| Biennials | 3rd or 4th | |
| Broccoli | 1st | Cancer, Pisces, Libra, Scorpio |
| Brussels sprout | 1st | Cancer, Scorpio, Pisces, Libra |
| Buckwheat | 1st or 2nd | Capricorn |
| Bulbs | 3rd | Cancer, Scorpio, Pisces |
| Bulbs for seed | 2nd or 3rd | |
| Cabbage | 1st | Cancer, Scorpio, Pisces, Libra, Taurus |

| Plant | Phase/Quarter | Sign |
|---|---|---|
| Cactus | | Taurus, Capricorn |
| Canes (raspberry, blackberry and gooseberry) | 2nd | Cancer, Scorpio, Pisces |
| Cantaloupe | 1st or 2nd | Cancer, Scorpio, Pisces, Libra, Taurus |
| Carrot | 3rd | Taurus, Cancer, Scorpio, Pisces, Libra |
| Cauliflower | 1st | Cancer, Scorpio, Pisces, Libra |
| Celeriac | 3rd | Cancer, Scorpio, Pisces |
| Celery | 1st | Cancer, Scorpio, Pisces |
| Cereals | 1st or 2nd | Cancer, Scorpio, Pisces, Libra |
| Chard | 1st or 2nd | Cancer, Scorpio, Pisces |
| Chicory | 2nd, 3rd | Cancer, Scorpio, Pisces |
| Chrysanthemum | 1st or 2nd | Virgo |
| Clover | 1st or 2nd | Cancer, Scorpio, Pisces |
| Corn | 1st | Cancer, Scorpio, Pisces |
| Corn for fodder | 1st or 2nd | Libra |
| Coryopsis | 2nd or 3rd | Libra |
| Cosmo | 2nd or 3rd | Libra |
| Cress | 1st | Cancer, Scorpio, Pisces |
| Crocus | 1st or 2nd | Virgo |
| Cucumber | 1st | Cancer, Scorpio, Pisces |

| Plant | Phase/Quarter | Sign |
|-------|---------------|------|
| Daffodils | 1st or 2nd | Libra, Virgo |
| Dahlias | 1st or 2nd | Libra, Virgo |
| Deciduous trees | 2nd or 3rd | Cancer, Scorpio, Pisces, Virgo, Taurus |
| Eggplant | 2nd | Cancer, Scorpio, Pisces, Libra |
| Endive | 1st | Cancer, Scorpio, Pisces, Libra |
| Flowers | 1st | Libra, Cancer, Pisces, Virgo, Scorpio, Taurus |
| Garlic | 3rd | Libra, Taurus, Pisces |
| Gladiola | 1st or 2nd | Libra, Virgo |
| Gourd | 1st or 2nd | Cancer, Scorpio, Pisces, Libra |
| Grape | 2nd or 3rd | Cancer, Scorpio, Pisces, Virgo |
| Hay | 1st or 2nd | Cancer, Scorpio, Pisces, Libra, Taurus |
| Herbs | 1st or 2nd | Cancer, Scorpio, Pisces |
| Honeysuckle | 1st or 2nd | Scorpio, Virgo |
| Hops | 1st or 2nd | Scorpio, Libra |
| Horseradish | 1st or 2nd | Cancer, Scorpio, Pisces |
| Houseplants | 1st | Libra, Cancer, Scorpio, Pisces |
| Hyacinth | 3rd | Cancer, Scorpio, Pisces |
| Iris | 1st or 2nd | Cancer, Virgo |
| Kohlrabi | 1st or 2nd | Cancer, Scorpio, Pisces, Libra |

| Plant | Phase/Quarter | Sign |
|-------|---------------|------|
| Leek | 1st or 2nd | Cancer, Pisces |
| Lettuce | 1st | Cancer, Scorpio, Pisces, Libra, Taurus |
| Lily | 1st or 2nd | Cancer, Scorpio, Pisces |
| Maple tree | 2nd or 3rd | Virgo, Taurus, Cancer, Pisces |
| Melon | 2nd | Cancer, Scorpio, Pisces |
| Moon vine | 1st or 2nd | Virgo |
| Morning glory | 1st or 2nd | Cancer, Scorpio, Pisces, Virgo |
| Oak tree | 2nd or 3rd | Virgo, Taurus, Cancer, Pisces |
| Oats | 1st or 2nd | Cancer, Scorpio, Pisces, Libra |
| Okra | 1st | Cancer, Scorpio, Pisces, Libra |
| Onion seed | 2nd | Scorpio, Cancer, Sagittarius |
| Onion set | 3rd or 4th | Libra, Taurus, Pisces, Cancer |
| Pansy | 1st or 2nd | Cancer, Scorpio, Pisces |
| Parsley | 1st | Cancer, Scorpio, Pisces, Libra |
| Parsnip | 3rd | Taurus, Capricorn, Cancer, Scorpio, Capricorn |
| Peach tree | 2nd or 3rd | Taurus, Libra, Virgo, Cancer |
| Peanut | 3rd | Cancer, Scorpio, Pisces |
| Pear tree | 2nd or 3rd | Taurus, Libra, Virgo, Cancer |
| Pea | 2nd | Cancer, Scorpio, Pisces, Libra |

| Plant | Phase/Quarter | Sign |
|---|---|---|
| Peony | 1st or 2nd | Virgo |
| Pepper | 2nd | Cancer, Pisces, Scorpio |
| Perennials | 3rd | |
| Petunia | 1st or 2nd | Libra, Virgo |
| Plum tree | 2nd or 3rd | Taurus, Virgo, Cancer, Pisces |
| Poppy | 1st or 2nd | Virgo |
| Portulaca | 1st or 2nd | Virgo |
| Potato | 3rd | Cancer, Scorpio, Taurus, Libra, Capricorn |
| Privet | 1st or 2nd | Taurus, Libra |
| Pumpkin | 2nd | Cancer, Scorpio, Pisces, Libra |
| Quince | 1st or 2nd | Capricorn |
| Radish | 3rd | Cancer, Libra, Taurus, Pisces, Capricorn |
| Rhubarb | 3rd | Cancer, Pisces |
| Rice | 1st or 2nd | Scorpio |
| Rose | 1st or 2nd | Cancer, Virgo |
| Rutabaga | 3rd | Cancer, Scorpio, Pisces, Taurus |
| Saffron | 1st or 2nd | Cancer, Scorpio, Pisces |
| Sage | 3rd | Cancer, Scorpio, Pisces |
| Salsify | 1st or 2nd | Cancer, Scorpio, Pisces |

| Plant | Phase/Quarter | Sign |
|---|---|---|
| Shallot | 2nd | Scorpio |
| Spinach | 1st | Cancer, Scorpio, Pisces |
| Squash | 2nd | Cancer, Scorpio, Pisces, Libra |
| Strawberry | 3rd | Cancer, Scorpio, Pisces |
| String bean | 1st or 2nd | Taurus |
| Sunflower | 1st or 2nd | Libra, Cancer |
| Sweet pea | 1st or 2nd | |
| Tomato | 2nd | Cancer, Scorpio, Pisces, Capricorn |
| Shade trees | 3rd | Taurus, Capricorn |
| Ornamental trees | 2nd | Libra, Taurus |
| Trumpet vine | 1st or 2nd | Cancer, Scorpio, Pisces |
| Tubers for seed | 3rd | Cancer, Scorpio, Pisces, Libra |
| Tulip | 1st or 2nd | Libra, Virgo |
| Turnip | 3rd | Cancer, Scorpio, Pisces, Taurus, Capricorn, Libra |
| Valerian | 1st or 2nd | Virgo, Gemini |
| Watermelon | 1st or 2nd | Cancer, Scorpio, Pisces, Libra |
| Wheat | 1st or 2nd | Cancer, Scorpio, Pisces, Libra |

# 2004 Gardening Dates

| Dates | Qtr. | Sign | Activity |
|---|---|---|---|
| Jan. 1, 12:02 am-<br>Jan. 3, 12:58 pm | 2nd | Taurus | Plant annuals for hardiness. Trim to increase growth. |
| Jan. 6, 1:38 am-<br>Jan. 7, 10:40 am | 2nd | Cancer | Plant grains, leafy annuals. Fertilize (chemical). Graft or bud plants. Irrigate. Trim to increase growth. |
| Jan. 7, 10:40 am-<br>Jan. 8, 12:38 pm | 3rd | Cancer | Plant biennials, perennials, bulbs, and roots. Prune. Irrigate. Fertilize (organic). |
| Jan. 8, 12:38 pm-<br>Jan. 10, 9:37 pm | 3rd | Leo | Cultivate. Destroy weeds and pests. Harvest fruits and root crops for food. Trim to retard growth. |
| Jan. 10, 9:37 pm-<br>Jan. 13, 4:38 am | 3rd | Virgo | Cultivate, especially medicinal plants. Destroy weeds and pests. Trim to retard growth. |
| Jan. 15, 9:33 am-<br>Jan. 17, 12:18 pm | 4th | Scorpio | Plant biennials, perennials, bulbs and roots. Prune. Irrigate. Fertilize (organic). |
| Jan. 17, 12:18 pm-<br>Jan. 19, 1:24 pm | 4th | Sagittarius | Cultivate. Destroy weeds and pests. Harvest fruits and root crops for food. Trim to retard growth. |
| Jan. 19, 1:24 pm-<br>Jan. 21, 2:11 pm | 4th | Capricorn | Plant potatoes and tubers. Trim to retard growth. |
| Jan. 21, 2:11 pm-<br>Jan. 21, 4:05 pm | 4th | Aquarius | Cultivate. Destroy weeds and pests. Harvest fruits and root crops for food. Trim to retard growth. |
| Jan. 23, 4:29 pm-<br>Jan. 25, 10:06 pm | 1st | Pisces | Plant grains, leafy annuals. Fertilize (chemical). Graft or bud plants. Irrigate. Trim to increase growth. |
| Jan. 28, 7:46 am-<br>Jan. 29, 1:03 am | 1st | Taurus | Plant annuals for hardiness. Trim to increase growth. |
| Jan. 29, 1:03 am-<br>Jan. 30, 8:18 pm | 2nd | Taurus | Plant annuals for hardiness. Trim to increase growth. |
| Feb. 2, 9:03 am-<br>Feb. 4, 7:50 pm | 2nd | Cancer | Plant grains, leafy annuals. Fertilize (chemical). Graft or bud plants. Irrigate. Trim to increase growth. |
| Feb. 6, 3:47 am-<br>Feb. 7, 4:03 am | 3rd | Leo | Cultivate. Destroy weeds and pests. Harvest fruits and root crops for food. Trim to retard growth. |
| Feb. 7, 4:03 am-<br>Feb. 9, 10:12 am | 3rd | Virgo | Cultivate, especially medicinal plants. Destroy weeds and pests. Trim to retard growth. |
| Feb. 11, 2:58 pm-<br>Feb. 13, 8:39 am | 3rd | Scorpio | Plant biennials, perennials, bulbs, and roots. Prune. Irrigate. Fertilize (organic). |
| Feb. 13, 8:39 am-<br>Feb. 13, 6:35 pm | 4th | Scorpio | Plant biennials, perennials, bulbs and roots. Prune. Irrigate. Fertilize (organic). |
| Feb. 13, 6:35 pm-<br>Feb. 15, 9:14 pm | 4th | Sagittarius | Cultivate. Destroy weeds and pests. Harvest fruits and root crops for food. Trim to retard growth. |
| Feb. 15, 9:14 pm-<br>Feb. 17, 11:27 pm | 4th | Capricorn | Plant potatoes and tubers. Trim to retard growth. |
| Feb. 17, 11:27 pm-<br>Feb. 20, 2:27 am | 4th | Aquarius | Cultivate. Destroy weeds and pests. Harvest fruits and root crops for food. Trim to retard growth. |

| Dates | Qtr. | Sign | Activity |
|---|---|---|---|
| Feb. 20, 2:27 am-<br>Feb. 20, 4:18 am | 4th | Pisces | Plant biennials, perennials, bulbs, and roots. Prune. Irrigate. Fertilize (organic). |
| Feb. 20, 4:18 am-<br>Feb. 22, 7:45 am | 1st | Pisces | Plant grains, leafy annuals. Fertilize (chemical). Graft or bud plants. Irrigate. Trim to increase growth. |
| Feb. 24, 4:30 pm-<br>Feb. 27, 4:22 am | 1st | Taurus | Plant annuals for hardiness. Trim to increase growth. |
| Feb. 29, 5:12 pm-<br>Mar. 3, 4:18 am | 2nd | Cancer | Plant grains, leafy annuals. Fertilize (chemical). Graft or bud plants. Irrigate. Trim to increase growth. |
| Mar. 6, 6:14 pm-<br>Mar. 7, 5:31 pm | 3rd | Virgo | Cultivate, especially medicinal plants. Destroy weeds and pests. Trim to retard growth. |
| Mar. 9, 9:03 pm-<br>Mar. 11, 11:57 pm | 3rd | Scorpio | Plant biennials, perennials, bulbs, and roots. Prune. Irrigate. Fertilize (organic). |
| Mar. 11, 11:57 pm-<br>Mar. 13, 4:01 pm | 3rd | Sagittarius | Cultivate. Destroy weeds and pests. Harvest fruits and root crops for food. Trim to retard growth. |
| Mar. 13, 4:01 pm-<br>Mar. 14, 2:51 am | 4th | Sagittarius | Cultivate. Destroy weeds and pests. Harvest fruits and root crops for food. Trim to retard growth. |
| Mar. 14, 2:51 am-<br>Mar. 16, 6:10 am | 4th | Capricorn | Plant potatoes and tubers. Trim to retard growth. |
| Mar. 16, 6:10 am-<br>Mar. 18, 10:26 am | 4th | Aquarius | Cultivate. Destroy weeds and pests. Harvest fruits and root crops for food. Trim to retard growth. |
| Mar. 18, 10:26 am-<br>Mar. 20, 4:29 pm | 4th | Pisces | Plant biennials, perennials, bulbs, and roots. Prune. Irrigate. Fertilize (organic). |
| Mar. 20, 4:29 pm-<br>Mar. 20, 5:41 pm | 4th | Aries | Cultivate. Destroy weeds and pests. Harvest fruits and root crops for food. Trim to retard growth. |
| Mar. 23, 1:10 am-<br>Mar. 25, 12:35 pm | 1st | Taurus | Plant annuals for hardiness. Trim to increase growth. |
| Mar. 28, 1:23 am-<br>Mar. 28, 6:48 pm | 1st | Cancer | Plant grains, leafy annuals. Fertilize (chemical). Graft or bud plants. Irrigate. Trim to increase growth. |
| Mar. 28, 6:48 pm-<br>Mar. 30, 1:07 pm | 2nd | Cancer | Plant grains, leafy annuals. Fertilize (chemical). Graft or bud plants. Irrigate. Trim to increase growth. |
| Apr. 4, 3:52 am-<br>Apr. 5, 7:03 am | 2nd | Libra | Plant annuals for fragrance and beauty. Trim to increase growth. |
| Apr. 6, 6:24 am-<br>Apr. 8, 7:50 am | 3rd | Scorpio | Plant biennials, perennials, bulbs, and roots. Prune. Irrigate. Fertilize (organic). |
| Apr. 8, 7:50 am-<br>Apr. 10, 9:33 am | 3rd | Sagittarius | Cultivate. Destroy weeds and pests. Harvest fruits and root crops for food. Trim to retard growth. |
| Apr. 10, 9:33 am-<br>Apr. 11, 11:46 pm | 3rd | Capricorn | Plant potatoes and tubers. Trim to retard growth. |
| Apr. 11, 11:46 pm-<br>Apr. 12, 12:33 pm | 4th | Capricorn | Plant potatoes and tubers. Trim to retard growth. |

| Dates | Qtr. | Sign | Activity |
|---|---|---|---|
| Apr. 12, 12:33 pm-<br>Apr. 14, 5:24 pm | 4th | Aquarius | Cultivate. Destroy weeds and pests. Harvest fruits and root crops for food. Trim to retard growth. |
| Apr. 14, 5:24 pm-<br>Apr. 17, 12:24 am | 4th | Pisces | Plant biennials, perennials, bulbs, and roots. Prune. Irrigate. Fertilize (organic). |
| Apr. 17, 12:24 am-<br>Apr. 19, 9:21 am | 4th | Aries | Cultivate. Destroy weeds and pests. Harvest fruits and root crops for food. Trim to retard growth. |
| Apr. 19, 9:43 am-<br>Apr. 21, 9:10 pm | 1st | Taurus | Plant annuals for hardiness. Trim to increase growth. |
| Apr. 24, 9:56 am-<br>Apr. 26, 10:14 pm | 1st | Cancer | Plant grains, leafy annuals. Fertilize (chemical). Graft or bud plants. Irrigate. Trim to increase growth. |
| May 1, 2:03 pm-<br>May 3, 4:38 pm | 2nd | Libra | Plant annuals for fragrance and beauty. Trim to increase growth. |
| May 3, 4:38 pm-<br>May 4, 4:33 pm | 2nd | Scorpio | Plant grains, leafy annuals. Fertilize (chemical). Graft or bud plants. Irrigate. Trim to increase growth. |
| May 4, 4:33 pm-<br>May 5, 5:08 pm | 3rd | Scorpio | Plant biennials, perennials, bulbs, and roots. Prune. Irrigate. Fertilize (organic). |
| May 5, 5:08 pm-<br>May 7, 5:17 pm | 3rd | Sagittarius | Cultivate. Destroy weeds and pests. Harvest fruits and root crops for food. Trim to retard growth. |
| May 7, 5:17 pm-<br>May 9, 6:46 pm | 3rd | Capricorn | Plant potatoes and tubers. Trim to retard growth. |
| May 9, 6:46 pm-<br>May 11, 7:04 am | 3rd | Aquarius | Cultivate. Destroy weeds and pests. Harvest fruits and root crops for food. Trim to retard growth.. |
| May 11, 7:04 am-<br>May 11, 10:52 pm | 4th | Aquarius | Cultivate. Destroy weeds and pests. Harvest fruits and root crops for food. Trim to retard growth. |
| May 11, 10:52 pm-<br>May 14, 6:02 am | 4th | Pisces | Plant biennials, perennials, bulbs, and roots. Prune. Irrigate. Fertilize (organic). |
| May 14, 6:02 am-<br>May 16, 3:57 pm | 4th | Aries | Cultivate. Destroy weeds and pests. Harvest fruits and root crops for food. Trim to retard growth. |
| May 16, 3:57 pm-<br>May 19, 12:52 am | 4th | Taurus | Plant potatoes and tubers. Trim to retard growth. |
| May 19, 12:52 am-<br>May 19, 3:47 am | 1st | Taurus | Plant annuals for hardiness. Trim to increase growth. |
| May 21, 4:35 pm-<br>May 24, 5:07 am | 1st | Cancer | Plant grains, leafy annuals. Fertilize (chemical). Graft or bud plants. Irrigate. Trim to increase growth. |
| May 28, 11:22 pm-<br>May 31, 3:08 pm | 2nd | Libra | Plant annuals for fragrance and beauty. Trim to increase growth. |
| May 31, 3:08 am-<br>Jun. 2, 3:52 am | 2nd | Scorpio | Plant grains, leafy annuals. Fertilize (chemical). Graft or bud plants. Irrigate. Trim to increase growth. |
| Jun. 3, 12:20 am-<br>Jun. 4, 3:12 am | 3rd | Sagittarius | Cultivate. Destroy weeds and pests. Harvest fruits and root crops for food. Trim to retard growth. |

| Dates | Qtr. | Sign | Activity |
|---|---|---|---|
| Jun. 4, 3:12 am-<br>Jun. 6, 3:10 am | 3rd | Capricorn | Plant potatoes and tubers. Trim to retard growth. |
| Jun. 6, 3:10 am-<br>Jun. 8, 5:38 am | 3rd | Aquarius | Cultivate. Destroy weeds and pests. Harvest fruits and root crops for food. Trim to retard growth. |
| Jun. 8, 5:38 am-<br>Jun. 9, 4:02 pm | 3rd | Pisces | Plant biennials, perennials, bulbs, and roots. Prune. Irrigate. Fertilize (organic). |
| Jun. 9, 4:02 pm-<br>Jun. 10, 11:49 am | 4th | Pisces | Plant biennials, perennials, bulbs and roots. Prune. Irrigate. Fertilize (organic). |
| Jun. 10, 11:49 am-<br>Jun. 12, 9:37 pm | 4th | Aries | Cultivate. Destroy weeds and pests. Harvest fruits and root crops for food. Trim to retard growth. |
| Jun. 12, 9:37 pm-<br>Jun. 15, 9:44 am | 4th | Taurus | Plant potatoes and tubers. Trim to retard growth. |
| Jun. 15, 9:44 am-<br>Jun. 17, 4:27 pm | 4th | Gemini | Cultivate. Destroy weeds and pests. Harvest fruits and root crops for food. Trim to retard growth. |
| Jun. 17, 10:37 pm-<br>Jun. 20, 11:05 am | 1st | Cancer | Plant grains, leafy annuals. Fertilize (chemical). Graft or bud plants. Irrigate. Trim to increase growth. |
| Jun. 25, 6:50 am-<br>Jun. 25, 3:08 pm | 1st | Libra | Plant annuals for fragrance and beauty. Trim to increase growth. |
| Jun. 25, 3:08 pm-<br>Jun. 27, 12:13 pm | 2nd | Libra | Plant annuals for fragrance and beauty. Trim to increase growth. |
| Jun. 27, 12:13 pm-<br>Jun. 29, 2:15 pm | 2nd | Scorpio | Plant grains, leafy annuals. Fertilize (chemical). Graft or bud plants. Irrigate. Trim to increase growth. |
| Jul. 1, 2:01 pm-<br>Jul. 2, 7:09 am | 2nd | Capricorn | Graft or bud plants. Trim to increase growth. |
| Jul. 2, 7:09 am-<br>Jul. 3, 1:22 pm | 3rd | Capricorn | Plant potatoes and tubers. Trim to retard growth. |
| Jul. 3, 1:22 pm-<br>Jul. 5, 2:26 pm | 3rd | Aquarius | Cultivate. Destroy weeds and pests. Harvest fruits and root crops for food. Trim to retard growth. |
| Jul. 5, 2:26 pm-<br>Jul. 7, 7:03 pm | 3rd | Pisces | Plant biennials, perennials, bulbs, and roots. Prune. Irrigate. Fertilize (organic). |
| Jul. 7, 7:03 pm-<br>Jul. 9, 3:34 am | 3rd | Aries | Cultivate. Destroy weeds and pests. Harvest fruits and root crops for food. Trim to retard growth. |
| Jul. 9, 3:34 am-<br>Jul. 10, 3:51 am | 4th | Aries | Cultivate. Destroy weeds and pests. Harvest fruits and root crops for food. Trim to retard growth. |
| Jul. 10, 3:51 am-<br>Jul. 12, 3:45 pm | 4th | Taurus | Plant potatoes and tubers. Trim to retard growth. |
| Jul. 12, 3:45 pm-<br>Jul. 15, 4:40 am | 4th | Gemini | Cultivate. Destroy weeds and pests. Harvest fruits and root crops for food. Trim to retard growth. |
| Jul. 15, 4:40 am-<br>Jul. 17, 7:24 am | 4th | Cancer | Plant biennials, perennials, bulbs, and roots. Prune. Irrigate. Fertilize (organic). |

| Dates | Qtr. | Sign | Activity |
|---|---|---|---|
| Jul. 17, 7:24 am–<br>Jul. 17, 4:56 pm | 1st | Cancer | Plant grains, leafy annuals. Fertilize (chemical). Graft or bud plants. Irrigate. Trim to increase growth. |
| Jul. 22, 12:39 pm–<br>Jul. 24, 7:08 pm | 1st | Libra | Plant annuals for fragrance and beauty. Trim to increase growth. |
| Jul. 24, 7:08 pm–<br>Jul. 24, 11:37 pm | 1st | Scorpio | Plant grains, leafy annuals. Fertilize (chemical). Graft or bud plants. Irrigate. Trim to increase growth. |
| Jul. 24, 11:37 pm–<br>Jul. 26, 10:48 pm | 2nd | Scorpio | Plant grains, leafy annuals. Fertilize (chemical). Graft or bud plants. Irrigate. Trim to increase growth. |
| Jul. 28, 11:57 pm–<br>Jul. 30, 11:54 pm | 2nd | Capricorn | Graft or bud plants. Trim to increase growth. |
| Jul. 31, 2:05 pm–<br>Aug. 2, 12:34 am | 3rd | Aquarius | Cultivate. Destroy weeds and pests. Harvest fruits and root crops for food. Trim to retard growth. |
| Aug. 2, 12:34 am–<br>Aug. 4, 3:59 am | 3rd | Pisces | Plant biennials, perennials, bulbs, and roots. Prune. Irrigate. Fertilize (organic). |
| Aug. 4, 3:59 am–<br>Aug. 6, 11:26 am | 3rd | Aries | Cultivate. Destroy weeds and pests. Harvest fruits and root crops for food. Trim to retard growth. |
| Aug. 6, 11:26 am–<br>Aug. 7, 6:01 pm | 3rd | Taurus | Plant potatoes and tubers. Trim to retard growth. |
| Aug. 7, 6:01 pm–<br>Aug. 8, 10:33 pm | 4th | Taurus | Plant potatoes and tubers. Trim to retard growth. |
| Aug. 8, 10:33 pm–<br>Aug. 11, 11:20 am | 4th | Gemini | Cultivate. Destroy weeds and pests. Harvest fruits and root crops for food. Trim to retard growth. |
| Aug. 11, 11:20 am–<br>Aug. 13, 11:30 pm | 4th | Cancer | Plant biennials, perennials, bulbs, and roots. Prune. Irrigate. Fertilize (organic). |
| Aug. 13, 11:30 pm–<br>Aug. 15, 9:24 pm | 4th | Leo | Cultivate. Destroy weeds and pests. Harvest fruits and root crops for food. Trim to retard growth. |
| Aug. 18, 6:09 pm–<br>Aug. 21, 12:37 am | 1st | Libra | Plant annuals for fragrance and beauty. Trim to increase growth. |
| Aug. 21, 12:37 am–<br>Aug. 23, 5:08 am | 1st | Scorpio | Plant grains, leafy annuals. Fertilize (chemical). Graft or bud plants. Irrigate. Trim to increase growth. |
| Aug. 25, 7:46 am–<br>Aug. 27, 9:08 am | 2nd | Capricorn | Graft or bud plants. Trim to increase growth. |
| Aug. 29, 10:33 am–<br>Aug. 29, 10:22 pm | 2nd | Pisces | Plant grains, leafy annuals. Fertilize (chemical). Graft or bud plants. Irrigate. Trim to increase growth. |
| Aug. 29, 10:22 pm–<br>Aug. 31, 1:46 pm | 3rd | Pisces | Plant biennials, perennials, bulbs, and roots. Prune. Irrigate. Fertilize (organic). |
| Aug. 31, 1:46 pm–<br>Sep. 2, 8:16 pm | 3rd | Aries | Cultivate. Destroy weeds and pests. Harvest fruits and root crops for food. Trim to retard growth. |
| Sep. 2, 8:16 pm–<br>Sep. 5, 6:24 am | 3rd | Taurus | Plant potatoes and tubers. Trim to retard growth. |

| Dates | Qtr. | Sign | Activity |
|---|---|---|---|
| Sep. 5, 6:24 am-<br>Sep. 6, 11:10 am | 3rd | Gemini | Cultivate. Destroy weeds and pests. Harvest fruits and root crops for food. Trim to retard growth. |
| Sep. 6, 11:10 am-<br>Sep. 7, 6:50 pm | 4th | Gemini | Cultivate. Destroy weeds and pests. Harvest fruits and root crops for food. Trim to retard growth. |
| Sep. 7, 6:50 pm-<br>Sep. 10, 7:06 am | 4th | Cancer | Plant biennials, perennials, bulbs, and roots. Prune. Irrigate. Fertilize (organic). |
| Sep. 10, 7:06 am-<br>Sep. 12, 5:16 pm | 4th | Leo | Cultivate. Destroy weeds and pests. Harvest fruits and root crops for food. Trim to retard growth. |
| Sep. 12, 5:16 pm-<br>Sep. 14, 10:29 am | 4th | Virgo | Cultivate, especially medicinal plants. Destroy weeds and pests. Trim to retard growth. |
| Sep. 15, 12:54 am-<br>Sep. 17, 6:25 am | 1st | Libra | Plant annuals for fragrance and beauty. Trim to increase growth. |
| Sep. 17, 6:25 am-<br>Sep. 19, 10:30 am | 1st | Scorpio | Plant grains, leafy annuals. Fertilize (chemical). Graft or bud plants. Irrigate. Trim to increase growth. |
| Sep. 21, 1:35 pm-<br>Sep. 23, 4:10 pm | 2nd | Capricorn | Graft or bud plants. Trim to increase growth. |
| Sep. 25, 6:55 pm-<br>Sep. 27, 10:57 pm | 2nd | Pisces | Plant grains, leafy annuals. Fertilize (chemical). Graft or bud plants. Irrigate. Trim to increase growth. |
| Sep. 28, 9:09 am-<br>Sep. 30, 5:24 am | 3rd | Aries | Cultivate. Destroy weeds and pests. Harvest fruits and root crops for food. Trim to retard growth. |
| Sep. 30, 5:24 am-<br>Oct. 2, 2:55 pm | 3rd | Taurus | Plant potatoes and tubers. Trim to retard growth. |
| Oct. 2, 2:55 pm-<br>Oct. 5, 2:54 am | 3rd | Gemini | Cultivate. Destroy weeds and pests. Harvest fruits and root crops for food. Trim to retard growth. |
| Oct. 5, 2:54 am-<br>Oct. 6, 6:12 am | 3rd | Cancer | Plant biennials, perennials, bulbs, and roots. Prune. Irrigate. Fertilize (organic). |
| Oct. 6, 6:12 am-<br>Oct. 7, 3:23 pm | 4th | Cancer | Plant biennials, perennials, bulbs, and roots. Prune. Irrigate. Fertilize (organic). |
| Oct. 7, 3:23 pm-<br>Oct. 10, 2:00 am | 4th | Leo | Cultivate. Destroy weeds and pests. Harvest fruits and root crops for food. Trim to retard growth. |
| Oct. 10, 2:00 am-<br>Oct. 12, 9:32 am | 4th | Virgo | Cultivate, especially medicinal plants. Destroy weeds and pests. Trim to retard growth. |
| Oct. 13, 10:48 pm-<br>Oct. 14, 2:10 pm | 1st | Libra | Plant annuals for fragrance and beauty. Trim to increase growth. |
| Oct. 14, 2:10 pm-<br>Oct. 16, 4:58 pm | 1st | Scorpio | Plant grains, leafy annuals. Fertilize (chemical). Graft or bud plants. Irrigate. Trim to increase growth. |
| Oct. 18, 7:07 pm-<br>Oct. 20, 5:59 pm | 1st | Capricorn | Graft or bud plants. Trim to increase growth. |
| Oct. 20, 5:59 pm-<br>Oct. 20, 9:38 pm | 2nd | Capricorn | Graft or bud plants. Trim to increase growth. |

| Dates | Qtr. | Sign | Activity |
|---|---|---|---|
| Oct. 23, 1:13 am-<br>Oct. 25, 6:24 am | 2nd | Pisces | Plant grains, leafy annuals. Fertilize (chemical). Graft or bud plants. Irrigate. Trim to increase growth. |
| Oct. 27, 1:37 pm-<br>Oct. 27, 11:07 pm | 2nd | Taurus | Plant annuals for hardiness. Trim to increase growth. |
| Oct. 27, 11:07 pm-<br>Oct. 29, 11:11 pm | 3rd | Taurus | Plant potatoes and tubers. Trim to retard growth. |
| Oct. 29, 11:11 pm-<br>Nov. 1, 9:53 am | 3rd | Gemini | Cultivate. Destroy weeds and pests. Harvest fruits and root crops for food. Trim to retard growth. |
| Nov. 1, 9:53 am-<br>Nov. 3, 10:32 pm | 3rd | Cancer | Plant biennials, perennials, bulbs, and roots. Prune. Irrigate. Fertilize (organic). |
| Nov. 3, 10:32 pm-<br>Nov. 5, 12:53 am | 3rd | Leo | Cultivate. Destroy weeds and pests. Harvest fruits and root crops for food. Trim to retard growth. |
| Nov. 5, 12:53 am-<br>Nov. 6, 10:00 am | 4th | Leo | Cultivate. Destroy weeds and pests. Harvest fruits and root crops for food. Trim to retard growth. |
| Nov. 6, 10:00 am-<br>Nov. 8, 6:23 pm | 4th | Virgo | Cultivate, especially medicinal plants. Destroy weeds and pests. Trim to retard growth. |
| Nov. 10, 11:05 pm-<br>Nov. 12, 9:27 am | 4th | Scorpio | Plant biennials, perennials, bulbs, and roots. Prune. Irrigate. Fertilize (organic). |
| Nov. 12, 9:27 am-<br>Nov. 13, 12:56 am | 1st | Scorpio | Plant grains, leafy annuals. Fertilize (chemical). Graft or bud plants. Irrigate. Trim to increase growth. |
| Nov. 15, 1:33 am-<br>Nov. 17, 2:39 am | 1st | Capricorn | Graft or bud plants. Trim to increase growth. |
| Nov. 19, 5:38 am-<br>Nov. 21, 11:11 am | 2nd | Pisces | Plant grains, leafy annuals. Fertilize (chemical). Graft or bud plants. Irrigate. Trim to increase growth. |
| Nov. 23, 7:16 pm-<br>Nov. 26, 5:25 am | 2nd | Taurus | Plant annuals for hardiness. Trim to increase growth. |
| Nov. 26, 3:07 pm-<br>Nov. 28, 5:10 pm | 3rd | Gemini | Cultivate. Destroy weeds and pests. Harvest fruits and root crops for food. Trim to retard growth. |
| Nov. 28, 5:10 pm-<br>Dec. 1, 5:50 am | 3rd | Cancer | Plant biennials, perennials, bulbs, and roots. Prune. Irrigate. Fertilize (organic). |
| Dec. 1, 5:50 am-<br>Dec. 3, 6:00 pm | 3rd | Leo | Cultivate. Destroy weeds and pests. Harvest fruits and root crops for food. Trim to retard growth. |
| Dec. 3, 6:00 pm-<br>Dec. 4, 7:53 pm | 3rd | Virgo | Cultivate, especially medicinal plants. Destroy weeds and pests. Trim to retard growth. |
| Dec. 4, 7:53 pm-<br>Dec. 6, 3:46 am | 4th | Virgo | Cultivate, especially medicinal plants. Destroy weeds and pests. Trim to retard growth. |
| Dec. 8, 9:43 am-<br>Dec. 10, 11:54 am | 4th | Scorpio | Plant biennials, perennials, bulbs, and roots. Prune. Irrigate. Fertilize (organic). |
| Dec. 10, 11:54 am-<br>Dec. 11, 8:29 pm | 4th | Sagittarius | Cultivate. Destroy weeds and pests. Harvest fruits and root crops for food. Trim to retard growth. |

| Dates | Qtr. | Sign | Activity |
|-------|------|------|----------|
| Dec. 12, 11:42 am-<br>Dec. 14, 11:10 am | 1st | Capricorn | Graft or bud plants. Trim to increase growth. |
| Dec. 16, 12:24 pm-<br>Dec. 18, 11:40 am | 1st | Pisces | Plant grains, leafy annuals. Fertilize (chemical). Graft or bud plants. Irrigate. Trim to increase growth. |
| Dec. 18, 11:40 am-<br>Dec. 18, 4:52 pm | 2nd | Pisces | Plant grains, leafy annuals. Fertilize (chemical). Graft or bud plants. Irrigate. Trim to increase growth. |
| Dec. 21, 12:52 am-<br>Dec. 23, 11:32 am | 2nd | Taurus | Plant annuals for hardiness. Trim to increase growth. |
| Dec. 25, 11:38 pm-<br>Dec. 26, 10:06 am | 2nd | Cancer | Plant grains, leafy annuals. Fertilize (chemical). Graft or bud plants. Irrigate. Trim to increase growth. |
| Dec. 26, 10:06 am-<br>Dec. 28, 12:14 pm | 3rd | Cancer | Plant biennials, perennials, bulbs, and roots. Prune. Irrigate. Fertilize (organic). |
| Dec. 28, 12:14 pm-<br>Dec. 31, 12:33 am | 3rd | Leo | Cultivate. Destroy weeds and pests. Harvest fruits and root crops for food. Trim to retard growth. |

# 2004 Dates to Destroy Weeds and Pests

| Date | Time | Date | Time | Sign | Qtr. |
|------|------|------|------|------|------|
| Jan. 8 | 12:38 pm | Jan. 10 | 9:37 pm | Leo | 3rd |
| Jan. 10 | 9:37 pm | Jan. 13 | 4:38 am | Virgo | 3rd |
| Jan. 17 | 12:18 pm | Jan. 19 | 1:24 pm | Sagittarius | 4th |
| Jan. 21 | 2:11 pm | Jan 21 | 4:05 pm | Aquarius | 4th |
| Feb. 6 | 3:47 am | Feb. 7 | 4:03 am | Leo | 3rd |
| Feb. 7 | 4:03 am | Feb. 9 | 10:12 am | Virgo | 3rd |
| Feb. 13 | 6:35 pm | Feb. 15 | 9:14 pm | Sagittarius | 4th |
| Feb. 17 | 11:27 pm | Feb. 20 | 2:27 am | Aquarius | 4th |
| Mar. 6 | 6:14 pm | Mar. 7 | 5:31 pm | Virgo | 3rd |
| Mar. 11 | 11:57 pm | Mar. 13 | 4:01 pm | Sagittarius | 3rd |
| Mar. 13 | 4:01 pm | Mar. 14 | 2:51 am | Sagittarius | 4th |
| Mar. 16 | 6:10 am | Mar. 18 | 10:26 am | Aquarius | 4th |
| Mar. 20 | 4:29 pm | Mar. 20 | 5:41 pm | Aries | 4th |
| Apr. 8 | 7:50 am | Apr. 10 | 9:33 am | Sagittarius | 3rd |
| Apr. 12 | 12:33 pm | Apr. 14 | 5:24 pm | Aquarius | 4th |
| Apr. 17 | 12:24 am | Apr. 19 | 9:21 am | Aries | 4th |
| May 5 | 5:08 pm | May 7 | 5:17 pm | Sagittarius | 3rd |
| May 9 | 6:46 pm | May 11 | 7:04 am | Aquarius | 3rd |
| May 11 | 7:04 am | May 11 | 10:52 pm | Aquarius | 4th |
| May 14 | 6:02 am | May 16 | 3:57 pm | Aries | 4th |
| Jun. 3 | 12:20 am | Jun. 4 | 3:12 am | Sagittarius | 3rd |
| Jun. 6 | 3:10 am | Jun. 8 | 5:38 am | Aquarius | 3rd |
| Jun. 10 | 11:49 am | Jun. 12 | 9:37 pm | Aries | 4th |
| Jun. 15 | 9:44 am | Jun. 17 | 4:27 pm | Gemini | 4th |
| Jul. 3 | 1:22 pm | Jul. 5 | 2:26 pm | Aquarius | 3rd |
| Jul. 7 | 7:03 pm | Jul. 9 | 3:34 am | Aries | 3rd |
| Jul. 9 | 3:34 am | Jul. 10 | 3:51 am | Aries | 4th |

| Date | Time | Date | Time | Sign | Qtr. |
|---|---|---|---|---|---|
| Jul. 12 | 3:45 pm | Jul. 15 | 4:40 am | Gemini | 4th |
| Jul. 31 | 2:05 pm | Aug. 2 | 12:34 am | Aquarius | 3rd |
| Aug. 4 | 3:59 am | Aug. 6 | 11:26 am | Aries | 3rd |
| Aug. 8 | 10:33 pm | Aug. 11 | 11:20 am | Gemini | 4th |
| Aug. 13 | 11:30 pm | Aug. 15 | 9:24 pm | Leo | 4th |
| Aug 31 | 1:46 pm | Sep. 2 | 8:16 pm | Aries | 3rd |
| Sep. 5 | 6:24 am | Sep. 6 | 11:10 am | Gemini | 3rd |
| Sep. 6 | 11:10 am | Sep. 7 | 6:50 pm | Gemini | 4th |
| Sep. 10 | 7:06 am | Sep. 12 | 5:16 pm | Leo | 4th |
| Sep. 12 | 5:16 pm | Sep. 14 | 10:29 am | Virgo | 4th |
| Sep. 28 | 9:09 am | Sep. 30 | 5:24 am | Aries | 3rd |
| Oct. 2 | 2:55 pm | Oct. 5 | 2:54 am | Gemini | 3rd |
| Oct. 7 | 3:23 pm | Oct. 10 | 2:00 am | Leo | 4th |
| Oct. 10 | 2:00 am | Oct. 12 | 9:32 am | Virgo | 4th |
| Oct. 29 | 11:11 pm | Nov. 1 | 9:53 am | Gemini | 3rd |
| Nov. 3 | 10:32 pm | Nov. 5 | 12:53 am | Leo | 3rd |
| Nov. 5 | 12:53 am | Nov. 6 | 10:00 am | Leo | 4th |
| Nov. 6 | 10:00 am | Nov. 8 | 6:23 pm | Virgo | 4th |
| Nov. 26 | 3:07 pm | Nov 28 | 5:10 pm | Gemini | 3rd |
| Dec. 1 | 5:50 am | Dec. 3 | 6:00 pm | Leo | 3rd |
| Dec. 3 | 6:00 pm | Dec. 4 | 7:53 pm | Virgo | 3rd |
| Dec. 4 | 7:53 pm | Dec. 6 | 3:46 am | Virgo | 4th |
| Dec. 10 | 11:54 am | Dec. 11 | 8:29 pm | Sagittarius | 4th |
| Dec. 28 | 12:14 pm | Dec. 31 | 12:33 am | Leo | 3rd |

# 2004 Egg-Setting Dates

| Dates to be Born | Qtr. | Sign | Set Eggs |
|---|---|---|---|
| Jan. 6, 1:38 am-Jan. 8, 12:38 pm | 2nd | Cancer | Dec. 16 |
| Jan. 23, 4:29 pm-Jan. 25, 10:06 pm | 1st | Pisces | Jan. 2 |
| Jan. 28, 7:46 am-Jan. 29, 9:04 pm | 1st | Taurus | Jan. 7 |
| Feb. 2, 9:03 am-Feb. 4, 7:50 pm | 2nd | Cancer | Jan. 12 |
| Feb. 24, 4:30 pm-Feb. 25, 9:55 pm | 1st | Taurus | Feb. 3 |
| Feb. 29, 5:12 pm-Mar. 3, 4:18 am | 2nd | Cancer | Feb. 8 |
| Mar. 22, 10:10 pm-Mar. 24, 5:29 pm | 1st | Taurus | Mar. 1 |
| Mar. 28, 1:23 am-Mar. 30, 1:07 pm | 1st | Cancer | Mar. 7 |
| Apr. 3, 11:52 pm-Apr. 5, 5:26 pm | 2nd | Libra | Mar.13 |
| Apr. 19, 9:43 am-Apr. 20, 3:36 pm | 1st | Taurus | Mar. 29 |
| Apr. 24, 9:56 am-Apr. 26, 10:14 pm | 1st | Cancer | Apr. 3 |
| May 1, 2:03 pm-May 3, 12:49 pm | 2nd | Libra | Apr. 10 |
| May 21, 4:35 pm-May 24, 5:07 am | 1st | Cancer | Apr. 30 |
| Jun. 17, 10:37 pm-Jun. 20, 11:05 am | 1st | Cancer | May 27 |
| Jun. 25, 6:50 am-Jun. 26, 7:41 pm | 2nd | Libra | Jun. 4 |
| Jul. 22, 12:39 pm-Jul. 24, 5:54 pm | 1st | Libra | Jul. 1 |
| Aug. 18, 6:09 pm-Aug. 20, 9:39 pm | 1st | Libra | Jul. 27 |
| Aug. 29, 10:33 am-Aug. 31, 1:46 pm | 2nd | Pisces | Aug. 8 |
| Sep. 15, 12:54 am-Sep. 16, 9:31 pm | 1st | Libra | Aug. 26 |
| Sep. 25, 6:55 pm-Sep. 27, 10:57 pm | 2nd | Pisces | Sep. 4 |
| Oct. 23, 1:13 am-Oct. 25, 6:24 am | 2nd | Pisces | Oct. 2 |
| Nov.19, 5:38 am-Nov. 21, 11:11 am | 2nd | Pisces | Oct. 29 |
| Nov. 23, 7:16 pm-Nov. 25, 11:37 pm | 2nd | Taurus | Nov. 2 |
| Dec. 16, 12:24 pm-Dec. 18, 4:52 pm | 1st | Pisces | Nov. 25 |
| Dec. 21, 12:52 am-Dec 23, 8:41 am | 2nd | Taurus | Nov. 30 |
| Dec. 25, 11:38 pm-Dec. 28, 12:14 pm | 2nd | Cancer | Dec. 4 |

# Companion Planting Guide
## Plant Helpers and Hinderers

| Plant | Helped By | Hindered By |
|---|---|---|
| Asparagus | Tomato, parsley, basil | |
| Bean | Carrot, cucumber, cabbage, beet, corn | Onion, gladiola |
| Bush bean | Cucumber, cabbage, strawberry | Fennel, onion |
| Beet | Onion, cabbage, lettuce | Pale bean |
| Cabbage | Beet, potato, onion, celery | Strawberry, tomato |
| Carrot | Pea, lettuce, chive, radish, leek, onion | Dill |
| Celery | Leek, bush bean | |
| Chive | Bean | |
| Corn | Potato, bean, pea, melon, squash, pumpkin, cucumber | |
| Cucumber | Bean, cabbage, radish, sunflower, lettuce | Potato, herbs |
| Eggplant | Bean | |
| Lettuce | Strawberry, carrot | |
| Melon | Morning glory | |
| Onion, leek | Beet, chamomile, carrot, lettuce | Pea, bean |
| Garlic | Summer savory | |
| Pea | Radish, carrot, corn cumumber, bean, turnip | Onion |
| Potato | Bean, corn, pea, cabbage, hemp, cucumber | Sunflower |

| Plant | Helped By | Hindered By |
|---|---|---|
| Radish | Pea, Lettuce, Nasturtium, Cucumbers | Hyssop |
| Spinach | Strawberry | |
| Squash, Pumpkin | Nasturtium, Corn | Potatoes |
| Tomatoes | Asparagus, Parsley, Chives, Onions, Carrot, Marigold, Nasturtium | Dill, Cabbage, Fennel |
| Turnip | Pea, Bean | |

## Plant Companions and Uses

| Plant | Companions and Uses |
|---|---|
| Anise | Coriander |
| Basil | Tomato; dislikes rue; repels flies and mosquitos |
| Borage | Tomato and squash |
| Buttercup | Clover; hinders delphinium, peony, monkshood, columbine |
| Chamomile | Helps peppermint, wheat, onions, and cabbage; large amounts destructive |
| Catnip | Repels flea beetles |
| Chervil | Radish |
| Chives | Carrot; prone to apple scab and powdery mildew |
| Coriander | Hinders seed formation in fennel |
| Cosmos | Repels corn earworms |
| Dill | Cabbage; hinders carrot and tomato |
| Fennel | Disliked by all garden plants |
| Garlic | Aids vetch and roses; hinders peas and beans |
| Hemp | Beneficial as a neighbor to most plants |
| Horseradish | Repels potato bugs |

| Plant | Companions and Uses |
|-------|---------------------|
| Horsetail | Makes fungicide spray |
| Hyssop | Attracts cabbage fly away from cabbages; harmful to radishes |
| Lovage | Improves hardiness and flavor of neighbor plants |
| Marigold | Pest repellent; use against Mexican bean beetles and nematodes |
| Mint | Repels ants, flea beetles and cabbage worm butterflies |
| Morning glory | Corn; helps melon germination |
| Nasturtium | Cabbage, cucumbers; deters aphids, squash bugs, and pumpkin beetles |
| Nettle | Increase oil content in neighbors |
| Parsley | Tomatoes, asparagus |
| Purslane | Good ground cover |
| Rosemary | Repels cabbage moths, bean beetles, and carrot flies |
| Sage | Repels cabbage moths and carrot flies |
| Savory | Deters bean beetles |
| Sunflower | Hinders potatoes; improves soil |
| Tansy | Deters Japanese beetles, striped cucumber beetles, and squash bugs |
| Thyme | Repels cabbage worms |
| Yarrow | Increases essential oils of neighbors |

# 2004 Weather Forecast

### by Kris Brandt-Riske

Astrometeorology—astrological weather forecasting—reveals seasonal and weekly weather trends based on the cardinal ingresses (Summer and Winter Solstices, and Spring and Autumn Equinoxes) and the four monthly lunar phases. The planetary alignments and the longitudes and latitudes they influence have the strongest effect, but the zodiacal signs are also involved in creating weather conditions.

The components of a thunderstorm, for example, are heat, wind, and electricity. A Mars-Jupiter configuration generates the necessary heat and Mercury adds wind and electricity. A severe thunderstorm, and those that produce tornadoes, usually involve Mercury, Mars, Uranus, or Neptune. The zodiacal signs add their energy to the planetary mix to increase or decrease the chance of weather phenomena and their severity.

In general, the fire signs (Aries, Leo, Sagittarius) indicate heat and dryness, both of which peak when Mars, the planet with a similar nature, is in these signs. Water signs (Cancer, Scorpio, Pisces) are conducive to precipitation, and air signs (Gemini, Libra, Aquarius) to cool temperatures and wind. Earth signs (Taurus, Virgo, Capricorn) vary from wet to dry, heat to cold. The signs and their prevailing weather conditions are listed here:

> **Aries:** Heat, dry, wind
> **Taurus:** Moderate temperatures, precipitation

**Gemini:** Cool temperatures, wind, dry
**Cancer:** Cold, steady precipitation
**Leo:** Heat, dry, lightning
**Virgo:** Cold, dry, windy
**Libra:** Cool, windy, fair
**Scorpio:** Extreme temperatures, abundant precipitation
**Sagittarius:** Warm, fair, moderate wind
**Capricorn:** Cold, wet, damp
**Aquarius:** Cold, dry, high pressure, lightning
**Pisces:** Wet, cool, low pressure

Take note of the Moon's sign at each lunar phase. It reveals the prevailing weather conditions for the next six to seven days. The same is true of Mercury and Venus. These two influential weather planets transit the entire zodiac each year, unless retrograde patterns add their influence.

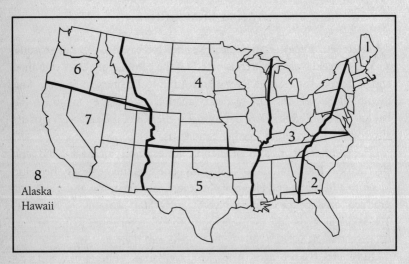

## Seasonal Weather Forecast

### Winter

**Zone 1:** Blizzard potential, especially in New England; wind and cold with precipitation throughout much of the zone.

**Zone 2:** Seasonal temperatures prevail, and precipitation is below normal in most areas except north, which is also colder.

**Zone 3:** Cold, cloudy weather dominates as major storms move through the zone; more seasonal east with less precipitation.

**Zone 4:** Significant precipitation northwest; drier west and central; cold throughout the zone; stormy east with blizzard potential.

**Zone 5:** Cold with storms moving through the zone from the west; low pressure systems increase tornado potential; eastern areas experience the greatest impact of high winds.

**Zone 6:** Storms generate above average precipitation throughout the zone; temperatures are seasonal to below and at times frigid.

**Zone 7:** Storms in western and central areas move east, bringing significant precipitation throughout the zone; temperatures are seasonal to below.

**Zone 8:** Eastern and central Alaska are cloudy, windy, cold, and stormy with above normal precipitation; drier and warmer west. Temperatures range from normal to above in Hawaii, except during stormy periods, which generate increased precipitation and unseasonably cool weather.

## Spring

**Zone 1:** Mostly fair and dry south; cold and dry north with a better chance for precipitation.

**Zone 2:** Temperatures are normal to below; dryness prevails with warmer conditions later in the season.

**Zone 3:** Heavy precipitation, thunderstorms, tornadoes, and wind throughout much of the zone; cooler and drier east.

**Zone 4:** Cold, windy, and dry west; warmer with increased precipitation and tornado potential in central areas; cloudy and cool east with periodic severe storms and tornadoes.

**Zone 5:** Windy and dry west, with temperatures above normal west and central; cooler east where cloudiness prevails; thunderstorm and tornado potential are highest central, where precipitation is above normal.

**Zone 6:** Cold with intermittent storms west; central and eastern areas are windy and seasonal with precipitation normal to below.

**Zone 7:** Conditions are generally cold and cloudy north coast; fair south with periods of cool and cloudy weather; desert areas are seasonal to above normal and dry, as are areas to the north.

**Zone 8:** Flood potential accompanies above normal precipitation in central and eastern Alaska; wind, cloudy skies, and temperatures normal to below dominate in the west; warmer east. Temperatures in Hawaii are seasonal to above with rainfall that ranges from normal to below.

## Summer

**Zone 1:** Temperatures range from normal to above; precipitation normal to below; drier north; strong thunderstorms south; windy.

**Zone 2:** Normal to above temperatures prevail make conditions ripe for hurricanes, thunderstorms, and tornadoes; heavier precipitation north.

**Zone 3:** Temperatures normal to below with abundant precipitation from significant storms that generate tornadoes, especially east and northeast; hurricane potential in the Gulf.

**Zone 4:** Windy and dry central with temperatures normal to above central and west, which sees more precipitation; cooler east with periods of higher temperatures and increased precipitation.

**Zone 5:** Above normal temperatures and windy with average precipitation west; some areas see flash floods; drier and hot central and east.

**Zone 6:** Dryness, fair skies, and above normal temperatures prevail except in some coastal areas, where it's cooler with more precipitation; windy with storms, cloudy skies, and cooler temperatures east.

**Zone 7:** Fair skies and normal to above temperatures with a greater chance of precipitation north; hot and dry in the east desert and mountain areas, but with periodic strong storm systems; southern California is hot and dry later in the season.

**Zone 8:** Temperatures are normal to below in Alaska with periods of high temperatures and dryness; overcast skies and storms with flood potential east, but warmer. Dry with normal to above temperatures at times in Hawaii; hurricane potential medium.

## Autumn

**Zone 1:** Cloudy, cool, storms, and hurricane potential dominate with heavy precipitation in some areas; temperatures seasonal to cool.

**Zone 2:** Thunderstorm, tornado, and hurricane potential high throughout the zone—especially south, which also experiences dry periods; cool and cloudy north; windy.

**Zone 3:** Severe thunderstorms with hail and tornadoes east; seasonal to cool throughout much of the zone, especially west, where storms bring wind and cloudy conditions.

**Zone 4:** Cold east with early frost and storms; more seasonal conditions west and central, although cool and windy; increased precipitation northwest from storms; cloudiness prevails.

**Zone 5:** Temperatures are seasonal to cool; mostly fair and dry, although severe thunderstorms spawn tornadoes.

**Zone 6:** Fair, windy, and dry with temperatures normal to above west and central; storms east and in mountain areas produce significant precipitation.

**Zone 7:** Hot in the desert with precipitation and flash floods; coastal areas are windy, with storms north; temperatures normal to above throughout the zone; storms generate increased precipitation east and in mountain region.

**Zone 8:** Central and western Alaska are warmer than areas to the east, which are cloudy and cool; significant precipitation central with fog and flood potential; stormy east.

# Weekly Forecasts

## January 1-6

**Zone 1:** Windy and cold with precipitation north; not as cold south with drizzle, freezing rain, and snow.

**Zone 2:** Dry, temperatures seasonal to above; mostly fair with a chance for precipitation later in the week.

**Zone 3:** Cold and clear east; partly cloudy west and south with a chance for precipitation.

**Zone 4:** Cold wave throughout much of the zone; windy central with precipitation; partly cloudy to overcast east with precipitation; heavy precipitation northwest and west with blizzard potential.

**Zone 5:** Windy with temperatures seasonal to below; partly cloudy with precipitation; thaw and flood potential near end of week.

**Zone 6:** Heavy precipitation inland and mountains; windy and cool with precipitation on coast.

**Zone 7:** Heavy precipitation in mountain region with blizzard potential extending south as storm approaches from west and moves through the zone; cold.

**Zone 8:** Precipitation and overcast eastern Alaska; windy and stormy later in the week with seasonal temperatures west; seasonal to cool in Hawaii; windy west; precipitation and cloudy east.

## January 7-14

**Zone 1:** Very windy and cold with precipitation as front moves north.

**Zone 2:** Windy with precipitation and variable cloudiness, then clearing, fair, and warmer.

**Zone 3:** Temperatures normal to above, fair to partly cloudy and mostly dry; chance of precipitation; windy and cooler east.

**Zone 4:** Precipitation and windy as a front moves east into the Plains out of the northwest; east central cool and partly cloudy to cloudy; warmer east, thaw.

**Zone 5:** Storm with freezing rain, sleet, and snow west and central; warmer east with partly cloudy to cloudy skies.

**Zone 6:** Partly cloudy, breezy, temperatures gradually warming; overcast skies with precipitation east, becoming fair and warmer.

**Zone 7:** Overcast with precipitation east as front moves through the area; fair to partly cloudy and warmer west; precipitation in the mountains.

**Zone 8:** Overcast and stormy in Alaska; seasonal and cloudy with precipitation in Hawaii.

## January 15-20

**Zone 1:** Cold with precipitation south; warmer northeast and then cooler with precipitation as storm moves north.

**Zone 2:** Cold with precipitation ranging from drizzle to snow, mostly cloudy.

**Zone 3:** Heavy precipitation, cold, and overcast as storm centers south; cold and cloudy northeast with precipitation.

**Zone 4:** Stormy and cold east as front moves into the area; warmer west, cloudy and seasonal.

**Zone 5:** Seasonal to cool east, cloudy, precipitation; warmer west.

**Zone 6:** Stormy, windy, and cold with heavy precipitation west; partly cloudy to cloudy east, windy, seasonal temperatures.

**Zone 7:** Cold and stormy coastal front moves into central and eastern areas of the zone, bringing increasing clouds and precipitation; cloudy and warmer south with precipitation.

**Zone 8:** Cold throughout Alaska with precipitation west; drier and windy east; seasonal to cool with precipitation in Hawaii.

## January 21-28

**Zone 1:** Cold north; cloudy and windy south with precipitation.

**Zone 2:** Fair, warmer south, coastal fog, mostly dry.

**Zone 3:** Fair and mild with variable clouds east; windy west.

**Zone 4:** Cold with precipitation, some heavy, central and east, then clearing, warmer and windy.

**Zone 5:** Cold with precipitation, some heavy; warmer east and cloudy.

**Zone 6:** Partly cloudy to cloudy along coast with precipitation, then clearing; warmer inland with variable clouds and precipitation east.

**Zone 7:** Mostly fair and mild in coastal areas with some fog and precipitation; temperatures normal to above south; desert is unseasonably warm, partly cloudy, and breezy.

**Zone 8:** Overcast, cold, windy, and stormy in Alaska; Hawaii is cool and windy with scattered precipitation.

## January 29-31

**Zone 1:** Partly cloudy with seasonal to above temperatures.

**Zone 2:** Seasonal temperatures and increasing clouds as a southerly air flow brings a low pressure system.

**Zone 3:** Fair and humid south with increasing clouds and precipitation; seasonal north with precipitation and partly cloudy to cloudy skies as a low pressure develops.

**Zone 4:** Fair and seasonal west; Plains dry with above normal temperatures; cooler east with partly cloudy to cloudy skies and precipitation.

**Zone 5:** Fair and seasonal west; above normal temperatures central; precipitation east with seasonal to above temperatures and variable clouds.

**Zone 6:** Clear to partly cloudy and cool; windy and cooler east.

**Zone 7:** Overcast and cool west, fair and cool east after precipitation.

**Zone 8:** Seasonal and windy with variable clouds in Alaska, and precipitation east; Hawaii is cloudy and cool with precipitation.

## February 1–5

**Zone 1:** Precipitation and variable clouds; colder northeast.

**Zone 2:** Overcast with precipitation—some heavy, then clearing and cold.

**Zone 3:** Significant precipitation fueled by southerly air flow with flood potential, overcast skies, and tornadoes possible.

**Zone 4:** Precipitation followed by cooler temperatures; heaviest precipitation west and east; colder east.

**Zone 5:** Front brings cooler temperatures with precipitation; colder east.

**Zone 6:** Variable clouds and cool with precipitation; colder east with heavier downfall.

**Zone 7:** Cool and cloudy with precipitation throughout zone as front moves east; stormy east and in mountain region with heavy precipitation.

**Zone 8:** Precipitation, seasonal temperatures, and partly cloudy to cloudy skies in Alaska; windy and warm in Hawaii.

## February 6–12

**Zone 1:** Cold and overcast with heavy precipitation.

**Zone 2:** Cloudy and stormy throughout much of the zone, especially inland and Florida; cooler temperatures.

**Zone 3:** Precipitation—some heavy—with flood potential west; front moves east, bringing precipitation throughout zone; warmer east.

**Zone 4:** Variable clouds west, high winds, precipitation and tornado potential; cloudy with precipitation and flood potential east.

**Zone 5:** Windy, cool, fair, and seasonal.

**Zone 6:** Seasonal to cool; colder east with precipitation.

**Zone 7:** Temperatures seasonal to above west; cooler east with variable clouds, precipitation, and windy.

**Zone 8:** Fair and seasonal in Alaska with precipitation east; warm west in Hawaii; cooler and windy with scattered showers east.

## February 13–19

**Zone 1:** Heavy precipitation under overcast skies; stormy northeast.

**Zone 2:** Fair, clear, and windy with a chance for precipitation south; then clearing and mostly fair.

**Zone 3:** Fair with partly cloudy skies and unseasonably warm temperatures south; windy central; precipitation northeast.

**Zone 4:** Cold and partly cloudy to cloudy west; warmer and fair with temperatures seasonal to above central ; colder north; chance of precipitation east.

**Zone 5:** Mostly fair and warmer with a chance for precipitation; rising temperatures and precipitation increase flood potential east.

**Zone 6:** Coastal fog, cold, and precipitation—some heavy—east; warmer west.

**Zone 7:** Mostly fair and warm southern coast; cloudy northern coast with precipitation extending east into the mountains, where conditions are cold and stormy.

**Zone 8:** Cold with precipitation throughout much of Alaska, heaviest west; fair and seasonal in Hawaii with increasing clouds, warmer, and precipitation midweek.

## February 20–26

**Zone 1:** Stormy and then clearing and warmer as low pressure dissipates.

**Zone 2:** Seasonal, partly cloudy to cloudy inland; warmer, dry, and fair along coast and south.

**Zone 3:** Precipitation near end of week with rising temperatures; windy central and warm; cloudy and cooler northeast.

**Zone 4:** Cloudy, cool, precipitation; warmer central with scattered precipitation and thunderstorms; cooler east with precipitation and tornado potential.

**Zone 5:** Precipitation, above normal temperatures, thunderstorms with tornado potential central and east; cloudy west with cooler temperatures later in the week.

**Zone 6:** Fair, dry, unseasonably warm; thaw and precipitation increases flooding east and in mountains.

**Zone 7:** Unseasonably warm, dry, windy; hot in desert.

**Zone 8:** Heavy precipitation central Alaska and cold; cloudy and warm with increased precipitation in Hawaii.

## February 27–29

**Zone 1:** Seasonal to cool, fog, and a chance of precipitation north.

**Zone 2:** Partly cloudy and cool; warmer and mostly dry with scattered precipitation south.

**Zone 3:** Precipitation north; warmer and fair east; partly cloudy and cooler northeast.

**Zone 4:** Fair and seasonal west; precipitation central and cold.

**Zone 5:** Fair and warm west; cooler east and mountains, overcast, precipitation.

**Zone 6:** Temperatures above normal with high pressure and coastal fog; cooler east and in the mountains with precipitation under cloudy skies.

**Zone 7:** Fair to partly cloudy west; cooler east and mountains under overcast skies with precipitation.

**Zone 8:** Precipitation and seasonal temperatures in Alaska; partly cloudy, showers, and seasonal in Hawaii.

## March 1–5

**Zone 1:** Precipitation and seasonal temperatures.

**Zone 2:** Partly cloudy and seasonal with a chance for precipitation.

**Zone 3:** Increased precipitation and cold west; fair to partly cloudy east; warmer south.

**Zone 4:** Temperatures seasonal to above west; partly cloudy to cloudy east, where precipitation is heavy in some areas.

**Zone 5:** Seasonal and fair west; cloudy with precipitation central; increasing clouds east as a front moves into the areas, bringing heavy precipitation.

**Zone 6:** Seasonal temperatures and variable clouds with precipitation central and east.

**Zone 7:** Cool and overcast with precipitation east; fair and seasonal west.

**Zone 8:** Seasonal; precipitation eastern Alaska; temperatures seasonal to above in Hawaii with a chance for precipitation.

## March 6–12

**Zone 1:** Partly cloudy to cloudy, windy and cool with precipitation.

**Zone 2:** Scattered precipitation, cooler, and windy north; warmer south with variable cloudiness.

**Zone 3:** Partly cloudy to cloudy; warmer east and mostly fair.

**Zone 4:** Partly cloudy, windy, mostly dry, temperatures seasonal to above west; cooler and dry central; variable clouds, cool and scattered precipitation east.

**Zone 5:** Fair and dry with temperatures normal to above west; precipitation and cooler east.

**Zone 6:** Precipitation west and central, cool and damp with variable clouds; stormy in the mountains; fair and warmer east.

**Zone 7:** Cloudy and cool west with precipitation that moves into central zone; fair and warm east; hot in desert region.

**Zone 8:** Precipitation, but mostly clear and seasonal with coastal fog in eastern Alaska; warm and seasonal in Hawaii with variable clouds and scattered showers.

## March 13-19

**Zone 1:** Windy and cloudy with precipitation throughout region; cold north.

**Zone 2:** Temperatures seasonal to above; precipitation throughout the zone but heaviest on the coast; drier inland.

**Zone 3:** Warm with precipitation, some heavy, west and central; windy and cloudy east with precipitation and possible flooding.

**Zone 4:** Fair, warm, and dry west and central; cooler east with precipitation—some heavy—with flood potential; then warming.

**Zone 5:** Unseasonably warm and dry west; cooler east with variable clouds, precipitation, and flood potential in some areas.

**Zone 6:** Overcast and cool with precipitation, which is heavier east; mountains are stormy, cooler, and windy.

**Zone 7:** Cloudy, windy, cool and stormy west, central, and mountain region with increased precipitation; chance for precipitation east.

**Zone 8:** Cold and mostly dry in Alaska with precipitation east; Hawaii is breezy with temperatures seasonal to above.

## March 20-27

**Zone 1:** Cloudy with precipitation north; partly cloudy south with precipitation; windy.

**Zone 2:** Warm, humid, chance of precipitation.

**Zone 3:** Fair, warm, and mostly dry with a chance of precipitation; temperatures normal to above; windy.

**Zone 4:** Partly cloudy northwest with precipitation; fair and dry west; stormy east with thunderstorms later in the week as temperatures rise across the Plains; tornado potential south and central with some areas seeing significant precipitation.

**Zone 5:** Severe thunderstorms midzone and east with high winds, tornado potential, and increased precipitation in some areas.

**Zone 6:** Cool and partly cloudy west with precipitation later in the week; precipitation central, east, and in the mountains.

**Zone 7:** Seasonal to warm and fair west; cloudy east with precipitation; coastal fog.

**Zone 8:** Overcast, stormy, cool, and some precipitation in Alaska; seasonal in Hawaii with variable clouds and precipitation.

## March 28-31

**Zone 1:** Temperatures normal to below; stormy north.

**Zone 2:** Dry and fair to partly cloudy north; scattered precipitation midzone and south with rising temperatures.

**Zone 3:** Fair to partly cloudy north; cloudy south and midzone with thunderstorms and tornado potential.

**Zone 4:** Windy and partly cloudy west and central with a chance for precipitation west; increasing cloudiness east and cooler with precipitation.

**Zone 5:** Temperatures above normal and dry; more seasonal and humid east; breezy and partly cloudy.

**Zone 6:** Cool west; stormy central with lower temperatures east.

**Zone 7:** Seasonal, then turning cool after a storm in the west; fair, warm, and windy east.

**Zone 8:** Windy, cold, and stormy western and central Alaska, warmer east; breezy with seasonal temperatures and scattered precipitation in Hawaii.

## April 1-4

**Zone 1:** Seasonal and mostly fair with rising temperatures.

**Zone 2:** Fair, warm, and mild.

**Zone 3:** Cloudy, precipitation, and cool west and central; warmer east; humid west and Gulf with precipitation later in week.

**Zone 4:** Windy, partly cloudy, seasonal temperatures throughout zone; warmer east with increasing clouds and end-of-week precipitation.

**Zone 5:** Dry with unseasonably warm temperatures west and central; precipitation, warm, and humid east.

**Zone 6:** Precipitation west; fair to partly cloudy and mostly dry central and east.

**Zone 7:** Warming trend boosts temperatures west; seasonal, windy, and dry east.

**Zone 8:** Windy and cool with precipitation in Alaska; breezy, fair, and seasonal in Hawaii before becoming cooler with precipitation east.

## April 5–10

**Zone 1:** Warm, precipitation with significant downfall in the north, then turning cooler.

**Zone 2:** High winds, thunderstorms, and tornado warnings throughout the zone.

**Zone 3:** Windy, humid, and warm with precipitation west; high winds and severe thunderstorms with tornado potential east and north.

**Zone 4:** Windy and cool west with thunderstorms; seasonal but dry in the Plains; precipitation, windy, and cooler east.

**Zone 5:** Temperatures above normal throughout the zone with wind and scattered thunderstorms.

**Zone 6:** Stormy, cloudy, and cool with high winds east and central; seasonal west and fair.

**Zone 7:** Precipitation throughout much of the zone, stormy in the mountains; partly cloudy to cloudy east and windy; hot in desert region.

**Zone 8:** Stormy, windy, and cold central and eastern Alaska, warmer west; windy and warm with precipitation in Hawaii.

## April 11–18

**Zone 1:** Precipitation, overcast, and cool, north; warmer south and mostly fair.

**Zone 2:** Fair and mild with chance for precipitation.

**Zone 3:** Stormy with high winds west; seasonal and windy, turning cooler east.

**Zone 4:** Unseasonably cool in the Plains with precipitation—some heavy—windy and stormy west.

**Zone 5:** Temperatures seasonal to above and windy west; precipitation central and east; stormy with increased precipitation, then cooler, in the Mississippi Valley.

**Zone 6:** Seasonal to cool with precipitation west and central; partly cloudy and warm east, then cooling.

**Zone 7:** Temperatures above normal, variable cloudiness, scattered precipitation west and central; cooler east.

**Zone 8:** Fair to partly cloudy and windy with temperatures seasonal to below in Alaska; overcast and cooler western Hawaii, fair and seasonal east with precipitation.

## April 19–26

**Zone 1:** Cold, cloudy, and windy with precipitation.

**Zone 2:** Cloudy with precipitation, temperatures seasonal to cool, windy.

**Zone 3:** Humid, fair, increasing temperatures, and windy south; cloudy, cool, and windy with precipitation north and east.

**Zone 4:** Precipitation west; normal to cool temperatures and mostly dry central and east.

**Zone 5:** Scattered thunderstorms with high winds and tornado potential, then cooler.

**Zone 6:** Chance of precipitation west and central; windy and mostly fair and dry central and east.

**Zone 7:** Partly cloudy with high winds west and in mountains; precipitation east; increasing temperatures in desert region.

**Zone 8:** Cloudy and windy with precipitation in Alaska as warm temperatures turn cool; precipitation, warm, cloudy, and windy in Hawaii.

## April 27–30

**Zone 1:** Seasonal; precipitation south; cooler and partly cloudy to cloudy skies, windy and stormy north.

**Zone 2:** Warm and humid with thunderstorms, tornado potential, and increased precipitation with possible flooding.

**Zone 3:** Precipitation and seasonal to cool temperatures west; thunderstorms, some heavy precipitation, and cool north and east.

**Zone 4:** Fair and seasonal west; thunderstorms in the Plains region with high winds and tornado potential and above normal temperatures; more seasonal east with chance for precipitation.

**Zone 5:** Rising temperatures breed thunderstorms with tornado potential and high winds central and east, then cooler; fair and warm west.

**Zone 6:** Precipitation west; fair central; cloudy, windy, and cooler east.

**Zone 7:** Windy with precipitation in northern California; fair to partly cloudy and seasonal south; cooler east as clouds increase.

**Zone 8:** Overcast, cool, and stormy in Alaska; Hawaii is warm, windy, and cloudy with precipitation.

## May 1–3

**Zone 1:** Increasing clouds and scattered precipitation; temperatures seasonal to cool.

**Zone 2:** Warmer south with increasing clouds and precipitation; cooler north.

**Zone 3:** Fair and seasonal; variable cloudiness with precipitation east; warm and humid south.

**Zone 4:** Windy with thunderstorms and tornado potential in the Plains; seasonal west and warm as temperatures rise; cooler east.

**Zone 5:** Fair and seasonal west; thunderstorms with tornado potential and above normal temperatures in the Plains.

**Zone 6:** Fair, seasonal, and windy; cloudy and cooler east with precipitation.

**Zone 7:** Dry and warming west; cloudy with precipitation east.

**Zone 8:** Overcast, cold, precipitation in Alaska; seasonal temperatures, cloudy skies and precipitation in Hawaii.

## May 1–4

**Zone 1:** Cool to seasonal temperatures and partly cloudy.

**Zone 2:** Above normal temperatures, partly cloudy but mostly dry with scattered thunderstorms and tornado potential inland; cooler north before a warming trend; heavy precipitation with possible flooding throughout much of the zone; humid.

**Zone 3:** Precipitation throughout much of the zone; thunderstorms with tornado potential in Ohio Valley and south with heavy downfall; cooler and partly cloudy northeast; temperatures above normal south.

**Zone 4:** Precipitation, windy, and cool west; scattered clouds in Plains region, but mostly dry; windy east with a chance for precipitation.

**Zone 5:** Windy with scattered thunderstorms, tornado potential and variable cloudiness west and central; mostly dry, fair, and cooler west.

**Zone 6:** Chance of precipitation and cool temperatures west, warming by week's end; partly cloudy central; seasonal, windy, and dry east.

**Zone 7:** Partly cloudy to cloudy, precipitation, and windy west; dry, fair, temperatures seasonal to above east.

**Zone 8:** Windy and cool with precipitation in Alaska; Hawaii is breezy and warm with variable cloudiness.

## May 11–18

**Zone 1:** Precipitation—some heavy, cloudy and windy south; seasonal conditions north under partly cloudy skies.

**Zone 2:** Temperatures cool after precipitation, some heavy with flood potential.

**Zone 3:** Seasonal temperatures and dry west; precipitation east and north.

**Zone 4:** Partly cloudy, temperatures normal to above west; windy east; mostly dry throughout zone.

**Zone 5:** Windy and dry with normal to above temperatures.

**Zone 6:** Above normal temperatures west; cooler and partly cloudy to cloudy central and east with precipitation.

**Zone 7:** Temperatures above normal west; cloudy and cooler with precipitation north central and in the mountains; seasonal, dry, and partly cloudy east.

**Zone 8:** Alaska is cold and windy east, seasonal with a chance for precipitation west; fair and dry with seasonal temperatures in Hawaii.

## May 19–26

**Zone 1:** Partly cloudy and humid with temperatures normal to above.

**Zone 2:** Hot, dry, and windy with scattered thunderstorms.

**Zone 3:** Hot and humid throughout much of the zone with scattered thunderstorms.

**Zone 4:** Above normal temperatures, windy, dry; scattered thunderstorms central and east, humid.

**Zone 5:** Windy, above normal temperatures, mostly dry, with only scattered thunderstorms east.

**Zone 6:** Cloudy, cool, and stormy west; partly cloudy central area; fair, warmer and windy east.

**Zone 7:** Cloudy, cool, and stormy in northern California; warming trend south and central; desert hot and mostly dry.

**Zone 8:** Cold in eastern Alaska, seasonal west, coastal area expect fog; seasonal but dry in Hawaii, cooler east.

## May 27–31

**Zone 1:** Partly cloudy, seasonal temperatures, chance for precipitation.

**Zone 2:** Hot, windy, humid, scattered thunderstorms—some severe with tornado potential.

**Zone 3:** Humid, scattered thunderstorms with tornado potential, above normal temperatures, and windy.

**Zone 4:** Hot and humid, windy, scattered thunderstorms with tornado potential.

**Zone 5:** Cloudy with showers, scattered thunderstorms and above normal temperatures west and central; humid with scattered thunderstorms, high winds and tornado potential east.

**Zone 6:** Cool and fair with variable cloudiness; warming trend late week.

**Zone 7:** Mostly dry, cool with scattered thunderstorms central, then warmer; partly cloudy, warm and dry east.

**Zone 8:** Fair and dry with temperatures seasonal to above in Alaska; breezy and fair in Hawaii, warmer east.

## June 1-8

**Zone 1:** Scattered thunderstorms, mostly fair.

**Zone 2:** Windy, cloudy, precipitation south; drier north.

**Zone 3:** Temperatures seasonal to above, mostly dry, windy; scattered thunderstorms with tornado potential Ohio Valley and south.

**Zone 4:** Hot, scattered thunderstorms with tornado potential, humid; greater chance for precipitation west; cloudy and muggy east.

**Zone 5:** Hot, scattered thunderstorms with tornado potential, humid throughout much of the zone.

**Zone 6:** Cool, cloudy, windy, precipitation west and central; warmer east with a chance for precipitation.

**Zone 7:** Temperatures above normal and mostly dry; precipitation west; hot and muggy east.

**Zone 8:** Windy and cool with precipitation in Alaska; Hawaii is mostly fair and warm, windy east with precipitation.

## June 9-16

**Zone 1:** Rising temperatures, mostly dry with scattered showers and windy north.

**Zone 2:** Temperatures seasonal to above, chance for precipitation, but mostly fair.

**Zone 3:** Hot throughout the zone, cooler east with scattered thunderstorms and windy.

**Zone 4:** War and dry west; windy and hot Plains with scattered thunderstorms.

**Zone 5:** Hot and dry west; humid, scattered thunderstorms, some severe with high winds, central and east.

**Zone 6:** Partly cloudy west, warm, precipitation, some heavy; hot inland with chance for precipitation central.

**Zone 7:** Hot, dry, and partly cloudy throughout most of the zone; precipitation northern coast.

**Zone 8:** Alaska is cloudy with precipitation and seasonal temperatures; humid, partly cloudy, showers and temperatures normal to above in Hawaii.

## June 17–24

**Zone 1:** Precipitation south and partly cloudy to cloudy; fair and cooler north; windy throughout the zone.

**Zone 2:** Humid, windy, temperatures seasonal to above with chance for showers and thunderstorms north.

**Zone 3:** Humid, scattered showers and thunderstorms with temperatures seasonal to above, but dryness prevails.

**Zone 4:** Precipitation and cooler temperatures northwest; hot in the Plains with scattered thunderstorms; dry west; chance for precipitation east.

**Zone 5:** Cloudy with seasonal to above normal temperatures; hot and humid east with thunderstorms.

**Zone 6:** Warm with precipitation east; dry central; chance for precipitation east, temperatures seasonal to above.

**Zone 7:** Coastal precipitation; warming trend west; dryness and heat prevail throughout most of the zone; east cooler with variable cloudiness and chance for precipitation and thunderstorms south.

**Zone 8:** Partly cloudy to cloudy and cool in Alaska, precipitation east; warm, variable cloudiness, chance for precipitation in Hawaii.

## June 25–30

**Zone 1:** Mostly fair and dry; hot south; chance for precipitation north.

**Zone 2:** Hot, especially north, partly variable cloudiness, scattered showers and thunderstorms.

**Zone 3:** Scattered thunderstorms and showers, seasonal to above normal temperatures; humid west and south, drier east.

**Zone 4:** Scattered showers and thunderstorms, windy, temperatures seasonal to above.

**Zone 5:** Hot and dry west; humid with scattered thunderstorms central and east—some severe with high winds—then cooler.

**Zone 6:** Windy, dry, temperatures seasonal to above; chance for precipitation west.

**Zone 7:** Hot and dry.

**Zone 8:** Cool and cloudy with precipitation central and eastern Alaska, warmer west; seasonal with showers and variable cloudiness in Hawaii.

## July 1–8

**Zone 1:** Increasing clouds bring precipitation, some heavy with flood potential, humid; cooler north.

**Zone 2:** Scattered thunderstorms and showers, seasonal to above normal temperatures, and humid.

**Zone 3:** Humid and partly cloudy west; temperatures seasonal to above; increasing clouds with precipitation east.

**Zone 4:** Hot with scattered thunderstorms west and central; humid east with chance for showers.

**Zone 5:** Windy west; showers and scattered thunderstorms throughout zone; hot.

**Zone 6:** Temperatures seasonal to above, then cooling with increasing clouds and precipitation.

**Zone 7:** Warm west; precipitation central and north; desert hot and dry.

**Zone 8:** Cloudy and cool with precipitation eastern Alaska, seasonal west and windy; increasing clouds in Hawaii with precipitation west, east is windy and warmer.

## July 9–16

**Zone 1:** Seasonal; cooler and partly cloudy with chance for precipitation north; scattered thunderstorms south.

**Zone 2:** Humid, thunderstorms, tornado potential south; rising temperatures as the week progresses; windy north with scattered thunderstorms.

**Zone 3:** Humid, potential thunderstorms and tornadoes throughout most of the zone; severe thunderstorms with possible tornadoes and flooding Ohio Valley; hot west and most of the zone by week's end.

**Zone 4:** Showers west; hail and thunderstorms with tornado potential east; seasonal to above normal temperatures.

**Zone 5:** Temperatures seasonal to above, scattered showers and thunderstorms, humid; windy east.

**Zone 6:** Fair and seasonal central and west; cooler east with gradual warming.

**Zone 7:** Fair with seasonal to above normal temperatures throughout most of the zone; scattered showers and thunderstorms in the mountains.

**Zone 8:** Precipitation in central and eastern Alaska, warmer west; warm in Hawaii with showers.

## July 17–23

**Zone 1:** Seasonal to above temperatures, fair, and scattered thunderstorms.

**Zone 2:** Scattered showers and thunderstorms, seasonal to above normal temperatures.

**Zone 3:** Cloudy west with thunderstorms; seasonal to above normal temperatures; precipitation northeast.

**Zone 4:** Seasonal to above normal temperatures; windy west; humid east and cloudy with thunderstorms.

**Zone 5:** Hot, humid, chance for precipitation east.

**Zone 6:** Precipitation, some heavy, central; partly cloudy and seasonal.

**Zone 7:** Precipitation west and central with variable cloudiness; temperatures seasonal to above.

**Zone 8:** Precipitation and warming trend in eastern Alaska, seasonal west with precipitation; showers and temperatures seasonal to above in Hawaii.

## July 24–31

**Zone 1:** Partly cloudy to cloudy, windy, and humid.

**Zone 2:** Hot and windy south; fair and dry.

**Zone 3:** Temperatures seasonal to above, humid; partly cloudy west; mostly dry.

**Zone 4:** Humid, showers, and scattered thunderstorms central; fair west; partly cloudy east; seasonal to above normal temperatures.

**Zone 5:** Temperatures seasonal to above, showers and thunderstorms—some severe with heavy precipitation and high winds.

**Zone 6:** Partly cloudy, chance for precipitation, temperatures seasonal to cool.

**Zone 7:** Windy, partly cloudy to cloudy; precipitation west.

**Zone 8:** Fair in Alaska, windy east; warm with showers in Hawaii.

## August 1-6

**Zone 1:** Seasonal with a chance for precipitation south.

**Zone 2:** Increased precipitation in coastal areas with possible flooding and tropical storm/hurricane; muggy.

**Zone 3:** Precipitation—some heavy with flood potential—throughout the zone; muggy.

**Zone 4:** Windy west with precipitation; fair central; windy east.

**Zone 5:** Scattered storms west; fair and seasonal central; windy east.

**Zone 6:** Seasonal west; cooler with partly cloudy skies, wind, and precipitation east.

**Zone 7:** Temperatures seasonal to above; chance for precipitation west; cloudy skies and monsoon storm with high winds in the desert.

**Zone 8:** Stormy central Alaska; mostly fair with some precipitation east; stormy conditions cool temperatures in Hawaii, followed by warm trend.

## August 7-14

**Zone 1:** Cool north with chance for frost; fair and warmer south.

**Zone 2:** Fair and warm.

**Zone 3:** Cool, windy, and cloudy west with precipitation; warmer east with chance for precipitation.

**Zone 4:** Hot with precipitation west and central; cooler east and cloudy with precipitation; chance for frost north.

**Zone 5:** Precipitation and warm west; cooler and windy central; hot and humid east.

**Zone 6:** Fair, partly cloudy to cloudy, temperatures seasonal to cool; windy west with precipitation.

**Zone 7:** Fair west; partly cloudy to cloudy in other areas with chance for precipitation; seasonal temperatures.

**Zone 8:** Variable cloudiness and precipitation eastern Alaska; coastal fog, fair central and west; fair, warm and humid in Hawaii with chance for showers east.

## August 15–22

**Zone 1:** Heavy precipitation north and cold; warmer south and partly cloudy.

**Zone 2:** Fair and warm; partly cloudy north.

**Zone 3:** Fair to partly cloudy, and warm.

**Zone 4:** Cloudy and stormy west; possible frost north; partly cloudy and mostly fair east.

**Zone 5:** Stormy west and central with high winds, possible hurricane; seasonal, partly cloudy, and humid east.

**Zone 6:** Seasonal, partly cloudy, fog west; precipitation central and east with variable cloudiness.

**Zone 7:** Precipitation throughout most of the zone, seasonal temperatures.

**Zone 8:** Windy with precipitation in western Alaska; fair east; warm and mostly fair in Hawaii.

## August 23–28

**Zone 1:** Precipitation, windy, and cool north; fair to partly cloudy south.

**Zone 2:** Fair to partly cloudy, warm, scattered showers; cooler north.

**Zone 3:** Warm, partly cloudy to cloudy west with scattered showers; fair west.

**Zone 4:** Stormy and cool with potential for frost west; fair east.

**Zone 5:** Cloudy and cool with precipitation west; fair and seasonal central and east.

**Zone 6:** Cool with chance for frost central; precipitation and wind east.

**Zone 7:** Partly cloudy north; warmer east.

**Zone 8:** Windy with precipitation western Alaska, warmer east; showers, warm and windy in Hawaii.

## August 29–31

**Zone 1:** Fair and cool north; cloudy and warmer south.

**Zone 2:** Cloudy, windy, and precipitation.

**Zone 3:** Increasing clouds and wind east; partly cloudy, warm, windy west.

**Zone 4:** Fair west and cool; warmer east and windy with scattered precipitation.

**Zone 5:** Breezy, cool, and fair to partly cloudy with precipitation; windy east.

**Zone 6:** Seasonal, partly cloudy with a chance for precipitation west; fair east.

**Zone 7:** Seasonal to above temperatures, and fair to partly cloudy.

**Zone 8:** Fair to partly cloudy and seasonal in Alaska; warm and fair in Hawaii.

## September 1-5

**Zone 1:** Windy with precipitation south; fair to partly cloudy and cool north.

**Zone 2:** Precipitation—some heavy—under cloudy skies; high winds.

**Zone 3:** Windy with precipitation, some heavy, under overcast skies.

**Zone 4:** Warming trend west and central; seasonal east with chance for precipitation.

**Zone 5:** Fair to partly cloudy with seasonal temperatures; cooler east with a warming trend later in the week.

**Zone 6:** Overcast with heavy precipitation west; increasing clouds central; fair to partly cloudy east.

**Zone 7:** Seasonal and fair to partly cloudy.

**Zone 8:** Warming trend in Alaska with scattered precipitation and variable cloudiness; fair to partly cloudy with scattered showers in Hawaii.

## September 6-13

**Zone 1:** Windy with precipitation; cooler north.

**Zone 2:** Windy with increasing cloudiness and precipitation—some heavy.

**Zone 3:** Precipitation across most of zone—some heavy—along with clouds and wind.

**Zone 4:** Showers and thunderstorms likely, windy as front moves through the zone.

**Zone 5:** Precipitation throughout the zone, potential for high winds heaviest in central and east; hurricane potential.

**Zone 6:** Breezy, partly cloudy, and precipitation west; fair central and east; windy east.

**Zone 7:** Cloudy and cooler with showers northern California; fair central; partly cloudy east and breezy.

**Zone 8:** Stormy central Alaska, warmer east, cooler west with precipitation; showers, windy and partly cloudy in Hawaii.

## September 14-20

**Zone 1:** Cloudy with significant precipitation, and possible hurricane.

**Zone 2:** Precipitation—some heavy—throughout most of zone, especially north with tornado potential; possible hurricane.

**Zone 3:** Fair and seasonal west; thunderstorms—some severe—with tornado potential and heavy preeipitation and flood potential east.

**Zone 4:** Fair and seasonal west and east; windy, cooler, and cloudy central, then warming.

**Zone 5:** Fair west; windy, and cooler with precipitation central and east, followed by warming trend.

**Zone 6:** Heavy precipitation west; breezy and fair to partly cloudy central and east.

**Zone 7:** Increasing clouds with precipitation west; fair and seasonal central and east.

**Zone 8:** Precipitation and cooler eastern Alaska, warmer and partly cloudy west; fair to partly cloudy, warm, chance for showers in Hawaii.

## September 21-27

**Zone 1:** Partly cloudy, windy, with some precipitation.

**Zone 2:** Mostly fair and seasonal; cooler and partly cloudy north.

**Zone 3:** Partly cloudy with scattered precipitation; cold north with frost potential.

**Zone 4:** Temperatures seasonal; scattered precipitation west and central; cooler north-central and east with chance for frost and precipitation.

**Zone 5:** Hot; thunderstorms west and central, which sees heaviest precipitation; partly cloudy east and cooler.

**Zone 6:** Cloudy, windy; warmer east; scattered precipitation west and central.

**Zone 7:** Windy; scattered precipitation west and central.

**Zone 8:** Windy, cloudy, precipitation in Alaska; warm with variable cloudiness and showers in Hawaii.

## September 28-30

**Zone 1:** Cloudy with precipitation north; seasonal south.

**Zone 2:** Thunderstorms and warm south; cooler, fair and seasonal north.

**Zone 3:** Cloudy west with precipitation; thunderstorms and warmer central; fair and seasonal east.

**Zone 4:** Partly cloudy with chance for precipitation west; fair, and seasonal in Plains region; cooler north with frost potential; cloudy east with precipitation.

**Zone 5:** Scattered precipitation west; fair central and east; cooler east.

**Zone 6:** Fair to partly cloudy; precipitation, windy, cloudy central and east.

**Zone 7:** Windy, variable cloudiness with precipitation west; thunderstorms central and east; cooler at higher elevations with frost.

**Zone 8:** Partly cloudy to cloudy in Alaska with precipitation west; variable cloudiness, warm and showers in Hawaii.

## October 1-5

**Zone 1:** Fair and seasonal.

**Zone 2:** Fair and warm.

**Zone 3:** Partly cloudy to cloudy west; fair and seasonal east.

**Zone 4:** Warm with precipitation and variable cloudiness; increasing clouds east.

**Zone 5:** Warming, partly cloudy to cloudy with precipitation.

**Zone 6:** Mostly fair and seasonal north; warming trend east; cloudy with precipitation in central region.

**Zone 7:** Warm, partly cloudy to cloudy, and some scattered precipitation.

**Zone 8:** Windy, cool, variable cloudiness and precipitation in Alaska; warm, fair, breezy with showers in Hawaii.

## October 6-12

**Zone 1:** Fair to partly cloudy and windy, chance for precipitation.

**Zone 2:** Variable cloudiness with precipitation; cool north.

**Zone 3:** Windy, cool, and partly cloudy to cloudy with precipitation.

**Zone 4:** Stormy and cold west in the mountains and western Plains region; windy throughout the zone with variable cloudiness.

**Zone 5:** Windy, cloudy, precipitation west and central; fair to partly cloudy east.

**Zone 6:** Fair to partly cloudy; windy and cooler east.

**Zone 7:** Windy, warm, and fair; variable cloudiness central and east with chance for precipitation.

**Zone 8:** Windy and cooler with precipitation in central and eastern Alaska, warmer west; showers, warm, and windy in Hawaii.

## October 13–19

**Zone 1:** Increasing clouds and wind with precipitation.

**Zone 2:** Windy and cloudy with precipitation throughout zone, followed by declining temperatures.

**Zone 3:** Chilly with frost likely west, variable clouds and scattered precipitation; cloudy and cold with precipitation central; precipitation east.

**Zone 4:** Fair and seasonal, windy; much cooler east with precipitation.

**Zone 5:** Fair to partly cloudy with normal to above temperatures; windy and more cloudiness with scattered precipitation central; cooler east.

**Zone 6:** Overcast, windy, and cold with precipitation as front moves from west into central region of the zone; fair and seasonal east.

**Zone 7:** Cold with increasing clouds and precipitation west; fair and seasonal east.

**Zone 8:** Cloudy and cold with precipitation in Alaska; windy and showers in Hawaii.

## October 20–26

**Zone 1:** Cool and windy with precipitation; warmer south.

**Zone 2:** Fair to cool, windy, partly cloudy, scattered precipitation.

**Zone 3:** Cool, damp, and windy with precipitation in west and central region; fair and cool east with chance for precipitation.

**Zone 4:** Cold, cloudy, windy with precipitation across the zone.

**Zone 5:** Cloudy and cool with precipitation throughout the zone and temperatures seasonal to below.

**Zone 6:** Cloudy, cool, and windy with precipitation west; cold and stormy central and east.

**Zone 7:** Cloudy, windy, and stormy west and central; cool east with precipitation under overcast skies.

**Zone 8:** Overcast, heavy precipitation, and cold in Alaska; cloudy, seasonal, showers in Hawaii.

## October 27-31

**Zone 1:** Fair and seasonal; cooler north.

**Zone 2:** Precipitation west and south, seasonal to cool; fair and windy north.

**Zone 3:** Variable cloudiness, windy, and some precipitation.

**Zone 4:** Fair to partly cloudy and seasonal to cool; chance for precipitation east.

**Zone 5:** Windy, fair to partly cloudy, cool.

**Zone 6:** Precipitation west and windy; fair and windy central and east; cold east.

**Zone 7:** Windy west; precipitation north; fair south and central; cold east.

**Zone 8:** Windy, cold, and fair in Alaska; warm, breezy, fair to partly cloudy, showers in Hawaii.

## November 1-4

**Zone 1:** Fair to partly cloudy with seasonal temperatures.

**Zone 2:** Precipitation with seasonal to cool temperatures.

**Zone 3:** Partly cloudy to cloudy across much of the zone with scattered precipitation.

**Zone 4:** Fair with temperatures seasonal to above west; variable cloudiness and cooler with some precipitation central and east.

**Zone 5:** Fair west; cooler with precipitation and increasing clouds central and east.

**Zone 6:** Scattered precipitation west and central, becoming cooler; seasonal to cool under fair to partly cloudy skies east.

**Zone 7:** Fair to partly cloudy; scattered precipitation west; cool and windy east.

**Zone 8:** Precipitation western Alaska, windy east and mostly fair and cool; fair and breezy with scattered precipitation in Hawaii.

## November 5-11

**Zone 1:** Cold and stormy with high winds.

**Zone 2:** Precipitation, windy, and variable cloudiness with cooler temperatures.

**Zone 3:** Fair to partly cloudy throughout most of zone; cool, windy, cloudy, precipitation east.

**Zone 4:** Stormy northwest; fair and seasonal in Plains region with precipitation east under cloudy skies.

**Zone 5:** Cool west before a warming trend; fair to partly cloudy central and east; precipitation east.

**Zone 6:** Fair to partly cloudy with precipitation west; windy, cooler, and stormy central and east as front moves through the zone.

**Zone 7:** Windy and mostly fair west with precipitation north; windy throughout the zone; stormy mountains and east.

**Zone 8:** Cold, fair, and windy in Alaska, stormy west; windy with precipitation in Hawaii.

## November 12–18

**Zone 1:** Cold with precipitation.

**Zone 2:** Fair and seasonal; partly cloudy north.

**Zone 3:** Cloudy, windy, precipitation west; fair east.

**Zone 4:** Cloudy, precipitation, windy, temperatures seasonal to below; warmer east.

**Zone 5:** Windy west and central; cloudy and cool with precipitation throughout zone.

**Zone 6:** Fair and seasonal west; cooler central with partly cloudy to cloudy skies; cold with precipitation east.

**Zone 7:** Seasonal to cool with variable cloudiness; precipitation mountains and east, followed by cooler temperatures.

**Zone 8:** Windy, cloudy, precipitation, seasonal temperatures in Alaska; cooler temperatures follow precipitation in Hawaii, variable cloudiness.

## November 19–25

**Zone 1:** Cloudy with precipitation; very windy and cold north.

**Zone 2:** Cool and fair south; cool and cloudy with precipitation north.

**Zone 3:** Cloudy and cold with precipitation throughout zone; very cold east.

**Zone 4:** Fair to partly cloudy west and central; precipitation east and cold under cloudy skies.

**Zone 5:** Partly cloudy to cloudy; warmer west; cold east with precipitation.

**Zone 6:** Overcast and heavy precipitation west and central, followed by clear and cold weather; windy and cold east.

**Zone 7:** Precipitation throughout with cooler temperatures as a front moves through the zone.

**Zone 8:** Windy and seasonal to cool in Alaska with precipitation central and west; scattered showers, windy, and seasonal in Hawaii.

## November 26–30

**Zone 1:** Cold and overcast north; precipitation throughout zone.

**Zone 2:** Seasonal to cool and fair; precipitation and colder north.

**Zone 3:** Fair to partly cloudy and seasonal; colder northeast with precipitation.

**Zone 4:** Partly cloudy, windy, and chance for precipitation west and central; cold east.

**Zone 5:** Chance for precipitation west, windy, and cool; warmer central and partly cloudy; cool east.

**Zone 6:** Fair west; partly cloudy central and east with precipitation; cool.

**Zone 7:** Partly cloudy to cloudy west and central; fair east; seasonal temperatures.

**Zone 8:** Cold with precipitation central and east; seasonal in western Alaska; showers and seasonal to cool in Hawaii.

## December 1–3

**Zone 1:** Cold and fair to partly cloudy.

**Zone 2:** Precipitation and cloudy south; fair and cold north.

**Zone 3:** Cloudy west; precipitation central; cold and fair east.

**Zone 4:** Windy, wet, and stormy west and central; fair east.

**Zone 5:** Stormy west and central with tornado potential; partly cloudy and windy east as front approaches.

**Zone 6:** Fair and cool west; cloudy with precipitation in mountains; seasonal east.

**Zone 7:** Cloudy and stormy west and central; fair east.

**Zone 8:** Precipitation, overcast and stormy eastern Alaska, seasonal west; cloudy with showers in Hawaii.

## December 4–10

**Zone 1:** Fair and seasonal south with chance for precipitation; colder north with precipitation.

**Zone 2:** Seasonal to cool with precipitation south; fair north.

**Zone 3:** Windy, cloudy, cold with heavy precipitation west and central; fair to partly cloudy east and cold.

**Zone 4:** Cloudy, cool, and windy with precipitation heaviest in the east.

**Zone 5:** Cloudy with precipitation; windy.

**Zone 6:** Windy and fair to partly cloudy west and central with scattered precipitation; cold and clear east.

**Zone 7:** Windy and cool with precipitation northern California; fair central and east; cold east.

**Zone 8:** Windy, cold, fair to partly cloudy in Alaska; seasonal in Hawaii.

## December 11–17

**Zone 1:** Cold and windy with precipitation.

**Zone 2:** Cloudy and cool with precipitation.

**Zone 3:** Windy, cold, and variable cloudiness with precipitation west and central; cold and overcast with precipitation northeast.

**Zone 4:** Cloudy with precipitation throughout zone; windy and cold east.

**Zone 5:** Partly cloudy to cloudy west; windy and cool central; cloudy east; precipitation throughout zone.

**Zone 6:** Variable cloudiness with precipitation west and central; fair and warmer east.

**Zone 7:** Cloudy, cool, and windy with precipitation west; fair with seasonal to above temperatures east.

**Zone 8:** Cold, windy, and clear in Alaska; breezy, fair, and seasonal to cool in Hawaii.

## December 18–25

**Zone 1:** Windy, cool, partly cloudy to cloudy.

**Zone 2:** Fair to partly cloudy; warm south; cooler north with wind and precipitation.

**Zone 3:** Stormy west and central; seasonal and fair east.

**Zone 4:** Cold, windy, and stormy across the Plains.

**Zone 5:** Windy and cold with precipitation throughout zone; stormy with heavy downfall and cold east.

**Zone 6:** A front brings precipitation to western and central portions of the zone, followed by cooler temperatures; mostly seasonal and fair east.

**Zone 7:** Cloudy with precipitation west and central; warmer south and cloudy; fair east.

**Zone 8:** Variable cloudiness with precipitation in Alaska; cloudy, showers, and cooler in Hawaii.

### December 26-31

**Zone 1:** Cloudy with precipitation; heavy downfall north.

**Zone 2:** Stormy and cold with heavy precipitation and tornado potential.

**Zone 3:** Variable cloudiness and cold west; cold and stormy central and east; tornado potential.

**Zone 4:** Partly cloudy to cloudy throughout zone with precipitation—some heavy.

**Zone 5:** Variable cloudiness with precipitation west and central; seasonal and partly cloudy east.

**Zone 6:** Cool and fair west; overcast with precipitation—some heavy in central region; cold and stormy east with increased precipitation.

**Zone 7:** Cloudy with precipitation west; colder north and east; windy throughout as front moves across zone.

**Zone 8:** Stormy throughout most of Alaska; cold east; cloudy, warm, and windy with showers in Hawaii.

# Weather for 2004 Sporting Events

## Super Bowl XXXVIII, February 1 in Houston, Texas

Originally called the AFL-NFL Championship and later nicknamed the Super Bowl, the game has grown into a major national event with millions of TV viewers and partyers. The first match, held January 15, 1967, in Los Angeles, was not a sellout, despite the $12 ticket price. About 60,000 people watched the Green Bay Packers beat the Kansas City Chiefs, 35–10.

### The Weather Forecast

An overall cold, cloudy and wet winter in Houston sets the trend for Super Bowl weekend. Pack sweaters, raincoats, and umbrellas if you're headed south to see this year's championship game at the Houston Astrodome.

## Daytona 500, February 15 in Daytona Beach, Florida

Stock car racing fans have flocked to Daytona Beach, Florid, since the 1930s to see what has become NASCAR's premier annual event. Previously run on a 4.1-mile beach and road course, Daytona International Speedway has been home to the event since 1959. The first winner at the new track was Lee Petty with an average speed of 135.521.

## The Weather Forecast

Fans and racers at the Daytona 500 will see fair to partly cloudy skies with temperatures that range from cool to seasonal as the wind picks up. Increasing midday clouds signal precipitation, but chances are good for showers to hold off until the evening.

## Masters Tournament, April 8-11 in Augusta, Georgia

The Augusta National golf course is home to the Masters, a tournament first hosted in 1934. Since then, it has become the most prestigious of the four annual major professional golf tournaments with the winner being awarded the coveted green jacket. The tournament wasn't held during World War II, when cattle and turkeys were raised on the grounds.

## The Weather Forecast

This year, golfers will have one eye on the sky as cold, windy, cloudy conditions signal the threat of rain. Showers and thunderstorms move through the area April 8-10 and, although a warming trend begins on April 11, weather is still cool and windy with a chance for precipitation.

## Kentucky Derby, May 1 in Louisville, Kentucky

Churchill Downs, home of the Kentucky Derby, was constructed through the sale of 320 membership subscriptions of $100 each. Aristides won the first race, held May 17, 1875. Today, the 1¼-mile race nets the winner nearly $1 million and, in 2002, enthusiasts wagered more than $79 million on the race.

## The Weather Forecast

Although showers, thunderstorms, and tornado warnings dominate the weather forecast in the days prior, the risk of rain diminishes on Derby Day. There is still, however, a chance for showers, and spectators and jockeys can expect wind and variable cloudiness. Thunderstorms are likely the night before.

## Indianapolis 500, May 27 in Indianapolis, Indiana

Indy cars and race fans will feel the effects of a cold front from the northwest that brings increasing cloudiness, showers, and thunderstorms as the day progresses. For Indianapolis residents, the pattern is all too familiar, since spring weather is mostly cold, windy, and wet.

## The Weather Forecast

Rain has been a factor in only ten races since the first Indianapolis 500 in 1911, when Ray Harroun won with an average speed of 74.602 miles per hour and claimed a purse of $14,250. Today's winners, whose checks are nearer $1.5 million, complete the 200 laps in about half the time at triple the speed. A. J. Foyt, who started in thirty-five races, holds the title of the most wins—four.

## U.S. Open Tennis Tournament, August 23–September 5 in Flushing, New York

The inaugural event in August 1881 in Rhode Island was called the U.S. National Singles Championship. It was limited to men until 1887, when the first women's championship was held in Philadelphia. Grass courts were used until 1973, and Forest Hills was home to the tournament from 1915 until 1978, when the switch was made from clay to hard courts. The first men's winner was Richard Sears, who repeated his success for the next six years. Ellen Hansell won the first women's title.

## The Weather Forecast

Summer temperatures range from seasonal to above with precipitation on the light side in Flushing, a pattern that prevails during the U.S. Open finals September 4–5. Mostly fair to partly cloudy and windy, scattered showers and thunderstorms are possible. Players can expect cooler conditions in the days leading up to the finals.

### About the Author

Kris Brandt Riske is an astrologer and author who serves on the National Council for Geocosmic Research Board of Directors and holds professional certification from the American Federation of Astrologers (PMAFA). She has a master's degree in journalism. The author of *Astrometeorology: Planetary Power in Weather Forecasting*, Kris also writes for AMI astrological publications and allpets.com, and has had numerous articles published in popular astrology magazines. Kris is an avid auto racing fan, although NASCAR is her favorite and she'd rather be a driver than a spectator.

# Planetary Cycles, Weather, and Astrometeorology

*by Valerie Vaughan*

Weather has always determined the general well-being of humans. When the weather changes, so, too, the water supply changes, as well as the success of food crops, and the need for appropriate clothing or shelter. From the age of hunting and gathering to the development of animal domestication and agriculture, weather conditions have been a major factor in human survival. But our ancestors were clever; they figured out that weather changed periodically, as did the Sun, Moon, and planets. Changes in the weather were observed to follow cycles that matched the movement of celestial bodies. With this recognition of geo-cosmic cycles, weather prediction was possible, and changes could be anticipated, which increased the odds for human survival. The observation and measurement of celestial phenomena and weather conditions were brought together as one study—astrometeorology.

Astrometeorology has been practiced for at least 4,000 years. Throughout this period, astrologers have studied how weather cycles correlate with the motions of all the celestial bodies, including the Sun, Moon, and planets. As readers of the *Moon Sign Book* know, there are important lunar influences on our weather. However, there is also much to learn about the planets. This article will focus on what astrologers have discovered about the planetary influences on our weather, as well as the confirmation given by some modern scientists.

Babylonian astrologers were among the first to link the planetary motions and the weather as well as the related effect on agriculture. The recorded their observations in *cuneiform* (wedge-shaped characters) writing. One cuneiform from about 1600 B.C. says, "If Venus appears in the east on the sixth day of the month of Abu, rains will be in the heavens. . . . On the eleventh of the month Duzu, Venus flares up in the west, and the crops will prosper." In a later text, dating from 668 B.C., a Babylonian astrologer wrote, "When Venus appears in the fifth month, there will be rain, and the crops of the land will prosper." It is important to note that nearly one thousand years separate these two very similar predictions. While modern critics of astrology claim that such predictions were based on superstition, we have to wonder how this tradition could have been maintained for such a long period without any evidence whatsoever that it "worked."

These ancient astrologers were meticulous in their recording and measurement of cycles. According to one ancient writer, the Babylonians expected the same weather to occur in cycles of twelve years, as did good crops, famine, and pestilence. Twelve years is close to the synodic period (the time it takes to travel once through the zodiac) of Jupiter. This fact was well-known to the Babylonians. Among their texts we find observations and predictions that refer to correlations between Jupiter's cycle and the weather, as well as its outcome, agricultural productivity. Examples of texts include: "When Jupiter appears at the beginning of the year, in that year corn will be prosperous," and "When Jupiter appears in the third month, the land will be devastated and corn will be expensive." The Babylonians realized there was a connection between weather and the economy. Bad weather caused ruined crops, and the result was economic trouble.

Eventually, the Babylonians' knowledge of astrology was passed to the ancient Greeks, who made further discoveries about planet-weather correlations. One of the early Greek astrometeorologists was Theophrastus, a student of Aristotle. Around 280 B.C., he wrote *Concerning Weather Signs*, in which he mentioned the influence of the planet Mercury on the weather. He stated that cold is increased when Mercury is visible in winter, and that more heat is indicated when Mercury is visible in the summer. (Mercury is visible only when it is at "greatest elongation," that is, when it reaches its greatest angular separation from the Sun, which is about 18 degrees.)

Another contributor to astrometeorology was the great astrologer Claudius Ptolemy, who lived around A.D.150 In his book *Tetrabiblos*, Ptolemy wrote about the tradition of observing the Sun, Moon, and planets for signs of weather. He described Saturn's effect on the weather as cooling and drying, and Mars effect as drying and burning. According to Ptolemy, Jupiter's effect is to heat and humidify, as well as to produce fertilizing winds. Venus is also connected with humidifying. Mercury's effect is varying—sometimes drying, sometimes wet—and changes are rapid between those two conditions. Ptolemy states that Saturn is related to extreme cold, freezing, corrupted air, gloominess, and destructive snowstorms. As he explained, the natural result is that Saturn is also associated with loss or scarcity of crops through hail, pests, storms, or flooding, and the subsequent famine that follows poor crops.

After listing the various weather conditions associated with each planet, Ptolemy reminds the reader of the complexity of weather forecasting.

> "Such are the effects produced by each planet by itself. However, when associated with each other by different aspects or sign placement, and with a corresponding tempering of their individual powers, there is a mixture of their natures, and this is complicated. It is of course a hopeless and impossible task to mention the proper outcome of every combination, for there is such a variety of them. Consequently, questions of this kind would reasonably be left to the enterprise and ingenuity of the astrologer, in order to make the particular distinctions."

It is important to note here that the challenge of interpreting the numerous complex factors that determine weather did not alter over time.

Today's meteorologists (both the astrologers and scientists) still complain of exactly the same difficulties.

Another important figure in the history of astrometeorology was Johannes Kepler. Most people know Kepler as an "early scientist" from the seventeenth century. What the science books don't tell you is that he was also a serious, accomplished astrologer. Kepler practiced astrometeorology and made weather predictions for almanacs based on planetary aspects. But he also recognized that astrometeorology cannot make proper forecasts that are based solely upon astrological theory; that is, without making any observations of physical weather phenomena. In one of his books, Kepler listed seventeen examples of weather observations to support his theory that a Sun-Saturn conjunction causes unusual coldness.

Kepler kept a regular weather diary from 1621 to 1629, and he compared his weather records with the angular separations (aspects) between the planets. For example, he found that heavy rains coincided with Venus being at greatest elongation (its greatest degree separation from the Sun, about 45 degrees). In one of his books on astrology, he wrote:

> "Saturn has an excess of humidity and is deficient in heat. Its influence gives wet winters. Mars is likened to dry heat; Venus will humidify more than it warms; Mercury produces more heat than humidity. The power of Saturn and Jupiter to humidify is greatest at conjunction or opposition with the Sun. Venus and Mercury will humidify the most at superior conjunction (with the Sun) and least at inferior conjunction."

(These terms refer to relative positions of the planets. Inferior conjunction occurs when Mercury or Venus is on the near side of the Sun; that is, when the planet is between the Earth and the Sun. Superior conjunction occurs when Mercury or Venus is on the far side of the Sun; that is, when the Sun is between the Earth and the planet.)

Kepler also considered the effects of planets when they were at apogee and perigee (i.e., when they were positioned at greater or lesser distances from the Earth). He thought that their power to warm was greater when they were closer to the Earth, a factor related to the planets' apparent speed of motion. He wrote:

> "When planets move most slowly, they have the greatest effect, and this is why they are so strong when stationary, even when they are at apogee. In this regard, Mercury's station is the most

effectual, for this planet, being at other times the fastest moving, loses the most motion. The station of Mercury mainly stirs up winds, and in some places, snow or rain."

Another seventeenth-century scientist who studied astrometeorology was the Englishman John Goad. In his own time, he was well-known and respected, but today few people have heard of him. However, thanks to the scholarly investigations of astrologer Bruce Scofield (a regular writer for the *Moon Sign Book*), we have information about this important contributor to astrometeorology. In 1686, Goad published *Astro-Meteorologica*, a major work on the astrological principles of weather. In this comprehensive, 500-page book, Goad compared weather records with the aspects between the Sun, Moon, and planets.

Among Goad's observations for the weather, he noted that Mercury seemed to be a rainy planet, though he added that the ancients considered it windy. He reasoned that, being in London, he could not speak confidently for the influence of Mercury in a different part of the world. He also found that the conjunction of Mercury and Venus frequently coincided with rains and storms, and that Jupiter appeared to be associated with drought. He observed that drought and cold weather were common when Jupiter and Saturn were in conjunction. A Mars-Jupiter conjunction brought "monstrous frosts." When Mars and Jupiter were in opposition in winter (and sometimes in springtime), they produced "cold, frosty mornings, while in summer they bring thunder with violence, wind, rain, and hail."

Like Kepler, Goad was a scientist who supported his statements with evidence. For instance, concerning his observation that cold temperatures were produced by Saturn in aspect to the Sun or Venus, he recorded the "horrid frosts" that had taken place during the Sun-Saturn conjunctions of the late 1660s. Goad agreed with a very ancient tradition that when Saturn and Mars were in aspect to each other, there was generally severe weather, including great winds, storms, lightning, and thunder. He also found that conjunctions of Mars and Saturn induced an "excess of rain."

Another source of information on astrometeorology is the almanac, which first appeared in the sixteenth century, flourished during the following centuries, and is still popular today. Today's almanacs are incidentally a convenient place to find dates for "greatest elongation" and "inferior/superior conjunction," positions which are not usually listed in astrology books.

There is no question that the weather predictions of most almanacs printed before modern times were based on astrological theory. It is only in more recent times that the writers of almanac predictions claim that they use "secret weather formulas," which they cannot divulge. This raises the question of whether modern almanac weather forecasters still use astrology—hidden under the guise of "secret formulas."

The answer is quite obvious to the experienced astrologer who examines the weather predictions and concurrent planetary aspects printed side-by-side in the columns of today's almanacs. For example, on the March page in the 1999 Old Farmer's Almanac, the conjunction of Moon, Venus, and Saturn just prior to the Spring Equinox is accompanied by this weather ditty: "Astronomers may say it's spring, but winter's having one last fling!" This particular planetary alignment is well-known to astrometeorologists as an indicator of a cold, wet snowstorm. True to the prediction, a serious snowstorm hit the entire East Coast of the U.S. at this time. A similar example is found on the March page of the 2002 edition, where a Moon-Saturn conjunction on the Vernal Equinox stands next to the weather prediction, "wintry blast." The prediction was also fulfilled. On this first day of spring of 2002, snow fell throughout the northeastern U.S.

During the twentieth century, there have been numerous scientific studies that support astrometeorology. The following are a few examples, but the interested reader may find many more listed in Earth Cycles: The Scientific Evidence for Astrology by Valerie Vaughan.

In the early 1920s, Henry Ludwell Moore, a professor of economics at Columbia University, found a large number of eight-year cycles in various meteorological and economic phenomena, such as rainfall records and crop production. He proposed that the cause was the planet Venus in its eight-year periodic motion with respect to the Earth and Sun (eight Earth years of 365 days is equal to five cycles of 584 days, the synodic cycle of Venus). He also suggested that Venus at inferior conjunction would produce disturbances in terrestrial weather. In the 1960s, the famous Edward R. Dewey researched cycles and confirmed Moore's ideas. Dewey found eight-year cycles in sixty-three different phenomena, including rainfall and barometric pressure.

In 1946, a scientist named Sydney Wood pointed out several long-term meteorological cycles based on the movement of the planets, which he believed were more reliable for use in weather forecasting than short-term cycles. Among the cycles he discussed was the thirty-three to thirty-four-year cycle, whereby the Sun, Venus, Earth, and Mars return to the same position relative to each other. He gave as an example the droughts that occurred in Chicago in 1867, 1901, and 1934.

In the 1980s, climatologists Rhodes Fairbridge and John Sanders showed that the Earth's climate is affected on long-term time scales by variations in planetary orbits. They found a twenty-year weather cycle that is caused by solar changes, which are in turn due to the alignments and motions of Jupiter and Saturn. Fairbridge and Sanders concluded that the orbital relationships between the Sun and planets were an important factor in determining cyclical changes in Earth's climate.

Most of today's scientists believe they are discovering new ideas about the cosmic sources of weather change. In many studies, however, they are merely confirming what astrologers have known for thousands of years—that what happens here on earth (including the weather) is connected to what is going on in the heavens. Modern scientists take credit for discovering these geocosmic connections, and meanwhile they look with disdain upon astrology.

Astrology, including astrometeorology, developed over thousands of years in tandem with human survival. The sobering truth is that human survival depended on understanding the concept of geocosmic connection—otherwise known as the astrological principle "As above, so below." It is entirely possible that if earlier humans had paid less attention to geocosmic cycles,such as the planetary influences on weather, our species might not be here today. Perhaps we should be grateful that our ancestors were not as "scientifically minded" as the modern skeptics who laugh at the "superstitious" cultures that paid homage to the stars.

## About the Author

Valerie Vaughan obtained her B.A. from Vassar College and a master's degree in information science. She is a professional science reference librarian and a certified astrologer (C.A., Level IV, NCGR). She has published numerous articles and books on the scientific basis of astrology and the astrological roots of science. Her writings can be accessed at www.onereed.com.

## For Further Reading

*Earth Cycles: The Scientific Evidence for Astrology* by Valerie Vaughan, (OneReed Publications, 2001).

"John Goad: Astrological Research Pioneer" by Bruce Scofield, *NCGR Journal*, Winter 1986–87.

# Gardening Styles of the Zodiac

*by Maggie Anderson*

Take a walk through your neighborhood and note the wide variety of gardening styles. Some contain a bounty of blooms and others appear very utilitarian, designed more for the ease of mowing lawns than for beauty. A few will display delightful surprises—an unexpected specimen plant or curious yard ornament. Many seem welcoming to children but others might as well have a "Keep off the Grass" sign posted. If you're curious enough to get a peek, you'll discover these many differences in gardening styles extend to backyards also. Who grows tomatoes? Who would rather plant canna bulbs in their private spaces? Astrology can assist inquiring minds that want to know. Check the gardening profile for each element (fire, air, earth, and water) as well as your individual Sun sign that follows.

# Fire Signs

The cosmic job of the fire signs (Aries, Leo, Sagittarius) is to inspire and motivate. These creative gardeners design and plant patriotic displays of red, white, and blue petunias in the shape of flags. They'll raise masses of blooms for one-of-a-kind Rose Bowl parade floats. Believing the natural world should be as much fun for adults as for children, their vegetable gardens have a playful quality to them: bean-pole teepees for little people's powwows, and corn maze displays.

# Air Signs

Air signs (Gemini, Libra, Aquarius) enjoy the intellectual challenge of keeping a garden. They're seldom satisfied to plant on a flat piece of ground in a straight row. Raised beds, window boxes, and ornately designed patio and roof gardens are trademarks of the air signs. Any activity that promotes social interaction pleases them, so expect to find a comfortable bench for two strategically placed in their lawns. Fragrant plants are their specialty, aroma being every bit as important to them as visual appeal. Nicotiana, lavender, and mint will have a special spot in air sign gardens.

# Earth Signs

No sign of the zodiac enjoys digging in the dirt as much as earth signs (Taurus, Virgo, Capricorn). They have an need to touch growing things and that includes nearly every plant in the horticultural world. It's earth signs that hug trees in parks and press flowers of remembrance into their diaries. Putting food on the table is also one of their specialties. When garden plots are small, they'll mix mesclun and sage with flowers. If space is abundant the earth signs will produce bountiful harvests of a wide variety of edibles.

# Water Signs

In gardening, as with other areas of their lives, water sign gardeners (Cancer, Scorpio, and Pisces) trust their instincts. Their gardens have an otherworld quality to them, as if inspired by angels. Who better to build a backyard lily pond than members of the water element? If they don't have naturally flowing water on site, they'll make do with a small man-made pond. Occasionally, their back yard gardening spaces are compromised by the presence of a very large swimming pool. White and pale blue blooms suit them best.

# Aries (March 20 to April 20)

Always on the go, Aries prefer maintenance-free gardens, the kind other family members can take care of while they wander off to explore the countryside. They're more given to vast expanses of lush green lawn than to elaborate plantings. After all, one must keep space open for a good game of volleyball! Red is their favorite color and it will show up somewhere on the Aries homestead, perhaps in a big pot of scarlet geraniums. This hot-blooded sign loves peppers. They often grow salsa gardens in order to have a supply of their favorite varieties. They'll forgo beans and carrots in favor of habanera peppers any day.

# Taurus (April 20 to May 21)

When astrologers refer to gardeners with a green thumb, we're talking about Taurus. The first time you view the garden of a Taurus, you'll be convinced that gardeners are born, not made. No matter how small their living quarters, members of this sign will be surrounded by greenery, inside and out. Their motto: "No planting space will go unplanted." Everything grows around this earth sign, and the more fragrant and sensual the better. Lush with color, roses are this sign's specialty as are pastel cutting flowers. Taurus vegetable gardens always produce more than he or she can consume, so expect to find members of this sign setting up shop at your local Farmer's Market.

# Gemini (May 21 to June 21)

A Gemini's garden can literally take your breath away! The twins are as energetic as two people are, and that's especially obvious in their flower beds. No monochromatic color schemes for them! Every color of the rainbow will be represented in their gorgeous flower gardens. This sign of the zodiac will display plants with variegated leaves and multicolored flower heads. Geminis are intellectuals and their gardening style communicates the best of their horticultural knowledge. As one of the sociable signs, their garden areas are visual gifts to their neighborhoods.

## Cancer (June 21 to July 22)

Cancers are one of the parental signs of the zodiac. Crabs lovingly nurture their delicate blooms, treating each cucumber plant and gorgeous gardenia as one of their "babies." No growing thing is ever rejected. Friends on the move will abandon house plants on Cancer's doorstep, confident they'll be adopted into a loving home. Cancer's gardens usually contain plants collected from friends and family members over many years. This sign, being ruled by Moon, will be the first in the neighborhood to produce a Moon Garden of white and silvery foliage. Kitchen gardens are almost a must for Cancers as they're wonderful cooks too!

## Leo (July 22 to August 23)

It's easy to find a garden belonging to a Leo: they're listed on the maps of your city's annual Garden. This fire sign is happy to take you on a tour of his or her well-manicured mini–Garden of Versailles, complete with elaborate fountains. They'll show you many rare plants with large blooms, the kind found in the gardens of royalty. Plantings around a Leo's homes are the biggest and the best specimens available. Giant red canna lilies, breathtaking redbud trees, and red maples will have a prominent place in their yards. Leos love to design outdoor spaces where people can have fun. This includes something special for children, like a playhouse surrounded by towering sunflowers. Golf course greenery is another Leo specialty.

## Virgo (August 23 to September 22)

Humble Virgo produces a modest garden: not too big or showy, but very functional. Expect to find many examples of edible landscaping around their homes. This group knows that flowering purple kale is not only a gorgeous fall plant but that it makes delicious soup, too! Virgos are also the best record keepers of the zodiac. They may be the only gardeners with up-to-date maps of planting spaces to facilitate proper rotation of crops. Virgos will methodically write down planting dates, seed and plant varieties, weather conditions, and harvest success in their gardening diaries. An avid reader, Virgo will study horticultural books and articles, learning all about each variety before lovingly digging it into the ground.

## Libra (September 22 to October 23)

For Libra, gardening is a labor of love. They will strive to create a fragrant, romantic atmosphere, indoors and out. Libras display vases of fresh cut flowers as well as light, ferny house plants in their living spaces. Beautiful floral displays decorate the fronts of their homes as well as the back, the delight of both guests and passersby. Members of this sign will gift their favorite people with bouquets of homegrown roses and Baby's breath, a subtle reminder of love and other affairs of the heart. Their pastel flower beds are planted with entertaining in mind. This sign is more likely than any other to host a garden party or hold a marriage ceremony under a back yard arch of pink roses. Their gardening signature will be a love seat hidden away among the blooms.

## Scorpio (October 23 to November 22)

You'll know you're held in special esteem if a Scorpio invites you for a stroll through his or her garden. Scorpios value their privacy and are more likely than other zodiac signs to have a secret garden. The front of a Scorpio's home won't reveal what lies in the back yard. Fences will hide garden spaces, a place where they can retreat from the busy, inquisitive world. This sign specializes in intense-colored flowering plants—like right red tulips and black Iris—and hidden, winding garden paths. You'll find water flowing somewhere in their gardens, too, either through a small, man-made pond or a fountain. All greenery will be kept well under control. Scorpios strive for a manicured look in their gardens with benches for quiet meditation.

## Sagittarius (November 22 to December 21)

Gardening is a challenge for the Sagittarian, who loves the natural world but dislikes staying home to tend a garden. Therefore, Sagittarians develop into one of two types of gardeners—those who plant as they go, like Johnny Appleseed; or those who cultivate self-sufficient plants. Never one to bow to public opinion, Sagittarians may be the only one on their block to establish a lawn of prairie grasses. Cactus gardens are another favorite for those who live in a southern climate. It's rumored that the first zen sand garden was arranged by a Sagittarian anxious to avoid weeding chores and hit the road. This is a playful sign so their lawns are uncrowded to better accommodate a game of darts or badminton.

## Capricorn (December 21 to January 20)

A Capricorn's well-known frugality is reflected in his or her gardening style. They are the original seed-savers—not for the purpose of preserving heritage variety plants, but to save money. Fortunately, the results are the same. These gardens are practical first and only then is attractiveness considered. Potatoes will be planted before peonies and turnips before tulips. They appreciate a flat garden bed and straight rows for vegetables because this makes for efficient hoeing and tilling. Capricorns enjoy problem solving and thrive on hard work. They'll tackle challenging soil and spaces and transform them into functional gardens. When time is short, however, Capricorn will fill in grassy spots with colored rocks. Capricorn's gardening signature is a big boulder placed on the edge of their property.

## Aquarius (January 20 to February 18)

If you're looking for someone to organize a community garden, call on the waterbearers—Aquarians. They know the value of teamwork and they love to garden as part of a group. No one likes gadgets as much as an Aquarian, either. Their gardens are high tech, complete with automatic watering systems and motorized compost bins. Members of this sign will buy the latest widgets designed to trap chipmunks and repel marauding blue jays. Aquarians will spend hours trying to eliminate cutworms and potato beetles from their vegetable gardens, not so much because the flowers or garden produce inspires them, but rather, this sign refuses to be outsmarted by rodents and insects. An Aquarian's favorite color is green, so don't expect to find large blocks of color in their gardens. You'll be able to view your reflection in their gazing ball though.

## Pisces (February 18 to March 20)

People with a Pisces Sun sign plant without design and achieve magnificent results worthy of a spread in the best gardening magazines. Their colorful cottage gardens and other welcoming outdoor spaces are the envy of their neighbors. All this comes with seemingly little effort. Pisces simply sows wherever the spirit leads, says a little prayer, and lets sunshine and rain do the rest. It's hinted at that Pisceans gardens are rescue centers for ailing plants. Sad, rusty roses will be given a second chance under the gentle care of this sign. They will coach shy flowering vines up trellises until they reach the very top. They'll also try to find good homes for the excess perennials in their own gardens. If no one wants the extra plants, the Pisces gardener will dig them into a nice spot in the city park (late at night) where they can eventually be enjoyed by large groups of people.

### About the Author

Maggie is an astrologer, writer, and gardener. She makes her home in the Heartland—Mount Vernon, Iowa, where she maintains a full-time astrological practice and teaches classes in astrology. Maggie has two specialties: one involves "all affairs of the heart," which allows her to utilize her experience as a family therapist when counseling astrology clients. Her interest in world affairs is evident in the mundane astrology writings on her website, www.astromaggi.com.

# Harvesting Corn by the Moon

## by Daniel B. Brawner

They say the Moon is cold. And it looks cold. But I had a feeling the Moon held the secret to how I was going to stay warm this winter. As a traditional symbol of regeneration, the Moon is an appropriate instrument for calculating the proper times for planting and harvesting. When the time is right for planting during the Moon's twenty-eight-day cycle, life goes into the ground. And in the fullness of the Moon at harvest, life comes out of the ground.

Once you find yourself in sync with that cosmic rhythm, you will want to take it to ridiculous extremes. Just as the Moon continuously renews itself, so do cabbages, cucumbers, box elder bugs, babies, and deer. In your mind, you see a swirling vortex of celestial energy pursuing a relentless cycle that, if you will only step into its path, will slurp you up to the heavens.

In a blinding flash of epiphany, it becomes clear the Moon is telling us that we all play a part in this "music of the spheres" and that, as regular and certain as a Bach intervention, the cosmic harmony supports our lonely note and keeps it from going sour. Hunger and cold can be smoothed away if we learn to get in step with the Moon's message of regeneration.

I figure it all boils down to energy. The Sun and Earth's energy make food grow. We consume the food to fuel our bodies. That's fine for curing hunger, but what about the cold?

Then I thought, metabolism of food is a kind of combustion that keeps us warm on the inside. Why shouldn't we use food to keep us warm on the outside? Looking out the window of my home in Iowa, I saw walnut trees and grass and . . . acres and acres of corn. What if corn could be made to release its energy to make us warm on the outside? It would have to be cooked well done. Very well done. Okay, burned.

## A Stove that Burns Food

I was afraid to let anybody know what I was up to. So, about a month ago when my dad came over and saw me building a giant wooden box in my garage, I was hesitant to discuss the matter.

"What are you making?" Dad asked with mild curiosity.

The box stood on 4 x 4 inch posts two feet off the floor and reached nearly to the rafters. It was seven feet on each side, externally reinforced with 2 x 4s fastened together and internally cross-braced for strength. Tough-looking carriage bolts gleamed at all the stress points. It was built like a bridge.

"Oh," I said evasively, "it's a corn crib."

My dad just nodded, as if that's what he figured it was. Here I had slaved over this thing for three days. The least he could do was ask what it was for. Finally, he inquired, "Have a lot of corn, do you?"

I couldn't take the suspense any longer myself, even if he could. Yes, I told him, I have about 10,000 pounds of corn coming. I'm taking out my wood stove and installing a new high-tech corn-burning stove.

In recent winters, astronomical gas prices and an area-wide firewood shortage sent me searching for an alternative source of heat. I looked for corn stoves at a store in nearby Cedar Rapids. Since they didn't carry such things, they set about condemning the entire concept. I pointed out that stoves that burn shelled corn operate at around 94 percent efficiency and can heat a 2,000 square-foot home on a bushel a day. Corn produces about 500,000 Btu's per bushel, while propane makes around 100,000 Btus per gallon. With corn prices at two dollars a bushel, you'd have to buy propane at forty cents a gallon to get a better value than corn. They thought I would be happier with one of their $3,000 wood stoves.

I replied that since burning corn does not produce much $CO_2$ or any visible smoke, it is essentially non-polluting and does not make creosote that necessitates periodic chimney cleaning. And best of all, unlike wood stoves, a corn stove burns all night without stoking so you wake up to a warm house.

"Oh yeah?" said one of them, clearly stumped. "Well, where are you going to get the corn?"

Last year, of Iowa's 55,875 square miles, 18,750 square miles were planted in corn. That's about one-third of the entire state. It amounted to approximately 1.7 billion bushels. *The Iowan* magazine observes that if Iowa were a country, it would be the world's third largest producer of corn, behind the rest of the United States and China. The European Union would be fourth.

Where would I find corn in Iowa? "You know," I said, backing out the door, "you really ought to get some windows in this place."

Oil suppliers in the Middle East think of Americans as infidel dogs. It makes me nervous buying necessities from somebody who hates me. So, I like the idea of using home-grown fuel. I bought my corn from Jim and Carol Brennaman of Mount Vernon who are extremely nice people and have never driven their tractor into a skyscraper.

A stove that burns food is nothing new at my house. Still, I was excited when the delivery truck arrived with my corn stove. The only trouble was, the semi had no lift gate.

"How tough are you?" the driver asked. "This baby weighs 350 pounds."

A better question would have been, "How strong are you?" because, when the huge crate slipped out of my hands and landed on me, I was able to get off the ground under my own power, proving that although I wasn't strong or even very bright, I was tough.

Fortunately, my new stove was unharmed. Until the bruises on my leg (and ego) heal, I won't be going for any Olympic weightlifting records. But at least I'll be warm.

## Warming Myself by the Moon

Getting back to the Moon: those who know about lunar gardening say that corn should be planted while the Moon is waxing, usually during the first quarter. It is often favorable to plant corn when the Moon is in Libra, an auspicious time for creative ventures that bear rich rewards. Libra is also associated with the lower back and it should not be necessary to explain why this is an appropriate sign for planting.

Since I don't actually raise the corn I burn, I must assume that my friends the Brannaman's plant during the correct lunar cycle. But commercial farmers are busy folks. And a lot of stuff can come up, besides the Moon. Still, somehow the corn always turns out beautiful. So I'm sure there is a special formula for adding just the right amount of anhydrous ammonia to compensate for being out of phase with the Moon.

I realize that my agricultural requirements are not the same as the typical lunar gardener since I'm not concerned with the taste of my corn. I only care how hot a fire it will make. So, for me, one of the most critical phases of the growing cycle is when to harvest.

I may be breaking new ground here, but when harvesting corn for fuel, I recommend that it be performed when the Moon is in a fire sign, say in the middle of October. And, if possible, the corn should be harvested during a waning Moon. Harvesting peat during a waxing Moon is said to result in moist fuel and smoky fires and the same must be true for corn. Harvesting corn during a Full Moon also gives a chance for excessive moisture to get into your corn bin—along with excessive mice that can better see what you're up to.

If you've done the proper lunar planning, your harvested corn should have an ideal moisture content of 11 or 12 percent. A local grain elevator will be able to test your corn accurately. If it happens that your corn is not dry enough, just have them throw it into one of those gigantic gas-fired grain dryers until it is. That's what everybody else does.

Tonight, I am watching what would have been one of the most spectacular Leonid meteor showers for decades to come. The late fall air is crisp and cold and a light wind rustles the remaining pin oak leaves by the river where I watch for the next streak of light through the night sky. There is a Full Moon—a harvest Moon—that hides all but the brightest of the meteors. But I don' t mind. If it wasn't for that Moon, I wouldn't have a warm place to go home to.

## About the Author

Daniel B. Brawner is an award-winning humor columnist and the author of a New Age mystery novel, *Employment Is Murder*. His trusty corn stove keeps him warm through the icy Iowa winters, and although his friends think he's naturally loony, Dan still has to check his Moon facts at www.astromaggi.com.

# How Plants Tell Time

## by Valerie Vaughan

Plants can measure the passage of time. Most plants normally respond to a twenty-four-hour rhythm, as we know from observing the daily opening and closing of flowers. In a great many plants, flowering also occurs on an annual basis—only at a certain time of the year. The onset of flowering in a particular species is often timed with uncanny accuracy to occur a regular time of the year, despite fluctuations in the weather.

There is one plant that follows a very long cycle—a type of bamboo that grows in Argentina. This bamboo has a life pattern of thirty years, from seed to seed. The plant grows for twenty-nine years, then produces flowers and seeds one year later. Astrologers might wonder if the biological clock of this plant is being triggered by the Saturn cycle. (Saturn takes twenty-nine to thirty years to move once through the zodiac.)

However, most plants follow a daily schedule. At the same time each evening, some houseplants, such as mimosa, fold up their leaves for the night. Many wild plants, such as clover and wood sorrel, do the same. Botanists say the reason for this leaf folding is unknown. It may happen to reduce heat loss from the plant during the cooler nighttime temperatures. Another theory is that it prevents the leaves from mistaking other light (such as strong moonlight) for the dawn of another day.

Plants open their flowers to lure insect pollinators with their nectar. Even plants that keep their flowers open all the time conserve energy by only producing nectar at certain times of the day. Insects that feed on this nectar must have a very well-developed time sense if they are to survive. Honeybees show a remarkable ability to synchronize their activities with the opening times of specific flowers.

Plants need sunlight in order to turn carbon dioxide into energy (a process called photosynthesis). A plant's leaves are arranged to detect the length of daylight, which varies from season to season. Some plants, including carnations, radishes, scarlet pimpernels, and clover produce flowers in the spring when daylight is lengthening. This type is called "long-day plants." Other plants flower during the shortening days of autumn and are known as "short-day plants." This type includes chrysanthemum, poinsettia, corn, and coffee. There are also other plants that flower at any time regardless of day length, including dandelions, sunflowers, tomatoes, and potatoes.

Despite the terms "short-day" and "long-day," botanists have discovered that the cue these plants are following is actually the length of darkness during nighttime. Scientists believe that plants are measuring the interval elapses between the reception of two successive light signals—dusk on one day and dawn on the following day. In other words, plants can tell what season it is—spring with shortening hours of darkness; summer with the shortest hours of darkness; autumn with lengthening hours of darkness. This ability to tell time is a controlling factor in the development and behavior of plants. Night length is the key to leaf growth, color change, and shedding, as well as winter bud formation.

Many plants need a period of dormancy before they can leaf and flower. The timing of this period is often influenced by the temperature, which is determined by season. The spreading leaf canopy of trees in the spring is initiated in part by temperature. However, the change of foliage color among deciduous trees in the autumn is not controlled by temperature but by the length of daylight.

The reason that some plants can only grow in certain latitudes is because they have a very specific requirement for daylight. For instance, ragweed plants produce flowers when the daylight period is equal to fourteen and one-half hours and the night is nine and one-half hours long. In some areas of the Midwest, the days are the right length for ragweed to grow and produce seeds. But in northern Maine, the daylight period is longer than fourteen-and-one-half hours for most of the summer. By the time the daylight shortens to that length in Maine, the weather has turned too cool. The ragweed dies before it can produce seeds. Likewise, the chrysanthemum requires an uninterrupted period of about thirteen hours of darkness (an autumn night) before it will flower.

Many plants open and close their flowers at set times each day. The daisy opens its flowers at dawn. Goat's beard, also known as "John-go-to-bed-at-noon" closes at midday. The dandelion opens its flowers in the morning and closes them in late afternoon. Its seed heads are actually called "clocks" in some rural areas. Many plants are so reliable about their timing that floral clock gardens have been designed, with flowers arranged in order of their opening and closing times, and in the shape of a clock face (circle) or sundial (semicircle). Carl Linnaeus, the great eighteenth-century botanist, planted a time-keeping flower garden that he called "Flora's Clocks."

## A Flower Clock Garden

| | |
|---|---|
| 6 am | Spotted cat's ear opens; water lily opens |
| 7 am | Dandelion opens; African marigold opens; St. John's wort opens |
| 8 am | Mouse-ear hawkweed opens; scarlet pimpernel opens |
| 9 am | Field marigold opens; sowthistle closes |
| 10 am | Common nipplewort closes |
| 11 am | Star of Bethlehem opens |
| 12 pm | Passionflower opens; goat's beard closes |
| 1 pm | Proliferous pink closes |
| 2 pm | Scarlet pimpernel closes |
| 3 pm | Hawkbit closes |
| 4 pm | Bindweed closes |
| 5 pm | White water lily closes |
| 6 pm | Evening primrose opens |

# Gardening by Zodiac Sign and Moon Phase

*by Janice Sharkey*

I magine that you have to grow your own food to survive. You would choose a growing method that gave you the best chance for a successful harvest. Gardeners have always worked with time—daytime and the seasons—but there is another time: Moon time. For centuries gardeners have been aware of the link between the phases of the Moon and its effect on plants. They learned that the power of the Moon to pull on the waters of this Earth also has a subtle effect on the internal waters of plants. It has now been scientifically proven[1] that germination increases when seeds are sown around a New Moon rather than at random times.

## A Time to Plant, A Time to Reap

The Moon takes about twenty-nine days to go around the Earth. This cycle is divided into four phases: waxing, Full Moon, waning, and New Moon. Each phase has its allotted gardening tasks. Ideally, it is better to wait a day or so either side of a New or Full Moon before planting. A waxing Moon helps to push moisture up into the leaves and parts of the plant growing above ground. This makes a New Moon the optimum time to sow and plant leafy plants, especially those that generate seeds inside like sweet

---

1. For more information about the effect the Moon's phase has on planting, see Nicholas Campion's, *The Practical Astrologer*, (New York: Abrams, 1989). This title is out of print, but it can be purchased used.

peas or tomatoes. A waning Moon will draw moisture downward to the root. Hence, the best time to plant root crops, biennials, and bulbs that need a solid grasp of the soil is during a waning Moon. The latter phase, when the least water is retained in the plant—the seven days after a Full Moon—is a better time for doing chores like weeding and mowing.

The Moon passes through each zodiac sign in approximately two days. Each sign belongs to one of the four elements: fire, earth, air, and water. Each element has a different affect on different biological parts of the plant. You can obtain maximum benefits if you plant in the right phase of the Moon and also consider the element and sign the Moon is in.

## Astrological Biology

In medical astrology each major organ of the body is ruled by a zodiac sign. Aries rules the head and eyes; Gemini rules the shoulders, arms, hands, and nervous system, and so on. Each major biological function of plants also comes under a particular sign and planetary rulership.

**Aries** influences seed production. Plants germinated under an Aries Moon will be more prone to go to seed.

**Taurus** rules food storage. It is especially good to plant under a Taurus Moon when plants need to survive a long winter via their root system.

**Gemini** governs the vascular system. Planting under a Gemini Moon will facilitate the flow of water and sap through the plant.

**Cancer** rules the principles of growth in the green foliage, stalk, leaf, or vine. Cancer is the best sign to plant or sow under for abundant, succulent crops.

**Leo** rules the curtailing function in the cycle of a plant's growth, which is very necessary so that a plant concentrates on producing seed and ensuring its future survival. Like Aries, Leo is a poor sign to plant under. But it is an excellent time to cut back growth, as in weeding and pruning tasks.

**Virgo**, as you would expect, governs the digestive process within a plant, helping it to distribute energy for healthy growth.

**Libra**, true to its Venus-ruled nature, relates to flowering and the need to attract pollinating insects to ensure the plant's reproductive capacity. If you want an abundant flowering garden, plant under a Libra Moon.

**Scorpio** relates to the sexual organs in plants. Planting under a Scorpio Moon promotes sturdy growth.

**Sagittarius** influences a plants ability to bear fruit, an important function in many plants.

**Capricorn** rules the skin and bones in the human body, similarly, it rules the bark and structural material of a plant. Capricorn also rules the hormones that control the dominance of top branches so that they grow faster and produce a symmetrical shape. An excellent time to plant ornamental shrubs is under a Capricorn Moon.

**Aquarius** influences the base of the plant stem—the part between the roots and the upper stem. True to the Aquarian nature, anything planted during an Aquarian Moon tends to be shock resistant. So any transplanting should be done then.

**Pisces** rules the feet. Likewise, Pisces governs hydrotropism, which relates to the water seeking function in the root system—a function vital to the continued survival of a plant.

## Linking Plants and the Four Elements

In astrology, one fundamental belief is that the universe consists of four basic elements: fire, air, earth, and water. Mystic and biodynamic gardener Rudolf Steiner worked out a system of correspondences between these four elements and what he considered the four primordial organs of the plant:

1. The seed/fruit that contains the basic blueprint of genetic material, such as DNA. Seed/fruit is associated with the element fire and is typified by fruits such as the tomato.

2. The flower is associated with the element air. Flowers, such as the dandelion, actually reach into the atmosphere to receive pollen from either airborne insects or the wind.

3. The leaf is governed by the water element. Leafy lettuce or cabbage are good examples of this type of plant.

4. The earth element, as you would expect, corresponds to the root of the plant and all that grows in the earth. Root crops, such as carrot or potato, come under this type of growth.

A lifetime of research lead Maria Thun, an authority on biodynamics, to one main conclusion about the effects of the Moon on growing plants. She concluded that:

> "Each of the twelve zodiac signs has a special relation with one of the four life forces which are manifest in the elements earth, water, light-air, and fire. All four forces can be seen to have an effect on the life body for the growth and development of plants."

This powerful force of planetary influence is also evident in its effect upon the actual shape and direction that plants grow in. A fundamental premise of astrology is that all living matter on this planet Earth is influenced by the cosmic energy emanating from above. The classical astrologers (such as William Ramsey, b.1626; and Nicholas Culpeper, b. 1616) believed that every type of fauna or flora shares characteristics with their ruling planet. They used two models for planetary rulership of plants: a medicinal one, and one based upon the philosophical doctrine of affinity. This latter concept permeated the medieval world—it is the essence of the macrocosm-microcosm dictate: as above, so below.

Culpeper tended to observe medicinal uses of various plants. Jupiter, for example, rules the maple, which has medicinal properties thought to heal Jupiter-ruled diseases such as liver diseases, or trouble with the thigh muscles.

Ancient apothecaries knew a thing or two about healing and it is likely that they grew some of their own herbs or, like Culpeper, they knew exactly which hedgerow to go to get a particular healing plant. The natural seasons of gardening and harvesting draw us closer to our own natural rhythms. The herb tea you drink, that aroma that lifts your senses, or the herbal bath you bathe in will heal you more than once if you have grown the herbs yourself. Using plants as therapy is part of the holistic experience keeping us grounded with Mother Earth and aware of the very cycle of life. Gardening by the cycle of the Moon adds a further dimension to the pleasure of planting, bringing us even closer to the cyclical pulse of the living cosmos.

## Mother Moon

One more step toward being in tune with nature and ourselves is to create a Moon garden, a natural living space that reflects our individual intuitive spirit.

Most of us know our Sun sign. (It relates to our core energy in a way that is similar to its effect on plants.) Yet, few of us realize the importance of our Moon sign, which represents our emotional and instinctive needs. Like the ebb and flow of water within plants, the emotional tides within humans varies with each passing phase of the Moon, depending on the zodiac sign your natal Moon is in. (Check your natal chart.)

In astrology the Moon symbolizes mother and nurturing, which can also be reflected in the very essence of our dependency upon nature for sustenance and ultimate survival. If you know your Moon sign, you can design a Moon garden to reflect the zodiac sign of your Moon. You can choose plants that are ruled by that sign, and extend the concept to include associated colors and materials, too.

There is a wealth of materials from Saturn-like granite to Cancer's reflective theme of using mirrors in garden design. As with throwing a pebble into a pond, the ripple effect of ideas extends out as you plunge into the hidden depths to discover your Moon sign and begin to recreate these traits into your personal garden space.

Every garden should be unique, bearing its own identity. Yet is it also interesting to create a theme or style that reflects your Moon sign. We can learn from our ancient ancestors who linked the motion of the Moon to beneficial planting. The wisdom of the stars can inform us about nature—be it human or plant—and how to nurture it.

In the next section, you will find some suggestions for making your own Moon garden.

## Garden Design Ideas
### Plants and Planting by Sign

| Sign | Rulership | Plants |
|------|-----------|--------|
| Aries | Mars | Clematis, euphorbia, tomatoes, anemone, phormium, peppers. |
| Taurus | Venus | Mint, maidenhair fern, oxalis, hosta, cowslip, lady's mantle. |
| Gemini | Mercury | Cotton lavender, lily of the valley, pulmonaria, oregano. |
| Cancer | Moon | Willow, lettuce, wallflower pumpkin, flag iris, lunaria. |
| Leo | Sun | Rosemary, heliotrope, vines, sundew, marigold, palm tree |
| Virgo | Mercury | Hazel, almond, inula, carrot, valerian, lavender, parsley |
| Libra | Venus | Rose (Damask), hollyhocks, daffodils, cherry, apple |
| Scorpio | Pluto | Ginseng, nicotiana, rheum, Venus flytrap, cyclamen |
| Sagittarius | Jupiter | Acer, maple, achillea, hyssop, salvia, chestnut tree, houseleek |
| Capricorn | Saturn | Aconite, ivy, pansy, hellebore, daphne, yew, erica, comfrey |
| Aquarius | Uranus | Tillsandia (airplant), sterlizia, Chilean bell flower, bromeliads |
| Pisces | Neptune | Watercress, waterlily, lotus, mushrooms, caltha palustris |

# Other Design Elements for Your Moon Garden

| Sign | Element | Image | Materials | Color |
|---|---|---|---|---|
| Aries | Fire | Spiky | Iron, diamond | Red |
| Taurus | Earth | Sensual, edible, practical | Copper, emerald, pottery | Pink |
| Gemini | Air | Light/shade, sound, movement | Mercury, agate, figurines, chimes | Yellows |
| Cancer | Water | Reflective mood rooms | Glass, mirrors, pearl, bamboo willow | Silver, gray blue |
| Leo | Fire | Classical, loving | Ruby, gold, solar | Sun colors |
| Virgo | Earth | Medicinal, tidy | Mercury, nickel, sardonyx, | Navy, green, hazel |
| Libra | Earth | Floral scented | Copper, sapphire, | Pastels, jade |
| Scorpio | Water | Wild bog | Steel, iron, opal hessian, reeds | Dark red, maroon |
| Sagittarius | Fire | Natural, free expansive | Tin, topaz. | Dark blue purple |
| Capricorn | Earth | Structured, low maintenance | Stonework, granite, silver | Black, gray brown |
| Aquarius | Air | Modern, minimalist | Aluminum | Turquoise |
| Pisces | Water | Tranquil, private, escapist | Hydropower, wood tin, bloodstone. | Sea green. |

## About the Author

Janice Sharkey is a dedicated astrological gardener. She studied and gained the certificate from the London Faculty of Astrological Studies, giving her a good grounding in astrology. She practices Moon and organic gardening, opening her garden for charity once a year as part of the Scottish Organic Gardens Weekend in July. She designs gardens to reflect an individual's birth chart and has clients from as near and far as the U.K. and U.S.A. Her hobbies include pottery and making astrological themes in stained glass. She is currently working on a Virgo theme featuring the harvest Moon, which will be built into a garden. When she is not stargazing or planting, she's looking after her two kids, Rose and David.

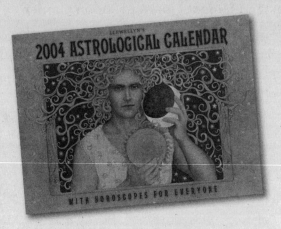

# Your On-the-Go Pocket Planner

The planets are on the move—and so are you. Slip this compact cosmic database into your pocket or purse and be able to make plans wherever you are. Note your daily appointments—and even schedule into next year. You'll find everything you need to plan for success right at your fingertips:

- Daily signs, phases, & aspects of the Moon
- Each week of 2004 on a two-page spread
- Each month of 2005 on a two-page spread
- Two-year ephemeris and aspectarian for 2004–05
- Void-of-course Moon table
- Time zone chart
- Retrograde table

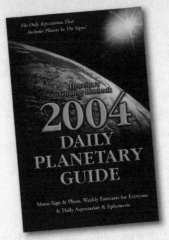

# Practice Herbal Magic

Learn how to use the potent energy of herbs for natural health and beauty, and in cooking crafts and magic. This bountiful guide presents time-honored traditions and fresh ideas for cultivating and practicing herbal wisdom. Featuring over twenty-five articles from nationally recognized herbalists, including:

- "Gardens by Moonlight" by Carrie Moss
- "Herbal Wines and Liqueurs" by Chandra Moira Beal
- "An Herbal Sleeping Potion" by Edain McCoy
- "Lunar Herbs and Your Health" by Jonathan Keyes
- "Making Herbal Bookmarks" by Elizabeth Barrette
- "Gathering Garlic" by S. Y. Zenith
- "The Buckeye Nut" by Robert Place
- "Crafting Magical Herbal Perfumes" by Peg Aloi

**LLEWELLYN'S 2004 HERBAL ALMANAC**
336 pp. • 5 ¼″ x 8″
0-7387-0127-0/J124 • $7.95, $12.50 Can.
To order call 1-877-NEW-WRLD

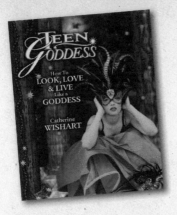

# Notes